ADVANCED THEORY AND PRACTICE IN SPORT MARKETING

ADVANCED THEORY AND PRACTICE IN SPORT MARKETING

Eric C. Schwarz and
Jason D. Hunter

ELSEVIER

AMSTERDAM • BOSTON • HEIDELBERG • LONDON • NEW YORK • OXFORD
PARIS • SAN DIEGO • SAN FRANCISCO • SINGAPORE • SYDNEY • TOKYO
Butterworth Heinemann is an imprint of Elsevier

Butterworth-Heinemann is an imprint of Elsevier
Linacre House, Jordan Hill, Oxford OX2 8DP, UK
30 Corporate Drive, Suite 400, Burlington, MA 01803, USA
525 B Street, Suite 1900, San Diego, CA 92101-4495, USA

First edition 2008

British Library Cataloguing in Publication Data
A catalogue record for this book is available from the British Library

Library of Congress Cataloging-in-Publication Data
A catalog record for this book is available from the Library of Congress

ISBN: 978-07506-8491-0

For information on all Butterworth-Heinemann publications
visit our web site at books.elsevier.com

Typeset by Charon Tec Ltd (A Macmillan Company), Chennai, India
www.charontec.com

Printed and bound in *USA*

08 09 10   10 9 8 7 6 5 4 3 2 1

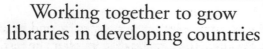

Working together to grow
libraries in developing countries

www.elsevier.com | www.bookaid.org | www.sabre.org

ELSEVIER   BOOK AID International   Sabre Foundation

Loughborough
College

ACKNOWLEDGMENTS, DEDICATIONS, AND EPIGRAPHS

Marketing is the Oxygen of Business – Neil Parmenter

hence…

Sport Marketing is the Oxygen of Sport Business!

DR. ERIC C. SCHWARZ

I would like to dedicate this book to the memory of my father, Rolf Schwarz. His wisdom, intelligence, and strength are foundations of my being, and I hope somewhere he is looking down and is proud of this project, of what I have accomplished, and who I have become as a person.

I am personally indebted to my wife, Loan, whose love and support has been unconditional during the writing of this book, and always. I could not have completed this project without her calming influence and belief in my abilities. I love you and thank you!!!

I would also like to acknowledge the love and support of my mother, Charlene, who has always been there to lend a hand during times of turmoil, an ear in times of confusion or frustration, a voice as one of my biggest supporters, and has always shown unconditional love to me. Thank you for everything you have done to help me be where I am today!

In addition, I would like to show my appreciation to my best friend and co-author of this book, Jason Hunter. We have been through a lot over the past 20 years of friendship, getting through numerous obstacles and having many successes. I thank you for your efforts on this book and for your friendship.

I owe thanks to Mariann, my wonderful wife, and three children, Zachary, Morgan, and Jake. Without their time and encouragement, there would not have been enough hours in the day to complete this project. I also would like to thank my friend, colleague, and co-author Eric Schwarz. Eric and I have known each other for 20 years, since back when we both received our undergraduate degree from Plymouth State University in New Hampshire. I am very thankful for the educational base and opportunities that Plymouth provided for me, and for the lasting friendships that developed from there.

Finally, I owe special thanks to my parents Jay and Merrylyn Hunter. I owe all that I am today to them. Without their love, support, and moral judgment, I would have never seen the true benefits of education and strength of family.

We would be remiss if we did not acknowledge those people associated with the completion and publication of this book. First, we would like to thank Dennis McGonagle from Butterworth-Heinemann/Elsevier in Boston. We had just lost our book contract with another company because they were sold, and Dennis had a foresight to see the value this book could bring to the overall body of knowledge in sport education. Thank you for believing in our concept and making this book a reality. Next to thank would be Fran Ford from Butterworth-Heinemann/Elsevier in Oxford. We could not have completed this book without your input, professionalism, and overall diligence!!! You have been a breath of fresh air after previous bad experiences with publishers, and we are forever grateful that you were our partner in this project. Thank you. Special thanks goes to Mani (Praba) Prabakaran from Charon Tec in India for your outstanding handling of the editorial and typesetting stages of producing this book. Finally, thank you to Julie Trinder, Stephen Pegg, and the rest of the team at Butterworth-Heinemann/Elsevier for your assistance in making this book a reality!!!

CONTENTS

PART VI THE FUTURE OF SPORT MARKETING

PREFACE

The field of sport marketing is infused in virtually all aspects of sport management. As such, it is inevitable that many students will be involved in some aspect of sport marketing during their career. This book is being published with the sport management educator and student in mind, specifically aimed at those whose sport management program is housed in the business and/or management department. Most sport marketing books restate concepts learned in an introductory marketing course prior to getting into sport marketing. This is appropriate for sport management programs housed in a department other than business and/or management. However, for sport management programs housed in a business and/or management division, where virtually all students have already taken principles of marketing course, the book is simply repetitive. *Advanced Theory and Practice in Sport Marketing* strives to go beyond the introductory marketing course by expanding the knowledge of the student with advanced marketing theory related to research, consumer behavior, ethics, logistics, products, advertising, sponsorship, promotions, sales management, e-business and e-commerce, and international and global marketing.

The other aspect of this book is the application of real-world situations into the text. Professors talk about what goes on in the field of sport marketing based on their limited experience. Advanced Theory and Practice in Sport Marketing publishes what goes on in the real world of sport marketing by having professionals in the field provide first-hand accounts of how they entered the field of sport marketing, information about what their current job entails, and advice to students who wish to enter the field of sport marketing. This allows the instructor to better prepare the student for life in the sport marketing profession. It is the goal of the author to have this book become a resource that sport marketing educators, students, and professionals will utilize as an everyday reference tool in pursuit of their goals.

The book reflects the authors' extensive research and varied experiences in the field of sport marketing. Dr. Schwarz has worked in and with professional, amateur, and non-profit sport organizations, as well as from the business aspects of sport marketing specifically related to consulting work in sport facility and event management. He has conducted and presented research in sport marketing and experiential learning in the United States, Canada, Europe, and Australia. In addition, from June 2006 to August 2007 he was on sabbatical conducting research in leisure marketing and designing a postgraduate course in Applied Sport management at the University of Ballarat in Australia. Dr. Hunter supplements this knowledge by bringing extensive experience from the physical education, athletics, and coaching realm, as well as being a former owner of a sport retail firm and a sport facility.

Part I of the book serves to provide an overview of sport marketing, including a basic review of those topics commonly covered in an introductory marketing course. The remainder of this text will provide the reader a framework understanding of sport marketing by connecting traditional marketing to sport marketing. Each chapter will cover a specific aspect of traditional marketing and applying it to the field of sport marketing.

RESEARCH

The reader will expand their knowledge of the concepts of market segmentation, positioning, and demand analysis, and using that knowledge to develop basic capabilities in advertising research, competitive analysis, and strategic outcomes assessment in sport marketing. Inclusive of this will be the development and implementation of focus group research, survey research, and experimental studies; the identification, retrieval, and analysis of secondary data; the utilization of qualitative and quantitative research methodologies; and the application of the research method. Inclusive of this will be a description of research services within sport marketing research, including but not limited to studies of customer satisfaction, economic impact, need assessment, organizational behavior, and risk assessment.

INFORMATION SYSTEMS

The reader will gain an appreciation of the use of information systems for sport marketing goals and objectives through structure, organization, and communication. Inclusive of this will be an examination of sport consumer relationship management for both Internet and non-Internet environment using strategic database and software marketing, with the goal of being able to identify market opportunities, develop targets, and manage and evaluate promotional efforts in sport.

CONSUMER BEHAVIOR

The reader will learn how to utilize basic cultural, personal, social, and psychological principles to explain how those factors directly affect individual purchasing and consumption behavior of participants, fans, spectators, volunteers, community and corporate partners. Additionally, there will be an examination of the various types of sport consumer studies, and how individual and environmental factors, socialization, and participation directly influence the decision making process for sport consumption. Inclusive of this examination will be an analysis of the expected demographic, psychographic, geographic, and behavioristic characteristics of the sport consumer.

PRODUCT MANAGEMENT

The reader will learn how to distinguish, identify, and classify the various elements of sport products and services, and the stages of the sport product life cycle. In addition, the concepts of branding, licensing, images, marks, and positioning will be identified as related to the sport product.

SALES MANAGEMENT

The reader will be presented with an overview of the strategies and techniques for promoting and selling the sport product, including sales theory models, promotion theory paradigms, and promotion application in sport marketing. Additionally, the distribution process of the sport product will be covered, including an analysis of the distribution principles related to time, place, and possession, as well as the process for selecting distribution systems.

PURCHASING AND SUPPLY CHAIN MANAGEMENT

The reader will be presented with numerous logistical functions that a sport business must manage, including inventory management, team and equipment transportation, warehousing, order processing, and information systems. Both network design and global logistics will be analyzed as a part of this focus. Additionally, there will be an explanation of the importance of the integration of these various systems, and the effects that integration has on the overall viability of the sport industry.

PROMOTIONS AND COMMUNICATION MANAGEMENT

The reader will learn about understand the other elements of the sport promotion mix, including licensing, publicity, personal contact, incentives, and atmospherics. The reader will know how to incorporate sport promotion activities into an integrated communications plan, how to plan an event, create pricing, location, and distribution strategies, and how to cost effectively promote them. Areas to be covered will include sports information, media relations, public relations, and community relations. In addition, indirect (word-of-mouth) and direct (sales) promotional strategies will be covered in relationship to positioning, building brand equity, increasing credibility, and enhancing image transfer and association.

ADVERTISING

The reader will be provided an overview of the methods for bringing public attention to the sport product or business through print, broadcast, or electronic media. This will include a comprehensive examination of copy and design, media planning and buying, portfolio development, video production, broadcast advertising development, billboard/outdoor advertising development, and graphic design. The reader will also discover how to integrate the field of sport and the engagement of interdisciplinary thinking as it related to all areas of communication. Special emphasis will be placed on journalism, audiovisual communications, development communications, telecommunications, and mass communications.

SPONSORSHIP

The reader will gain an appreciation of the significant role sponsorship plays in the sport promotional mix. Through an explanation of the history of sport sponsorship, the reader will gain an understanding of the various areas of sport sponsorship, including governing body sponsorship, team sponsorship, athlete sponsorship, broadcast sponsorship, facility sponsorship, and event sponsorship. Through the articulation of corporate and brand goals, the reader will also learn about the various criteria for sponsorship, and how they are utilized in choosing the companies to partner with, developing sponsorship packages, and engaging in sponsorship negotiations.

RETAIL MANAGEMENT

The reader will gain an understanding of sport retailing and sport retail management through a presentation of various retail strategies and a strategic approach to retailing in the sport field. Inclusive of this chapter will be the concepts of strategic retail management; the factors and skills associated with situation analysis; the manners to target customers and gathering information; concepts associated with choosing a retail location; the concepts related to managing a retail business; the concepts related to merchandise management and pricing; the various ways of communicating with the customer; and integrating and controlling all aspects of the retail strategy.

E-BUSINESS AND E-COMMERCE

The reader will gain an understanding that in the 21st century, e-business and e-commerce have become staples within the field of sport marketing. Information will be offered regarding the factors that drive modern business through digital technologies. Inclusive of this will be concepts of managing digital enterprises via the Internet, the World Wide Web, and Intranets, including C2B and B2B, as well as potential future technologies. In addition, how sport businesses utilize electronic means to overcome barriers of geographic boundaries to market, produce, and deliver services will be covered.

INTERNATIONALIZATION AND GLOBALIZATION

The reader will gain an appreciation of the ever-growing internationalization and globalization of marketing in and through sport. This will be accomplished through an examination of the implementation of policies, procedures, and strategies within the parameters set forth by cultural, economic, political, and legal constraints of various worldwide markets.

ENTERPRISE MARKETING MANAGEMENT

The reader will gain an appreciation for this growing aspect of sport marketing. Though effective and efficient sport marketing is increasingly important due to tough competition and growing global opportunities, it has long been an island in most sport organizations, disconnected from core business processes and reliant on customized information technology that hampers communication and collaboration with other departments. This chapter will tie the topics from previous chapters to concepts such as brand architecture, investment measurement, and how to engineer creativity, and demonstrate how enterprise marketing management and customer relationship management work together to produce optimal sport marketing efforts by sport entities.

PEDAGOGICAL FEATURES

Advanced Theory and Practice in Sport Marketing enhances learning with the following pedagogical devices:

- Each chapter opens with a Chapter Outline and a list of Chapter Objectives.
- Illustrations, photos, and charts throughout the text that clarify text material and enhance learning.
- Key terms appear alphabetically at the end of the book in the Glossary.
- Each chapter will have at least one case study embedded within the chapter to enhance critical thinking as related to real-world concepts associated with the text material. Suggested discussion topics associated with each case study allow the learner to apply theoretical knowledge to the scenarios.
- At the end of each chapter, there is a real-world case written by professionals from the field of sport marketing. These experts are from academia, professional sports leagues and teams, amateur sport organizations, and corporate sport. The information they provide will provide the learner with knowledge of how the individual entered the specific area of sport marketing, about the real world of sport marketing, and advice of what the learner can do to better prepare themselves for entry into the specified area of sport marketing.
- A comprehensive Conclusion at the end of each chapter that reviews the Chapter Objectives and pertinent information from the chapter.
- A Test Bank that includes Multiple Choice Review Questions and Discussion Questions to allow students to check their comprehension of the chapter's main concepts.

CRITICAL THINKING

One of the most important skills for students to develop through their college and university years is critical thinking. This mental process of analyzing and evaluating information is used across all disciplines, and serves as a process for reflecting on the information provided, examining facts to understand reasoning, and forming conclusions and plans for action.

The authors of this book have provided a series of opportunities for students to enhance their critical thinking skills while also verifying their understanding of the materials presented in this text. For each chapter, there are 10 multiple choice questions that provide students the opportunity to verify their comprehension of the chapter's main concepts. To supplement that verification, there are also four discussion questions. These questions, which can be used as essay topics or in-class discussion issues by instructors, are based on the information provided in the chapter, the research available in the specific aspect of sport marketing, and the education and experiences of the authors.

In addition, each chapter has a minimum of one case study focusing either on the ethical or global nature of the specific sport marketing topics. These cases are a collection of "real-world" situations modified with a sport marketing twist to provide the student with the maximum opportunity to analyze, evaluate, and ponder possible solutions to the ethical or global situation. Suggested discussion topics associated with each case study will help the student focus their efforts on key theoretical aspects from the chapter, and apply that knowledge to deal with the specific scenario.

This text provides a unique opportunity for critical thinking in association with sport marketing in the corporate or professional setting. "From Theory to Practice" cases appear at the end of each chapter, written by professionals in the field of sport marketing. They provide information about how the individual entered the specific area of sport marketing, the professional world of sport marketing, and advice of what the learner can do to become better prepared for entry into the specified area of sport marketing.

SUPPLEMENTS

Advanced Theory and Practice in Sport Marketing provides the instructor with the following teaching aids:

- PowerPoint presentations for each chapter.
- An electronic test bank.
- Suggested discussion questions associated with the case studies embedded in each chapter.

ABOUT THE AUTHORS

Dr. ERIC C. SCHWARZ

Dr. Schwarz has been a member of the faculty within the Division of Business and Management at Daniel Webster College since 2000. Currently holding the rank of Associate Professor, he serves as the Program Coordinator, and is the faculty advisory for the Daniel Webster College Society for Sport Management. During the 2006–2007 school year, he took a sabbatical leave to serve as a Visiting Senior Lecturer and Researcher at the University of Ballarat in Australia. His responsibilities included teaching classes, conducting research in leisure and professional sport marketing, and developing a postgraduate program in Applied Sport Management.

Dr. Schwarz received a B.S. degree in Physical Education from Plymouth State University in 1991; a M.Ed. in Administration and Supervision from Salisbury University in 1992; and an Ed.D in Sport Management from the United States Sports Academy in 1998.

Prior to coming to Daniel Webster College, Dr. Schwarz had worked with a variety of sport-related organizations in high school athletics, college athletics, and campus recreation programming. He also owned his own summer camp, clinic, and coaching training business.

Since coming to Daniel Webster College, in addition to his teaching and administrative responsibilities, he has been focused on research, consulting, and experiential learning. Dr. Schwarz has presented on various topics in sport marketing and experiential learning at conferences in the United States (SMA, EBEA), Canada (NASSM), Europe (EASM), and Australia (SMAANZ). Dr. Schwarz has been most active with the Sport Marketing Association, where he has been a regular presenter, and has had two articles published in the conference book of papers. In addition, a group of his undergraduate students finished in first place in the undergraduate poster competition at the 2004 conference in Memphis, and won the case study competition in 2005 in Arizona.

Dr. Schwarz has been involved with numerous consulting projects, including being an independent consultant in facility management and marketing for three sport facilities in New Hampshire, the development of a new retail management plan for a minor league baseball team in New Hampshire, and an economic impact analysis for a Senior PGA Tour event in Massachusetts. Dr. Schwarz also serves as an expert witness in Physical Education and Sport Management for a lawyer in New Hampshire.

The importance of experiential learning for both students and professors is critical in the fields of sport marketing and management. The student gains practical experience that allows them to apply the theory learned in the classroom in a real-world setting. It allows the professor to understand the most current practices in the field, thus allowing them to provide the most current information to students. Dr. Schwarz lives that philosophy through his work with various organizations. Some of the events include the Boston Marathon, the NHL All-Star Game FanFest, the NBA Jam Session FanFest, and NASCAR at New Hampshire International Speedway.

Dr. Schwarz currently lives in Merrimack, New Hampshire with his wife Loan.

DR. JASON D. HUNTER

Dr. Hunter is a 1990 graduate of Plymouth State University with a B.S. in Physical Education; earned his Masters Degree in 1993 from the United States Sports Academy in Sports Management; and in 2005 completed a Ph.D. in Educational Administration from Madison University.

Dr. Hunter has dedicated his life to teaching and coaching at the collegiate level. At Plymouth State University, he served as the director of recreation, assistant baseball and women's soccer coach, and head women's softball coach. He also supervised the recreation component of a new 9 million dollar campus recreation and student union building. Co-owner of D&M Sports, a sporting goods retail store, Dr. Hunter joined his love and knowledge for sports to providing quality sporting goods equipment to the community.

In 1997, Dr. Hunter became the head coach of baseball and women's soccer at New England College, where he also served as an assistant athletic director and faculty member. In 2000, he relocated to Illinois to become the head men's and women's soccer coach and faculty member at North Central College. In 2003, he moved to the College of DuPage to become a faculty member in physical education and the women's soccer coach. Dr. Hunter recently has been granted tenure in this position. In addition, he has been selected as Coach of the Year five times and Adidas Central Coach of the Year in 2005.

Dr. Hunter is developing a Sports Management Program at College of DuPage and also serves as a senator for the faculty association. He has also presented at regional, national, and international conferences.

Dr. Hunter is the father of three wonderful children, Zachary, Morgan, and Jake and the husband to Mariann Hunter, the love of his life. They reside in Montgomery, Illinois.

SPORT MARKETING: THE BASICS

1

INTRODUCTION TO SPORT MARKETING

CHAPTER OUTLINE

CHAPTER OBJECTIVE

The reader will be able to:

- Provide an overview of sport marketing.
- Define what sport marketing is, how it is connected to the business of sport, and the relationship to traditional marketing.
- An introduction to the 3 C's of marketing analysis (consumer, company, and competition) and STPD (segmentation, targeting, positioning, and delivery).

3

WHAT IS SPORT MARKETING?

Prior to describing what sport marketing is, we should take a look at the definitions of the two root words: "sport" and "marketing."

Sport – Or Is It Sports?

First we look at the concepts of sport and sports. Sport is defined as activities, experiences, or business enterprises that center on athletics, health and wellness, recreation, and leisure time opportunities. Some of the common misconceptions about sport include (1) there needs to be a competitive situation, (2) the offering must have a standard set of rules, and (3) participants need specialized equipment and facilities. This is true of sports, which simply refers to individual, dual, and team sports activities such as soccer, baseball, golf, and tennis. Sport is an all-inclusive term covering all aspects that go beyond the playing field, including all the various operations that make the games happen.

Sport and Business

Now we look at how the concept of business ties into these previous definitions. Business is defined as individuals or organizations that seek to make a

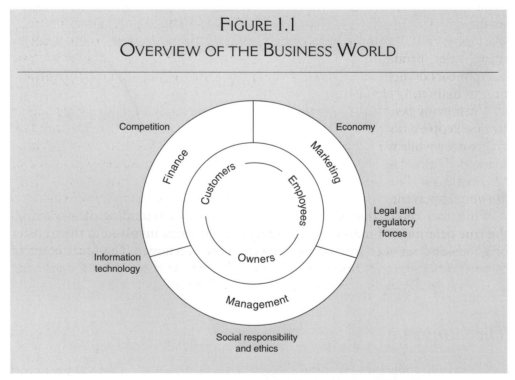

FIGURE 1.1
OVERVIEW OF THE BUSINESS WORLD

Source: Ferrell, O.C. and G. Hirt (2003). *Business: A Changing World*, 4th ed., p. 5. New York: McGraw-Hill.

profit by providing products and services that satisfy the needs, wants, and desires of the consumer. The business world, as documented in Figure 1.1, covers a wide variety of aspects. The internal factors include the primary business activities of management, marketing, and finance, which are centered on business owners, employees, and customers. The external factors include competition, the economy, information technology, legal and regulatory forces, and social responsibility and ethics.

The definition of business and the internal and external factors in the business world are mirrored in the profession of sport management and administration. With regard to whether sport administration or sport management is more appropriate, it seems as though more programs as business utilize the term management over administration; however, there is no significant difference between the meanings of the two terms when it comes to the field of sport. The only difference tends to be curricular based, and will vary from institution to institution. Therefore, when looking at this field, the major of sport management, and in some cases sport administration, is of greater interest to business educators. This is defended by the following definition of sport management: the collection of skills related to the planning, organizing, directing, controlling, budgeting, leading, and evaluation of an organization or department whose primary product or service is related to sport and its related functions.

Marketing

Now that we have a definition of sport, as well as a basis for its relationship to the business world, what is marketing? There is often confusion on what marketing truly is. Marketing is often defined by its components, such as advertising, sales, promotions, product management, pricing, publicity, etc. These components do not define what marketing is – they act to enhance the application of marketing elements.

When many people think of marketing, they are really thinking of marketing tactics. People associate marketing with tactics, including the television commercials we see while watching sporting events, the between play promotions during live sporting events, and the information published in newspapers or broadcast on a newscast. But tactics in marketing are similar to the tactics of sport. They are very important, but useless without having a sound basis of knowledge.

While this knowledge is a sound basis for the understanding of marketing, the true definition of marketing is simply the functions involved in the transfer of goods and services from the producer to the consumer. The focal point of these functions are in three specific areas known as the 3 C's of marketing analysis: the consumer, the company itself, and the competition.

The Consumer

Who is the consumer? Is it the shopper who visits stores, either in person or via an online capability, in search of merchandise or bargains? Is it the buyer who knows what they want and makes the purchase? How about the customer who repeatedly purchases a commodity or service? It is these three and much more. By definition, a consumer is an individual or organization that purchases or obtains goods and services for direct use or ownership. As marketing professionals, we strive to please all of these consumers to maximize sales of products and services, and hence maximize profit. But how do we reach these consumers?

Segmentation

Segmentation is the concept of dividing a large, diverse group with multiple attributes into smaller groups with distinctive characteristics. These distinctive groups have similar needs and desires, and hence will respond to marketing efforts in similar manners. The concept of segmentation is basic to all marketing efforts, as the goal of segmentation is to identify the market.

One of the biggest challenges for marketing professionals is to determine the appropriate segment to market. Some of the major factors utilized to choose a segment includes:

- What is the size of the segmented market?
- What is the purchasing power of the segmented market?
- How can the marketer be sure that the product is what the consumer wants?
- Is it worth marketing the product to the chosen segment?
- What tactics should be used to attract the segment to purchase the sport product?

To answer these questions, marketers utilize the four bases of segmentation: the consumer's state of being, the consumer's state of mind, product usage by consumers, and product benefits as perceived by consumers.

The consumer's state of being is the concept of belonging to a specified class or group. In marketing, the major states of being include location, age, income level, gender, race and ethnicity, and sexual orientation. Geographic location is utilized to determine the spread of population as related to the distribution and usage of a product. Age helps to differentiate the needs and interests of consumers, as they differ throughout the lifespan. Income levels help the marketer determine probable standard of living of the demographic, which in turn influences the manner in which a product is marketed. An example of this would be that a teenage inner-city basketball player who plays at the Rucker from Harlem will be marketed to differently as compared to the suburban soccer mom, and in comparison to the 10-year-old alternative sports fan who is influenced by anything related to skateboarding and BMX bikes. As marketing becoming more global in nature, understanding the intricacies of various race and ethnic markets is integral to marketing success. In addition, marketing based on sexual orientation is an emerging market; however, there is still some controversy as to whether this should be viewed as a separate and distinct market.

The consumer's state of mind deals with the individual cognitive processes involved in marketing. Among the most prevalent concerns to marketers are individual personality traits, lifestyle changes that are evident throughout the lifespan, and the individual preferences and perceptions of consumers, which are wide and varied.

Product usage by consumers deals with the consumption rates by the various market segments. Central to this concept is the Pareto Principle, otherwise known as the 80/20 rule. The Pareto Principle is generally applied to vendors or customers in a retail setting. This rule assumes that 20% of the customers generate 80% of the sales, or that 80% of merchandise comes from 20% of the vendors.

Product benefits as perceived by consumers go beyond the consumer's state of mind to look specifically at the assessment by the consumer as to the advantages the products provided to them. The consumer will always ask the question "What is in it for me?" By understanding the consumer's viewpoint, it allows marketers to (1) describe the products more efficiently and effectively in marketing collateral, (2) better prepare salespeople as to how to sell products, and (3) provide evidence as to how to better differentiate products.

Targeting

In the marketing world, we strive or aim for satisfying our desired market through the concepts of exchange and relationships. The purpose of targeting is to find the best way to get a product's image into the minds of consumers, and hence entice the consumer to purchase the product. The research and development processes described earlier are utilized at this stage to enter the product into the market. This is accomplished through a detailed analysis of the marketing mix, otherwise known as the 4 P's of marketing: product, price, place, and promotion (see Figure 1.2). The *product* may be tangible (goods) or intangible (services), and decisions are made based on concepts such as branding, functionality, and quality. *Price* is the amount of money or goods asked for in

FIGURE 1.2
THE MARKETING MIX

Product   Price

Target market

Place   Promotion

Source: www.netmba.com/marketing/mix.

exchange for something else. *Place* deals with the methods of distributing the product to consumers. *Promotion* represents how information about the product is communicated to customers, with a goal of receiving positive response from the consumer, and results in product sales.

Note: Later in this chapter, we will elaborate on this concept, and show how in the realm of sport, the elements of marketing are expanded to the 5 P's of sport marketing by moving publicity/public relations out of the category of promotion, since it is such a large factor in the marketing of sport.

Positioning

Positioning is how a company seeks to influence the perceptions of potential and current customers about the image of the company and its products and services. This is accomplished by applying the 4 P's of marketing with the goal of strategically placing the product or service firmly in the mind of the consumer. We often talk in society about the concept of "making a good first impression." In positioning, the goal is to get the consumer's mind to react to the implementation of the marketing mix in a positive manner. By creating this knowledge, consumers will develop an impression that is often difficult to change. Hence, if the marketer can send a message that is consistent with what the consumer already believes (the consumer's perceptions); the product will become easier to sell. An example would be a Detroit Red Wings advertising campaign concentrating on Detroit being known as Hockeytown. Hockey consumers are already aware of this fact, and the marketers can play off of this knowledge.

One of the best ways to position a product in the consumer's mind is to be first on the scene. People want who they perceive is first in the market, or the best in the market. This concept of being number one often can overcome other shortcomings of products.

However, not all products can be first on the market, or number one in the market. So how do you position these other products so the consumer will buy? This is most often accomplished by claiming a unique position in the market. Through applying the marketing mix, the marketer will strive to carve this uniqueness into the mind of the consumer, so that they feel they are getting something different and worthwhile for their hard earned money. In general, when there is a clear market leader, it is often extremely difficult to knock off the king of the mountain. By not challenging the market leader head-on, a company can increase their market share through marketing their uniqueness as compared to that industry leader. To market their uniqueness, marketers look to cater to the specific benefits of the product. In order to do this, often the product must be sold at a low price, as people when viewing new products will value low initial price more than quality.

Delivering

Delivery is the concept of producing or achieving what is desired or expected by the consumer. Through the concepts of segmentation, targeting, and positioning, a framework is created to allow the industry to utilize marketing to deliver an awareness of products to potential consumers. The previous concepts are the development phase and the start of the implementation phase of the marketing concept. Delivery is the completion of the implementation phase, and the start of the management aspect, where the creative and process aspects of the marketing discipline are applied.

The remainder of this book will focus on the delivery of the marketing concept. Understanding the consumer is central to the ability to engage in marketing. Marketers must know how consumers behave, their motivations, their perceptions and preferences. Marketers must have an awareness of their attitudes, their knowledge, and their emotions. Also, marketers must have the ability to segment the market, analyze the target market, position the product, and deliver it to consumers.

The Company

What do we need to know about the company itself? The framework for this is the SWOT analysis, which looks at the internal strengths, internal weaknesses, external opportunities, and external threats of the organization (Figure 1.3).

For starters, the framework of understanding is in the first two parts of a SWOT analysis: internal strengths and internal weaknesses. The strengths of a company are its resources and capabilities that can be used to develop a competitive advantage. A competitive advantage is where a company sustains profits above the average for the specific industry. Competitive advantage is usually looked at in two ways: cost advantage (when a company can deliver the same benefits as competitors at a lower cost) and differentiation advantage (when a company can deliver benefits that exceed those of other products in the specific industry). By understanding these concepts, a marketer can gain a better understanding of the company itself. In addition, the marketing professional

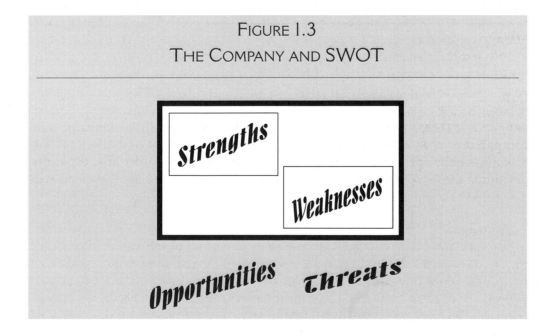

FIGURE 1.3
THE COMPANY AND SWOT

Strengths

Weaknesses

Opportunities   Threats

can implement a more effective and efficient marketing effort by maintaining or improving on strengths, while seeking ways to improve on and eliminate weaknesses. Examples would include having limited time, staff, or funding.

The Competition

Finally, what do we need to know about the competition? The framework of competition is in the last two parts of a SWOT analysis: external opportunities and external threats. By evaluating opportunities and threats, a company can evaluate their current status in the market, and determine which direction the company should be heading. This is most often guided by an organizational mission, through an evaluation of organizational and management options, and outlining the goods and/or services to be marketed. The opportunities are the marketplace openings that exist because others have not entered or capitalized on that part of the marketplace. Threats are those environmental factors that can negatively affect the marketing of a product if the company does not react to them.

The Marketing Plan

All of the previous information is then compiled into a marketing plan. A marketing plan starts with primary and secondary market research. It is very dangerous to start a marketing plan without appropriate research by assuming what the intended market wants and needs. Primary market research is gathering your own data through observation, surveys, interviews, and focus groups. Secondary market research uses published information including industry profiles, trade periodicals, and demographic profiles to determine the scope of your market.

The next part of the marketing plan focuses on economics. The key factors when identifying the economy of your market includes the following:

- What is the total size of the market?
- What percent share of the market do you intend to capture?
- What is the current demand within the market?
- What are the current and future trends of the market?
- Is there growth potential within the market?
- What are the barriers to entering the market, and how will the company overcome those barriers?
- How could changes in industry itself, the economy, technology, and governmental regulations affect your company and force changes in your marketing efforts?

The following section should describe the product(s) and/or service(s) to be marketed. Three key concepts that should be articulated in the plan for each product or service should be: (1) a description of the most important features of the product/service, with particular consideration given to what differentiates it from other products/services; (2) a description of the benefits, specifically considering what the product/service will do for the consumer; and (3) a description of the post-sale services (warranties, service contracts, delivery options, consumer support, and refund policies).

Now we need to detail the demographics of our customers. For individuals, we consider such items as age, gender, race/ethnicity, location, income level, social class, occupation, and education. For business consumers we consider the industry, location, size, and preferences.

Next we detail the competition. It is important to remember in this section to list all competitors (indirect and direct), and differentiate the level of competitiveness – whether they compete across the board, or only in certain product areas. In this section, there must also be a comparison of how your product(s) or service(s) will compare with the competition. This competitive analysis will help determine your competitive advantages and disadvantages, and provide data to help determine the best way to market your products within the industry.

After this information has been compiled, a niche can be defined. A niche is a special area of demand for a product or service. On a large scale, companies such as Nike and Reebok design and market athletic shoes for each different sport, and often with specialized models based on specific athletes. On a more direct scale, a niche marketing scheme would be offering specialized golf products such as customized club, designer balls and tees, and associated golf gadget to subscribers of Golf Magazine. These niches are then used to develop the marketing strategy. Inclusive of this strategy development are the elements of the marketing mix, including:

- The method for setting prices and associated pricing strategies (price).
- The distribution channels to be utilized to sell products and services (place).
- The method for getting information to potential consumers (promotion).

Now that a description of the products, services, customers, markets, and strategy has been completed, the final element of the marketing plan is a sales forecast. Usually this is completed in two ways. First, a "best-case scenario," should provide a realistic expectation of sales. Second, a "worst-case scenario," should provide the minimum expectation of sales irrespective of what happens.

INTRODUCTION TO ETHICAL DECISION MAKING IN SPORT MARKETING

Funding for Boys and Girls Club

The local Boys and Girls Club has struggled for years to raise enough funds to support its programs and services. Support from public and private financial sources has significantly declined, resulting in a decrease in available budgetary money by 23% over the last 2 years. The local economy is stagnant, especially since many of the major employers have laid off employees during the last 5 years. The General Manager of the Boys and Girls Club

Continued

is a salaried employee of the organization, and has worries that if things do not turn around, that the Boys and Girls Club may have to either reduce programming or close down.

One day, the General Manager was approached by a new Board member with a novel fundraising idea. This Board member is a local attorney in private practice, and also represents the local sports arena. The Board member suggested that he could encourage the concessions manager at the arena to donate to the Club part of its proceeds on the sale of beer at six upcoming sports events. Convinced by previous sales figures that the revenues generated would more than cover costs, he thought the Club could pay the concessionaire for the arena a fee of $3000 for the first night and $2000 for each of the remaining nights in exchange for the beer service concession. Therefore, for these six evenings, the Club would pay the concessionaire at the arena a total of $13,000 for the privilege of running the concession stand. The concessionaire would guarantee that the Club would net at least $500 each night.

The General Manager discussed the idea with the Chairman of the Club's Board of Directors, and at a subsequent Board meeting the idea was approved. One week after the last of the six events, the Club received $16,000 in cash (their $13,000 investment plus $3000 in net profit).

At the next Board meeting, a proposal was presented that encouraged the Club enter into a much more formal relationship with the concessionaire at the arena. Several clauses of the contract were discussed, including:

- The Boys and Girls Club will apply for a Class A Liquor License to sell malted beverages at the arena. The concessionaire will furnish the arena's beer services facilities, fixtures, supplies (exclusive of the malted beverages), and utilities for $2800. The concessionaire will provide 19 people to operate the concession stand at the rate of $7.85 per hour per person. All personnel shall be supervised and controlled by the Club, and shall be trained to dispense malted beverages.
- During each event, the Club shall have on site at least two of its own Board members who will supervise the concession operation.
- The concessionaire will provide the Club with eight tickets per event for its exclusive use. This would come out of the concessionaire's personal allocation from the arena.
- The concessionaire will indemnify and hold the Club harmless for any claim or cause of action whatsoever arising out of the Club's activities pursuant to this agreement.
- The concessionaire guarantees that the Club will net at least $500 per sporting event.

The Club's Board was now uniformly enthusiastic about the proposed contract. As a result, a contract between the concessionaire and the Board of the Boys and Girls Club was signed.

Source: Adapted from Dubinsky, J. E. (1997). Practical ethics: a case study. In *Ethical Issues in Partnerships Between Businesses and Nonprofit Organizations*. Retrieved from http://www.corcom.org/publications.htm.

Suggestion Discussion Topics

1. You are the General Manager of the Boys and Girls Club. Assume philosophically and ethically that you do not agree with using alcohol proceeds to sponsors the youth organization. Part of your reasoning includes that you preach in your programming the dangers of under-age drinking. Considering both the organizational and marketing-based issues related to this situation, what would you do in this situation where your Board has now agreed to use the sales of alcohol beverages to fund programming for the Club?
2. One of the fastest growing fundraising efforts is based on the popularity of Texas Hold'Em, a popular version of poker. Events take place in towns all over the country, and a portion of the proceeds go to the sponsoring charity for the evening. The charity is required to provide the dealers for the evening. If they cannot find enough people, they can sign up members of the poker organization as members of the charity, and then they can deal in the event. The charity also needs to be present at the end of each evening to write checks to the winners. You are the General Manager of the Boys and Girls Club considering utilizing this as a fundraising opportunity. What are the pros and cons of sponsoring such an event? Is it ethical to use proceeds from gambling for youth programming? What are the marketing implications for your organization?

BOTTOM LINE – WHAT IS SPORT MARKETING?

In conclusion, [marketing is the study of the consumer, the company, and the competition, specifically relating those areas to market segmentation, target markets, product positioning, and delivery of the product.] Then to engage in marketing, we use the various tactics of marketing, which will be elaborated upon throughout the remaining chapters of this text.

OK – then what is sport marketing? Based on the definition of "sport" and "marketing," it shows how complex both concepts are. Therefore, it is safe to assume that combining the two concepts to get sport marketing is probably even more complex. This is very true, because sport marketing is a process of developing and implementing activities related to the production, pricing, distribution, promotion, and publicizing of a sport product. These sport products run the gambit, from sport drinks to sport clothing with team logos, to ticket packages. The goal of this process is to satisfy the needs and wants of consumers, achieve the goals and objectives of the company in relation to their philosophy, mission, and vision, and stay ahead of the competition to maximize your product's and company's potential. With this complexity come certain characteristics that make the sport product unique.

CONCLUSION

The purpose of this chapter is to provide the reader with an overview of the evolution of sport marketing. First we investigate what sport marketing is by defining the root words. Sport is defined as activities, experiences, or business enterprises that center on athletics, health and wellness, recreation, and leisure time opportunities. The association of sport with business (individuals or organizations that seek to make a profit by providing products and services that satisfy the needs, wants, and desires of the consumer) helps to develop an understanding of the field of sport management as the collection of skills related to the planning, organizing, directing, controlling, budgeting, leading, and evaluation of an organization or department whose primary product or service is related to sport and its related functions. The marketing aspect of sport focuses on the functions involved in the transfer of goods and services from the producer to the consumer.

The focal point of these functions is in three specific areas known as the 3 C's of marketing analysis: the consumer, the company itself, and the competition. The consumer is an individual or organization that purchases or obtains goods and services for direct use or ownership. To reach sport consumers, sport marketing professional go through a series of processes. Segmentation is the concept of dividing a large, diverse group with multiple attributes into smaller groups with distinctive characteristics. Targeting seeks to find the best way to get a product's image into the minds of consumers, and hence entice the consumer to purchase the product. This is accomplished by focusing on the 4 P's of marketing – product, price, place, and promotion – and the evolution of publicity as a 5th P. Positioning focuses on how a company seeks to influence the perceptions of potential and current customers about the image of the company and its products and services. Delivery is the concept of producing or achieving what is desired or expected by the consumer.

With regard to the company and competition, the framework is centered on the SWOT analysis. The managerial function of the company itself is most concerned with internal strengths and weaknesses. The leadership of the company tends to focus on the external opportunities and external threats posed by competition and the environment. All this information is then compiled into a marketing plan, and enhanced with primary and secondary research, economic and financial consideration, and an evaluation of the products and services to be offered.

FROM THEORY TO PRACTICE

Frank Supovitz, Senior Vice President, Events

National Football League
New York, New York

In my opinion, I have the best job in the world. Sometimes, it seems like one of the toughest, but it is certainly the best. In my position as Senior Vice President of Events for the National Football League, I manage a department that is responsible for the planning and management of the Super Bowl, Pro Bowl, and the NFL Draft, among many other programs. We work closely with the host cities, stadiums, hotels, sponsors, broadcasters, and support venues that are needed to successfully execute these events, sometimes many years in advance.

Getting to this point in my career was partially a function of being in the right place at the right time, but also about being open to the many exciting possibilities a career can take. That did not mean taking any job that came my way. I evaluated every opportunity to determine whether a new job might provide me with new challenges for my experience and expertise, and whether I could imagine myself happy in a new pursuit not a year later, but 10 years later.

I grew up in Queens, and worked evenings after school as an usher at Radio City Music Hall. That part-time job turned into a 16-year run at the Hall, advancing through the ranks through the operations department, then marketing, and finally to director of special events. There, I applied my experience in entertainment marketing with the knowledge of staging corporate, sports, and civic events to projects including the halftime show for Super Bowl XXII. From there, I worked on the US Olympic Festival, the Goodwill Games, and other major programs, eventually ending up at the National Hockey League in 1992. There, I was responsible for NHL All Star Weekend, the Stanley Cup, and the NHL Draft, among many other events. After 13 seasons in hockey, I moved from pucks to pigskin, moving to the National Football League in 2005.

What does it take to plan a Super Bowl? Start with 3–5 years of working with local business and governmental leaders to prepare a city to host 150,000 inbound visitors, preparing the stadium for the nation's most watched annual event, managing ticketing for more than 70,000 fans, contracting more than 20,000 hotel rooms, hundreds of motor coaches, and tens of thousands of parking spaces. Many elements the public never sees, such as securing two practice facilities with the same playing surface as the stadium, hotels for the competing teams' accommodations and offices, and a media center to house more than 100 radio stations and the NFL Network broadcasting live throughout the week, as well as work space for thousands of accredited reporters and writers. We design and construct tented or indoor hospitality space for up to 8000 corporate guests, more than 150,000 square

Continued

feet of space for two major parties, a million square-feet home for the NFL Experience fan festival, and banner and décor programs for city streets, the stadium, hotels, and other event facilities. We are also concerned with the presentation of the game on the field and scoreboard, create a 300-feet hardened security perimeter around the stadium, and manage a program to credential thousands of game day workers. While this list is by no means complete, it provides a tiny snapshot of why it takes hundreds of people and a number of years to prepare for one game on one day.

None of it is possible without the help of our business partners, and it is also our job to ensure that our sponsors get the best possible value from their association. It is so much more than sponsor signage on site, an ad in the program, or public address announcements. Each sponsor wants their product, service, and message to rise above the clutter, targeting a specific audience, and encouraging sampling or purchase. The trick is to involve sponsors in a meaningful way so they feel a sense of ownership in our events. Visa, for instance, offers special and exclusive experiences in which cardholders can win a chance to tour the Super Bowl field before the game, watch the halftime show from the field, or bring Gatorade to the bench (involving yet another sponsor). General Motors is featured as a sponsor of the post-game ceremonies during which the Super Bowl MVP wins a Cadillac. Pepsi offers fans and visitors a concert series in the host city. Each of these partners activate their sponsorships with involving and unique experiential marketing programs that their association with the NFL can offer because we understand that our relationship is a true partnership in which both parties can richly benefit.

The pursuit of success in your sports marketing and management career will follow many of the same philosophies as building success on the field. Expand your playbook by staying current with the market and learning all you can about how this amazing business works. Keep your eyes open for changing developments and trends that will help you punch through obstacles and challenges, and be prepared to respond quickly to opportunities.

Settle for no less than excellence in everything you do. The competition for the best positions is fierce!

MANAGING THE SPORT MARKETING MIX

CHAPTER OUTLINE

CHAPTER OBJECTIVES

The reader will be able to:

- Understand how the sport marketing mix is implemented and managed.
- Recognize the concepts that make sport marketing unique.
- Expand the traditional marketing mix into the 5 P's of sport marketing.
- Appreciate the intricacies of the sport marketing plan.

WHAT MAKES SPORT MARKETING UNIQUE?

When we look at sport marketing and what makes it unique, we must complete an in-depth analysis of those market forces that are utilized to meet the needs and wants of the consumers, while ensuring success for the company. What makes this different than traditional marketing? In theory, there is no difference. However in practice, there is a world of difference. The primary sport product, and hence the market, is traditionally demand based, whereas most generic products are marketed based on need.

THE CHARACTERISTICS OF SPORT MARKETING

Sport Can Be a Consumer Good, a Consumer Service, a Commercial Good, or a Commercial Service

Sport is an end product that is produced for mass consumer appeal for spectators and participants. The primary sport product can be both tangible and intangible in nature. At the same time, businesses and corporate entities use sport as a way to reach their consumers and to sell their respective products and services. They also utilize sport (specifically events) as a reward system for their employees. An example of this would be having an employee night at the local ballpark or arena to reward the employees for their hard work. An additional reward system could be offered if the company owned a corporate suite at the facility. The organization could reward those with the highest level of production with the ability to watch event from the suite.

The Principal Sport Product Is Perpetually Intangible, Subjective, and Variable

The consumer experience is constantly subjective because it is subject to various levels of interpretation. This makes it very difficult for the sport marketer because with so many different consumer perceptions, it becomes challenging to guarantee the satisfaction of consumers.

Additionally, since there is no predictability of the results of sport, and there is no guarantee of the quality of play from the participants, it again becomes challenging for the sport marketer to guarantee the satisfaction of the consumer.

Sport Has an Appeal that Is Extensive and Permeates All Aspects of Life

This provides the sport marketer a range of target markets, and thus requires the sport industry to create variations of products. These variations must represent the innumerable demographics of consumers, including age, sex, income level, race/ethnicity, and geographic location.

Sport Is Normally Publicly Consumed and Consumer Satisfaction Is Directly Affected by the External Environment

The consumption of sport usually involves social interaction. According to numerous studies conducted, there is a strong correlation between social identification, affiliation with a team, and the decision to attend sport events. In fact, the research shows that less than 2% of collegiate and professional sport spectators attend events alone. As a result of this, sport marketers must create products and activities that enhance group attendance, and hence facilitates consumer satisfaction.

The Chief Sport Product Elicits a Strong Emotional Connection

Customers have a strong personal identification, both positive and negative, with elements of the sport product. The sport marketing professional must be able to market products to both sides of this affiliation.

The Sport Consumer Believes that They Are the Experts When It Comes to Knowledge of the Product

Usually the manufacturers of a product are the experts about that product. In turn, consumers usually trust the opinion of the company producing the product, or the industry where the product is sold. Not so in sport, where the consumer believes they are the expert. An example of this is the concept of the "Monday Morning Quarterback" – where fans look back on the game and pass judgment on what the players or coaches should have done. This is intensified by the number of media outlets – websites devoted to sports (especially fantasy sports), sport radio, 24-hour sport television networks, back page newspaper coverage, etc.

The Sport Product (in an Event Form) Is a Perishable Commodity

In this form, there is no true inventory. The sport event is produced and consumed at the same time. Therefore, the sport marketer must pre-sell the event. To accomplish this, the sport marketing professional must "sell" anticipated performance and projected potential.

As With Most Demand-Based Products, the Consumer Demand for the Main Sport Product Can Vary Greatly

With most products, we consider the economic concept of supply and demand. The main sport product is demand based. This makes it difficult for the sport marketer to develop strategies, as they must read the minds of consumers and identify their needs and desires as related to the sport product.

Sport Organizations Concurrently Compete and Cooperate

While sport organizations compete on the court or field, they cooperate away from the competition to assure stability and existence. This challenges sport marketing professionals to market the sport product with both in mind. A great example of this would be the rivalry between the Boston Red Sox and the New York Yankees. While they often compete with each other in the standings, the field of play, and in the minds of fans, they must rely on each other for games to take place on the field. If the Red Sox chose not to show up for a game at Yankee Stadium, there would be no event.

Most of the Marketing Effort Is Not Placed on the Primary Sport Product; It Is Placed on Product Extensions

Since marketing professionals have little or no say about the prima~~ry~~ ~~prod~~uct, they must use product extensions to get the message about the product into the public eye. The main example of a product extension is merchandise. Product extensions serve as a major revenue generation for sport organizations at all levels.

Exposure from the Mass Media Has Resulted in a Reduced Emphasis on Traditional Sport Marketing

The oversaturation of sport in the mass media has resulted in an evolution in the traditional method of controlling and coordinating the marketing mix. This exposure is called publicity. The expanded public relations efforts have forced marketers who traditionally viewed the marketing mix as the 4 P's of marketing evolve their theory into the 5 P's of sport marketing: product, price, place, promotion, and publicity (Figure 2.1).

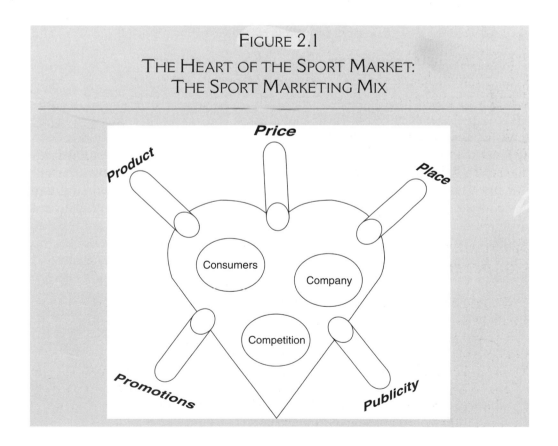

FIGURE 2.1

THE HEART OF THE SPORT MARKET:
THE SPORT MARKETING MIX

THE SPORT MARKETING MIX

The heart of the sport market is the sport marketing mix. Central to our understanding of the sport marketing mix are the three areas of marketing analysis – the consumer, the company, and the competition. These "chambers" of the heart must be understood so that the marketing mix can be controlled, coordinated, and implemented within the overall marketing effort. As reviewed earlier in Chapter 1, our analysis of consumers includes segmentation, targeting, positioning, and delivery. For the company, we analyze internal strengths and weaknesses, as well as competitive advantages including cost and differentiation. As far as competition, we consider external opportunities such as marketplace openings, and external threats such as environmental factors.

Once we understand the components of the sport market, we can now manipulate our efforts through the elements of the marketing mix. As discussed earlier in the chapter, there is a significant difference in the traditional view of the marketing mix when it comes to sport. As a rule in marketing, the marketing mix was always viewed as the 4 P's of marketing. However, in sport marketing, there is an expanded role that publicity/or public relations play. These are the methods and activities utilized to establish and promote awareness with the public by disseminating information through various media outlets. With this expanded role of publicity, that aspect has been broken away from being a part of promotion into its own elements. Hence, the sport marketing mix has evolved into the 5 P's of sport marketing: product, price, place, promotion, and publicity.

The successful interaction of the marketing mix with the target, as well as between the elements themselves, is crucial to a successful marketing effort. This interaction has a direct affect on the sport marketing professional's decision making process. Included in this process is the realization that interactions are not always positive in nature. How does the sport marketer deal with this?

This is where strategy comes into play. The marketing mix can only be utilized if it is in conjunction with understanding the 3 C's of competitive analysis (the chambers of the heart of sport marketing): the consumer, the company, and the competition. We talk about segmentation, targeting, positioning, delivery, differentiation, marketplace openings and environmental factors – but how do we develop a strategy that takes into account all the facts that are important, while having a full understanding of the cross-impact of all of these factors? Unfortunately, many in the field of sport marketing do not know how, or do not wish to spend the time. They often make decisions based on unfounded, preconceived notions, or knee-jerk reactions. However, there are a series of questions, falling into three categories, which if answered can provide the information necessary to make more effective and efficient decisions related to the sport marketing mix as a whole:

- *Product impact*
  - What is the level of impact the marketing effort will have?
  - Will the product increase the return on investment?

- Would the introduction of a broader product range increase the possible return on investment?
- *Potential risks*
  - What is the probability the marketing effort will be successful?
  - Is it based on a theory that success has a low or high probability of occurring?
  - Are competitors likely to respond with a better option?
  - What are the risks of not pursuing the marketing strategy and being left behind?
- *Feasibility*
  - Is the marketing effort feasible from a technical point of view (enough resources – space, staff, and customers)?
  - Is the marketing effort feasible from a financial point of view (affordability, cash flow and net income implications)?
  - Is the marketing effort feasible from a political point of view (support from stakeholders)?

Once these questions have been answered, the sport marketing professional can then effectively create a value chain for the effort. Adding value is a crucial factor in marketing a product. The goal is to identify, evaluate, and understand the consumer's value chain and investigate the potential impact of the organization's value chain on the consumer. The value chain shows the amount of value that is added during the marketing process, which in turn facilitates differentiation. Differentiation is the concept of being creating and demonstrating distinct and specialized characteristics of sport products and services as compared to those of its competitors. In the sport market, efforts toward differentiation are centered on the following:

- *Purchasing*: quantity discounts, package deals.
- *Products*: improve features of extensions such as merchandise.
- *Distribution*: faster delivery, ease of purchasing products, increase opportunities to purchase the product.
- *Marketing communication activities*: public relations, media relations, community relations.
- *Sales activities*: appropriate pricing of products, selling products with the features consumers need and want.
- *Customer service activities*: convey product information to customers, availability to effectively and efficiently deal with customer problems and questions.

Sport marketing differentiation strategies are doomed to fail if the product feature is not perceived as an influencing or determining factor by the consumer. This includes charging a price that consumers perceive as being too high relative to the additional features, or that the features have not been well conveyed to the consumer. Basically, if there is no understanding of or attempt to identify how consumers define value, the marketing professional cannot implement an appropriate marketing plan, and hence the goal of differentiation will fail. This, in turn will affect the profitability of the organization, which eventually could lead to its downfall.

THE ESCALATOR CONCEPT

To stay on the cutting edge of providing value for the sport consumer, the sport marketing professional strives to establish ways to gain new consumers into the sport market while enticing current sport consumers to become more involved with the sport product. Earlier with regard to product usage we talked about the Pareto Principle, otherwise known as the 80/20 rule. The utilization of the 80/20 rule by marketers is fundamental to the development of segments. But how do marketers then develop the segment over time? The concept that is essential to this development process is the escalator concept. This concept is utilized to represent the movement of consumers to higher levels of involvement with a specified product. This concept is diagrammed in Figure 2.2.

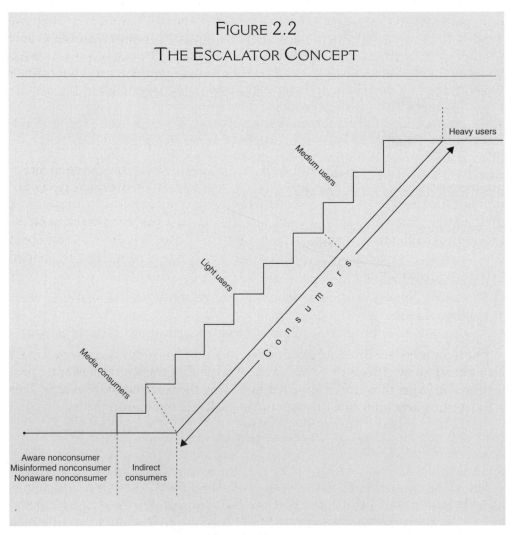

FIGURE 2.2
THE ESCALATOR CONCEPT

Source: Mullin, B. J., S. Hardy, and W. A. Sutton (1999). *Sport Marketing*, 2nd ed., p. 36. Champaign, IL: Human Kinetics.

Nonconsumers

A nonconsumer is an individual who does not use a good or service. There are three levels of nonconsumers that the sport marketing professional must attempt to identify with. The nonaware nonconsumer is an individual who does not know about the sport product, and therefore is not a user of the sport product. The sport marketer strives to get this demographic aware of the product so they might choose to become a consumer in the future. The misinformed nonconsumer is an individual who is aware of the sport product, but does not purchase because based on the information they do not associate themselves with the sport product. The aim of the sport marketing professional is to change this image of the product in the mind of the misinformed nonconsumer by providing information that creates an association with the sport product. The aware nonconsumer is probably the most difficult to address, because they have knowledge of the sport product and its benefits, and have chosen not to consume the sport product. Often, these aware nonconsumers are so knowledgeable, they can sense when the sport marketer is trying to influence them. The sport marketer must attempt to change perceptions about a sport product, which involves a detailed understanding of this aware nonconsumer's value chain. Getting this type of nonconsumer on the bandwagon often takes a lot of effort.

Indirect Consumers

Indirect consumers in the sport market are those who utilize the sport product from a distance through the use of intermediate or intervening opportunities. For the sport product, this may include only watching sport on television, only being a part of a fantasy league, or only purchasing peripheral products such as hats and shirts. The goal of the sport marketer is to entice these sport consumers to increase their level of involvement by purchasing more peripheral products, or more realistically, attending events in person.

Light Users

The light users are those who are actively involved as indirect consumers, but also attend an event one or twice a year. The goal of the sport marketing professional is to get them more involved by having them attend more events. This is most often accomplished through ticket packages and group plans.

Medium Users

The medium user is even more involved. They probably attend as many as half of the events related to the sport product. The sport marketers attempts to entice this sport consumer to move to the top of the "escalator" by showing them the benefits of having season tickets, leasing a sky box, or attending a hallmark event (Super Bowl, All-Star Game) associated with the sport product.

Heavy Users

Heavy users are sport organizations bread and butter. These are individuals who are fully engaged in the culture of the organization at a maximum consumer level. The sport marketing professional must work to maintain this level of expectation through their efforts, continually apprising the heavy user that they are important and receiving the maximum benefits.

The key is to strive to increase the level of involvement in the sport product over time, while limiting having anyone fall off or go down the escalator. However, it is important not to forget those who do reduce their involvement. By understanding their reasons for decreasing the connection with the sport product, sport marketers learn valuable lesson to improve of their tactics as to work toward preventing a reoccurrence of this dip in image and involvement.

Another challenge sport marketers face is that, depending on the sport product, individuals can fall on different part of the escalator. For example, one individual may be a heavy user for football, but a light user of basketball, and an aware nonconsumer for baseball. Marketing efforts not only must differ based on the level of consumer or nonconsumer, but also must differ for each sport product. With so many sport products on the market, the task for the sport marketing professional is challenging and never-ending.

DEVELOPING A SPORT MARKETING PLAN

Now that we have an understanding of the different levels of sport consumers and nonconsumers, a sport marketing plan must be developed to address their needs and wants. Sport marketing plans are comprehensive frameworks for identifying and achieving a sport organization's marketing goals and objectives. The process used in developing a sport marketing plan is a 10-step process.

Step 1: Identifying the Purpose of the Sport Marketing Plan

All individuals involved with a sport organization must be involved in the process of writing mission and vision statements, as well as developing goals and objectives. This is to ensure that all members of the sport organization will be committed to carrying out the plan acting in accordance with the organizational philosophy.

Step 2: Analyzing the Sport Product

The sport product is three-dimensional – tangible goods, intangible support services, and the game or event itself:

1. Goods include tangible items such as clothing (e.g., shoes, licensed apparel) and equipment (e.g., bats, balls, racquets).

2. Intangible support services include activities or programs that are supplementary to sport but necessary for its operation (e.g., game officials, operations staff, office support).
3. The game or event itself is composed of two parts – the main product and the product enhancements:
   - The main product of the event is the actual competition taking place.
   - The product enhancements are the extras during the event, such as the mascot, music, halftime entertainment, concessions, and cheerleaders. These serve to enhance the overall experience for the customer.

Step 3: Forecasting the Market Climate

Assessing the sport climate requires examining internal and external factors as they affect marketing efforts. Assessing the past market climate enables managers to identify factors associated with successful or failed marketing efforts. Forecasting the future market climate requires reexamining the organization's mission. This involves the aforementioned SWOT (strengths, weaknesses, opportunities, and threats) analysis – assessing the strengths and weaknesses of an organization or event and the opportunities and threats faced by an organization or event.

Step 4: Positioning the Sport Product

When positioning the product, the sport marketing professional must take into account six distinct markets for sport: three are considered primary markets and three are considered secondary markets:

- *Primary markets*
  - *Participants*: athletes, coaches, and game officials.
  - *Spectators*: stadium attendees, television viewers, radio listeners, and newspaper or magazine readers.
  - *Volunteers*: social hosts at sport events, statisticians, and team managers.
- *Secondary markets*
  - *Advertisers*: use sports to target and communicate their products to large groups of spectators.
  - *Corporate sponsors*: use sports to target and communicate positive and distinctive images about their products to large groups of spectators.
  - *Athletes' endorsements of products and licensed products*: personalities and celebrities or distinctive symbols, logos, or trademarks encourage consumers to perceive products as popular or prestigious.

Step 5: Segmentation and Targeting Consumers

This step involves grouping consumers according to common characteristics. Segmentation is most commonly analyzed using demographics, psychographics, or based on media preferences. Demographic segmentation refers to grouping sport consumers based on their age, gender, income, race or ethnicity, education, and place of residence. Psychographic segmentation refers to influencing the consumers' attitudes, interests, and lifestyles. Market segmentation based on media preference categorizes consumers based on their sport media preferences (such as television, radio, Internet, magazines, or publications). This helps to identify smaller groups to be targeted, and allows the sport marketer to develop an effective and efficient strategy to reach the target market.

Step 6: Packaging the Sport Product

This is the way the consumer will view the sport product. Since consumers view products in different ways, it is necessary to present the sport product in different ways. Packaging tangible or industrial sport products involves explaining the benefits of the products such as the strength and longevity of metal bats, comfort and safety of helmets, or the expanded sweet spot of over-sized tennis rackets. Packaging the core product of sport (the game or event itself) involves communicating about the expectations of the product and providing information before the point of purchase. Another aspect of product packaging is the manner in which product enhancements (discussed in Step 2) are included in the overall sport experience.

Another aspect of packaging the sport product is the associated licensed merchandise. For example, many sport teams and events offer goods such as hats, T-shirts, jackets, and other apparel. They also offer non-apparel such as novelty items and sport memorabilia that are perceived as extensions and representations of the respective teams.

Also utilized to package the sport product is sponsorship. Sponsorship involves an agreement between a sport organization and a corporation where the corporation pays a fee to the sport organization to acquire rights to affiliate with the organization or an associated event for the purpose of deriving benefits from the partnership. Sponsorships can help corporations increase sales, change attitudes, heighten awareness, and build and maintain positive relationships with consumers. An example of this would be the college football Bowl Championship Series – where it is the Tostitos Fiesta Bowl, the Nokia Sugar Bowl, the FedEx Orange Bowl, and the Rose Bowl presented by Citi.

Step 7: Pricing the Sport Product

Price is the factor that is most visible and flexible, especially as a result of sales, discounts, rebates, and coupons. Creating a strategy for pricing is integral to the success of the sport organization because it has a significant impact on the success of the overall sport marketing plan.

Sport marketers must consider the 3 C's described early in the chapter within the "heart of sport marketing": the company itself, the sport consumer, and the competition. In addition, pricing is directly affected by the external factors including government regulations, the economic climate, and politics.

Step 8: Promoting the Sport Product

Promoting sport products involves implementing a mix of activities that will communicate the preferred image of the sport product to selected targets, educate the target audience about the sport product and its benefits, and ultimately persuade the sport consumer to purchase the product. The following elements compose a promotion strategy:

- *Advertising*: Presenting a one-way paid message about the sport product (newspapers, magazines, television, radio, direct mail, scoreboards, in-arena signage, pocket schedules, game programs, posters, and outdoor advertising).
- *Community relations*: Activities and programs arranged by a sport organization to meet the interests and needs of the public and, by doing so, establish good faith relationships with the public (youth sport clinics, athlete autograph signing opportunities, and collecting food items at arenas to help people in the community).
- *Media relations*: Maintaining positive relations with networks and individuals in the media to obtain positive media exposure for a sport product (schedule informal and formal information sessions with media representatives).
- *Personal selling*: Direct face-to-face communication with individuals, groups, or organizations to sell tickets, luxury suites or boxes, or sponsorships.
- *Promotions*: Activities and inducements to encourage consumers to purchase the sport product (giveaways, coupons, free samples, cash refunds, contests, and raffles).
- *Public relations*: A sport organization's overall plan for communicating a positive image about its product to the public, including implementing community and media relations activities and programs.
- *Sponsorship*: Forming a partnership between sport organizations and corporate entities as a form of promotion.

Step 9: Distribution (Place) of the Sport Product

Place refers to the location of the sport product (stadium, arena), the point of origin for distributing the product (ticket sales at the stadium, sales by a toll-free telephone number), the geographic location of the target markets (global, national, regional, state, communities, cities), and other channels that are important to consider regarding whether target audiences may access the product (such as time, day, season, or month in which a product is offered, as well as the media distribution outlets consumers may use to receive the product experience). Factors related to the physical location of the sport can have a favorable or unfavorable impact on the marketing plan as well.

Step 10: Evaluation and Feedback about the Sport Marketing Plan

This evaluation requires obtaining feedback (from inside and outside the organization) about the marketing plan. The feedback must then be analyzed and evaluated. The evaluation should focus on determining the extent to which the plan helped the organization achieve its mission by acting in accordance with the core values of the organization.

MOUNTAIN DEW AND THE X GAMES

In an interview with Carolyn Sy, Marketing Analyst for PepsiCo, she discusses how the product line Mountain Dew brand is involved in sponsoring and producing alternative sports events, and how they have benefited from their relationship with these sports.

During the summer of 1995, the American public added two terms to its vernacular that would become a staple to describe America's youth for the next decade: extreme and Mountain Dew. In the summer of 1995, ESPN launched its first Olympics for alternative sports. The Extreme Games, later renamed to the X Games, debuted in Providence/Newport, Rhode Island and neither ESPN nor PepsiCo has been the same since.

The Extreme Games were born from an idea by ESPN's Director of Programming, Ron Semiao. Sitting in his home on his sofa one Sunday afternoon, Semiao realized that extreme sports were emerging not only in participation, but also in a competitive nature. From this idea a phenomenon was created. Today, that phenomenon has turned into a lucrative event that millions of television viewers watch twice a year (summer and winter). This phenomenon spun from a couch side brainstorm, has not only become lucrative for ESPN, but for its sponsors as well (ESPN.com).

No X Games sponsor has reaped more reward from the event's success than has Mountain Dew. Mountain Dew, the original "extreme" sponsor, has received financial as well as brand awareness and recognition success only paralleled by MasterCard's sponsorship of FIFA's World Cup. Just as Semiao saw alternative sports as a way for ESPN to connect with the 12–24-year-old demographic, PepsiCo did also. Pepsi had been in limbo with its "alternative" brand of soda, Mountain Dew. The company saw these types of sports as its opening to the youth market.

Mountain Dew became the Extreme Games' first title sponsor, and has stayed with ESPN as a title sponsor. Mountain Dew was there for the transformation of the Extreme Games into the X Games. Mountain Dew was there for the formation of the first Winter X Games, and was also there when ESPN decided to take the event global. By staying on board with ESPN and keeping its title sponsorship package, Mountain Dew has created brand awareness, recognition, and loyalty with ESPN's X Games' demographic.

Over the past decade, Pepsi has used the success it has had with its branding effort of Mountain Dew through alternative sports, and has continued it into a vertically integrated platform within the alternative sports industry. Today, Mountain Dew is not only branded nationally via the X Games, but the brand is also integrated into the alternative sports' culture at the regional and local level as well.

On a regional platform, Mountain Dew sponsors the Vans Triple Crown Series. These events feature the world's top alternative athletes participating in premier venues throughout North America in six disciplines: skateboarding, wakeboarding, BMX, freestyle motocross, surfing and snowboarding. Sponsoring regional events allow Mountain Dew to gain a more intimate connection with its consumers. Consumers now see Mountain Dew as not just a title sponsor of major corporate media events, but as a company that truly cares about the development of alternative sports and athletes.

This passion to connect with its young consumers in the alternative sports arena is evident through Mountain Dew's local sponsorship campaign. Mountain Dew's Free Flow Skatepark Tour is a grassroots level campaign specifically aimed at the development of alternative sports and athletes. The tour makes stops at 18 skateparks across the United States and is targeted for the amateur alternative athlete who is looking to accelerate his/her athletic career. At each stop, three contest winners are crowned and given the opportunity to join the Mountain Dew Free Flow Team. Mountain Dew provides the team members with money and equipment so that they can make an effort to progress their skateboarding abilities. It is grassroots campaigns such as this that enables Mountain Dew to stay credible within the alternative sports industry, and maintain high brand awareness and loyalty.

Source: Adapted from Schwarz, E. C., D. Blais, and K. Detjen (2003) [Interview with Carolyn Sy, Marketing Analyst, PepsiCo]. *In the New Face of Sport Marketing: Goodbye Michael Jordan, Hello Tony Hawk*. Gainesville, FL: Presented at the Inaugural Sport Marketing Association Conference.

Suggested Discussion Topics

1. The case discusses the successes of Mountain Dew at the local, regional, and national level. The case also describes inviting the world's top alternative athletes to participate in the Vans Triple Crown Series at various venues in North America. Assume you are the Director of Event Marketing for Mountain Dew, and you have been asked to determine where the best place would be to hold the Vans Triple Crown Series outside North America. Looking at the series of questions

Continued

discussed in the chapter about developing a strategy in congruence with the sport marketing mix (product impact, potential risk, and feasibility), explain in detail the location you would choose for this event and the process followed for making that decision.

2. Utilizing the 10 steps for developing a sport marketing plan, create an annotated outline for marketing this event in the location chosen.

WHY THE THEORY AND PLANS DO NOT ALWAYS WORK

All the sport marketing plans in the world are great in theory, but they do not always work. The major reason for this is having a lack of vision. There is a tendency to look for instant gratification – what is going to be successful right now. This lack of foresight in sport marketing ventures is known as a marketing myopia. A summary of research shows that the major reasons there is a marketing myopia in sport are:

- There is a tendency to produce and sell goods, rather than identify needs and satisfy customers. This is a result of sport organizations failing to spend time and money on quality market research, which in turn has lead to a major shortfall in data collection and analysis.
- There is a belief that winning equals sales, which in most cases is not true.
- There is confusion between what marketing is and what promotions are.
- Sport organizations tend to be shortsighted – the "I want it now" principle.
- Since there is such an overabundance of people wishing to enter the sport field, starting salaries are often very low. There is an effort to offset these low salaries by including commissions, but the lack of guaranteed income scare many quality potential marketers away.
- With sales being driven by quotas and commissions, organizations tend to put little emphasis on training, tactics, and sales as a strategy. If a sport marketer can sell, only then will time be put in. This has created a slow growth of professional sport marketing staff.

CONCLUSION

Sport marketing is unique for numerous reasons, but most importantly because the primary sport product, and hence the market, is traditionally demand based, whereas most generic products are marketed based on need. These concepts are elaborated upon in the chapter, as well the impact of the sport marketing mix, the escalator concept, and the elements of the sport marketing plan.

Sport marketing is unique to traditional marketing in numerous ways:

- The sport product takes many forms including a consumer good, a consumer service, a commercial good, or a commercial service.
- The main sport product is perpetually intangible, subjective, and variable.
- Sport and hence the sport product has an appeal that is wide and varied.
- The sport product is normally publicly consumed and consumer satisfaction is directly affected by the external environment.
- Sport product elicits strong emotional connections.
- Sport consumer believes that they are the experts when it comes to knowledge of the product.
- The sport product is a perishable commodity.
- Since the sport product is demand based, the consumer demand for the main sport product varies greatly.
- Sport organizations concurrently compete and cooperate.
- Sport marketing efforts focus more on product extensions than the primary sport product.
- Influences from mass media have resulted in a reduced emphasis on traditional sport marketing.

The oversaturation of sport in the mass media has resulted in an evolution in the traditional method of controlling and coordinating the marketing mix. This exposure is called publicity. The expanded public relations efforts have forced marketers who traditionally viewed the marketing mix as the 4 P's of marketing evolve their theory into the 5 P's of sport marketing – product, price, place, promotion, and publicity. Strategic implementation of the sport marketing mix can only be utilized if it is in conjunction with understanding the 3 C's of competitive analysis – the consumer, the company, and the competition in terms of product impact, potential risks, and feasibility. Ultimately this analysis seeks to determine how to provide value to the sport consumer, and enticing them to become more involved with the sport product. The concept that is essential to this development process is the escalator concept. This concept is utilized to represent the movement of consumers to higher levels of involvement with a specified product – whether they are nonconsumers, indirect consumers, light users, medium users, or heavy users.

Sport marketing plan must be developed and utilized to address the needs and wants of the sport consumer. Sport marketing plans are comprehensive frameworks for identifying and achieving a sport organization's marketing goals and objectives. The process used in developing a sport marketing plan is a 10-step process:

1. Identifying the purpose of the sport marketing plan
2. Analyzing the sport product
3. Forecasting the market climate
4. Positioning the sport product

5. Segmentation and targeting consumers
6. Packaging the sport product
7. Pricing the sport product
8. Promoting the sport product
9. Distribution (place) of the sport product
10. Evaluation and feedback about the sport marketing plan

Sport marketing plans are great in theory, but they do not always work. The major reason for this is having a lack of vision. There is a tendency to look for instant gratification – what is going to be successful right now. This lack of foresight in sport marketing ventures is known as a marketing myopia. Is it the goal of the sport marketing professional to avoid these pitfalls by engaging in a sport marketing effort that is efficient, effective, and addresses the wants and needs of the sport consumer.

From Theory to Practice

Brady Sadler, Director of Sales and Marketing

Manchester Wolves Professional Arena Football (Af2) Team
Manchester, New Hampshire

Like many young college students I was unsure of what I wanted to pursue in terms of a career. I was always told that the equation for a great job was finding something that you would love to do and then finding a way to get someone to pay you for doing it. To this end, I was interested in politics from the young age. My father was involved in town government and while in Junior High I volunteered for the 1992 presidential campaign. This was of course the year that Bill Clinton won the presidency and stopped a Republican run that had lasted over a decade. Clinton's campaign and promotion did not resemble the past races that my elementary school history books had taught me about. The PR for this campaign resembled a plan for a rock star more so than a politician. They were selling the image and branding of Bill Clinton, his energy and charisma, more than his stance on particular issues. New, young, fresh and in touch with society, that was his platform. It was truly an important period in the history of politics and an exciting time to be involved. I may not have even known it at the time but this was my first taste of marketing. The experience exposed me to aspects of advertising, media, event planning, cold calling, crisis management and a number of other skills I would later apply to my position in sports.

I stayed involved in politics in high school and held a number of positions with my class and student council. In these positions I learned to market myself as well as specific events that we planned. My high school also had a state-of-the-art video editing suite. I began to learn the basics of film editing and assisted in producing a video year book for my senior class. We marketed the sale of the video by making it known that every student in the class would be featured along with every sports team. This helped to make it appealing to all classes and even the teachers. Seeing the final product shown at random parties throughout the summer made me realize how much I enjoyed being involved with projects that entertained audiences.

My involvement was not always behind the scenes. I hosted some of our high school programming as well as my own segment on a public access show called Brady's News and Views. With this experience under my belt I decided that I would go to college for broadcast journalism. Though it was interesting, I soon learned that I did not like the production side of the video work as much as I liked marketing a product itself. I began taking more marketing-based classes and soon made that the focus of my major in communications. I had not totally lost sight of my interest in government and decided to minor in Political Science.

Upon graduation I accepted an internship with the Walt Disney Company. The College Program internship was one of the best experiences I have ever had. While in Orlando I was taken through a number of rigorous customer service training sessions. Mastering this skill would be something I would take with me and continue to apply every day of my life. The program gave me a chance to see how one of the most successful companies and brands in history operated. The company philosophy was that there were no employees. Every worker was considered a "cast member" and all patrons were referred to as "guests." Instead of working, we were told that we were putting on a "show." While onstage, anywhere that guests were permitted, every cast member had their part in the show. This instilled a sense of accountability in all that were involved. On a daily basis my part in the show required a variety of responsibilities from welcoming guests, explaining safety precautions, giving tours, and even putting guests on rides. Additional opportunities such as seminars with company leaders and departmental shadowing programs were always available. Interns were encouraged to seek these out and I certainly did. This taught me that an experience can really provide whatever one is willing to put into it.

I got my start in professional sports through networking. I talked with anyone in business that would take the time to answer some questions. I went on a few job interviews just for the sake of it and had a chance to learn about some different companies. A month or so into this networking phase I was introduced to the general manager of the Mohegan Wolves Arena Football team. My father had attended a Rotary Club meeting where the General Manager was giving a presentation and made the connection. On the day of our first meeting I learned that the team was starting a call center dedicated to tickets sales. I was offered a part time job on the spot and decided to give it a go. During the orientation stage we learned about the sport of Arena

Continued

Football, the different ticket plans and the pricing structure. Next, to help us prepare for anything we might encounter when calling, we role-played potential phone scenarios. The compensation plan consisted of an hourly wage, commission and bonuses for added motivation. The sales board, displayed for everyone to see, created a competitive atmosphere. Although the nightly 4-hour calling shift could be extremely dull and monotonous, I developed some great phone skills. I would later learn from a well-established business mogul that the phone can be a businessperson's best tool.

Week after week I was consistently atop the leader board in sales. Being from Connecticut, I used my hometown roots to help drive sales and began to inquire about group sales and sponsorship. These were not sales that fell under our job description so the initiative was immediately recognized. I was also given the opportunity to become the production assistant for the team's weekly television show. This was a volunteer position but I knew the experience was more valuable then any pay could have been. Before long I was offered a full-time position as the team's Director of Group Sales and Marketing. I was not very excited to stay in Connecticut but I knew that the opportunity was unique and the experience would be worth the sacrifice.

At the end of my first season in Connecticut the team was purchased by a group of businessmen and relocated to Manchester, New Hampshire. Most all of the staff and the local partnering organizations were not aware that this move was going to take place until only a week or two before it was officially announced. I was given the opportunity to move along with the club or take on a position with another team already established in the league. I chose to move with my team because I wanted to gain the experience of working in a completely new market. I was in for more than I could ever imagine. I came to find out that starting a new team is very similar to running a political campaign.

The team had to be introduced to the public, gain their respect and to win their support. This was even more challenging because many citizens of this new state had never even heard of Arena Football. The NFL was hugely popular, but few knew whether or not we were bringing legitimate professional football or an unorganized and contrived product that resembled the XFL. Our mission became proving ourselves as a sport and organization.

We began with a press conference at the team's new arena. Opening 2 years prior, the building was already one of the busiest in the world for its size and represented re-growth and prosperity in a city that was experiencing a renaissance. During our first official public appearance as an organization it was important to position ourselves with this great arena and everything it meant to the people of the city.

On that day I was introduced to the eight local owners, all of which had grown up in the area and become very successful in their respective businesses. Although the team was not yet established, the ownership group had been laying the groundwork for sponsorship, season ticket sales, media connections, charitable alliances and political influence all their lives. By aligning ourselves with the ownership group we had some immediate legitimacy, though there was a lot of work to do before we would be established. It became my job to essentially build off of the foundation that was laid by the owners. Although my position would require involvement in corporate sponsorships, media buying, event planning, public relations and much more, there was never a day that ticket sales did not play a major role in what I was doing.

Tickets are the lifeline of every team. Without the fans and consistent attendance it is impossible to operate the business. A team's season ticket base is its bread and butter. Year after year these fans will not only attend all of your games, but if treated right will act as ambassadors for your organization. I would encourage anyone who is interested in a career in sports to immediately learn about ticket sales. No matter what aspect of a front office you are working for, there will come a time when someone will ask you a question about tickets. A basic understanding of the process will help maintain the professionalism that your team will inevitably strive for. This professionalism is in essence customer service. The skills I learned during my tenure at Disney had prepared me to deal with almost any fan problem or inquiry. Even if I did not have the answer they were looking for or could not fix the problem, I had been trained to make the person feel that they were extremely important and do everything that I could to rectify the situation. This takes good communication, planning, patience, and pride in ones organization.

Over the course of the off season it was very apparent that everything we were doing was leading up to our first event. Having a well prepared and properly trained staff was very important to our show. By "show" I mean the ancillary things that go on during game days outside of the games themselves. For our team the goal was not to provide eight home games but to put on eight major events. Each event began with a free outdoor pre-game concert. Also on the plaza was a 50-feet rock climbing wall that we acquired by partnering with a local climbing gym. Upon entrance to the arena each fan received a great giveaway item. From bobble heads to touchdown towels, these items contained the logos of companies that had paid us to distribute them to fans. Once inside fans were treated to face painting, balloon animals and a number of games and amusements on the concourse. Team introductions consisted of pyrotechnics, a light show and 20 Harley Davidson's escorting a professional dance team. During the game the video board provided additional entertainment while a blimp flew over fans dropping gift certificates and coupons. After the game fans were invited onto the field to meet the players, coaches, and dance team members for autographs and pictures. A field goal kicking station was also set up so that fans could

Continued

experience what the players had just demonstrated. Each event offered something for everyone in the family to enjoy even if they were not a football fan.

Opening night was a momentous occasion. Although most of us had not slept in weeks, the crew rallied and we put on a fairly good show. Luckily many of the mistakes were behind the scenes, and there were many of them. I began preparing a list of individual responsibilities for everyone on my staff. They included in-depth descriptions of what was expected and when it was to be done. When the crowd is screaming, the music is blaring and the team is on the field, it can be very easy to get caught up and forget what one is supposed to do. This is the most important thing that I took away from my experience working for the team. Leave nothing to chance and provide safety nets for your staff. If presented in the right manner, people will appreciate and respect the attention to detail.

Note: In September 2005, Brady was hired as an Account Executive for the marketing and public relations firm Griffin, York, and Krause. The firm manages a number of local, national and international accounts in a variety of areas including sport organizations, political campaigns, governmental agencies, and multi-brand corporations.

II

UNDERSTANDING THE SPORT CONSUMER

SPORT MARKETING RESEARCH

3

CHAPTER OUTLINE

CHAPTER OBJECTIVES

The main objective of this chapter is to expand on the concepts of market segmentation, positioning, and demand analysis to develop basic capabilities in advertising research, competitive analysis, and strategic outcomes assessment, in sport marketing. Inclusive of this will be an analysis of the sport marketing research process including the development and implementation of focus group research, survey research, and experimental studies; the identification, retrieval, and analysis of secondary data; the utilization of qualitative and quantitative research methodologies; and the application of the research method. The chapter will conclude with a description of research services within sport marketing research, including but not limited to studies of customer satisfaction, economic impact, need assessment, organizational behavior, and risk assessment.

Specifically, the reader will be able to:

- Recognize the purpose and uses of sport marketing research.
- Distinguish between the steps of the sport marketing research process, including realizing the importance of each step and the development process associated with those steps.
- Know the variety of research services in sport marketing research and how to access them.
- Understand the difference between sport marketing research and online sport marketing research.

WHAT IS SPORT MARKETING RESEARCH?

Sport marketing research is the collection and analysis of information about sport consumers, market niches, and the effectiveness of sport marketing initiatives. This is accomplished by first identifying and defining market opportunities and threats, and then designing, implementing, managing, and evaluating marketing actions via the marketing plan. Sport marketing research is a 10-step process as follows:

1. Determining the need for sport marketing research
2. Defining the problem
3. Establishing sport marketing research goals and objectives
4. Choosing the appropriate research methodology
5. Identifying sources of information and determining methods for collecting data
6. Designing data collection forms
7. Determining sample size
8. Collecting data
9. Examining data and drawing conclusions
10. Preparing and presenting the final research report

SPORT MARKETING RESEARCH PROCESS

Determining the Need for Sport Marketing Research

Research is needed for many purposes within sport marketing. In some cases, research is conducted when there is a lack of information about what is going on within the targeted market, and the organizations cannot make informed decisions about their marketing efforts. In other cases, research is utilized to examine the perceptions of sport consumers in relation to a myriad of areas ranging from attendance at events to sponsorship and brand awareness. Sport marketing research is even needed when there is existing information, but the application of the information is unknown.

The purpose of sport marketing research is twofold. First, it is used to determine if there are opportunities in the market for the sport organization to take advantage of. This may include a lack of competition in the overall, a market niche void of competition, or an opportunity to offer better products or services than that of the current members of the segment. Second, it is utilized to determine the threats to the sport organization. This involves an evaluation of marketing performance and determining whether the marketing efforts are working. If they are not, the sport marketing professional then must modify current marketing strategies, or create new marketing actions.

Sport marketing research ultimately will significantly decrease the uncertainty in making marketing decision. Unfortunately, many sport organizations are not willing to spend the time necessary to conduct appropriate sport marketing research. Some of the reasons include a lack of time, funding, or resources. However, a major reason that most sport organizations do not conduct research is because they do not know how to in an efficient and effective manner. Those who enter the sport marketing profession with a clear understanding of how to manage the sport marketing research process become a significant asset to the sport organization.

Another major problem is not being able to separate being a marketing manager and a marketing researcher. In larger organizations, these may be two separate positions – the marketing manager controls the marketing resources and efforts of the sport organization, whereas the marketing researcher investigates the needs of the sport organization and plans for meeting those needs. However in most sport organizations, the sport marketing manager must also conduct the research for the organization. Therefore, it is imperative that the sport marketing professional know how to separate those roles.

The role as a sport marketing researcher is to generate and ask questions, and develop the techniques necessary to accomplish the task at hand. The sport marketing researcher must view the organization in an unbiased manner – they cannot let politics or emotional involvement with the organization affect their research. If bias enters the equation, there may be invalid, unreliable data that will prevent appropriately defining the problem or determining the most suitable method for solving the problem.

In general, the sport marketing researcher is conducting a cost–benefit analysis to determine the loss to the organization if the problem is not addressed. Therefore, sport marketing research is conducted when problems or changes in the market takes place, new marketing objectives are implemented that result in changes in marketing action, there is an opportunity to secure a competitive advantage in the market, or there is a need to reevaluate the status of your competition.

Defining the Problem

Once it has been determined that there is a need to conduct sport marketing research, the problem must be defined. This is the most important step in the sport marketing research process. Without a clear understanding of the purpose for the research, appropriate goals cannot be developed, actions cannot be planned, and a solution cannot be achieved.

One of the major problems within sport marketing today is confusing symptoms of problems with the actual problem itself. An example of this would be a baseball team seeing a 10% decline in ticket sales. Typical conclusions that have been drawn include increasing the amount of advertising, offering ticket promotions, or give rewards or incentives to customer who attend (example: $1 off French fries at McDonald's after the game). However, has the organization actually determined the problem? These snap decisions are typical with sport organizations because of lack of time, money, or resources. However, if the organization simply took stock of the situation, sat back, and completed some basic research, they could determine the true problem and direct their marketing efforts accordingly.

So how do we define the problem? First there must be a full evaluation of the sport organization, including history and culture, products and services, strengths and weaknesses, perceived opportunities and threats, resources available, and any recent marketing strategy changes. The researcher must also understand what the overall mission, goals, objectives, and vision for the sport organization are. By evaluating all this information, the sport marketing researcher can get a full understanding of the sport organization, and potentially discern patterns or deviations from norms.

After assessing the organizational situation, the sport marketing researcher then clarifies the situation in terms of indicators of change. Some of these indicators include changes in sales volume, market share, profit, and complaints. The sport market researcher cannot look at each indicator at face value only – often they must delve into each indicator in significant detail to determine any potential underlying causes of the problem.

As the researcher collects this information, they are evaluating all the data in an effort to pinpoint actual problem. For every problem, there is an underlying cause of that problem. Therefore, as the data is evaluated, indicators that are determined not to be a cause of the problem are eliminated from consideration. This allows the sport marketing researcher to narrow the focus and target the most likely causes of the problem by creating a list of probable causes. These probable causes will eventually lead to the development of the true problem statement.

After these probable causes are determined, the sport marketing researcher must come up with potential solutions to address these causes and hence resolve the problem. These solutions can range from changing the price of a product or service, improving service, modifying products, implementing new promotions, and making changes to the channels of distribution. A caution when making these changes – the sport marketer must ensure that the solution does not have a negative impact on other parts of the sport organization.

Establishing Sport Marketing Research Goals and Objectives

The aforementioned potential solutions are then articulated in terms of research goals and objectives. Sport marketing research goals are the list of items that need to be accomplished to rectify a problem. The objectives are the steps that will be undertaken to accomplish each goal.

These goals and objectives formulate the backbone of the sport marketing research plan.

Research goals and objectives must be accurate, detailed, clear, operational, and measurable. To facilitate the development of these goals and objectives, the sport marketer must develop constructs and operational definitions, define or create relationships between those constructs, and identify the model(s) to be used to conduct the research. A marketing construct is the item which is to be examined or measured. The operational definition is how the construct will be measured. This is usually in a question format that will be used in a specific measuring tool. The sport marketer will then look for relationships between the constructs, which will identify significant links between two or more constructs and help in the development of concise outcomes. The development of these concise outcomes will then be logically ordered and research questions developed. At this point, the sport researcher will choose an appropriate research method to answer the research questions.

Choosing the Appropriate Research Methodology

The research method is a plan for a study that steers the collection and analysis of information gathered. There are two major sources of information in sport marketing research. Primary data is information collected by the sport marketer specifically for the research project. This is normally achieved through personal contact, either by mail, telephone, email, or face-to-face. The methodologies utilized in collecting this type of data will be discussed later in the chapter.

Secondary data is information that has been collected by another source or for another purpose prior to the current research project, and is being evaluated for use to solve the problem at hand.

The availability of secondary data is endless, so the sport marketer must understand the various classifications and sources of this data.

One of the common misconceptions is that secondary can only come from external sources from the sport organization, such as from the Internet and research studies. While these sources are very important, some of the most vital secondary data can be found within the sport organization. Data such as sales records, surveys and questionnaire administered by other departments, end-of-year reports, and program and operational evaluations can be utilized as a solid starting point for any research effort. In addition, internal databases that collect generic information for the sport organization can also be extremely valuable. All of this internal secondary data starts to tell a story about the sport organization, how it works, and possible directions to take the research.

As noted, external sources including the Internet and research studies are also valuable sources of secondary data. With regard to the Internet, it continues to be the fastest growing source of information not only for sport marketing research, but for all types of research. However, one of the cautions of using Internet-based information is guaranteeing the reliability of the source, and validity of the data. Almost anyone in the world can post something on the Internet. Determining the data that is most important to your organization, while ensuring that it is from an appropriate source is quite a challenge.

Hence this is why most researchers tend to use research studies. The sources are usually valid and reliable, accepted on a global scale across the industry, and are usually issued through a publisher, syndicated service, or database. Some of the major sources of secondary data in the sport marketing field include marketing journals such as *Sport Marketing Quarterly* (www.smqonline.com), online databases such as the Sport Business Research Network (www.sbrnet.com), sports marketing research companies such as American Sports Data (www.americansportsdata.com), and independent market research studies conducted by numerous corporations and organizations around the world. Some of the key demographic and general sources of secondary data often used in sport marketing include the United States Census Bureau (www.census.gov), the United State Government Printing Office (www.po.gov), the Survey of Buying Power (www.salesandmarketing.com), and Demographics USA published by Bill Communications. With the increasing popularity of lifetime sports and alternative sports, the Lifestyle Market Analyst (http://www.srds.com/front Matter/ips/lifestyle) published by SRDS has become an increasingly important tool in understanding lifestyle marketing, customer relationship marketing management, and consumer experience marketing management.

The type of primary or secondary data to be utilized depends on which one of the three major methods for conducting research is utilized: exploratory, descriptive, or causal.

Exploratory Research

Exploratory research is conducted when there is little or no information about an opportunity or threat. This is the most difficult methods of research because it is impossible to create a plan of action in advance, instead working with impressions and assumptions based on personal experience or expertise. The gathering of information is usually informal and unstructured. This means that the sport marketing researcher will collect as much data as possible in order to gain as much information about the situation as possible. As the problem becomes clearer, the collected data is evaluated and a determination of which information should be kept and which can be discarded is made. Eventually the problem will become evident, and a plan of action can be created. Sport marketing professional often do not wish to engage in this type of research because of the time needed to complete the process. They often would rather use a "best guess" scenario and hope they stumble upon the right conclusion. However, quality exploratory research can reveal significant background information, clarify problems, define concepts, generate hypotheses, and create a list of research priorities.

Descriptive Research

Descriptive research utilizes data that describes the "who, what, when, where, and how" of a potential problem. This information is very factual and accurate, but does not take into account the cause of the situation. Although this method is most often used in sport marketing circles via observations and surveys, there is still a major fear in conducting this type of research because of mathematics. Many people have a fear of numbers and commonly misinterpret the difference between math and statistics. Math involves the actual solving of equations, whereas statistics is the collection, organization, and interpretation of solved mathematical equations. If more people understood that descriptive research involves looking at what the numbers mean rather than solving equations, more sport marketing researchers would be willing to take more time conducting this type of research.

Causal Research

Causal research is utilizing experimentation and simulations to determine the cause-and-effect relationship between the sport organization and the problem at hand. This type of research is extremely complex because there is no certainty that the results are not being influenced by other variables. As a result of this, and the need for time, money, and resources, this type of research is rarely conducted by sport marketing professionals.

Identifying Sources of Information

The source of information will be directly affected by the type of research design. Qualitative research involves collecting, analyzing, and interpreting data by observing what people do, or how they answer open-ended questions. This research tends to involve a small number of respondents that represent a segment of the population. The respondents focus on the qualities of a sport product or service by articulating the values and beliefs they perceive the specific brand to have. In contrast, quantitative research involves collecting, analyzing, and interpreting data collected from a larger sample via a structured questionnaire or survey. The data is analyzed in statistical terms, and the results produced in a numeric form. At times, both qualitative and quantitative data will be used concurrently. This is known as pluralistic research.

The source of information to be utilized for a research study will depend on not only the research design, but also the type of primary or secondary data available, and the preferred method of collecting data.

Exploratory Sources of Information

Secondary Data Analysis
As implied earlier in this chapter, secondary data analysis involves using existing data that has been collected by another source or for another purpose

prior to the current research project. The secondary data that comes from sport research studies are usually classified in one of four categories. Narrow-Random studies are usually conducted by leagues, individual teams, and sponsors on an as-needed basis to gather specific information on consumer demographics, behaviors, attitudes, product use, and media consumption. Extensive-Random studies are usually only performed by large corporations because of the significant resources (money, time, and people) needed to broaden the study using a large or national sample. As a result of this cost, these types of studies are done on an irregular basis. Narrow-Standard studies deals with specific samples and populations, and are conducted on a regular basis to provide a clearer view of trends. Extensive-Standard studies are more generalized to a large or national sample and tend to look at categories in a generic sense without consideration for individual differences caused by culture, location, or demographic makeup.

Case Study Analyses

Case study analyses are a special type of secondary data analysis. Case studies are published accounts of situations that have occurred to a business or industry, and can be viewed to serve as a guide to answer current research questions. This allows the sport marketer gets a first-hand view of a similar situation and sees how another organization dealt with the circumstances. It is important, however, to use case studies with care. Even though situations may be similar, the solutions may not be viable or appropriate for the organization. Therefore, it is important to look at case studies and determine the relevancy to the current research questions. The more relevant the case is to the research being conducted, the more valid and reliable the solutions will be.

Focus Groups

Focus groups are an interview that involve 8–12 people at the same time in the same group, and is used to evaluate products and services, or to test new concepts. To plan for a focus group, the major objective of the meeting must be decided on. Once the main objective is chosen, the facilitator must design a series of questions (usually 6–8) that will serve to gain a better understanding about the stated objective.

When planning for the session, on average four questions can be asked per hour, as the focus group is basically a series of individual interviews. Therefore, most focus groups last between 1.5 and 2 hours. The best place to hold focus group sessions in a room free from distraction with good air flow and lighting, such as a conference room. Offering refreshments during the session would be appropriate.

It would be proper to provide an agenda prior to the meeting (1 week), and review that agenda at the start of session. At that time, setting ground rules for the focus group will keep the session flowing freely. Those ground rules should help keep the group focused, the meeting moving, and bring resolution to each question.

The make-up of the focus group should include individuals with similar characteristics, but do not know each other. The focus group members should have a willingness to be thoughtful in analyzing the questions, and to share their responses to the questions. The focus group members should also be willing to have the meeting recorded so the facilitator can review the meeting afterwards.

The job of the facilitator of the focus group is to welcome the members of the group, ask the questions, ask follow-up questions that are geared to clarifying the original answer, and ensure even participation from all members of the focus group. It is best that the facilitator have a knowledge of the concepts related to the objective, but should be independent from the organization to limit bias. At the end of the focus group meeting, the facilitator should thank everyone for their participation, and guarantee that they will receive a copy of the report from the meeting.

Experience Surveys

Experience surveys refer to collecting information from those whom are considered to be experts in the field of interest. These experts may be a part of a direct network, through recommendations of members of the direct network, or from research conducted about the area related to the research questions or objectives. These differ from traditional surveys in the fact that they are specifically fact finding in nature; therefore, the results are not being compared to other individuals or groups.

Projective Techniques

Projective techniques are used to allow respondents to verbalize their true opinions or beliefs about products and services. When asked directly, respondents often will not address their true attitudes or motivations due to assuming what the interviewer wants the answer to be, feeling pressure that their attitude or belief is not correct, or simply not wanting to have their name tied to their response. Projective techniques, such as tests using word association, sentence completion, or thematic perceptions can allow the respondent to answer in a non-threatening environment. Also utilized are third person techniques, such as role playing, allows the respondent to reply in terms of another.

Descriptive Sources of Information

Cross-Sectional Studies

Cross-sectional studies measures components from a sample within a population at a specific point in time. Since these are one-time measurements, they are often referred to as a snapshot of the population. The main type of cross-sectional study utilized in sport marketing research is a survey. Surveys can be administered in paper form or online, and are utilized to gather information from a sample. It is expected that the sample is representative of the entire population.

Longitudinal Studies

In contrast, longitudinal studies measures components from a sample within a population repeatedly over a period of time. These multiple measurements seek to show trends related to the research being conducted. Two major methods of longitudinal study are panels and market tracking studies.

Panels represent a group of individuals who have agreed to being involved with market research studies at periodic intervals to measure changes over time with a consistent sample. Panels may be continuous or discontinuous. Continuous panels are asked the same questions repeatedly over the period, hence tracking trends related to the specific objective. Discontinuous panels vary the questions asked, therefore allowing the researcher to track various related topics within a specific research area.

Market tracking studies do very much the same as panels, but without the human interaction. These studies measure one or more variables over a period of time using data available from other research studies.

Causal Sources of Information

Test Marketing

Most experiments in sport marketing take place in the real world. A common phrase utilized in sport marketing to describe these field experiments is "test marketing." Test marketing usually involves determining the sales potential of a new product or service, or the acceptance of a product previously entered into the marketplace. Test marketing for sport organizations often centers on the variability of the sport marketing mix and how changes may influence future sales.

Test marketing can take place via normal distribution channels, but because of the lack of time and resources, these experiments are usually outsourced to research firms who will conduct testing in one of the three ways. Controlled testing is where distribution of information or products will be through the research firm's predetermined number and type of distribution network. Electronic testing is a limited methodology involving a panel of sport consumers carrying a card that they present when making a purchase (or obviously their lack of product purchase). The information is then fed into a computer and results compiled. Simulated testing is even more limited in the fact that a small sample of data is collected from consumers, assumptions about the specific population made, and information about generic marketing programs collected. All the information is then put into a theoretical model, and likely results of sales volume and product interest are generated.

Secret Shopping/Mystery Shopping

Secret shopping (also known as mystery shopping) is a tool utilized in market research to investigate products and services of competitors by sending individuals to act as buyers. Usually what happens is a sport organization wants to measure the level of service offered by a competitor, or needs to collect data about specific products. The sport marketing professional will hire individuals to either act as shoppers or legitimately shop on behalf of the organization in return for either payment or the opportunity to keep what they purchase. Secret shoppers are: provided with the expected behaviors to be exhibited, questions and/or complaints to discuss, specific purchases to be made, and data to be recorded. Sport organizations then use this information to adjust pricing, modify services, or justify the methods already being utilized.

Determining Methods for Collecting Primary Data

As defined earlier in the chapter, primary data is information collected by the sport market researcher specifically for the research project through personal contact. The most basic method for collecting primary data is by observation. While it seems very simple and basic to watch someone or something, and then record what was seen or heard, it is easier said than done. In fact, most observations rely on recording devices ranging from tape recorders or video to the most basic of observational recording methods – written notes. The main importance of recording information in a tangible form is because while the mind is one of the most comprehensive computers known to man, the complexity of retrieving every detail of information on an "as-needed basis" is difficult and often lacking necessary intricate details.

For obvious reasons, the time and resources needed to conduct observations for all research is impossible. Therefore, other methodologies need to be utilized to conduct the extensive marketing research needed by sport organizations.

The Survey

The most common method used is the survey. Surveys are used to collect information from respondents about their attitude, values, opinions and beliefs via telephone, mail, face-to-face, and online. A survey can consists of anywhere between 5 and 500 questions, however those surveys that are concise and short, with directed, easy-to-answer questions usually reward the researcher with a larger amount of information that tends to be more reliable and valid.

There are a number of advantages to utilizing surveys for sport market research. First is the ability to standardize the survey. This allows for consistency in the measurement as all respondent will answer the same questions in the same order and following the same scale. Second, it is easy to administer a survey. In most cases the respondents fill out the survey without assistance from the researcher.

Surveys also allow the sport marketing researcher to gain information about concepts that are unobservable. From a demographic interest, we can solicit more accurate information about many topics including a person's income level, occupation, and distance traveled to the event. From a business standpoint, an example would be asking a question about how many times a person has attended a sporting event during the season. Unless we saw the person every time they entered the facility, or we have a computer tracking program that could accurately tell us who used a ticket, we would not know the answer. The response to the survey questions can be used to tell us where this customer falls on the "escalator," and how we can more effectively market toward that individual to entice them to make additional purchases.

The ease in which we evaluate the data received via surveys is also a great advantage. All the data from a survey can be statistically analyzed using computer processing programs such as Minitab and SPSS, or be evaluated by creating your own statistical analysis format using a spreadsheet program such as Excel. These programs offer the ability to process small and large amounts of information for tabulations, correlations, probabilities, and numerous other statistical analyses.

This also allows for coding of data to take into account individual, segment, and subgroup differences.

Types of Surveys

There are three major ways to collect data – self-administered surveys, interviews, and computer-administered surveys. Prior to initiating the process, the sport marketing researcher complete an analysis of (1) the time available to collect and analyze data and (2) the budget available to administer the survey. The sport marketing researcher will use this information to determine which data collection method will provide the highest quality amount of data within the stated constraints.

Self-administered Surveys

A self-administered survey is where an individual respondent completes the survey on their own. This is the most commonly utilized survey method because the cost is low, the respondent is under no pressure to complete the survey, and there is usually no undue influence placed on the respondent by the surveyor. However, the responses to the survey may not be totally accurate due to misunderstanding questions, not following directions in answering the survey, or just not fully completing the survey because of lack of time or interest. The two main types of self-administered surveys are mail surveys and drop-off surveys.

Mail surveys involve mailing the survey to potential respondents and encouraging them to fill out the questionnaire and returning it via mail. To entice respondents to take the survey seriously and increase the likelihood of a response, sport marketing researcher will often include a self-addressed, stamped envelope with the survey. Additionally, some will put a coupon or even a one-dollar bill in the envelope as an incentive.

Drop-off surveys are given to the respondent to fill out. Then the following option may be offered: (1) the researcher will come back at a later time to pick up the completed surveys; (2) a drop box will be set up for the respondent to return the completed survey; or (3) the ability for the respondent to return the completed survey by mail, fax, or email is provided.

Interviews

Interviews are basically person-administered surveys. The interviewer reads the questions and then records the answers from the respondent. This can be accomplished either in-person or via telephone. The advantages of this type of surveying include being able to build a rapport with the respondents so they are in a comfort zone, being able to ask follow-up or clarifying questions instantaneously, and the ability to control quality and adapt questions and methods throughout the process. On the other hand, since this type of surveying take a longer period of time, the use of this method has significantly decreased. The reason for this include the advent of computer technologies and their use in surveying, the limited amount of discretionary time people have to meet or talk, and the desire not to be bothered at home during family time to participate in a survey. Regardless, it is important to understand the various methods because while not as widely used, they are still important tools in the acquisition of data.

Telemarketing is the old-fashioned telephone call to a person's home. These can be administered in two ways. The most common method is the central location telephone interview. This is where a group of individuals work for a research firm or data collection company and make standardized interview calls to a list of individuals, businesses, or even just a series of phone number. Usually, a supervisor keeps track of the callers by listening in to the conversation and providing instant quality control to the telemarketer following a call. When a company does not have the ability to set up a call center, another method is where individual callers work from their home and has a list of people, business, or phone numbers assigned to them.

Another method of interviewing takes place as a result of our need to shop. Shopping intercept surveying occur when a researcher stops shoppers at malls, supermarkets, outlets, and other retail establishments to get individual opinions. Often times the shopper will be enticed with a discount or free item if they participate in the survey. The major limitation of this survey again involves time. Since the person you are interviewing is shopping, and often only has a set amount of time, the survey needs to be concise, and the enticement must be of interest to the consumer.

Computer-Administered Surveys

As mentioned earlier, with the advent of advanced computer technologies, surveying has entered a new era. In the latest data published by the Economics and Statistics Administration (www.esa.doc.gov):

- The rate of growth of Internet use in the United States is currently 2 million new Internet users per month.
- More than half of the United States population (54%) is now online using the Internet.
- Approximately 2/3 of the population in the United States used computers on a regular basis.
- Nearly one in two people use email on a regular basis.
- Over 1/3 of the American population (36%) use the Internet to search for products and services.

With these types of numbers, it was inevitable that surveying via this method would come. There are numerous advantages of computer-administered surveys. The main advantage is error-free data collection with speed. In addition, the sport marketing researcher can include pictures, videos, graphics, and other informational data to supplement the information provided to the respondent. The only downfall to computerized surveys is specifically for detailed surveys, where there may be some high set-up costs.

The most commonly used computer-administered surveys are online/Internet-based questionnaires. In some cases, individual respondents would be emailed the survey via attachment, and they would then download the survey, reattached, and reply. However, in most cases, respondents would go to a specific website to fill out the questionnaire. Sport marketing researchers would design and post the survey via the website, and the responses would be tabulated and forwarded by the Internet site company. Some of the most popular sites to use for surveys today are www.surveymonkey.com; www.zoomerang.com; www.surveyshare.com; and www.websurveyor.com.

Two other methods of computer-administered survey are computer-assisted telephone interviews (CATI) and fully computerized interviews. CATI is where the survey questions pop up on a computer screen, the interviewer reads the question to the respondent, the respondent gives the answer, and the interviewer enters the answer into the computer. Fully computerized interviews take the interviewer out of the equation. The respondent sits at the computer, questions show up on the screen, and the respondent enters their answer directly into the computer for tabulation.

Super Bowl Market Research

Claria is a pioneer and leader in behavioral marketing and personalization technology. Claria's proprietary behavioral marketing platform provided consumers with relevant content and offers based on their ordinary Web browsing and search behavior. Since its inception in 1998, Claria has served millions of online consumers and more than 1000 advertisers. By November 1999, Claria had revolutionized the online advertising industry by introducing its contextual and behavioral relevant online advertising model. A highly effective alternative to demographic targeting, this advertising method resulted in unparalleled ROI for advertisers.

One of Claria's former divisions (Feedback Research) provided full-service, custom marketing research programs and in-depth analytics of anonymous consumer Web usage patterns across a broad spectrum of the Internet. Feedback Research offered a breakthrough way of communicating one-to-one with tens of millions of consumers. Through the power of behavioral targeting, Claria was able to gather data from hard-to-reach consumers targeted based on their actual, not self-reported, online behavior.

Claria, through its Feedback Research division, conducted an independent, non-sponsored research study of its user base around advertising and sponsorship activities associated with the Super Bowl. The data Claria generated was comprised of Web analytics, where it analyzed Web traffic among the GAIN Network user base from December 1, 2003 through February 1, 2004 for all official NFL team Websites, popular football content sites (NFL.com; Superbowl.com; ESPN NFL; Yahoo! Sports NFL; and Sportsline NFL), and Super Bowl television advertiser sites. Search terms that were relevant to the NFL football and the Super Bowl were also monitored. The GAIN network was comprised of consumers who had agreed to become part by of the service, which allowed the user to receive more advertising (pop-up and banner ads) by choosing to download software that was supported by online advertising. Because there was a significant scale and a wide variety of applications to choose from, GAIN users shared the same overall demographic characteristics as ordinary Web users.

Claria analyzed Web traffic to determine trends for official NFL team Websites, as well as popular content domains. By looking at overall traffic, average viewer session per person, cross-traffic between sites, and the time of day when people visited the sites, insights were generated that created a clear understanding of how people used the Web in connection with the event.

Source: Adapted from prior content on http://www.claria.com.

Suggested Discussion Topics

1. Claria, through their Feedback Research division, was collecting primary research to analyze Web traffic of members using the GAIN Network, which incidentally is also owned by Claria. What would Claria have to do to use this information collected from users in an ethical manner for market research studies? Include in your answer what information it can use and disclose without permission, and what information requires permission from the user?
2. Assume that the data being used is generic in nature and does not need approval for use by Claria. However, make an assumption that the market research firm takes the collected data, puts it into a report, then sells that data to advertising firms. Is this an ethical practice? Why or why not? Support your answer with details and examples.

Designing Data Collection Forms

Regardless of the type of survey or interview to be administered, there are some constant functions that must be considered in designing a tool to collection data. What form should questions take? How are the results to be measured? Am I using the best scale of measurement? Can I guarantee reliability and validity?

Response Format for Questions

There are three fundamental response formats for questions. Closed-ended questions are when the sport marketing researcher provides specific options of answers for the respondent. Open-ended questions have no answer options provided by the sport marketing researcher to the respondent. Scaled-response questions utilized a scale developed by the sport marketing researcher, and the answers from the respondent are based on both their perception and the scale defined. Closed-ended survey questions may be developed utilizing two formats: dichotomous and multiple category. Dichotomous closed-ended questions require a choice of two responses, such as yes or no or (a) or (b). Multiple-category closed-ended questions are where there are more than two response options. These types of surveys are used most often by researchers because of the ease of administration, the limited amount of time needed to complete the survey, and the ease of tabulating results.

Open-ended survey questions tend to take longer to answer, as it requires the respondent to elaborate on their answers. This type of survey is also complex to tabulate as there are often no standard answers, and extended time is often needed to analyze the results. An unprobed format tends to be easier to tabulate and evaluate as the sport marketing research simply wants an exact response from the respondent. If the survey is developed in a probing format, the sport marketing researcher is giving the respondent a chance to elaborate on answers. While this may provide additional information, there is no guarantee that the data will be helpful to the study.

Scaled-response survey questions generally fall under two formats. If utilizing an unlabeled format, it is a numbered format where a descriptor is given to the endpoints. An example would be "Rate the service level of the following utilizing a scale of 1–5, where 1 is poor and 5 is excellent." A labeled format gives a descriptor for each level of the scale, such as:

1 = outstanding   2 = very good   3 = average   4 = need improvement
5 = unacceptable

So how does a sport marketing researcher choose the proper type of question and response format for their survey? The type of answer being looked for is the most important feature. After that, other considerations include what has been utilized in similar studies in the past; the method in which the data will be collected (i.e., telephone, mail, email, face-to-face); past history of how respondents prefer to answer questions; and the statistical analyses needed for reporting the findings.

Measuring Results

The way in which responses are measured provides you pertinent information about the subject being sought by the sport marketer. It also helps to provide parameter as far as what the information shows and what it does not show. These limitations help with the accuracy of disseminated information and serve to focus on the most important information needed by the sport organization. These parameters will also dictate the statistical analyses to be used by the sport marketing researcher.

There are two major considerations to consider when planning to measure responses. The first is the characteristics of the scale to be utilized. There are four main characteristics – description, distance, order, and origin. Description refers to how the scale is to be labeled. Distance represents the numeric range between responses. Order signifies the size of the scale descriptors (more than, less than, equal to). Origin deals with the starting point of the data. While many times the data starting point is "0", it is important to remember that in sport marketing research, the zero point may be an arbitrary point based on previous data. This is especially true in sales where commissions are not paid until reaching a certain sales level. Assuming a salesperson must make $50,000 in sales prior to receiving commissions; the zero point in this case is $50,000 in the mind of the salesperson.

The other consideration is the levels of measurement for the scales. In sport marketing research, there is a hierarchy of scales based on the number of characteristics evident. The most basic of scales is the nominal measurements of scale, where the responses only used labels, and hence only have the characteristic of description. Ordinal measurements of scale describe the data and rank order it. Interval measurements of scale use distance as descriptors to designate the range of responses, as well as ordering and describing the data. Ratio measurements of scale show all four characteristics, including a true zero point.

In sport marketing research, there are two major scales of measurement utilized for survey data. The first is the Modified Likert Scale in which respondents are asked to indicate their degree of agreement or disagreement on a symmetric agree–disagree scale for each of a series of statements. In sport marketing research, the most common form is the 5-point scale as follows:

$$1 = \text{strongly disagree} \quad 2 = \text{disagree} \quad 3 = \text{neutral} \quad 4 = \text{agree}$$
$$5 = \text{strongly agree}$$

The second is the Lifestyle Inventory, which centers on the measurement of psychographic data. This modified version of the Modified Likert Scale takes into account the values and personality traits of people as reflected in their unique activities, interests, and opinions toward their work, leisure time, and purchases.

The Questionnaire Development Process

Now that a framework for data collection methods has been describe, the development of the questionnaire can begin. The starting point is to determine the goals and objectives of the survey. The goals articulate the plan of what the sport marketing professional wishes to find out, and the objectives are the steps within the questionnaire that will seek to answer those questions. Once this has been determined, a review of the data collection methods is undertaken to determine the most appropriate form the questionnaire should take.

Designing the Questionnaire

The first step is designing a questionnaire in the development of the individual questions. When writing a question, one of the basics is to keep questions very specific, focusing on a single topic. Therefore, the questions should be brief, but directed. Also, the question should have universal interpretation. This will increase the level of reliability and validity of the responses. The best way to ensure this is to use basic vocabulary and simple grammar that is utilized across the majority of demographics within the population or sample.

There are also things that should be avoided when designing questions for a survey. The biggest "no-no" is making assumptions with questions. It is the job of the question designer to specify the criteria that judgments are to be based on; not allowing the respondent to assume the criteria. In addition, the questions need to be as general as possible. Questions that are too specific or utilize an example will direct the respondent to focus on the example instead of the broad application of the concept being questioned.

Questions should not be beyond the scope and understanding of the respondents. This includes the memory of the respondents – as most individuals remember things in generalities instead of in specifics. If questions are not general in nature, it may force the respondent to answer at two extremes, guess at the response they think the surveyor wants, or exaggerate the answer so it appears that the respondent is knowledgeable.

Three final "do not's" when designing questions. Do not ask questions that the respondent cannot relate to – such as asking a person which cable television station they watch sports on, but there is no choice for those who do not have cable. Second, avoid what is called "double-barreled" questions, where there are two questions within one. An example would be "Were you satisfied with the concessions and merchandise offered at the stadium?" If the answer is yes, were they satisfied with the food offering? Food taste? Beverage variety? Offerings in the pro shop? Service? You cannot tell from the answer to the question, and therefore the response is useless. Finally, questions should not be leading the respondent to a specific answer. To avoid this, avoid loading the question with statements or words that will direct the respondent into a biased response. An example would be "How did you like your experience at the game?" and the responses are (a) extremely well, (b) very good, (c) OK, and (d) not too well. Since only positive answers are provide (not too well still focuses on the positive – "well"), this is a biased and leading question (Figure 3.1).

FIGURE 3.1
QUESTION DESIGN

Do's	Do Not's
■ Focus on a single topic ■ Be very specific ■ Be brief and directed ■ Design questions with universal interpretation ■ Use basic vocabulary and simple grammar	■ Make assumptions with questions ■ Be specific with questions ■ Use specific example ■ Go beyond the understanding of the respondents ■ Force the respondent to guess at a response ■ Compel the respondent to exaggerate their answer ■ Ask questions that the respondent cannot relate to ■ Use "double-barreled" questions ■ Use leading questions

Once all the questions are created, an initial evaluation process is started to reword and rework questions. During this process, each question is evaluated based on the do's and do not's listed above, and modified if necessary. The goal is to ensure that the questions meet the standards set forth to decrease the potential of generating unreliable, inaccurate, or invalid responses.

Organizing the Questionnaire

There are four steps to organizing a questionnaire: the introduction, question sequencing, pre-coding, and the approval process. The introduction is usually a cover letter or paragraph at the top of the questionnaire giving general information about the study. The first item of consideration when writing the introduction is whether the sponsor of the study, or the individual/company administering the questionnaire, is to be identified. If they are identified, it is known as an undisguised survey. If they wish to remain anonymous, it is a disguised survey.

The next part of the introduction explains the purpose of the research. This should be a brief and simple one to two sentence explanation of the study. This is followed by one sentence explanation of how and why the respondent was chosen for this study.

The last part of the introduction is the part that makes or breaks the research – the request for participation in the survey. People have less discretionary time in today's society – what is going to make them take time out of their busy schedule and complete your survey? The answer is incentives! Incentives can range from money to product samples to discounts and coupons. For some, a copy of the study when completed is desired. The goal is to match the incentive to the respondents.

One other note with regard to the introduction ... there will be some who will only complete a questionnaire if they are guaranteed either anonymity or confidentiality. Anonymity assures the respondent that they will not be identified in conjunction with the data collected or the study. Confidentiality means that the researcher knows the individual respondents, but the name of the respondent will not be divulged, or information related to the study not attached to the individual, without the expressed consent of the respondent.

Once the introduction is completed, the questions will be sequenced. However, one step that is added in some questionnaires at this point is screening questions. Screening is the process by which a research can conduct a preliminary appraisal of the potential respondent to determine their suitability for the study. These questions are asked at the beginning of the questionnaire to eliminate those who do not meet the necessary qualifications for the study. For example, if this is a general questionnaire to determine perceptions of service and quality at a particular baseball stadium, a question might be "Have you attended a baseball game at this stadium?" If the response is no, then you would thank the respondent for their time and move on to another potential respondent.

Next is the sequencing of questions. Usually a questionnaire starts with warm-up questions. These questions are usually simple, easy to answer, and creates further interest in the study. An example of a warm-up question would be "How often have you attended a baseball game at this stadium?" After the warm-ups, transitions are used to let the respondent know that the format of the questions will be changing. For example: "For the next series of questions, you will be asked about your views of service and quality for various areas of the stadium." Sometimes, skip questions will be used as a part of this section. A skip question is where the answer to that question will affect which question to ask next. An example would be "Have you made a purchase from any merchandise booth with the stadium during this season?" If the answer is yes, they move on with the questionnaire; if the answer is no, the respondent would be directed to skip a series of questions about merchandising and move onto the next section.

As a rule, easier questions are placed earlier in the questionnaire, with complicated questions appearing toward the end. The reason for this is that once you have a respondent who has investing a period of time with the survey, the likelihood of them just not completing the questionnaire because of a difficult question is very low. Therefore, the sport marketing research uses the easy questions as a hook, and once hooked the respondent is committed. Another way to ensure that the respondent does not quit is to inform them that they are almost finished, as there are usually a limited number of difficult questions. An example of a complex question would be "Rate each of the following services on a scale from 1 to 7."

The last section of the questionnaire is classification and demographic questions. In years past, these questions were found at the beginning of a questionnaire, but studies have shown that asking for that information up front discourage people from completing surveys because they did not want to give personal information. Even if it was noted on the questionnaire that the section was optional, the perception of this information being at the front was that it was most important to the study. Therefore, now these questions appear at the end. The respondent has already provided the sport marketing researcher with information and now whether they wish to provide this information or not, the research has the data. The demographic and classification information is important to the research in order to do additional statistical analysis on the data, so it is important to ask questions that allow for anonymity and confidentiality should the respondent wish for that.

The next step in the questionnaire development process is pre-coding questions. This information is utilized to help in data entry and dissemination. The goal of pre-coding is to associate each possible response with a unique number and/or letter. Numbers are preferred because there are more statistical analysis programs that identify with numbers than with letters. The key is that the pre-coding cannot interfere with the respondent answering questions by confusing them. In fact, with the use of computer tabulation, most pre-coding is put into the statistical software instead of on the actual survey, and as data is entered the pre-coding will automatically be implemented.

The final step is to gain approval of the survey from the client. It is important to remember that although the sport marketing researcher may be the expert in the field, it is ultimately the client (i.e., the management of the sport organization) who must approve the research tool. Often this process requires explanation to the management, who may not understand the process.

Pre-testing and Revisions

After the questionnaire has been approved, the sport marketing researcher must make sure the questionnaire works through the process of pre-testing. In this process, the sport marketing research is actually conducting a "dry run" of the process by testing the survey on a small, representative sample of respondents. Usually, 5–10 respondents are used to not only answer the questions, but also ask the sport marketing researcher questions regarding confusions or misunderstandings. The sport marketing researcher will analyze these concerns and make revisions as necessary. Once revisions are finalized, the questionnaire is ready for mass use.

Questionnaire Development of the Future

One final note about questionnaire design – this process used to take a long period of time because of the lack of computer software available in the past. Question design was long and tedious. Data collection was dependent on people taking time at home or in a fast-moving environment (malls, offices, supermarkets). Data computation by hand took many man hours. But now with the Internet and other computer software, questionnaires are much easier. Data analysis through programs such as SPSS, Minitab, or most spreadsheet software cuts the computation time down to seconds instead of hours and days. Questionnaire development through programs such as www.surveymonkey.com; www.zoomerang.com; www.surveyshare.com; and www.websurveyor.com has cut down the design process significantly.

Determining Sample Size

A sample is the most basic element of sport marketing research, as it is the factors taken from a small group that is representative of the characteristics of an entire population. The population is the entire group that is defined as being under study as per the research questions. Information about populations, and hence samples, most often come from the census (www.census.gov).

A sport marketing researcher would start with a sample frame, which is a master list of the entire population (e.g., All Los Angeles Lakers fans who have attended at least one game at Staples Center). We then must realize that there may be errors in the listing, such as those season ticket holders who might be a corporation and give the tickets to various people who use them, individuals who buy tickets for someone else, and those who paid cash for the ticket may not even be in the database. This is known as the sample frame error – the degree to which the sample frame does not encompass the entire population.

From there we choose a sample. For example, Los Angeles Lakers season ticket holders. Again, there may be a sampling error, which is caused either by the method the sample is chosen, or by the size of the sample. In the scenario listed above, an error could be that a season ticket holder may not be a representative of a person who can only afford to go to one game per year, or that the season ticket holder sample may not statistically be a large enough sample to reliably and validly represent the entire Los Angeles Lakers ticket population.

However, the realization is that it is less expensive and time consuming to take a sample instead of attempting to survey the entire population. In addition, it would be almost impossible, even with computer assistance, to analyze the massive amount of data that would be generated from such a large population. Therefore, we use one of two methods of sampling – probability and non-probability.

Probability Sampling

Probability sampling is most often used in sport marketing research when looking at current customers. It utilizes random selection from the known population. There are four methods of probability sampling – simple random sampling, systematic sampling, cluster sampling, and stratified sampling.

Simple random sampling is where the sport marketing researcher uses some chance method that guarantees each member of the population has an equal chance to be selected into the sample. The most common of these are the blind draw method (pulling names out of a hat) and the random numbers methods (every member of the population is given a number and a computer generates a random list of numbers for the sample).

Systematic sampling is less time consuming than the simple random method. Starting with a list of the entire population, each is given a number. Then a skip interval is calculated. This skip interval represents how many names would be skipped when selecting the sample. This is calculated by taking the entire population list, and dividing it by the desired sample size. For example, let us say there are 10,000 ticket holders, and we want a sample size of 1000. The skip interval would be 10. Therefore, every 10th name on the list would be entered into the sample.

Cluster sampling is where the population is divided into groups, any of which could be considered as a representative sample. Most of the time clusters are based on demographics (geographic location, age range, sex, race). While this is a faster method of dividing groups, there cannot be a guarantee that the cluster is truly representative of the entire population.

Stratified sampling is utilized when there might be a large divergence in the population that would cause a skewed distribution. This skewed distribution is a result of extremes in the population – for example, if the majority of the population has an average income of $50,000 ± 25% ($37,500–67,500), but a significant percentage is making over $100,000. In this case, the population would be separate into different strata, and a sample would be taken from each.

Non-probability Sampling

Non-probability sampling is most often used in sport marketing research when there is no way to guarantee the representation in the sample. Therefore, the desired population does not have a guarantee of being a part of the sample. There are four methods of non-probability sampling – convenience sampling, referral sampling, judgment sampling, and quota sampling.

Convenience sampling is where the sport marketing researcher goes to a high-traffic area such as a mall or shopping center to survey potential respondents. Errors occur as a result of there being no guarantee that users will be within the population at the chosen location.

Referral sampling is where the respondents to a survey are also asked to identify other individuals who would likely qualify to take the survey. Again this is a biased sampling method as those who are not well known, not liked, or have caused conflict in the eyes of the respondent will not be included.

Judgment sampling occurs when the sport marketing researcher uses either their own opinion, or that of someone considered to be an expert, to determine who will be a part of the sample. This is a subjective method of sampling, therefore beliefs, feeling, attitudes, and perception could play a significant role, and hence may bias the sample.

Quota sampling goes a step further than judgment sampling, but also seeks to enhance convenience sampling. This method seeks to balance the proportion of selected respondent characteristics by setting quotas on how many individuals from a specific group can respond. Groups may be capped based on demographic features, product use, or service features utilized.

Examining Data and Drawing Conclusions

The goal of this section is to introduce the student to basic methods of describing the data and being able to draw basic conclusions utilizing one of five statistical analysis methods – descriptive, inferential, differences, associative, and predictive. All of these statistical methods are used to reduce the large quantity of data for use in drawing conclusions for the study. The data is summarized and explained in logical order, while communicating patterns of behavior or action and generalizing the sample to an entire population. It is recommended that individuals who wish to gain more extensive experience in data analysis take a market research class or a probability and statistics class.

Descriptive Analysis

Descriptive statistics are used early in the analysis of data and serve as a foundation for future, more detailed analysis of data. As the title states, descriptive statistics uses basic data reduction and summarization to describe the respondents, the sample, and the population. The methods utilized for descriptive analysis are mean, median, mode, frequency distribution, range, and standard deviation – each are defined in the chart below:

Mean	The average value of a set of numbers (sum of all responses/number of respondents).
Median	The middle value of a distribution (50th percentile).
Mode	The value occurring most frequently in the data.
Frequency distribution	The number of times a value occurs during the study. These distributions can be documented as individual cases (frequency), percentages, and running totals (cumulative).
Range	The distance between the lowest value and the highest value.
Standard deviation (SD)	Measures the spread of values throughout the data. For a normal curve, which is used most often, the midpoint is the mean and the standard deviation is measured from that point.

Inferential Analysis

Inferential statistics are used to generalize the results and draw conclusions simply based on the population characteristics and the data collected. This method is used to estimate values, test hypotheses, and determine significant differences. The two main methods for completing an inferential analysis are standard error and the null hypothesis. Standard error is used to measure the variability in the sample distribution. This is accomplished by taking the standard deviation from the mean and dividing by the total number of respondents (SD/N). This allows us to apply that error to determine the similarity or dissimilarity of the sample based on the spread of the distribution and the associated percentages. Also associated with the standard error are confidence intervals. These are utilized to calculate the degree of accuracy that the researcher prefers. Most researchers seek a 95% level of confidence in their studies.

Hypothesis testing is the articulated expectation of the sport organization, the sport marketer, or the sport marketing researcher. There is a five-step process to hypothesis testing as documented below:

- *Step 1*: Make a statement about something that exists within the population.
  The owner of an Af2 Arena Football Team states that attendance is only at 60% capacity because the community at large is not aware of the team's presence.

- *Step 2*: Draw a probability sample and determine a sample statistic (mean is most often used).
  The sport marketing department outsources to a market research firm and asks for a systematic sampling method to be used on residents within a 40 mile radius. At the end of the study, results show that 83% of the geographic target is knowledgeable about the team. Additional information shows that 61% of the respondents did not attend a game for two associated reasons – high ticket prices of arena football, and choosing to spend their discretionary money on the minor league baseball team in town.

- *Step 3*: Compare the statistic to the original statement (hypothesis).
  The 60% stated by the owner does not equate to the 83% stated by the research.

- *Step 4*: Decide if the statistic supports the hypothesis.
  The researched 83% does not support the owner's original statement.

- *Step 5*: If the sample does not support the hypothesis, reject it and revise.
  We reject the owner's statement and start a plan to address the reason why 40% of the arena is empty – including a review of ticket prices, and a modification of marketing and promotional efforts to address the competition.

Difference Analysis

Difference analysis is utilized when there are variations that exist between targeted groups. This is very apparent in sport marketing research, especially with the aforementioned escalator concept. Heavy users (season ticket holders, luxury suite owners) will view satisfaction with sport products and services very differently than light users (come to a game one or twice per year).

Two main statistical concepts are utilized to measure differences between groups. The first is the *t* test, which assesses whether the means of the two groups are statistically different than each other. Marketing efforts can be directed to the two groups in a similar fashion only if the difference between the means is statistically insignificant. The other test is the analysis of variance (ANOVA). ANOVA testing is utilized when there are more than two groups being compared.

Associative Analysis

Associative statistics evaluate whether two specific variables within a study are related. An example would be: are ticket promotions in the local newspaper resulting in more tickets purchased. There are three main methods for evaluating association – cross-tabulations, chi-square analysis, and Pearson product moment correlation:

Cross-tabulations	Basic tabular comparison method using raw data, frequencies, or percentages.
Chi-square	Known as a "goodness of fit" test; it seeks to take the obtained frequencies from the sample and compare them to the statistical hypothesis.
Pearson product moment correlation	Also known as the correlation coefficient; creates a linear association between two variables.

Predictive Analysis

Predictive statistics are used mainly by sport marketing researchers in prediction and forecasting of the future by evaluating previously collected data. A variety of regression analyses are utilized to engage in predictive analysis including bivariate regression analysis (two variables), and multiple regression analysis (more than two variables). Regression measures a dependent variable and its relationship to one (bivariate) or more (multiple) independent variables.

SPORT MARKETING POTENTIAL IN CHINA

This is a two part case study. This section will cover the marketing research efforts that targets consumers' influences and financial implications as being a worthwhile sport marketing effort. To implement effective marketing strategies in a specific country, it is pertinent to understand consumer behavior in that country, which will be covered as the second part of the case study and will appear in Chapter 5.

From the marketing research effort, a questionnaire was administered to 2155 mainland Chinese consumers in 10 selected cities, different economic, social, and personal factors in the China's environment are determined.

Continued

Introduction

With a quarter of the world's population and a fast growing economy, China is rapidly turning into one of the busiest market centers in the world. Sport marketing has the potential to emerge not only as an effective vehicle in imitating the development of the Chinese economy; it also affects the Chinese culture and lifestyle.

Since sport marketing in China has not been analyzed or researched, it is appropriate to study the consumer as well as general financial implications. A look at American success in sport marketing will be helpful. However, implementing such strategies in China creates special considerations because of the existence of cultural and economic differences between the two countries. This study attempts to identify the proper marketing strategies in China through an analysis of Chinese consumers' behavior, attitudes, and buying patterns.

Methodology

The methodology used in this study consisted of exploratory research of interviewing managers of retail outlets, secondary research of literature review, and primary research of a total of 4000 questionnaires distributed in 10 selected cities (Beijing, Chendu, Guangzhou, Nanjing, Qindao, Shanghai, Shenzhen, Tianjin, Xian, and Xiamen) in China. Questionnaires were administered to a judgmental quota sample and assigned to one of four age groups with equal males and females.

The rate of response was 53.9%; 2155 questionnaires were returned.

The analysis of the data includes editing, coding, analyzing coded observations, and interpreting results for solutions to the research problems. Tabulations and measures of central tendency were used to describe the distribution of characteristics in the subject population. Cross-tabulation and chi-square statistics were also used to show relationships between consumer segments.

Survey Findings

Eleven major factors affecting consumer purchasing emerged from the questionnaire data analysis:

1. *Purchasing reasons:* The major reason why people purchased sport products was "for exercise."
2. *Purchasing experience evaluation:* Approximately half of the respondents indicated that their purchasing experience was "positive."
3. *Income level relative to the expenses level:* The Chinese consumers' income levels range from less than $173 US per year to over $863 US

a year. The middle income level accounted for 72% of the respondents. However, most respondents indicated they spent "less than $40 US per year" on the purchase of sporting goods.

4. *Type of sporting goods purchased*: "Shoes" were the No. 1 favorite type of sporting goods for Chinese consumers. Females tended to purchase apparel; males were more likely to purchase all type of sporting goods.

5. *Product factors affecting purchasing*: "Quality," "style," and "price" were the three most important factors influencing purchasing decisions.

6. *Purchasing*: "Boy-and-girlfriend" had the most important influence in the decision process. "Parents" had the least important influence.

7. *Sources of information about where and how to purchase*: The major information channel for Chinese consumers was their "going to a shopping mall" experience.

8. *Influence of advertisements*: Of those responding to the survey, more than half said they either "occasionally" or "rarely" believe advertisements.

9. *Brands consumers prefer*: Adidas, Asics, Nike, and Reebok were identified by the Chinese consumers.

10. *Where goods purchased*: Most of those surveyed purchased their sporting goods from either "a sporting goods store" or "a department store."

11. *Time spent in sport activities*: Almost 90% of the Chinese consumers spent "less than 5 hours a week" participating in sport activities. However, three meaningful findings emerged: (1) those who participated "less than 5 hours per week" in sport activities spent more money purchasing sport products than those who participated "over 5 hours per week" in sport activities; (2) those in the income level of "$402 to $863 US" spent more time participating in sport activities; and (3) young adults and "unmarried" persons spent more time per week participating in activities than those who were "married" or elderly.

Source: Adapted from Geng, L., B. Lockhart, C. Blackmore, and R. Andrus (1996). Sport marketing strategy: a consumer behavior case analysis in China. *Multinational Business Review* 4(1): 147–154.

Suggested Discussion Topics

1. Utilizing a questionnaire for this type of research can be quite a challenge due to the spread of the 2155 mainland Chinese consumers in 10 selected cities, and the different economic, social, and personal factors in the China's environment. In a country of over 1 billion people with a land mass of over 9.5 million square kilometers (3.67 million square miles or the size of the United States) it is very difficult to determine an

Continued

appropriate sample. Considering the sampling methods discussed in the chapter, what methods of probability and non-probability sampling could have been used for this study? Explain in detail as to your reasoning why you belief this method could be used. Choose the one method you would use and explain why in terms of ensuring reliability and validity of the data collected.

2. Assume you are the Marketing Director of a sport apparel company who wishes to enter this market. By analyzing each of the 11 factors affecting consumer purchasing that emerged from the questionnaire data analysis, would you move forward with entering into this market? If yes, how would you proceed? If no, why not?

RESEARCH REPORTS AND SERVICES WITHIN SPORT MARKETING RESEARCH

Once all the information has been compiled, the results need to be communicated to the sport organization through a sport marketing research report. This report presents factual information based on research results, recommendations from the sport marketing researcher, and conclusions about what could happen if necessary change is not implemented. This report is then used by the management of the sport organization as a foundation for their decision making process. For this reason, the information presented in the sport marketing research report must be organized, concise, accurate, and clear. Visuals, including tables, pie charts, bar graphs, line graphs, maps, photos, and flow diagrams, can all be used to enhance the report and simplify the message for those who may not read it in its entirety. It would also be appropriate for the sport marketing researcher or professional to include an oral presentation with the report to highlight the most important sections.

Sport marketing research reports cover a wide range of area, including but not limited to customer satisfaction, economic impact, needs assessment, organizational behavior, and risk assessment. There are a number of publications and services available that focus on the field of sport marketing research, including the following.

Sample List of Sport Marketing Research Companies

- American Sports Data   www.americansportsdata.com
- C. Barnes and Company   www.barnesreports.com
- Beverage Marketing Corporation www.beveragemarketing.com

- EPM Communications, Inc.   www.epmcom.com
- Football Fans Central Limited   www.footballfanscensus.com
- Forrester Research, Inc.   www.forrester.com
- Hoovers, Inc.   www.hoovers.com
- IBISWorld   www.ibisworld.com
- Key Note Publications, Ltd.   www.keynote.com.uk
- Richard K. Miller and Associates   www.rkmillerinc.com
- Mintel International Group, Ltd.   www.mintel.com
- Plunkett Research, Ltd.   www.plunkettresearch.com
- Snapdata International Group   www.snapdata.com
- SportBusiness Group, Ltd.   www.sportbusiness.com
- Sport Business Research Network   www.sbrnet.com

Sample List of Sport Marketing Research Publications

- EPM Entertainment Marketing Sourcebook
- Plunkett's Sports Industry Almanac
- Spectator Sports Industry Report by Barnes Reports
- Sports Business Market Research Yearbook by Miller and Associates
- Sports Marketing and the Beverage Industry by the Beverage Marketing Corporation
- The Business of Sport Marketing by SportBusiness International Group

ONLINE AND WEB-BASED SPORT MARKETING RESEARCH

With the expansion of electronic technologies and the Internet, online and web-based sport marketing research has become more prevalent. The main reason the online and web-based technologies are becoming the preferred method for conducting research is because of its effectiveness (ease of use) and efficiency (minimal time and resources needed). There are numerous other advantages to online and web-based research, including:

- Can be effectively utilized at all stages of the sport marketing research process.
- Can be used for both qualitative and quantitative research.
- Can be used to administer surveys, as well as conduct observational research both in real time and asynchronously.
- Allow respondents to participate in a place of their choice (home, work, Internet café, etc.).
- Researchers and organizations can view data in real time.
- Researchers can provide supplemental information (videos, pictures, advertisements, simulations) for respondents to view and review as a part of the research.

There are also a number of challenges with online and web-based research. First, it is difficult to determine will full reliability and validity that the data collected is truly representative of the entire population. It is challenging to verify the authenticity of the person responding to the research. This is also true for the secondary information published on the web. It is important that researchers verify that the source of the information is reputable.

Another challenge is getting people to complete surveys via the web. Spam (unsolicited email) and pop-up advertisements have inundated online and web-based systems to the point of people downloading pop-up blockers, and having unknown email go to a junk email folder for deletion.

Many of these challenges have forced sport organizations to review the way in which they conduct research. This has resulted in more sport organizations investing time and resources into the creation of a sport management information system (SMIS). This structure consists of all aspect of the sport organization (people, equipment, goal and objectives, policies and procedures, etc.) being responsible for gathering, organizing, analyzing, evaluating, and distributing marketing information across the sport organization for the purpose of efficient and effective decision making. The next chapter of this book will discuss in detail the sport marketing information system.

CONCLUSION

This chapter introduces the reader to the concepts of sport marketing research. The chapter systematically goes through the steps of the sport marketing research process, focusing on the importance of each step and the development process associated with those steps.

The sport marketing research process starts with determining its need as a result of a lack of information available about a target market. As a result of a problem being defined, the sport marketing professional comes up with a list of potential solutions, which are then articulated in terms of goals and objectives, and then utilized to develop modified policies and procedures.

At this point, the sport marketing researcher must choose the appropriate research methodology based on the type of primary and secondary data available. Research will be conducted using one of three methods: exploratory research, descriptive research, or causal research. For each of these types of research, there are various sources of information. Exploratory research utilizes secondary data analysis, case study analysis, focus groups, experience surveys, and projective techniques. Descriptive research employs cross-sectional studies and longitudinal studies – including panels and market tracking studies. Causal research uses experiments and test marketing to secure information.

Often, the sport marketing researcher needs to collect additional primary data, which is secured through personal contacts via observations, self-administered survey questionnaires, person-administered surveys (interviews), and computer-administered surveys. The development of data collection forms, while in different tangible and intangible forms, are developed utilizing a similar process. The development process starts with determining the response format for the questions – either closed-ended, open-ended, or scaled-response. Once the response format for the questions is chosen, the sport marketing researcher must determine how the results will be measured. There are two major considerations to consider when planning to measure responses: the characteristics of the scale to be utilized and the levels of measurement for the scales.

Now that the response format and measurement scale has been determined, the survey questionnaire can be developed. Questionnaire development has become significantly easier with the introduction of computer technologies. Questionnaire development and data analysis software and websites have cut the design and computation time down significantly.

Once the survey questionnaire is developed, the sport marketing researcher must determine sample size. A sample is the most basic element of sport marketing research, as it is the factors taken from a small group that is representative of the characteristics of an entire population. A sample is chosen using one of two methods: probability sampling and non-probability sampling. Data is then examined statistically and conclusions drawn. There are five basic statistical methods employed in sport marketing research: inferential analysis, descriptive analysis, difference analysis, associative analysis, and predictive analysis.

The chapter also provides the reader with information regarding research report and services within sport marketing research, including information on sport marketing research companies and publications. In addition, the significant impact of online and web-based research is covered. While this method of research has become the preferred method for conducting research is because of its effectiveness, efficiency, and wide range of use throughout the sport marketing research process, there are challenges to its reliability and validity as a result of guaranteeing the authenticity of the person responding to the research, information being published by non-reputable sources, and the misconception of surveys as created by spam and pop-up advertisements.

In closing, it is important to note that with the complexity and variety of methods of research utilized in sport marketing, the conclusions drawn are consequently used in a wide variety of ways. Since the specific aspects of sport marketing varies widely, the use of collected research data will be discussed accordingly within each future chapter.

From Theory to Practice

Douglas Blais, Professor of Sport Management

*Southern New Hampshire University,
Manchester, New Hampshire*

I am currently a Full Professor of Sport Management in the School of Business at Southern New Hampshire University, and have a Ph.D. in Sport Management with a concentration in marketing from the University of Connecticut. I have had extensive experience conducting market research for

Continued

a variety of sport organizations including the Boston Celtics, Manchester Monarchs (AHL affiliate of the Los Angeles Kings), Bank of America Championship (PGA Champions Tours), Eastern Mountain Sports, Manchester Wolves (Arena Football 2), and the Verizon Wireless Arena. Sport marketing research is a crucial element to the success of a sport organization. Strong marketing research provides timely information to identify new opportunities, evaluate the current market, determine market segments, and aid in marketing mix decisions.

The Manchester Monarchs of the American Hockey League are consistently one of the top draws in the league. President Jeff Eisenberg contributes their success to understanding the needs and wants of their fans. The Monarchs have made a commitment to market research. The organization has conducted extensive market research in each of its first 5 years. This research takes on various forms including a brief fan survey conducted every game, focus groups, in-depth fan surveys, secret shoppers, and arena observations.

The in-depth survey has been one of the most critical elements in the organization's research. The surveys are administered during a mid-week game, a Friday night game, a Saturday night game, and a Sunday afternoon game, ensuring proper sampling. An example of the survey questions are below:

- What is your zip code?
- What are your favorite radio stations?
- Do you listen to the Monarchs on the radio?
- How many games do you expect to attend this year?
- What is the number of times you visit the Monarchs' website?
- Where do you obtain schedule information?
- What starting time for the games do you prefer?
- Who was the decision maker for attending the game?
- Please list your three favorite promotions.

The Monarchs use this information in a variety of manners. The Monarchs are able to give sponsors demographic information, determine which promotions to continue or eliminate, the effectiveness of their website to disseminate information, and the best ways to reach their target audience.

The in-depth survey allows the Monarchs to sample a large number of fans and obtain research on a number of areas. The focus groups, while limited to a much smaller sample, allow the Monarchs to obtain more qualitative research. The Monarchs annually conduct focus groups with season ticket holders, individual game attendees, and a sampling of fans with partial ticket plans. Fans are given the opportunity to express what they like best and least about the organization and game presentation. An example of information obtain during a focus group was the displeasure of fans when other fans left their seat during play. The research indicated that this was occurring more often in the 200 level compared with 100 (lower) level of the arena. The Monarchs developed additional announcements incorporating clips from the Seinfeld™ comedy show educating fans to wait for a stoppage in play before leaving or returning to their seats. Additional ushers were placed in the 200 level to apply this policy.

The Bank of America Championship used fan surveys to answer many of the same questions used in the Monarchs surveys. Additional research questions included:

- How the tickets were obtained (from a sponsor, own company, gift, promotion …).
- The number of days attending the tournament.
- Number of golf rounds played per year.
- Golf Handicap.
- Reason(s) for attending (fan of golf, meet players, business, family outing …).
- How they learned about the event.

The Bank of America Championship also conducted focus groups of fans that had attended in previous years and did not attend the past year. The focus group allowed for participants to voice their opinion as to why they stopped attending the event.

The above research aided to tournament officials in deciding how to best develop their marketing mix.

Students interested in conducting marketing research should:

- Be familiar with spreadsheet software (Microsoft Excel™) and statistical software (SPSS™).
- Volunteer with local organizations to conduct market research. Professional market research is expensive and many minor league and non-profit organizations cannot afford to hire a firm. Organizations such as the Special Olympics, YMCA, Boy and Girls Club, or your local organization (i.e., Kiwanis) that sponsors a running road race would all be interested in your services.
- By conducting this research, you will be able design, collect, analyze, interpret, and report your own findings.
- Understand the importance of the market research process in the success of any organization.

SPORT MARKETING INFORMATION SYSTEMS

CHAPTER OUTLINE

CHAPTER OBJECTIVES

The reader will be able to:

- Recognize the purpose and uses of sport marketing information system.
- Recognize the differences between the components of the sport marketing information system.
- Understand how the research system interacts with the internal reports system, the intelligence system, and the decision support system (DSS), as well as with each other, to implement a most efficient and effective sport marketing information system.

WHAT IS A SPORT MARKETING INFORMATION SYSTEM?

As stated at the end of the previous chapter, more sport organizations are investing time and resources into the creation of a sport marketing information system (SMIS). This structure consists of all aspect of the sport organization (people, equipment, goal and objectives, policies and procedures, etc.) being responsible for gathering, organizing, analyzing, evaluating, and distributing marketing information across the sport organization for the purpose of efficient and effective decision making.

The sport marketing research system was discussed in detail in Chapter 3, and serves as the foundation of the studies that are undertaken for specific problems. However, to have an efficient and effective sport marketing information system, there needs to be interaction from three other components: the internal reports system, the sport marketing intelligence system, and the sport marketing DSS.

The internal reports system involves information that is generated by the internal operations of the sport organization. Internal reports include all aspects of the accounting information system, including asset and liability management, revenue and expense operations, and administration of owner's equity. The sport marketing intelligence system involves the procedures and sources that the organization utilized to obtain everyday information about developments regarding external opportunities and threats. The sport marketing decision support system, or sport marketing DSS, encompasses the primary and secondary data previously collected by the sport organization, the tools and techniques utilized to interpret that data, and the process by which that information is used in the decision making process. The remainder of this chapter will focus on these three systems.

COMPONENTS OF A SPORT MARKETING INFORMATION SYSTEM

Internal Reports System

The internal reports system is the basic information system used by sport marketing professionals to examine the internal operations of the sport organization. The internal reports consist of all facets of the accounting information system, including asset and liability management, revenue and expense operations, and administration of owner's equity. This allows the sport marketing professional to review reports of orders, sales, costs, inventories, cash flows, receivables, payables, and debts on an ongoing basis. This information is available quickly, because most sport organizations produce these reports of financial management on a monthly, and even weekly, basis.

Any sport organization that has been in business for any period of time has more information available than they realize. Therefore, much of this information often remains under-utilized because the information does not leave the department it was created or collected by. The individuals in those various departments do not always realize how the data could help sport marketing in their decision making process. In addition, many sport marketing professionals fail to appreciate how information from other areas might help them and therefore do not request it.

The internal records that are of immediate value to marketing decisions are orders received, inventory, and sales invoices. By comparing orders received with invoices, a sport marketing professional can establish the extent to which the sport organization is providing an acceptable level of customer service. Evaluating inventory records with orders received helps a sport marketer determine whether the marketing efforts are addressing the current demand patterns, and if changes may need to be made. This often occurs with ticket sales for less desirable match-ups. For example, when the New York Yankees hosts the Boston Red Sox, there is usually not a ticket to be had. However, for other teams such as Tampa Bay or Kansas City, there is less of a demand to pay a premium price for those games. The sport marketing professional can look at ticket inventory levels, see which games are not selling, and design programs to entice customer to purchase tickets and attend the games.

However, there is a lot of information that the various departmental, managerial, and administrative areas within the sport organization can provide that would enhance the sport marketing information system. The following chart provides a sample list of internal operations that can provide internal report information to the sport marketing information system:

Organizational Area	Information to be Provided	Use of the Information
Accounting and finance	Product pricing and costing Marketing and sales expenses	Profitability potential by sport product or service
Customer service	Customer feedback on product reliability and performance	Ability to review files for new product or service ideas Ability to review problems that need to be addressed
Corporate planning	Goals and objectives for the sport organization	Measuring tool to determine progress toward attaining goals
Data processing	The system for organizing data	Understanding of the capabilities of the system Articulation of what the system needs to provide
Human resources	Background on sales and marketing employees Performance review data	Learning curve for salespeople Review criteria for future hires
Marketing department	Types of new sport products and services with market possibilities Customer response to current sport products and services Strategic marketing plans Promotional campaigns	Data for market analysis of current sport products and services for: ▪ Prospects ▪ Current customers

Continued

Organizational Area	Information to be Provided	Use of the Information
Merchandising/ ticketing	Inventory status	Forecast promotional needs to be attached to selected inventory
Sales department	Sales figures Feedback from customers	Streamline and improve methods of securing sales

Order-to-Payment Cycle

The focal point of the internal records system is order-to-payment cycle, which includes all of the activities associated with the completion of a business transaction. The process starts with a request for purchase. This request can range from a merchandiser or concessionaire placing an order with a supplier, to an individual clicking on buttons to find tickets online, to a fan placing an order for food at the concession stand. The request for purchase is any situation where a buyer wishes to make a purchase from a seller.

The cycle continues with the seller providing information on the price to be paid. For the merchandiser or concessionaire, it is the receipt of an invoice. For the sport consumer purchasing tickets online, it is the screen that tells how much the cost will be. At the concession stand, it is the vendor telling the customer how much it will cost for the food ordered. The order-to-payment cycle concludes with the payment and delivery of the products.

The more efficient and effective the cycle works, the more orders can be processed, the more sales can be transacted, and the potential for higher profit by the sport organization is realistic. From the standpoint of the sport marketing professional, access to the order-to-payment is crucial. The order-to-payment cycle spans most business processes. The sport marketing professional may need access to information from any of those processes at a given time based on a problem at hand. Therefore, the sport marketing professional can address market changes, opportunities, and threats more quickly. In addition, sport marketers can send messages to prospects and customers that the sport organization addresses consumer needs, wants, and desires quickly. This, in turn, has the potential of increasing sales and the image of the sport organization.

Point-of-Sale System

As with many sport marketing functions, time is of the essence. If a demand need is not addressed quickly, another organization will swoop in and take advantage of the opportunity. Therefore, many sport organizations have increased the speed in which sport marketing professional and management can access information by moving their internal report systems to a computer-based Intranet. Advances in technology have provided sport marketing professionals with more comprehensive information at their fingertips by providing instant access to information about their prospects and customers through sales information systems. These sales information computer systems for internal reports are also known as point-of-sale (POS) systems.

There is a variety of POS hardware that can collect information that can be ultimately used by the sport marketing professional. Some examples are as follows:

Name of Hardware	Variations of Hardware
Barcode scanner	Hand-held, hands-free, and countertop
Barcode printer	High-speed direct thermal and thermal transfer label printers
Receipt printer	High-speed thermal and impact receipt printers
Credit card reader	Standard
Check reader	Standard
Portable age/ID verifier	Identity verification via driver's license or state-issued/military ID
Palm pilots	With integrated barcode scanner or wireless communication
Cordless scanners	Long range and short range, cordless and wireless
POS keyboards	With integrated credit card or check reader
POS monitors	Touch screen

In addition, there are a number of software programs that take the information collected and disseminate that data into an easy-access format. Some examples of the software programs available include the following:

- eClub Logic by KI Software
- Intuit Quickbooks POS
- Microsoft Retail Management System
- Seta Systems Golf Club Management Software
- TangentPOS by Venue1
- Windward's SportsStorePOS for Retail Sport Stores

Data Mining of Transactional Data

One of the major growth areas in sport marketing is transactional data collected as a result of data mining. Data mining is the process of collecting and analyzing data from non-traditional perspectives, categorize the data, and summarize relationships. An example of this would be a baseball team using a fan loyalty reward card to analyze buying patterns at the stadium and associated merchandise outlets. They might discover that men who buy a ticket to the game on average also purchase two beers, approximately $15 of food, and spend about $10 on merchandise. It can also show what the most popular food and merchandise items are. It could also be used to offer promotions on low-selling items, and hence be able to move that merchandise out of inventory and replace with other types that may increase revenue.

This concept of data mining of transactional data has served as the foundation of current sport consumer relationship management programs, which will be discussed later in Chapter 15. Two companies engaged in data mining of transactional data for sport organizations are AIM Technologies and EDCS. AIM Technologies focuses on collecting information about the demographics and psychographics of fans, whereas EDCS's Top Prospect system collects information and translates purchases into a points system similar to a frequently flyer program for airlines. The more the fan uses their card, the more points they get, and the more benefits they receive. Under both programs, sport marketing professionals are able to use the data to design promotions and other specials through the programs.

These data mining efforts allow sport marketers to analyze and correlate hundreds if not thousands different segments that were targeted differently. However, with this mass of information, sport marketing professional can get lost in the quantity. The key is that each transaction is not of interest; the patterns and associations of transactions to evaluate areas where coordinated sport marketing efforts can be utilized save time and resources for the sport organization.

The data collected can also be utilized to grade the sport customer, which is another emerging method of sport marketing productivity. Most of the data collected is able to be given a grade or score, and hence sport marketing professionals can evaluate the success or failure of sport marketing campaign – just as a teacher would evaluate a research paper handed in by a student. As long as the sport marketer has developed outcomes that can be broken down into measurable terms, these grades can be used to more effectively and efficiently target potential and current sport consumers.

In addition to the grading of transactional data, sport marketing professionals must also categorize information using RFM (recency, frequency, monetary) analysis. RFM analysis is used to determine the most profitable customers for the sport organization based on: (1) if the customer has purchased recently; (2) how often the customer has made a purchase; and (3) how much the customer spends with the sport organization. This RFM analysis serves as the foundation for the Pareto Principle (or 80/20 rule) discussed in Chapter 1, where 80% of a sport organization's business comes from 20% of their customers. The RFM analysis also provides the sport marketer with the ability to conduct a long-term value analysis. Long-term value with regard to the sport consumer is an evaluation of what that sport consumer is worth to the sport organization in terms of sales and profit over a period of time. A long-term period usually refers to a minimum of 3 years, but can be as long as a lifetime.

The internal reports system serves as a framework for the sport marketing information system by allowing the sport marketing professional the ability to examine the internal operations of the sport organization and improve upon marketing efforts. Utilizing the information collected from various departments through inputs from the order-to-payment cycle; the POS system; and data mining, the sport marketing professional is better able to understanding the sport organization itself, and its relationship to prospective and current customers. However, as discussed in the introduction, this is only the second of four components that make up the sport marketing information system.

Sport Marketing Intelligence System

The sport marketing intelligence system is a set of procedures utilized by sport marketing professionals to secure everyday information about developments in the marketing environment regarding external opportunities and threats. In the last chapter, we discussed the difference between primary data and secondary data. The same concept applies in the sport marketing intelligence system – primary intelligence and secondary intelligence.

Primary intelligence is information collected by the sport organization through direct contact with customers, the distribution network, competitive analysis, and the internal sport organization itself. To enhance the collection and dissemination of primary intelligence, sport marketing professional will work with the sport organization in two ways. First, they can create an internal marketing information department that is responsible for being the central location for all data gathered from marketing research and collected via marketing intelligence. The department would be accountable for providing information throughout the sport organization to help enhance the marketing efforts in all areas. Second, the sport marketing department can work with the sales department to train salespeople not only to sell, but also to observe and report on the perceptions, values, and beliefs of customers.

Sport marketing professionals can also obtaining primary intelligence by communicating with all channel members (suppliers, manufacturers, and distributors), and work to share intelligence so that all have a detailed awareness of each other's activities. Having an integrated system of intelligence will help all parties to understand roles and create a more effective and efficient network.

Another method is to collect intelligence from competitors, especially those who have products in direct competition with the sport organization. Being aware of the opportunities and threats created by competition and addressing those issues promptly is crucial to success in sport marketing. Some of the methods used to collect competitive intelligence are drive-by and on-site observations such as secret shopping, cold calling the organization to obtain information by asking generic questions a normal customer would, and contacting community sources such as a chamber of commerce to secure additional information.

Secondary intelligence is information collected by the sport organization from previous published sources such as books, trade journals, newspapers, and reliable sources on the Internet. In addition, many sport organizations will purchase data from syndicated sources such as those discussed in Chapter 3.

The following chart provides a sample list of external area that can provide intelligence information to the sport marketing information system:

External Area	Information to be Provided	Use of the Information
Competition	Products and services offered Product and service literature	Offering comparisons Technology comparisons Opportunity analysis Threat analysis
Customers	Demographic, psychographic, and geographic profiles Sales data	Customer segmentation Customer profile analysis Product and service sales history

Continued

External Area	Information to be Provided	Use of the Information
Database and Internet information retrieval system	News abstracts about current events, industry news, products and services, the economy, and market analysis	Potential changes in product and/or service positioning Understanding of economic impact and the influence of current events on markets
Governmental (federal, State, and local) data	Industry comparisons Competitor comparisons Demographic and geographic comparisons Economic and financial data	Competitive analysis Market segment analysis Organizational profiling
Industry reports	Data analysis by industry Industry news	Industry growth statistics Trend analysis
Suppliers, wholesalers, and distributors	Market conditions General consumer analysis	Sales analysis Pricing changes Promotion ideas Segmenting and targeting Introduction of new products and/or services

Scanning of the Environment

Although the goal is to approach sport marketing intelligence in a deliberate fashion as described above, much of the actual collection of intelligence is mainly acquired through informal observations and conversations. The process is known as scanning. In sport marketing intelligence gathering, scanning can be undertaken in a number of ways. Formal scanning is a systematic search for information where there is a specific goal for the intelligence gathering. The scope of the search is narrow, but less rigorous that a full marketing research effort. Informal scanning involves a limited, unstructured effort in collecting data for a specific goal. This usually involves making inquiries to individuals on an impromptu basis. An example would be a sport marketer walking around a partially full stadium and just sitting down next to a fan and asking generic, yet structured questions to them about their satisfaction with the experience.

Semi-focused scanning is where there is no specific intelligence being sought or goal to attain, but a general inquiry is conducted to discover any piece of intelligence that may become evident. With this type of scanning, the sport marketing researcher usually limits where they will attempt to gather intelligence. For example, they may ask generic questions to full season ticket holders, but not to partial plans holders or fans that purchase single game tickets. A final type of intelligence search is unfocused scanning, where the sport marketing professional exposes their self to information they deem to be useful based on what they have read, heard, or seen. Although this activity is unfocused, it is an intentional attempt to gather intelligence. An example would be a sport marketer with a minor league baseball team reads in the local newspaper an editorial about a fan's displeasure with the concessions offered at the stadium. At the following home game, that sport marketer works their way around the facility, standing on various concession lines and talking informally with fans. The hope is to gather enough information to address the issues of concern with the concession stands.

Dissecting Intelligence from Scanning

Regardless of the method of scanning chosen by the sport marketing professional, there is a process for scrutinizing the information that has been collected. While the sport marketing researcher may be the leader of the scanning process, it is important to utilize as many resources as possible to collect data. In addition, it is important that all individuals involved in scanning the external environment be open-minded and unbiased in the gathering of marketing intelligence.

The first stage begins with an evaluation of the intelligence, and associating that information to relevant trends. These associations are analyzed using trend–impact analysis, which is a forecasting method that allows sport marketing researchers and the organization to track trends, apply the intelligence that has been collected to those trends, and examine the impact on potential future events that are a part of the overall organizational strategic plan. When determining whether to move forward or not, the sport marketer and the management of the sport organization must determine how advantageous moving forward would be; in other words, what is the probability of success? This is determined by looking at the feasibility of the organization to make any changes that are needed based on time and resources available. This is especially true in the marketing area as changes could directly affect advertising, promotions, consumer behavior, and methods for completing future market research.

The second stage starts when the organization agrees to move forward with change based on the intelligence. At this point, the sport marketing professional will work with the management of the sport organization to complete a cross-impact analysis, which examines the relationships between outcomes. The newly created outcomes from the previous stage (the future organizational impact) are correlated with current organizational impacts (philosophy, mission, goals, and vision).

Upon completion of the cross-impact analysis, the results are evaluated in terms of the organization's strengths and weaknesses. This third stage of entering the data into the internal part of the organization's SWOT (strengths, weaknesses, opportunities, and threats) analysis, with the objective of determining whether the changes coincide with the philosophy of the organization, requires the creation of additional or new goals and objectives, and/or necessitate a change to the vision for the sport organization. Changes to goals and vision may be appropriate within any sport organization. However, changes that impact organizational philosophy should be looks at very seriously as those changes may significantly shift the entire value and belief system of the organization.

If change is deemed to be appropriate, the fourth stage would be twofold. The sport marketing professional would draw up plans to evaluate the marketing impact of these changes. As the same time, the management of the sport organization will look to how to best integrate the changes within all aspects of the organizational strategic plan. The groups would then come together to make a final decision and make one of three choices:

1. *Opposition:* Decide that the change is not appropriate for the sport organization.
2. *Modification:* Take the necessary steps to integrate the changes across the sport organization. This often requires the sport marketing department to act quickly to inform relevant constituents (distribution network, customers, and media) of the changes. In addition, the sport marketing professional will need to examine how the changes affect the current marketing mix and segments, and to what new segments the sport organization could be opened to.
3. *Relocation:* The decision that takes place only in dire situations where the sport organization must change to a different market. This type of change is done only in extreme circumstances.

Sport Marketing Decision Support System

The sport marketing decision support system (DSS) is the fourth component of the sport marketing information system. The sport marketing DSS assists sport marketing professional and other decision makers within the sport organization by taking advantage of information that is available from the various sources. The sport marketing DSS comprises three major parts: (1) the primary and secondary data previously collected by the sport organization; (2) the approaches and methods utilized to decipher and explain the data; and (3) the process of utilizing the information in the decision making process of the sport organization. This coordination of data, systems, tools, methods, people, and infrastructure serve as a central clearing house for information used to make strategic decisions, control decisions, operational decisions, and marketing decisions.

The sport marketing DSS has an effect on both the decision process and the decision outcomes. These two components are interrelated since the outcome depends on the result of the decision process. The outcome for any decision in sport marketing must lead to a better performance in the marketplace by the sport organization. To accomplish that, the decision process must involve decision makers who can identify the core decision variables that have the strongest relationship to positive performance. This in turn will enhance the quality of decisions that are made.

High-quality decisions are made when the change in the selected marketing variable leads to higher profits, a stronger and more positive image, or increase sport consumer satisfaction. To test and determine whether those changes will work, those involved with the sport marketing DSS will run simulations by performing "what-if" analyses. Each outcome is usually integrated with each relevant element of the sport marketing mix to determine whether the desired effect would take place. However, sport marketing decision makers must make sure they understand their information-processing limitations. The human mind is limited in their ability to process and recall information. When there is an overabundance of information, the decision maker must spend an extensive amount of time organizing the information instead of solving the problems. This is especially true when there is irrelevant information included in the data. This slows down the process, and may divert the decision maker from quickly finding relevant data.

Key Factors of the Sport Marketing DSS

There are two factors that play an important role in the framework of the sport marketing DSS. The first factor is the cognitive abilities of the decision maker. Cognitive abilities refer to the perceptual and intellectual capabilities of individuals. These abilities include comprehension, judgment, learning, memory, and reasoning. Cognition has a direct effect on the decision making style of an individual and can be viewed from two extremes. High-analytical decision makers break down problems into smaller parts, resulting in a set of causal relationships. Then the decision variables are manipulated to address those relationships with the goal of reaching decisions that will provide optimal success for the sport organization. Low-analytical decision makers look at a problem as an absolute, and seek feasible solutions to the entire problem based only on past experiences and previously solved problems.

The second factor is the time pressures associated with decision making. Sport marketers realize that due to the ever-changing marketplace, acting fast is as important as acting correctly. Hence this time pressure has a direct effect on the ability to appropriately utilize the sport marketing DSS, since using it takes additional time and the benefits from the system focus on effectiveness rather than efficiency. Time pressure often reduces the amount of information searching and processing conducted by the sport marketing professional, which often results in simplifying strategies and being more conservative with decision making.

Engaging the Sport Marketing DSS

This is the most difficult component of the sport marketing information system to employ. Sport marketing professional tend to be highly analytical, and as a result of the profession of marketing in general, usually have a significant level of time pressure place upon them. As a result, many sport marketing schemes, promotions, and activities are not successful over the long term. The key is to expand the likelihood of long-term success. This is done by first addressing the changing environment quickly, and then engaging the sport marketing DSS to evaluate the change, make recommendations on further modifications, and implementing those recommendations within the sport marketing environment. However, it is important to remember that whatever decision is made, it must be able to interact with the other related sport marketing mix efforts including product strategies, sales efforts and pricing tactics, place distribution, and advertising and promotional plans.

ETHICS IN SPORT INFORMATION SYSTEMS: ALL-STAR VOTING

Now that professional sports have online All-Star voting, what would prevent someone from developing a program that could cast multiple votes for a single player or players?

For instance, in 1999 there was a gentleman who tried to cast thousands of votes on his favorite player. In most cases, the professional organization limits the number of votes that a single person or IP address can submit. Some of the parameters that vote counters search for are patterns or abnormalities such as, votes being cast too frequently from the same IP and the speed at which these votes are cast.

What if there was a program developed that would clone other IP addresses and cast votes at a rate that could account for human input. Most large corporations and governments employ highly paid computer programmers to prevent computer espionage. A large majority of these programmers have a hacking background.

To prevent this hacking, programmers have developed elaborate algorithms that should not allow hacking to occur. However, if a human created the algorithm, a human can find a way around it.

Why would someone spend their time trying to affect the outcome of a baseball or basketball roster? Herb Edelstein, a data warehouse and data mining analyst at Two Crows Corp. in Potomac, MD., said pattern recognition is vital to uncovering fraud.

"Discovering the difference between normal and abnormal behavior is the basis of fraud detection," Edelstein explained. "Systems with high transaction volumes, [such as] credit-card systems and stock trading, depend on pattern recognition for fraud prevention."

With the 2006 World Cup coming to Germany, fans that have purchased tickets needed to produce their passport in order for the ticket number and the passport number to be linked. The purpose of this link is to ensure the safety of the individual's attending the games and to end the scalping of tickets. Security is predicted to be the most stringent in any of athletic event in history.

Source: Deck, S. (1999). *Baseball Execs Spot All-Star Online Ballot Box Stuffing*. Retrieved from http://www.computerworld.com/news/1999/story/0,11280,36334,00.html.

Suggested Discussion Topics

1. Have information systems developed at such a fast rate that we have sacrificed integrity for speed? Why or why not?
2. What does the future hold for security at sporting events and how will marketing and management information systems play a role?

VALUE OF AN INTEGRATED SPORT MARKETING INFORMATION SYSTEM

A carefully designed sport marketing information system will produce information that is significant and useful to the sport marketing professional for making sport marketing decisions. It is important to understand that while the ultimate goal of the sport marketing information system is to help the sport marketing professional make better decisions in the shortest period of time possible, management wants a system that will provide a positive return on investment. One of the common misconceptions by management is that the cost, time, and appearance of needing extensive resources because of the involvement of all department and the need for a significant computer infrastructure, is not worth it. In fact, many organizations think that the sport marketing information system is a façade that makes the sport organization appear to be current by implementing the latest marketing ideas. However, just as with any product or service offered by the sport organization, we look at the information collected in terms of marginal cost vs. marginal value. Marginal cost is the total cost that is incurred based on the quantity produced. Marginal value is the worth to the sport organization of producing one more unit of the product in comparison to other products. Therefore, a sport marketing information system that is valuable to a sport organization must show that the value of the information being collected, analyzed, and used is equal to the cost of that information.

CONCLUSION

The purpose of a sport marketing information system is to collect the various data available in one place for use in making efficient and effective sport marketing decisions. A sport marketing information system is a structure of interacting people, infrastructure, and techniques to gather, sort, analyze, evaluate and distribute relevant, well-timed, accurate information for use by sport marketing professional to sport marketing plan development, implementation, and management.

The marketing research system, detailed in Chapter 3, is the process of designing, gathering, analyzing, and reporting information that is utilized to solve a specified sport marketing issue or problem. The other three systems are the internal reports system, the sport marketing intelligence system, and the sport marketing decision support system (DSS).

The internal reports system serves as a framework for the sport marketing information system by allowing the sport marketing professional the ability to examine the internal operations of the sport organization and improve upon marketing efforts. Utilizing the information collected from various departments through inputs from the order-to-payment cycle; the POS system; and data mining, the sport marketing professional is better able to understanding the sport organization itself, and its relationship to prospective and current customers.

The sport marketing intelligence system is a crucial element of the sport marketing information system because it opens the door to understanding the external environment that affects the sport organization. By using the primary and secondary intelligence collected through the various methods of scanning, and evaluating that data through the scanning dissemination process, the sport marketing professional gains a better understanding of the opportunities, threats, and trends that can affect the sport organization. In addition, this intelligence is utilized to enhance the internal reports of the sport organization, and can serve as a framework for future sport marketing research.

The sport marketing DSS assists sport marketing professional and other decision makers within the sport organization by taking advantage of information that is available from the various sources and using that information to make strategic decisions, control decisions, operational decisions, and marketing decisions. This system looks at both the decision process and the decision outcomes, with the goal of making changes in selected sport marketing that lead to higher profits, a stronger and more positive image, or increase sport consumer satisfaction.

The key factors of the sport marketing DSS are the perceptual and intellectual capabilities of the decision makers (cognitive abilities), and the time pressures associated with decision making. The most difficult component of the sport marketing information system to implement, the overall goal of this component is to make decisions that interact with all parts of the sport organization, as well as to the other related sport marketing mix efforts including product strategies, sales efforts and pricing tactics, place distribution, and advertising and promotional plans.

The sport marketing information system collects data from the marketing environment, including information from channels, competitors, customers, the economy, the law, markets, politics, and secondary research. The information is disseminated into one of three areas: the sport marketing research system, the internal reports system, and the sport marketing intelligence system. All that information is then fed into the sport marketing DSS to make strategic decisions, control decisions, operational decisions, and marketing decisions. The decisions must produce results that are valuable to a sport organization by showing that the information being collected, analyzed, and used is equal to the cost of that information.

FROM THEORY TO PRACTICE
Dr. Mark Friederich, Vice President of Research
The Bonham Group, Denver, Colorado

I was born in Rio de Janeiro, and grew up in Germany before moving 5000 miles to attend Colorado College to earn a Bachelor's degree. I also have earned both a Master's and Doctorate degree in Experimental Psychology from Brown University. My previous positions before coming to The Bonham Group included managing all end-user research for Qwest Dex (formerly US WEST Direct), and as Director of Market Research for INVESCO Funds Group.

In 1998, The Bonham Group identified a need in the marketplace to complement impressions-based analyses with additional quantitative and qualitative analyses, so we launched a market research division. It helped clients

Continued

understand attendee attitudes, gauge the impact of a sponsorship on a corporate brand and measure purchase intent. Original clients included ESPN Zone, adidas, and the East Coast Hockey League.

The Bonham Group Market Research Company has since done work for many major corporations (Nationwide, New York Life), sports leagues (NHL, LPGA, NFL), teams (San Diego Padres, Cleveland Indians), shopping centers (Westfield Shoppingtowns), and cultural entities (B&O Railroad Museum, National D-Day Museum).

At The Bonham Group, my main responsibilities are new product and business development and managing all research projects. Some of the high profile projects I have overseen have included:

- *The National Hockey League*: Market research studies gauging fan attitudes and avidity levels.
- *Anschutz Entertainment Group (AEG)*: Research designed to help AEG's MLS teams increase ticket sales, target fans more effectively, and obtain insights into fan motivations and needs, particularly among Hispanic fans of international soccer.
- *Nationwide*: Research to help the insurance/financial services provider understand and improve the impact of its title sponsorship of the PGA developmental tour.
- *The LPGA*: Fan segmentation study which provided a detailed understanding of fan attitudes, needs, and motivations to help the LPGA increase TV viewers and tournament attendees.
- *Miller Brewing Company*: Research designed to help Miller develop effective sports, concert, and other cultural sponsorship programs among the general population, with a key emphasis on Hispanic sub-segments.

So how does it all work? After completion of a contract, The Bonham Group's market research executives, in conjunction with client representatives, develop specific objectives for the study. We then devise a plan to meet the objectives, including the formulation of appropriate methodologies.

The next step is to go into the field to conduct custom primary research and/or conduct secondary research. After acquiring the data, the market research staff analyses and synthesizes it, and then presents it in preliminary form to an internal executive committee. Based on input from this committee and key market research personnel, we develop strategies and recommendations to maximize the usefulness of the data to the client. These are tailored specifically to the needs and objectives of the client and its industry. The data and our conclusions are then packaged in a formal document and presented to the client. Follow-up consultation is provided as appropriate.

We believe that reliable, "real-world" information helps corporations maximize value and properties generate additional revenues. Sports marketing needs may vary and evolve over time, but a creative and innovative approach to information analysis has ongoing and universal appeal.

5

SPORT CONSUMER BEHAVIOR

CHAPTER OUTLINE

CHAPTER OBJECTIVES

The reader will be able to:

- Utilize basic cultural, personal, social, and psychological principles to explain how those factors directly affect individual purchasing and consumption behavior of participants, fans, spectators, volunteers, community, and corporate partners.
- Examine the various types of sport consumer studies and how individual and environmental factors, socialization, and participation directly influence the decision making process for sport consumption.
- Analyze the expected demographic, psychographic, geographic, and behavioristic characteristics of the sport consumer.

WHAT IS SPORT CONSUMER BEHAVIOR?

Sport consumer behavior is the conduct that sport consumers display in seeking out, ordering, buying, using, and assessing products and services that the consumers expects will satisfy their needs and wants. In general, there are two major types of consumers that sport marketers want to understand. First is the personal consumer, who is an individual who buys goods and services for their own use. This personal use is not always limited to individual use – it often extends to household use, use by a family member, or use by a friend or colleague. An example of this extension would be a family buying a set of tickets to a game. Second is the organizational consumer, which is for profit or non-profit business or industry entity that buys goods, services, and/or equipment for the operations of the organization. An example of this would be a baseball team purchasing equipment, balls, and bat for use in practices.

INTERNAL FACTORS AFFECTING SPORT CONSUMERS: WHAT MAKES THEM TICK?

Personality of the Sport Consumer

From an individual standpoint, the sport marketer must be able to understand numerous concepts. The first of those is the consumers' self-concept. This self-concept goes beyond self-image; it includes recognizing who the sport consumer wants to be (ideal self), how the sport consumer believes they are viewed by others (perceived self), and how the sport consumer interacts with their reference group (reference group self). Sport marketers must also be aware of the stage in the life cycle the target is a part of. The sport consumer changes as they transition through life, which in turn modifies an individual's attitudes, values, and identities.

These concepts serve as the foundation for the individual personality. Personality is defined as the unique and personal psychological characteristics of an individual which reflects how they respond to their social environment. An individual's personality reflects their individual differences. While personality can change, it is generally permanent and consistent.

Personality has been examined by many theorists; however, a majority of sport consumers and consumer researchers in general tend to apply the personality theories of Sigmund Freud to consumer behavior. It is generally held in Freudian Theory that consumer purchases are a reflection of the personality of the consumer. Freud believed that the unconscious needs or desires of people motivate them to do something. In sport consumer behavior, that "something" is the purchase of a sport product. To understand Freudian Theory, the sport marketing professional must comprehend the three elements of the theory: the id, the superego, and the ego. The id is the primary process of the unconscious mind that focuses on gratification (such as instant gratification and release) and primitive instinctual urges (such as sexuality and aggression). The superego is the morality of an individual, which in turn formulates the ethical framework of individual values, beliefs, and codes of conduct. The ego is the balancing part of the mind between primitiveness and morality, which includes internal and external consciousness, individual character differences, and the relationship between emotions and actions.

The goal of the sport marketer is to arrive at an optimum stimulation level. According to the theory of optimal stimulation level, individuals attempt to adjust stimulation until their specific optimal level is reached. The sport marketing professional must be able to determine these changes in stimulation level as these variations will have a direct effect on the behavior of sport consumers.

There are two levels of sport consumer consumption that are directly affected by stimulation levels. The first is materialistic sport consumer. These individuals place a value of acquiring and showing off their accumulated sport products. These are the "I have to have it" sport consumers who believe that possessions equal status. Often times these materialistic sport consumers see their possessions as a representation of self. Having the sport product often improves their self image, or provides them with a higher status as viewed by their external influences.

The second is the fixated sport consumer, otherwise known as the fanatic. They have a strong interest in a particular sport product category and are willing to go to extreme lengths to secure items in that category segment. These individuals are willing to spend as much discretionary time and money as necessary to search for and purchase the specified sport product. While not all sport consumers fall into these two levels, the sport marketer will often target these demographics as they often result in the greatest return on marketing efforts.

The Learning Process of the Sport Consumer

Sport marketers must understand how the sport consumer learns. Some will want to learn about a specific offering prior to creating an opinion, and hence becoming involved with the sport product (learn → feel → do). An example would be someone who is interested in rugby – researches and learns how to play – then becomes a fan. Others will develop an attitude toward a sport product, then consume the product, and as a result of satisfaction, learn more about it (feel → do → learn). For example, a boy whose father is a football fan influences the boy to become a fan at an early age, and as he grows older he looks into the team and its history.

A third manner in which the sport consumer learns is by trying a sport product, and if satisfied learn more and develop a more detailed view of the sport product (do → feel and learn). This is evident in the example where someone with no prior interest in basketball participates in a pickup game with some friends, then enjoys the game and becomes a fan.

Sport marketers also have to educate the sport consumer where to buy, how to use, and how to continue using the sport product. This is most often accomplished through a process of teaching theory and providing experience to the sport consumer about purchase and consumption behavior of sport product. This learning process can be a result of a careful search of information (intentional) or by accident (incidental). Regardless, sport marketing professionals must use a number of techniques to educate the sport consumer. Through motivation (which will be examined later in this chapter), the sport marketer strives to influence the sport consumer toward a specific goal such as a purchase. Sport marketers often use signals, sounds logos, and associations to motivate the sport consumer. They also use reinforcement to entice the sport consumer to repurchase the sport product.

To effectively teach the sport consumer, the sport marketing professional must be aware of various learning theories – both behavioral (learning that takes place as a result of observable responses to external stimuli) and cognitive (based on problem solving and information processing).

Behavioral Learning Theories

Classical conditioning refers to the process of using an existing relationship between a stimulus and response to bring about the learning of the same response to a different stimulus. There are three strategic applications utilized by sport marketers regarding classical conditioning. First is repetition, which increases the connection with the sport product while at the same time preventing the sport consumer from overlooking the sport product. This has a direct relationship to exposure, which is a significant concern of sport marketers with regard to sport product awareness. It is generally accepted that three exposures to an advertisement is the minimum necessary for it to be effective.

The second application of classical conditioning is stimulus generation. This is the inability of the sport consumer to differentiate between similar stimuli.

In this respect, the sport marketer utilizes numerous techniques to differentiate the sport product through product extensions, branding, and licensing. The final application of classical conditioning is stimulus discrimination, where the sport consumer is able to perceive differences between sport products. This tells the sport marketer that they have accomplished effective positioning of the sport product.

Another behavioral learning process is operant conditioning. Sometimes also called instrumental conditioning, this is where no automatic stimulus–response relationship is involved, so the sport consumer must first be induced to engage in the desired behavior and then this behavior must be reinforced. This theory is more of a trial-and-error process when reinforcement plays a significant role to determine customer satisfaction. The goal is to provide the sport consumer with a favorable experience as related to the sport product in order to shape the learning of the sport consumer, and result in repeating the behavior (i.e., repeat purchase of the sport product).

Operant conditioning is widely utilized by sport organizations. The goal is to equate the activity, product or service with pleasure, entertainment and enjoyment. Think about your typical football game – why are there cheerleaders? How come music is played during intermissions? Why do they put trivia questions or other contests on the big screen? How about participatory activities such as "Fling-A-Football," where you get to throw a Nerf ball from you seat onto the field and hopefully land it on a target for prizes? Why do they have short pee-wee football games on the field during halftime? All of these are in an effort to engage the spectator over and above the game, entice them into a positive behavior, have them leave the facility with a feeling that they were entertained (even if their team lost), and encourage them to repeat their purchase behavior.

Cognitive Learning Theories

Cognitive learning focuses on the information processes that are important to the sport marketing professional. Primary in this focus is the concept of retention, which involves the ability to recall or recognize something that has been learned or experienced. Information is stored in the human memory either in the order it was acquired, or based on major categories. The sport marketer must be able to figure out how to retrieve those memories through marketing efforts, which in turn should aid in the retention of the sport consumer.

Another concept important to cognitive learning is involvement. Involvement was defined earlier in this chapter as creating a close connection with something. The sport marketer seeks to stimulate the process of acquiring knowledge about a sport product through media strategies. The strategies often are directed toward creating a relationship between the sport consumer and the sport product through persuasion. Marketing strategies that focus on the specific attributes of the product are used to persuade those sport consumers who are already highly involved with the sport product. For those who need to be persuaded to become associated with the sport product, alternate methods involving cues such as setting (playing in a new facility) and endorsements (equating a favorite player with a sport product) are used.

The sport marketing professional, regardless of theory, must be able to measure the effectiveness of consumer learning. This is accomplished through a number of measures. The most basic is through recognition and recall of the sport product through advertisements and other marketing collateral. This can be completed through aided or unaided recall. Another method is through an evaluation of cognitive responses, when an evaluation of the sport consumer's comprehension of the intended message is conducted. Similar to this are attitudinal measures and behavioral measures, where the feelings of sport consumers, and responses by sport consumers to promotions, are evaluated to determine the effectiveness of message delivery. The overall goal, regardless of method, is to determine whether the sport consumer has learned enough about the product to become brand loyal.

The Process of Motivating Sport Consumers

Motivation is the influence that initiates the drive to satisfy wants and needs. For the sport consumer, this is achieved through motives such as accomplishment, fun, improvement of skill, health and fitness, or the desire for affiliation with or love for a player or team. For the sport consumer, it goes beyond their needs and wants; it also involves tension and drive. Tension is mental or emotional stress, while drive is the desire to accomplish a task. When the sport consumer has a want or need, they stress about how they will fulfill it. The sport consumer then comes up with a plan to fulfill the need with influences from their own personality and learning process. The result is the creation of a behavior that will hopefully lead to the fulfillment of the want or need. This fulfillment then reduces tension and the sport consumer is satisfied.

Prior to understanding how motivation works, the sport marketing professional must recognize what motives are. A motive is an emotion or psychological need that acts to stimulate an action. Emotional motives involve the selection of goals according to individual or subjective criterion. Rational motives entail selecting goals based on objective criteria. In general, motives will never fully satisfy needs, because new needs develop as a result of the satisfaction of old needs. In other words, as individuals achieve their goals, they set new (and often higher) goals for themselves.

In general, in order to motivate the sport consumer, the sport marketing professional needs to focus on three specific needs: power, affiliation, and achievement. Power is where the sport consumer wants to have control over their environment. Sport marketers strive to provide this feeling to the sport consumer, but still keep control of the situation. Affiliation is the most basic concept of social interaction. Human beings need interaction with other human beings. Sport marketers make every effort to provide an atmosphere of this connectedness and belonging, not only with the sport product, but also with other users. Achievement involves the need for personal accomplishment. Sport consumers want to have feelings of self-fulfillment, high self-esteem, and prestige. Sport marketers work to control the attitude of the sport consumer and provide them the perception of a positive experience as related to the sport product.

How the Attitudes of the Sport Consumer Are Formed and Changed

An attitude is a state of mind or behavioral predisposition that is consistently favorable or unfavorable with respect to a product or situation. Attitudes are formed in many different ways, but most often they are formed either from personality factors or are learned from environmental influences. As mentioned at the end of the previous segment, sport marketers strive to control the attitudes of the sport consumer. But how is that accomplished?

There are a number of models for attitude formation and identification. The most prevalent of these is the tri-component attitude model, where cognitive, affective, and conative factors are considered. The cognitive component focuses on the knowledge and perceptions of the sport consumer that are acquired from a direct experience with an attitude object – in this case a person, behavior or event related to the sport product. The affective component involves the emotions or feelings of the sport consumer as related to the specific sport product. The conative component centers on the likelihood that the sport consumer will carry out a specific action or behavior as a result of the interaction with the attitude object.

Another model is the multi-attribute attitudes models. These series of models examine the makeup of sport consumer attitudes in terms of the attributes of the sport product. The first is the attitude-toward-object model, where the sport consumer will have a positive attitude toward the sport products they feel have an acceptable level of attributes that they want, and a negative attitude toward sport products they feel do not have what they are looking for. Next is the attitude-toward-behavior model, which states that the attitude of the sport consumer toward a specific behavior related to the sport product is a function of how strongly they believe that the action will lead to a specific outcome. The final model is the theory-of-reasoned-action model. This is a theory that interprets the interrelationship between attitudes, intentions, and behavior, which in turn should lead to better explanations and predictions of sport consumer behavior.

There are two other models of attitude formation that are utilized by sport marketing professionals. The trying-to-consumer model tries to account for an attempted purchase of the sport product by investigating personal and environmental barriers. The attitude-toward-the-ad model simply investigates the feelings and judgments of sport consumers based on their exposure to sport-related advertisement. The measurement involves the attitudes toward both the advertisement and the sport product.

Since different sport consumers may like or dislike the same sport product for different reasons, a practical framework for examining attitude functions of sport consumers can be very useful for the sport marketing professional. In general, there are four basic attitude functions sought in the sport consumer. The *ego-defensive function* suggests that since most sport consumers want to protect their self-images from inner feelings of doubt, they seek to replace their uncertainty with a sense of security and personal confidence. The *knowledge function* stresses that sport consumers usually have a strong need to know and understand the people and things with whom they come in contact. The *utilitarian function* states that when a sport product has been useful or helped the sport consumer in the past, the attitude toward that sport product tends to be favorable. The *value expressive function* maintains that attitudes are an expression or reflection of the sport consumer's general values, lifestyles, and outlook.

In understanding these functions, the sport marketing professional must understand the various strategies employed to implement attitude change. This can be accomplished in a number of ways, including:

- Changing the basic motivational function of the sport consumer.
- Associating the sport product with a respected group or sport event.
- Working out a conflict between two attitudes, preferably moving from negative to positive.
- Changing components of the multi-attribute attitudes model to meet the needs of the sport consumer.
- Altering the beliefs of sport consumers as related to the brands of the competitors of the specific sport product.

Sport consumer attitude formation and change has a direct relationship to the other behavioral concepts through attribution theory – which attempts to explain how people assign the concept of cause and effect to the sport product on the basis of either their own behavior or the behavior of other sport consumers. There are a number of issues related to attribution theory that have a direct effect on its implementation. They include:

- Self-perception theory suggests that attitudes develop as sport consumers look at and make judgments about their own behavior.
- Internal attribution is the sport consumer giving credit to their self for an outcome as a result of the sport consumer's own ability, skill, or effort.
- External attribution is the sport consumer giving credit to factors beyond their own control.
- The foot-in-the-door technique is based on the premise that sport consumers develop attitudes by looking at their own behavior.
- Attribution toward others is when the sport consumer feels that another person is responsible for either positive or negative sport product performance.
- Attribution toward things is when the sport marketers and researchers are trying to find out why a sport product meets or does not meet the expectations of the sport consumer.

These elements of attribution theory are qualitatively tested and measured by sport marketing professionals in a number of ways. First, through distinctiveness, the sport marketer can determine the distinguishing traits between sport consumers. Sport marketers can also track consistency over time, or repetition of purchasing patterns. Finally, the sport marketer can draw a consensus as to the attitude of the general sport consumer population.

The Perceptions Developed by Sport Consumers about a Sport Product

Perceptions involve gaining an understanding of the individual values, attitudes, needs, and expectations of the sport consumer by scanning, gathering, assessing, and interpreting those insights. For the sport consumer, perception involves the process of interpreting and selecting a sport product based on awareness obtained through any of the five senses, but especially via sight or hearing. Basically, it is the way the sport consumer sees the world around them. The three elements that formulate perception are sensations, images, and affections. Sensations are the most basic element of perception as they are the immediate and direct responses from the sensory organs. Images are the pictures that are formed in the mind to differentiate what is perceived. Affections are the actual emotions emitted as a result of the perception.

Perception can be viewed in three distinct manners. The first is perceptual selection, which is based on the previous experiences and the present state of mind of the sport consumers. Selective perception is made up of a number of sub-concepts including selective exposure, selective attention, perceptual defense, and perceptual blocking. Selective exposure deals with knowing that the sport consumer chooses whom they listen to, what they watch, and they only obtain specific types of information. Selective attention is that at any given point, a sport consumer can only digest so much information and that they only pay attention to those they believe are most important at the given time. Perceptual defense is when the sport consumer protects their self from an awareness of something unpleasant or threatening. Perceptual blocking is the process of the sport consumer putting up obstacles to prevent perceptions from influencing them.

The second manner is via perceptual organization. This is the concept of grouping perception in a manner so the individual sport consumer can interpret the perception and chart a plan of action. Unfortunately there are perceptual distortions which may prevent appropriate interpretation of perceptions. These may include similarities in physical appearances, stereotypes, misinterpreted first impressions, and jumping to conclusions. There is also a concept called the halo effect where a sport consumer may form an overall positive impression of a sport product because of one good characteristic, however, the sport consumer may not have the expertise to pass judgment in an effective manner to truly determine the quality of the sport product.

The third aspect of perception is interpretation. This is the area most sport marketing professionals concentrate on as this interpretation focuses on the imagery and emotions of the sport consumer, and gives the sport marketer information as to whether their marketing efforts are successful. This determination of sport consumer imagery focuses on positioning, price, quality, and risk.

Positioning involves establishing a specific image for a sport product in relation to competing products. A sport marketer will utilize perceptual mapping to determine the best position to enter the marketplace. This research method provides sport marketers the opportunity to graphically analyze perceptions concerning the attribute of specific sport products. Depending on the evaluation, a number of methods of positioning could be implemented to enter a sport product into the marketplace. For direct positioning, the sport marketer may position the sport product directly against the competition or position the sport product based on a specific benefit. More broad positioning efforts include positioning the product for several markets, and umbrella positioning – covering all aspects of the marketplace. There are even times where a sport marketer may position a product in an unknown position, taking a risk and hoping for the reward.

Pricing strategies are focused on perceived value of the sport product. Pricing based on perception is based on three factors: satisfaction, relationships, and efficiency. Central to this strategy is acquisition–transition utility. Acquisition utility represents the consumer's perceived economic gain or loss associated with the purchase of the sport product. This is determined by the utility of the sport product and the purchase price. Transaction utility deals with the perceived pleasure or displeasure associated with the financial aspect of the purchase by the sport consumer. This is based on the internal reference price of the sport consumer (the price they perceive, the sport product is valued) and the actual purchase price.

Perceived quality of sport products depends on the form the sport product takes. If a sport product is tangible in nature, the perceived quality come from internal beliefs and environmental influences. If the sport product is intangible or variable (as most sport services are), the product is viewed as perishable. In addition, because of the nature of the sport product, the quality is variably perceived due to the fact that the sport product is often produced and consumed at the same time. There is a direct correlation between price and quality, as the perception of price is an indicator of product quality. It is believed that if a sport product has a high price, then the sport product is of a higher quality.

Probably the least controllable factor of perception is risk. This is the extent of uncertainty perceived by the sport consumer as to the outcome of a specific purchase decision related to the sport product. These risks may include functional risk, physical risk, or financial risk. While the sport consumer cannot totally control risk, they can reduce the likelihood by staying up to date on the latest information about the sport product, staying loyal to known sport products, selecting sport products based on image, and searching for reassurance from external influences.

EXTERNAL FACTORS AFFECTING SPORT CONSUMERS: THE ENVIRONMENT IS EVERYTHING

For the business of sport, consumer behavior is a complex process because the sport organization has limited control over the end results. However, it is crucial to have a better understanding of the core environmental and individual elements that contribute to success in marketing sport. From an environmental standpoint, there are a number of external factors that the sport marketer has limited control over, but has the opportunity to manipulate to their advantage. These include targeting the consumer behavior of those associated with the sport consumer (family, friends, and colleagues), and the opportunity structure of sport. The opportunity structure of sport is critical to the development of marketing opportunities as it is the foundation of involvement in sport activities. The opportunity structure and the associated involvement are influence of geographic concepts such as climate and geography, and psychographic concepts such as norms, values, and beliefs.

However, the area of greatest interest is demographics. Demographics are the categories of traits that characterize a group of people. The generic categories that most sport marketing professionals look at are age, gender, race and ethnicity, household size, annual income, and geographic location. Age is an important factor because it is important to understand who in the family is responsible for decision making. While the parent may have the purchasing power, the children have the influencing power. In addition, younger people purchase items for different reasons than older people. This is also true for gender. Males tend to make more impulsive decisions, while female tends to be more analytical in their purchasing. Race and ethnicity is significant because of the variety of beliefs and values based on cultural differences. Household size will have a direct effect on purchasing power and the types of product they will purchase.

Geographic location, especially in sport, has a gigantic effect. For example, a baseball fan that live in Nassau County on Long Island, New York has two choices – go 15–30 miles to Yankee Stadium in traffic that could take 1–2 hours, or go 5–10 miles to Shea Stadium to see the Mets and not have to fight as much traffic. If a person does not have allegiance to one team or the other, the decision will be clear in most cases – take the shorter trip. However, if you are a fan of the New England Patriots or Boston Red Sox, where the team is marketed as a regional team for Maine, New Hampshire, Vermont, Massachusetts, Rhode Island and Connecticut, individuals will travel up to 6 hours to go to a game.

In sport marketing, especially with the expansion of global influences, these concepts are expanded beyond the traditional concepts to include culture, subculture, cross-culture, and social setting.

Culture

Culture is the principal attitudes, behaviors, values, beliefs, and customs that typify the functioning of a society. In sport consumer behavior, culture often regulates the level to which marketing efforts are accepted. The sport marketing professional must understand how sport consumers learn within their culture, and what factors affect their problem solving and decision making processes. Culture is "learned" in four distinct ways. Formal learning is typically classroom based and highly structured. Informal learning is an independent learning style where learning rests primarily in the hands of the learner. Incidental learning comes as a result of the activity the individual is participating in, such as task accomplishment, interpersonal interaction, sensing the organizational culture, trial-and-error experimentation, or even formal learning. Technical learning is the combination of education and training. The eventual goal is for the sport marketing professional to understand these cultural differences, so marketing efforts such as advertising can be directed in such a way that the sport consumers view the sport product as being socially acceptable.

There are two qualitative measurements utilized to assess culture and cultural learning: content analysis and consumer fieldwork. Content analysis is a method for systematically analyzing the content of print, verbal and/or visual communication to determine the current social values of a society. Consumer fieldwork involves site observation within a normal environment, often without the knowledge of the consumer, to observe behavior.

For the sport marketing professional, these two qualitative techniques seek to draw conclusions based on the attitudes and motivations of sport consumers. In sport marketing, these conclusions are used every day. When Ichiro came to the Seattle Mariners from Japan and Hideki Matsui came to the New York Yankees, new marketing opportunities arose immediately. Seattle's influence in the significant Japanese market in their city instantly increased. The New York Yankees started putting advertisements in Japanese in the stadium. Both resulted in more people from the Japanese culture going to games and buying merchandise.

This is also true of Yao Ming of the Houston Rockets, who has single handedly brought a new Asian-American fan base to basketball. The presence of Dominican Republic flags in the stands whenever Pedro Martinez pitches at Shea Stadium is evident, to the point where the team now has Latin American Heritage night. They have even expanded those cultural nights to a series of Theme, Community and Heritage dates, including Greek Night, Korean Night, Meringue Night, Italian Night, Pakistani Night, Irish Night, Hispanic Heritage Night, Jewish Heritage Day, Oktoberfest, and Polish Heritage Day.

Subculture

A subculture is a distinct cultural group differentiated by an identifiable segment within a larger population. Subcultures are usually identified based on their demographic segment – gender, age, geographic region, race, nationality, ethnicity, social class, occupation, and religion. Some would even argue that sport is a subculture. Market segmentation recognizes that different consumer groups have assorted wants and needs that justify the development and offering of different products and services. Sport marketers have utilized a variety of approaches to segment the sport, entertainment and leisure service and retail markets; however, each of the traditional segmentation approaches has limitations. Marketing methodologies, including segmentation strategies, need to mirror and harmonize with the target subculture.

International and Global Interaction: Cross-Culture

As transportation and technology innovation bring the far reaches of the world closer, there obviously becomes more interaction internationally and globally. This is especially true in the sport market. The United States has been known for hundreds of years as "the melting pot," but can be more aptly described today as a "mosaic" – many different cultures and subcultures overlapping to create the 21st century American society. As this interaction grows, the sport marketing professional learns to not only understand the similarities and differences among sport consumers, but often must learn the process of acculturation. Acculturation is the modification of a culture or subculture as a result of contact with a different culture. As more and more athletes come from overseas to the United States to play professional sport, the sport marketing professional must not only market to the behavioral aspects of the sport consumer, but also ever-expanding cultural aspects of the sport consumer. This forces the sport marketing professional to not only have a solid understanding of the business of sport, but also the humanities and social science aspects that can be directly related to this new global society.

Social Setting

While culture, subculture, and cross-culture issues are important to the sport marketing professional, ultimately the social setting is the most direct concern of the sport marketer. The understanding of these reference groups within the target market is ultimately going to determine those who will purchase the majority of the specific sport product. A reference group is a group – two or more people making up a unit – with which a sport consumer identifies with, and hence probably shares similar attitudes, values, and beliefs. In sport marketing we acknowledge four categories of reference groups: Normative reference groups are what individuals look to in order to determine how they should behave. In comparative reference groups, individuals look at other individuals and groups to compare and gauge their behavior to. Multiple reference groups reinforce the idea that an individual can access more than one reference group. Indirect reference groups are individuals or groups with whom a person identifies but does not have direct contact with.

When a sport consumer identifies himself as part of a reference group, they usually conform to the norms (attitudes, values, and beliefs) of that reference group. The sport marketing professional often targets elements of the reference group to spread the word about a sport product. This provides a vehicle to inform all members of the reference group about the sport product, and legitimize the decision to use the same sport product as the rest of the group. Sport marketers attempt to influence the members of the reference group as a whole by associating the sport product with factors such as attractiveness, credibility, and expertise. Sport marketers at the same time try to influence individual group members by marketing the sport product in terms of the need for affiliation, the need to be liked, and the fear of negative evaluation as related to the reference group.

The most powerful reference group in today's society is family. The function of the family includes emotional support, a suitable lifestyle, and a stable economic foundation. Families influence each other throughout the lifespan to make decisions about purchases. The sport marketer must understand the roles of the family decision making process to determine the best way to influence those sport consumers to purchase the sport product. There are five roles in the family decision making process:

- *Initiators* are any member of the family who can express the need for a product or service such as a boy asking his father to buy tickets to a baseball game.
- *Influencers* are people whose views carry some weight in the final decision. An example would be a mother suggesting to a father that it would be good to go on a family's outing to a baseball game.
- *Deciders* are family members who assume the responsibility for choosing the characteristics of the product and executing the decision with regard to the brand, the vendor, the timing and the payment method. This decision is based on the information collected in the previous stages. For example, the father deciding that the family will attend a minor league baseball game next week, and he will buy the tickets online.
- *Buyers* refer to the family member(s) who are physically involved in the process of purchasing a product. This would be the father actually going online and making the purchase. It is important to remember that the retailer still has an influence on the sport consumer. If the purchase is difficult because the website is too complex, the buyer may choose to go elsewhere.
- *Users* are the members of a family who are beneficiaries of the product. It is imperative to identify who actually qualifies as the end-user of the product, and how satisfied the user is with different aspects of the product. An example would be that the father purchases the tickets, but because he has to work, only the mother, son and his son's friend use the tickets.

Since so many members have influenced the purchase decision, it is possible that user satisfaction may vary on different counts ... which is reflected in their post-purchase behavior.... The users may or may not recommend the product to others on the basis of their satisfaction levels. This has serious implications for the marketer since word-of-mouth plays a very important role in the purchase of consumer durable products.

The sport marketing professional must have a keen understanding of the different social settings and social classes when attempting to influence the sport consumer. Depending on the social class, sport consumers from similar geographic areas may view the sport product very differently. Some may view the sport product in terms of being fashionable and a status symbol, while others may view the sport product as a treat or appropriate use of discretionary time and/or money. So once the sport marketer understands all of these factors, how do they actually go about influencing the sport consumer to purchase the sport product?

Consumer Behavior and Ethics: Good Corporate Citizenship

One of the most extensive studies of the perspectives of United States business leaders on corporate citizenship and the role of private business in society has been completed. A joint effort of The Center for Corporate Citizenship at Boston College and the United States Chamber of Commerce's Center for Corporate Citizenship, the research report is titled *The State of Corporate Citizenship in the United States: Business Perspectives in 2005*. The work was produced in cooperation with the Hitachi Foundation and updates a similar effort from 2003.

The survey instrument was sent to approximately 24,000 members of the United States Chamber and the Boston College Center, and it generated 1189 responses from companies of various sizes and industries. The research design oversampled large businesses in order to provide sufficient responses for separate analysis. The inclusion of members of the Boston College Center in the survey population also skews the results toward larger firms. As the goal of the Center is to "help business leverage its social, economic, and human assets to ensure both its success and a more just and sustainable world," companies having an interest in responsible business are likely to be overrepresented. Yet the findings are still remarkable in terms of the strength of the convictions of respondents. Focus groups provided additional insights into the motivations, challenges, and priorities of businesses across the country.

For purposes of the study, the authors define corporate citizenship as the commitment that a corporation makes to accomplish the following goals:

- Minimize risks by working to decrease the negative consequences of corporate activities on all stakeholder groups.
- Maximize benefits by contributing to societal and economic well-being.
- Be accountable and responsive to stakeholders, building understanding of the progress and setbacks that result from efforts to operate ethically.
- Institutionalize and integrate core values into operations. The findings of the 2005 study of the state of corporate citizenship include:
  - 92% of respondents believe that many companies do a great deal more for their communities than is talked about or known.
  - While 81% believe that corporate citizenship needs to be a priority for companies today, 80% agree it should be completely voluntary and not enforced through additional laws and regulations.
  - 69% believe the public has a right to expect good corporate citizenship.
  - 64% believe that corporate citizenship makes a tangible contribution to the bottom line.

Among large corporations, the portion of all companies having the above beliefs is even larger, ranging from 84% to 98%.

Continued

The involvement of private companies in socially related issues includes environmental protection, support of education, and economic development in poor communities. Large companies are likely to have a more expansive definition of their role in society and believe that human capital issues are most urgent. Large companies focus in particular on the role of business in supporting the health and safety, development, loyalty, diversity, and civic engagement of their employees. Ninety-eight percent of executives from large companies say their company's performance on social issues is important to their employees.

There was significant agreement by a majority of respondents as to how a number of corporate actions were important to the specific role of business in society. It is interesting, yet not unexpected, to note that "operating with ethical business practices" was far and away the action deemed most "critical" by respondents (62%). The following actions were believed to be either "critical" or "very important" by more than half the respondents:

- Operating with ethical business practices (93%).
- Ensuring employee health and safety (85%).
- Managing and reporting company finances accurately (84%).
- Maximizing long-term profits for owners/shareowners (73%).
- Providing jobs (66%).
- Providing employee benefits (63%).
- Protecting consumers (63%).
- Improving conditions in your community (55%).
- Protecting the environment (52%).

There was less agreement on the most important drivers of good corporate citizenship:

- It fits our company traditions and values (73%).
- It improves our reputation/image (56%).
- It is part of our business strategy (44%).
- It helps to recruit and retain employees (30%).

The concluding commentary from The State of Corporate Citizenship in the United States is that businesses realize they have an important role as stewards for shareowners and society alike. The question is not whether corporate citizenship fits into the day-to-day operations of a company but how.

Additional insight into the impact of business on society is provided by a global survey conducted by consultants McKinsey and Company and published in the online McKinsey Quarterly. The 4000+ survey respondents included more than a quarter CEOs or other C-level executives. Overwhelmingly, the study reported a belief that the role of corporations in society goes far beyond simply meeting obligations to shareowners. Only one in six agrees with the Milton Friedman premise that the sole focus of a corporation should be on higher returns to shareholders.

Study respondents believe that the broader concerns of corporations should include providing good jobs, making philanthropic contributions, and going beyond legal requirements to minimize pollution and other negative effects. But only 8% of executives think that large corporations champion social or environmental causes out of "genuine concern." Almost 90% agree that corporations are motivated by public relations, profitability, or some combination.

Senior executives view their expanding position in society as a risk rather than an opportunity. Issues they expect to have a negative effect in future years include providing pension, healthcare, and other retirement benefits; political influences; opposition to foreign investment and freer trade; pay incquality between senior executives and other employees; privacy and data security; and environmental issues including climate change. Issues providing an opportunity include demand for more ethically produced products, demand for healthier or safer products, human rights standards, job loss and off-shoring, and workplace conditions and safety.

In spite of the fact that executives view their leadership position in society as a burden, readers of this column will recall several previous discussions of how good citizenship is very closely aligned with superior financial performance. Good management provides proper rewards for all stakeholders.

"Leadership has less to do with any single individual ... than it does with the culture, norms, and value of the institution itself."

Source: Taken from Verschoor, C. C. (2006). Good corporate citizenship is a fundamental business practice. *Strategic Finance* 87(9): 21–22.

Suggested Discussion Topics

1. In the case above, the authors define corporate citizenship as the commitment that a corporation makes to accomplish a series of eight goals. Considering each of those goals, how would you design ethical standards within your marketing plan to ensure positive image for the sport organization, thereby creating positive attitudes, perceptions, and buying behaviors from consumers.

2. The final statement in the case was "leadership has less to do with any single individual ... than it does with the culture, norms, and value of the institution itself." What role does the sport marketing professional play in ensuring that marketing efforts related to the culture, norms, and value of the sport organization is articulated to the sport consumer? Discuss in terms of culture, subculture, cross-culture, and social setting.

THE MARKETING CONCEPT FOR SPORT

To deal with the inner workings of sport consumer behavior, the sport marketer must have a clear understanding of the marketing concept, which is a consumer-oriented philosophy that suggests that satisfaction of consumer needs provide the focus for product development and marketing strategy to enable the firm to meet its own organizational goals. The development of the marketing concept for sport is centered on three sub-concepts: sport production, the sport product, and the selling of sport. Sport production is centered on the premise that sport consumers are primarily interested in the availability of the sport product at reasonable prices. The sport product makes an assumption that sport consumers will purchase the offering with the highest quality, the best performance, and the most features. The selling of sport relates to a belief that sport consumers are not likely to buy a sport product unless they are enticed to do so. The combination of these ideas is central to the marketing concept for sport in that in order for a sport organization to be successful, the needs and wants of the target markets must be met at a higher level as compared to the competitors.

Who Are the Sport Consumers?

There are two major groups of sport consumers that sport marketers are concerned with: spectators and participants. Spectators are defined as individuals who observe a performance, such as a sporting event. When sport marketers consider this fairly narrow definition of spectators, their main concern is attendance at events. There are numerous factors that the sport marketing professional must consider to attract as many spectators as possible to a sport event.

A central factor to consider with spectators is motivation. Motivation (which will be discussed in more detail later in this chapter) is a psychological concept that stimulates an individual to work toward accomplishing a desired goal, which in turn gives purpose and direction to an individual's behavior. In sport, there are numerous motivational factors that influence spectators to attend an event. Intrinsic motivation is the desire to satisfy natural needs and interests, including knowledge, accomplishment, and experiences. Extrinsic motivation involves rewards or incentives used by an individual to bring about desired behavior in another person. Amotivation is where there is no influence intrinsically or extrinsically. Sport marketers must have a clear understanding of these motivational factors to entice the sport consumer to consume the sport product. Some of these factors include self-esteem enhancement, diversion from everyday life, entertainment value, eustress, economic value, esthetic value, the need for affiliation, and family ties.

On the other hand, the definition of participants tends to be broad in nature. By definition, participants are individuals who take part in an activity. However, the manner the participant takes part in the activity varies greatly. Participant consumer behavior is defined as actions performed when searching for, participating in, or evaluating the sport activities the consumer believes will satisfy their needs. As with the spectator, the participant has internal and external influences that affect their level of involvement in sport. Internally, the decision of the participant is affected by their personality, motivation, ability to learn, intrinsic perceptions, and personal attitudes. Externally, decisions are affected by culture, social class, reference groups, family, friends, peers, and colleagues.

Why Do People Consume Sport?

There are numerous individual and environmental factors that have an effect on consumer behavior. For the sport consumer, there are three subfactors that seem to have the most influence on the sport consumer: socialization, involvement, and commitment.

Socialization is defined as the process by which individuals acquire attitudes, values, and actions which are appropriate to members of a particular culture. In sport culture, sport marketers look at the process by which individuals develop and incorporate skills, knowledge, attitudes, and items/equipment necessary to perform sport roles.

Socialization in sport demands some type of involvement, which is defined as creating a close connection with something. Involvement in sport is as easy as ABC. Affective is the attitudes, feelings and emotions directed toward a sport activity, such as sadness when your team loses a playoff series. Behavioral are the actions or reactions directly related to the internal and external stimuli sport provides. For example, cheering and giving "high-five" with other people in a sports bar when your team makes a great play. Cognitive is the process of acquiring knowledge about a sport activity, including researching information on the Internet, listening to experts on sports radio, and asking questions about an activity to someone who understands that activity.

Commitment is the process by which an individual is emotionally or intellectually bound to a course of action. In sport, commitment refers to frequency, duration, and intensity of involvement in a sport. A sport marketer must understand the thought processes of the sport consumer as it relates to concepts such as willingness to spend their valuable discretionary money, time, and energy. This understanding of commitment directly relates to the concepts presented in Chapter 2 related to the escalator concept. As the sport consumer becomes more committed to the sport product, they move up the escalator. An example of this would be the 2003 Florida Marlins. During the regular season, the Marlins average only 22,792 fans per game, and that average went up significantly during the last month of the season when the team appeared to be headed to the playoffs. However, once they made the playoffs and made it to the World Series, they were averaged to 65,900 fans.

PROBLEM SOLVING AND DECISION MAKING

The previous sections provided a basic description of who the sport consumer is as well as their philosophy as to why they consume the sport product.

But the understanding of the values and beliefs of the sport consumer is useless if the sport marketing professional fails to understand how the sport consumer ultimately makes a decision. Hence, an analysis must be conducted of how the sport consumer determines what they want, and how the sport consumer sets goals and objectives that result in making a choice. This is the framework for the problem solving and decision making processes.

Problem Solving

Problem solving is a cognitive process by which an individual uses critical thinking to work out and answer a problem. To understand problem solving, the sport marketing professional must first understand the problem solving cycle. This is an organized, step-by-step approach that involves brainstorming, formulating various solutions, analyzing all solutions to determine a course of action, implementing the course of action, evaluating the success of the course of action, and repeating until an optimal solution is reached. The problem solving cycle involves the steps as shown in the diagram below:

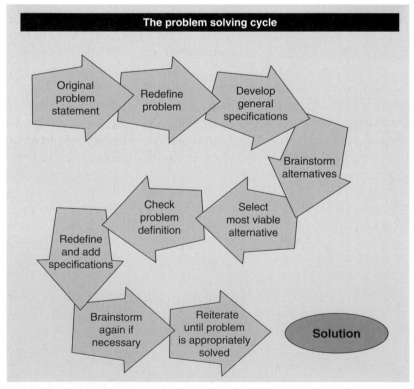

http://thayer.dartmouth.edu/teps/

The first step involves understanding the stated problem(s). These statements can be in many forms, from simple open-ended questions, to existing conditions in need of change.

- *Example – The GM comes to you to come up with a plan to increase attendance for the last month of the season. The team is in last place and attendance is down 15%.*

Second, the problem(s) needs to be redefined by the sport marketer in terms that are clear and void of bias. Often when individual customers encounter a problem, they put an internal spin on the necessity for a solution because of vested interest or perceived need. Sport marketing professionals seek to remove those biases so the root problems can be identified and solved with an optimal level of success.

- *Attendance is down 15%.*

The third step is to set general specifications. As the sport marketing professional gains an understanding of the problems at hand, a plan is created to focus on the core problems. This plan involves setting parameters for solving the problem, while considering constraints to the problem solving process such as legality and ethical issues. To ensure optimal effectiveness, the parameters must always be defined and justified, and if economics are involved, also quantified.

- *A 15% decrease in attendance does not only affect the team's bottom line in ticket sales. It also affects concessions, merchandising, parking, and potentially the morale of the players and coaches. The plan must address all of these areas. It also means there is probably no additional money to enact a plan.*

The fourth step is to identify alternative solutions. This is where the brainstorming process begins, ideas are contemplated, and a list of various possible solutions is created. This process often takes place in a group setting, without criticism, and with maximum creativity. The longer the list of possible solutions, the better the chance for success.

- *Some possible solutions include: buy one ticket get the second half off; meet and greet autograph sessions before and after the game; discounts at merchandise and concession stands; buy two tickets to a game and receive a voucher for one free ticket to a game next season (with the purchase of another ticket).*

Next, the most viable alternative must be selected. The solution list is analyzed in depth, determining the advantages and disadvantages of each alternative. The process for examining the alternatives involves categorizing the alternatives, determining a scale for critiquing each alternative, pooling the best alternatives, and then ranking those solutions from most desirable to least. This part of the problem solving process often involves experimentation and market research to justify the best option, and a clarification of unclear alternatives.

- *With concessions and merchandising already losing money, they may not be willing to decrease prices. Meet and greet sessions before the game may interfere with game preparation – after the game may be easier. Buy two, get one for next year eats into potential profits in the long term, and may not be looked upon too well by the ownership. Therefore, the most viable options are buy one get one half off, where at least there is the potential to get some revenue from tickets, and may help merchandising and concessions. Then supplement that with some free autograph times after the game (keeps people to the end even when the team may be losing and allows an opportunity to improve image.*

Once the best option has been determined, the sixth step involves the sport marketer revisiting the problem to ensure that the brainstorming process did not go off track, and that the option chosen has the best opportunity to solve the base problem. Upon completion of this redefinition, the next two steps take place. First (Step 7) involves refining and adding specifications that are directly related to the chosen alternative. Then (Step 8), a second brainstorming takes place to become more focused on the alternative chosen, and determine any sub-alternatives that may arise from the redefinition.

- *Seems like the plan can address the problem of attendance being down 15%. However, we note that there is one series of games against the World Champions, and we have already sold 80% of our seats for the series. Therefore, this offer needs to be limited to the series' where attendance is significantly less than average.*

The final step involves the implementation of the selected alternative. If the selected alternative works to solve the problem, you have succeeded! If the option does not work, the sport marketer must utilize the feedback and measurements provided to them, revise the problem solving methodology, and repeat the process until the problem is solved.

- *Create flyers, radio and TV spots promoting the discount. Put the information on the website. Make sure all members of the organization, especially the sales staff, of the promotion. Time the promotion so that there is a chance for purchase, but not too soon around the practically sold out series so those customers do not feel that they got a raw deal.*

Now that the generic problem solving cycle has been discussed, the sport marketing professional must understand how the sport consumer uses this process to solve problems. There are three levels of problem solving: routine response behavior, extensive problem solving, and limited problem solving. Routine response behavior has the lowest level of problem solving involvement by the sport consumer. In the mind of the sport consumer, there is no problem to solve because the sport product is frequently purchased and the perception is that there is little risk involved with the purchase of the sport product. An example of this would be purchasing tickets to a game. As a result of this habitual problem solving, there is limited information search, and the process of evaluating alternatives is eliminated. For the sport marketing professional, there is very little they must do with these sport consumers, and hence need to spend little money to develop marketing plans directed to this type of problem solvers.

Extensive problem solving is the other end of the spectrum – where the involvement in the problem solving process by the sport consumer is at the highest level. The sport consumer extensively evaluates the sport product, conducts a significant information search about the sport product, and refuses to enter the decision making process before having an abundance of alternatives to choose from. This might be when an active mogul skier is seeking to purchase a new pair of skis. The sport marketer must spend extensive money and resources geared toward this level of problem solving and must provide a broad spectrum of data in order to have this type of sport consumer consider the sport product.

In between these two extremes are the sport consumers who engage in limited problem solving. When a problem is recognized, they first complete an internal information search, relying on data they already know. They may then supplement their data with an external search, such as via the Internet, but this is not always necessary. This type of problem solver considers a limited number of alternatives, but those alternatives are more generic – involving alternative forms of entertainment. An example would be a person buying a new pair of shoes, but their purchasing is going to be limited to Nike, Reebok, and Adidas. The sport marketer must focus on selling the sport product by demonstrating that spending discretionary dollars on the specific sport product will provide value to the sport consumer.

Decision Making

Decision making is a cognitive process by which an individual consciously makes a tactical or strategic choice that results in executing an action. In sport consumer decision making, there are four views that are utilized by sport marketing professionals enabling them to understand this process. The economic view is a systematic process where sport consumers make the most rational personal choices and identify the resulting opportunity costs of involvement with the sport product. The passive view is where sport consumers are submissive to marketing efforts, and hence will not object or resist to the promotional efforts of sport marketers. The cognitive view is a knowledge-based form of decision making, where the sport consumer is a thinking problem solver that is not driven by their internal desires, but also not automatically shaped and controlled by environmental influences. The emotional view is simply based on the mood of the sport consumer. If they feel like purchasing the sport product, they will – it does not matter what efforts the sport marketer has employed.

Setting and Attaining Goals

In understanding these views, and prior to entering into the decision making process, sport marketing professionals must understand how sport consumers set and pursue their goals. The diagram below illustrates the sport consumer goal development process:

The first step is to set a goal, which is a specific task that will serve to meet the overall mission of an organization or individual. These goals are often generic

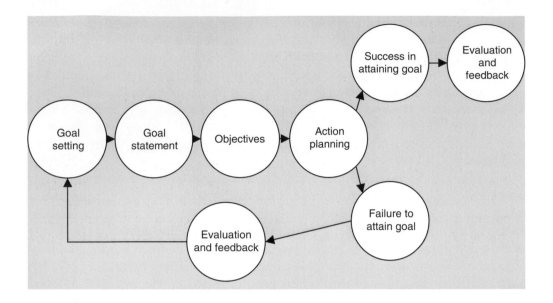

in nature. After you have a base goal, the second step is to clarify the goal by creating a goal statement. There are four major sections to a goal statement. The action is what you are going to accomplish. The object is the actual thing that will be acted upon. The amount is the quantification of the goal. The deadline is the time limitation on the attainment of the goal. An example of a goal statement for a sport consumer would be "To obtain a donation from the New England Patriots of signed memorabilia for the silent auction fundraiser by 2 weeks before the event." The action is "obtain," the object is "New England Patriots signed memorabilia," the amount is "donation" (implied no cost); and the deadline is "by 2 weeks before the fundraising dinner."

The third step would be to set objectives, which is the development of the specific steps an individual will take to attain the goal. Some objectives that might be set in conjunction with the goal statement from above would be: (1) mail a letter to the community relations department at the New England Patriots to request a donation; (2) contact a local sport memorabilia store to request a donation to the silent auction; and (3) attend an autograph signing by a New England Patriots player and obtain his signature on a piece of memorabilia.

The fourth step is the action process. This involves creating a plan of action to accomplish the goal. This includes determining what deliverables must be produced, how they will be produced, who will produce them, when the deliverables are to be ready, and initiating the use of the deliverable to attain the goal.

The fifth step is goal attainment or failure. Eventually, you will either accomplish the goal based on the objectives set forth, or the objectives failed to bring results. Either scenario leads directly into the sixth step – evaluation and feedback. At this point, if the goal is attained, an appraisal of the process is completed and a determination of final success is completed. If the goal was not attained, the appraisal process looks at why the objectives could not be accomplished, and a return to the first step is made for reevaluating the goal and setting a new course of action.

The Decision Making Process

As the sport consumer sets and attains goals, the decision making process begins. This process involves three stages: pre-purchase decision making (including problem or need recognition, pre-purchase information search, and evaluation of alternatives); the actual purchase, and post-purchase evaluation.

Pre-purchase Decision Making: Problem and Need Recognition

The first part of this first stage involves problem or need recognition. The making of a decision by the sport consumer is a result of wanting to move from an actual state to a desired state. The sport consumer will determine whether it is important to engage in the decision making process based on two considerations: (1) the size of the problem or need and (2) the importance placed on needing to make a decision.

Pre-purchase Decision Making: Information Search

Once the sport consumer determines that a decision needs to be made, they engage in the pre-purchase information search. At this time, the sport consumer seeks to obtain relevant information that will help resolve the problem. The sport consumer will utilize both internal sources and external sources to start making a decision. The information that is based on previous exposure and personal experience serves as a framework for the internal information search.

External sources are environmentally based, and come from a number of sources. Personal contacts such as friends, peers, relatives, co-workers, colleagues, neighbors, and salespeople; and impersonal sources such as newspaper and magazine articles, consumer reports, direct mail brochures, product advertisements, and websites are primary sources of information the sport consumer will utilize.

This often is in direct correlation to concerns about perceived value. There are a number of reasons that the sport consumer places value on a product including: whether the product is discretionary instead of necessary; the alternatives have both desirable and undesirable consequences; family members disagree on product requirements or evaluation of alternatives; product usage deviates from important reference group; the purchase involves ecological considerations; and there are many sources of conflicting information.[5]

Information from the actual sport product also has a direct effect on the pre-purchase information search. Some of these factors include time between purchases, changes in the make-up and style of the sport product, diversity of purchasing options, the actual price of the specific sport product, and the alternative brands and features available in the various sport product segments. The sport marketer has a direct effect on how the product is viewed by the sport consumer by understanding the individual differences of those consumers. This is often accomplished though an effective use of market research (Chapter 3) – especially demographic, psychographic and behavioristic characteristics.

There are also a number of other external sources that can serve to provide information that can aid in making a decision. Experiential learning about a product will vary from consumer to consumer. Those who have had a positive experience with a product will require less effort to make a decision. However, when the sport product is being purchased for the first time, the product is new to the market (hence no past experience), or the sport consumer has had an unsatisfactory experience with the product in the past, the sport marketer's efforts toward re-education of the sport consumer is often wide, varied, and detailed.

Another external source directly relates to the concept of social acceptability. When a sport product is socially visible, and other sport consumers purchase the sport product on a regular basis, there is a psychological reaction that entices other sport consumers to decide to purchase. On the other hand, a sport consumer may, in fact, avoid a desired product because of reference group or peer pressure. An example of this would be a Yankees fan living in Boston whose friends would not be too happy with him wearing Yankees merchandise.

Another concept within social acceptability involved gifting. Whether the purchase is for a gift for oneself or another person, it elicits gifting behavior. Gifting behavior falls into five sub-divisions:

Interpersonal gifting	Individual to individual	A father giving a skateboard to his child for his birthday
Intercategory gifting	Individual to another group	A Boys and Girls Club giving a skateboard to an underprivileged child
Intrapersonal gifting	Individual to self	A child buys a skateboard for their own use
Intergroup gifting	Group to another group	A school fundraiser collects skateboards to give to a local Boys and Girls Club
Intragroup gifting	Group to the group	An after-school program raises money and buys itself some skateboards

Gifting is a significant concept that sport marketing professionals must understand, as they can use these relationships to focus their marketing efforts. Some of the circumstances for gifting include celebration of accomplishment, a reward for completing a goal, having some extra discretionary income, or as a reward system to motivate individuals.

So how does the sport marketing professional effectively reach the sport consumer and influence the information being received? It is a difficult process in today's society because it seems that consumers are less loyal to sport products for a number of reasons including: (1) an overabundance of choices; (2) an oversaturation of available information; (3) a feeling that the sport consumer is entitled to the product at a reasonable price; (4) an aggravation with the commoditization of sport; and (5) insecurity about the stability of the sport product – especially in light of the 2004–2005 NHL strike.

Pre-purchase Decision Making: Evaluation of Alternatives

The purpose of this section is to use the information acquired during the information search in order to evaluate each alternative proposed. The criteria used to evaluate each alternative are based on the important features and characteristics of the specified sport product. There are three ways that sport consumers look at sport products. The evoked set is the sport product the sport consumer gives their greatest consideration to. The inept set is the sport product that the sport consumer excludes from purchase consideration. The inert set is the sport product that sport consumer is indifferent toward because they are perceived to have no significant advantage. The sport marketer strives to promote their sport product so that it falls within the evoked set of potential sport consumers.

This is accomplished by understanding the criteria used by the sport consumer to evaluate sport products, and then developing marketing strategies to meet the needs and desires of the sport consumer. These strategies are developed based on an understanding of the various sport consumer decision rules.

The compensatory decision rule is how a consumer evaluates each sport product in terms of each important attribute, and then chooses the sport product or brand with the highest overall rating. The non-compensatory decision rule is that the positive evaluation of an attribute of a sport product does not counteract a negative evaluation of another attribute belonging to the same product. The conjunctive decision rule is the sport consumer establishing a minimally acceptable grade for each attribute evaluated. For each sport product that falls below the established grade on any attribute, that sport product is eliminated from purchase consideration. The affect referral decision rule is a simplified decision rule by which sport consumers make a sport product choice based on previously established overall ratings of the sport product. These ratings are directly affected by brand awareness, advertisement, salesperson influence, emotions, feelings, and moods.

The Actual Purchase

Participation is the most important outcome of the decision making process, as this is when the sport consumer makes a purchase of the sport product. In sport, we are concerned with three types of purchases. A *trial purchase* is the concept of sampling of the sport product before repurchase. The goal of the sport marketing professional is to provide as positive experience as possible to entice this sport consumer to repurchase. A *repeat purchase* is the ensuing sales of the sport product after the initial purchase. The sport marketer is concerned with consumer satisfaction as related to this purchase because the higher the level of satisfaction, the higher the level of retention and repeat sales. *Long-term commitment purchases* are where the sport consumer is in a state of being bound emotionally or intellectually to a sport product. As with the repeat purchase, the sport marketer is concerned with satisfaction, however, they are going to offer additional incentives and programs to maintain the sport consumer as a high volume user of the sport product.

Post-purchase Evaluation

The work for the sport marketing professional does not end with the purchase – there is often significant work that goes into post-purchase evaluation. A primary concern that sport marketing professionals have is consumer satisfaction and dissatisfaction. As stated in the previous section, to maintain long-term commitment sport consumers and repeater purchasers, an evaluation of their satisfaction must often be completed. Of equal importance is consumer dissatisfaction, which can result from the sport consumer having a negative perception of the sport product, or the sport product not meeting pre-purchase expectations of the sport consumer.

To evaluate the outcome of the sport product, sport marketers look at six levels of assessment: (1) actual performance of the sport product matches the expectations of the sport consumer; (2) actual performance of the sport product significantly exceeds the expectations of the sport consumer; (3) actual performance of the sport product is significantly below the expectations of the sport consumer; (4) the sport consumer has a neutral feeling about the performance of the sport product; (5) actual performance of the sport product is better than expected (positive disconfirmation); and (6) actual performance of the sport product is worse than expected (negative disconfirmation).

Another significant concern during the post-purchase evaluation is cognitive dissonance. In general, the human mind tends to embrace thoughts that minimize the amount of conflict between cognitions, which may include attitudes, emotions, beliefs, or values. When two cognitions have a conflict between each others, the sport consumer falls into a state of cognitive dissonance. Sport marketers are very concerned with cognitive dissonance because people tend to subjectively reinforce decisions they have already made. Therefore, if the sport consumer feels they may have made the incorrect choice, they will change their perceptions to make their decision seem better. The sport marketer strives to prevent this conflict. If they cannot, the gear shifts toward reversing this modified decision so that the sport consumer repeats their purchase of the sport product.

Factors That Affect the Decision Process: Decision Variables and External Influences

During the decision making process, there are decision variables and external influences that have a direct effect on the end results of the process. Decision variables are those individual behavioral factors that make sport consumers unique. These qualities include (1) the personality of the sport consumer, (2) the learning process of the sport consumer; (3) the process of motivating sport consumer, (4) how the attitude of the sport consumer is formed and changed, and (5) the perceptions developed by sport consumers about a sport product. External influences are also known as the "circle of social influence." These external influences include (1) culture, (2) subcultures, (3) international and global interaction (cross-culture), (4) social setting, and (5) social class.

GLOBAL CONSUMER BEHAVIOR: CONSUMER INFLUENCES IN CHINA

This is the second part of a case study that started with the marketing research effort as discussed back in Chapter 3. As you may remember, a questionnaire was administered to 2155 mainland Chinese consumers in 10 selected cities, different economic, social, and personal factors in the China's environment are determined. Eleven major findings related to the unique behavior, attitudes, and buying patterns of Chinese sport consumers were determined. The marketing implications of the Chinese culture and lifestyle as related to findings were considered in terms of economic, social, and personal influences. These three categories have unique Chinese environmental and cultural meanings and thus need to be considered when engaging in marketing in China.

Economic Factors

Unlike the past, when most income was spent on basic necessities such as food and clothing, the current Chinese consumer spends more money on entertainment and durable goods. However, the general tendency of the Chinese consumer to have stronger purchasing power and the fact that their buying decisions reflect creative purchasing beyond bare necessities are not reflected in sport marketing. It could be concluded that not all Chinese consumers are willing to spend a certain percent of their income on sport products. This phenomenon can be explained either by consumers' lack of sufficient income or too high a price for sport products. On the other hand, however, a great potential exits for marketers who appeal to the Chinese consumers with creative strategies. Those who know desires and needs in specific areas, while being sensitive to economic restraints, may capture a slumbering Chinese market.

Social and Culture Factors

With the implementation of an "open-door policy" in China, the lifestyle of the Chinese people changes constantly. Several social and cultural trends may stimulate marketers to be optimistic about Chinese consumers:

- The most important trend is growing fitness consciousness. No matter the gender, age, occupation, and education of those surveyed, all tend to tie their purchase of sport products with exercise and entertainment.
- A second trend the survey revealed is a movement toward use of sport products for casual reasons. Chinese consumers are embracing a more casual and health-conscious lifestyle.
- There is a growing consumer preference for international products. The Chinese people, especially the younger generation, are very fond of wearing and using brand name sporting goods from around the world. Owning high grade sporting goods seems to be a symbol of wealth and a new fashion for those young consumers.

The social and culture trends just discussed will lead to different pricing, promotional, and distributional strategies. Since marketing principles are

Continued

applicable throughout the international arena, what has proved successful in the American market could basically be transferred and applied to the China market.

However, to implement a successful marketing strategy in China, several environmental differences must be taken into account:

- "Shopping on Sundays" is a hobby for Chinese consumers. Marketers should create an attractive shopping environment in a prestigious shopping center.
- Chinese consumers believe what they see rather than what they hear. They know that some imitation products exist in the market, and dishonesty in advertising is publicized. Marketers should increase their image by eliminating imitation products and dishonesty advertising.
- Although consumers' attitudes toward the international sport products are positive, devotion or loyalty to brands is subject to rapid change. Marketers should have a strategy to keep consumers' loyalty.
- Nonathletes have greater purchasing power than most athletes or sportspersons. Nonathletes buy sporting goods either to impress others or simply because their friends have those items. Marketers should consider how to design sport product with attractive sport features.
- The type of sporting goods desired by the older and younger generations is widely dissimilar. And a large gap exists between the desire to purchase and the ability to purchase sporting goods. It causes problems of bringing the right products to the right person and establishing an appropriate price policy.
- The purchasing decision of Chinese consumers is heavily influenced by social values and the social environment. Marketers should establish an educational program to either match or lead a social value.

Personal Factors

Because of recent social changes, Chinese consumers have learned much from other cultures. They are more independent and more knowledgeable about commerce and business. There are at least three particular changes which may create opportunities for marketers:

- The nuclear family has become the basic economic unit, and it has more power to make purchasing decisions. With the implementation of the "one child per family" policy in China, the nuclear family, consisting of parents with one child, has replaced the traditional clan family which consisted of two or more generations living as one family.
- Chinese wives are viewed as decision makers for goods purchased in families. Since wives control family finances, it is important to target wives.

- Individuals who live in the urban locations have stronger purchasing power. The Chinese government predicts that by the end of 1995, people in large urban areas will increase to 30% of the population. This modernization movement will undoubtedly create business opportunities.

Source: Adapted from: Geng, L., B. Lockhart, C. Blackmore, and R. Andrus (1996). Sport marketing strategy: a consumer behavior case analysis in China. *Multinational Business Review* 4(1): 147–154.

Suggested Discussion Topics

1. It has been generally accepted that a great potential exists in the Chinese sport market. However, questions concerning political stability, the uncertainty of economic development, and cultural differences have not only slowed Chinese sport marketing efforts, but have caused confusion and indecisiveness among sport marketers who strive to implement effective marketing strategies in China. How has the influence of Yao Ming playing for the Houston Rockets and the 2008 Summer Olympic Games being hosted by Beijing changed these views and improved sport marketing efforts in China?
2. Changes to the traditional management of the sport marketing mix had to be modified to accommodate the Chinese situation. They include (1) choosing target market segments; (2) determining the services and products to be offered; (3) selecting appropriate pricing strategies; (4) designing promotional programs; and (5) providing a proper distribution system. You are the international marketing manager for a sport organization of your choice. How would you address each of these areas?

INFLUENCING THE SPORT CONSUMER

What Is Opinion Leadership?

Sport marketing professionals strive to understand how the sport consumer solves problems and makes decisions. Sport marketers, once they gain this understanding, strive to find ways to influence the sport consumer. Influence is a central concept in the definition of leadership. Sport marketers seek to utilize opinion leadership, which is the process by which the sport marketer, or the opinion leader, informally influences the consumption actions or attitudes of sport consumers, who may be classified as opinion seekers or opinion recipients. The main reason that opinion leadership is an effective tool for sport marketers is that the sport consumer views the source of the information (the sport marketing professional) as being credible. Typically, the opinion leader is held in high esteem by those that accept their opinions.

There are a number of communication processes that can be used. This is representative of the interpersonal flow of sport communication. There are two models that we utilize in sport marketing. First is a modification of the two-step flow communication model, which is a direct method of communication from a source (owner of the sport product) to the sport marketer (opinion leader), then on to the sport consumer (opinion seekers and opinion receivers) through the mass media and networks. This is illustrated below:

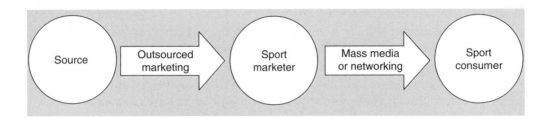

A hybrid of the previous model is a modification of the multi-step flow model of communication In this model, there is information flowing from the source (owner of the sport product) to the sport marketer (opinion leader), but also directly to the sport consumer (opinion seekers and opinion receivers). At the same time that sport consumers receive information about sport products, sport marketers and the owners of the sport product receive feedback from the sport consumers that can be used to more effectively and efficiently market the sport product. This is illustrated below:

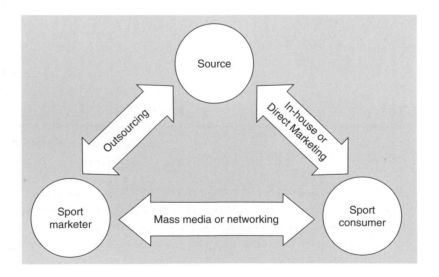

Viral Marketing

However, specifically from the viewpoint of the sport marketer, opinion leadership seeks to pass marketing messages about the sport marketer to as many people as possible, creating the potential for exponential growth with the influence the sport marketer has, as well as exposure of the sport product. This type of marketing is commonly called viral marketing, however, has also been referred to as buzz marketing or avalanche marketing.

There are six elements involved with viral marketing. While an effective strategy does not have to involve all six elements, the more elements it embraces, the more powerful the results are likely to be.

The first is to give away valuable products or services. People in general are naturally attracted to the word "FREE." This powerful word in all aspects of marketing will attract the attention of consumers. The goal of this first element is once you have the sport consumer hooked, you can then try to sell them additional sport products. This is very similar to the concept of "to make money you need to spend money." In this aspect of viral sport marketing, the sport product is given away with the goal of selling additional products in the future, and hopefully on a permanent basis.

The second element is to provide for an effortless transfer of the marketing message to others. This is accomplished by sport marketers by keeping the message short, hence making it easy to communicate to the potential sport consumers. In this day of the digital revolution, it has become increasingly easier to send and replicate these sport marketing messages through mediums such as websites, emails, digital television, digitized scoreboards, and on-site advertisements.

The next element is the case in which one can scale the marketing efforts from small to very large. As the marketing messages spread exponentially, more and more opinion seekers and opinion receivers will hear the message and potentially answer the message. The sport marketing strategy must be able to have the ability to answer potential questions about the sport product in response to the message, or in a best-case scenario, produce the sport product at an optimal level to deal with the response.

Fourth is to exploit common motivations and behaviors. As discussed earlier in this chapter, understanding the cognitive processes that are utilized to problem solve and make decision is crucial to success in sport marketing. The fifth element is to utilize existing communication networks. Many people may limit this element to media-based networking such as print, radio, television, or Internet. However, human networking still is the most powerful tool the sport marketer has to communicate sport products to potential consumers. Human networking is viral sport marketing opportunity for significant and valid exponential growth. Individuals have a broad network that consists of innumerable contacts including family, friends, peers, and colleagues. In addition, people have minor influences with people in society who they do not know, often based on an individual's position in society.

The final element is to take advantage of the resources of others. Sport marketers use many affiliated opportunities to get the marketing message out. In sport marketing, this can range from sponsorship of an event, to news and press releases that appear in newspapers or on the scroll across the bottom of a television screen, to having a link from another's website to your own. Sport marketers, while they wish to have as much control of the message as possible, need the assistance of outside sources to spread the message to a wider audience.

How To Measure the Effectiveness of Opinion Leadership

One of the key tasks of a sport marketer is to measure the outcomes of their efforts to determine the level of success of the marketing strategy. In the area of opinion leadership, sport marketers look at four key determinants of success: (1) did the marketing program influence sport consumers; (2) did the advertisements and other collateral materials stimulate sport consumer purchases; (3) was the spread of information about the sport product via word-of-mouth in an effective and controlled manner; and (4) was there a creation of a secondary level of opinion leader to further promote the sport product.

Another method of outcome assessment is related to determining whether the marketing efforts reached the opinion leaders in the target market. There are a number of ways to measure these outcomes. The self-designating method is the measurement used most often in marketing. It involves asking a series of AIO (activity, interest, and opinion) questions using surveys to have the respondent determine whether they view themselves as an opinion leader. The sociometric method is where a segmented population is asked to identify those individuals whom they give advice to, and to whom they go to for advice. This aid is identifying when people see themselves as opinion leaders, and when they see themselves as opinion seekers and opinion receivers. The key informant method is a form of data collection that involves individuals selected to participate in interviews or focus groups for the purpose of identifying those who are viewed as opinion leaders in society. A final method is the objective method, where individuals are put in a position of being an opinion leader, and an independent analysis of their efforts is conducted to determine success rate.

DIFFUSION AND ADOPTION PROCESSES

Now that we have a strategy for sending the message, how does the message spread to sport consumers? There are two major ways: the diffusion process and the adoption process.

The Diffusion Process

The diffusion process is where the acceptance of a sport product is spread through communication channels to sport consumers over a period of time. The four key elements within this process are the innovation of the sport product, the sport communication channels, the sport consumer social system, and the time period.

The innovation of the sport product begins with the first two stages of the product life cycle – introduction and growth. During this period, different constituencies are defining the sport product and giving it its own personality, including the producer itself, the product itself, the market, and the sport consumer. Many of these concepts will be discussed in more detail in Chapter 6 – Sport Product Management.

The sport communication channels are wide and varied, including print, radio, television, digital and Internet. These concepts will be addressed further in Chapter 9 – Communication Management in Sport. The sport consumer social system includes culture, subculture, cross-culture, group, reference group, and social class. This was discussed earlier in this chapter in the section about the external factors affecting sport consumers. Finally, time is relative. There are so many internal and external factors that affect time that it is specialized depending on the innovation of the product, the availability of sport communication channels, and the interest level for the sport consumer.

Of the four elements, the innovation of the product is the most significant in the diffusion process. The product characteristic is the only element the sport producer and the sport marketer has considerable control over. One reason has to do with relative advantage, which is the extent that potential sport consumers perceive a sport product as being superior to existing substitutes. Another reason has to do with compatibility. This is the level to which a sport consumer feels that a sport product is able to be integrated with their needs, values, and practices. A third reason is complexity – the degree to which the sport product is very intricate by nature, and hence difficult to understand or use. Fourth is trialability (or divisibility), which is the degree to which the sport product is able to be offered and tried by a number of people on a limited basis. A fifth and final way to control the sport product is through observability (or communicability). This is where the sport product is readily visible to and consumable by the sport consumer.

As a result of controlling the characteristics of the sport product, three distinct levels of innovation result. Continuous innovation is where a sport product is an improved or modified version of an existing product rather than being a totally new product. Traditionally, this alteration has had very little change on the consumption pattern of the sport product. A second level of innovation is called dynamic continuous innovation. This level takes continuous innovation a step further by actually having a changing effect on consumption patterns of the sport product. Finally, there is discontinuous innovation, where the sport product is entirely new, and there needs to be the establishment of consumption practices.

The Adoption Process

The adoption process is made up of the stages that the sport consumer passes through when making a decision to try/continue or not to try/not continue using a sport product. The diagram below illustrates these stages:

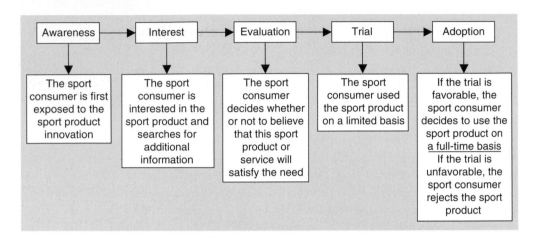

Now that we see what the adoption process is, where does the general population fall? The illustration below diagrams the five categories of adopters:

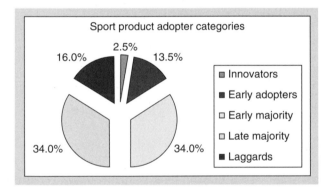

Innovators, who represent 2.5% of the overall population, are venturesome individuals who are willing to try new products. These consumers are usually highly educated, will use multiple information sources to make decisions, and are more willing to take risks. These consumers tend to stay within their own adoption category, and hence rarely communicate about products outside their adopter category.

Early adopters represent 13.5% of the overall population, and are usually the leaders in social settings. These individuals tend to be more integrated within local social systems, and hence tend to earn more respect than any other adopter category. Hence, the early adopter tends to be the most influential over people, which results in them being the ideal opinion leader and role model.

The early majority represents 34% of the overall population. These consumers tend to be extremely deliberate in their decision making and adopt new ideas/

product in an average amount of time. They usually do not hold leadership positions – they would rather be more of an opinion seeker.

Of an equal percentage are the late majority, who tend to be very skeptical of change. As a result, these adopters tend to be followers rather than leaders, and therefore the adoption process is usually as a result of either economic necessity or peer pressure. This group makes up a majority of opinion receivers – and hence tends to be followers of trends.

The final group, representing 16% of the overall population, are called laggards. These individuals are traditionalists in the truest sense of the word. They are happy with the status quo and are the last people to adopt an innovation. They are extremely happy in their comfort zone – living in the past and very suspicious of new products.

Getting the Message Out

Sport marketing professional utilizes the information from these analyses combined with opinion leadership strategies to influence the sport consumer into purchasing the sport product. By means of the diffusion process, the sport marketer seeks to influence sport consumers to accept and purchase a sport product by spreading information about the sport product through numerous communication channels (print, radio, TV, and Internet) over a period of time. By way of the adoption process, the sport marketing professional brings awareness of the sport product to the consumer, and influences the sport consumer to become interested in the sport product and hence search for additional information. The sport marketer continues to work toward influencing the sport consumer throughout the evaluation process and entices them to try the product. Ultimately, the sport marketer strives to have the sport consumer believe that the sport product meets and satisfies their needs, and resulting in the sport consumer purchasing and using the sport product.

CONCLUSION

Sport consumer behavior is the conduct that sport consumers display in seeking out, ordering, buying, using, and assessing products and services that the consumers expects will satisfy their needs and wants. In general, there are two major types of consumers that sport marketers want to understand – the personal consumer and the organizational consumer. The sport marketing professional must understand the internal and external factors that affect sport consumers. The internal factors that make the sport consumer tick include the personality of the sport consumer, the learning process of sport consumers, the process of motivating sport consumers, how the attitudes of the sport consumer are formed and changed, and the perceptions developed by sport consumers about a sport product. External factors resulting from environmental influences include culture, subculture, international and global interaction, social setting, and social class.

In order to effectively understand sport consumer behavior, sport marketing professionals must understand the marketing concept, which is a consumer-oriented philosophy that suggests that satisfaction of consumer needs provide the focus for product development and marketing strategy to enable the firm to meet its own organizational goals. The development of the marketing concept for sport is centered on three sub-concepts: sport production, the sport product, and the selling of sport. The marketing concept focuses on two major groups of sport consumers: spectators and participants. It also focuses on three individual and environmental factors that have an effect on why people consume sport: socialization, involvement, and commitment.

Problem solving and decision making techniques must be effectively utilized in order to efficiently analyze sport consumer behavior. This will allow the sport marketing professional to analyze how sport consumers determine what they want, and how they set goals and objectives that result in making a choice. The problem solving process is an organized, step-by-step approach that involves brainstorming, formulating various solutions, analyzing all solutions to determine a course of action, implementing the course of action, evaluating the success of the course of action, and repeating until an optimal solution is reached. The decision making process involves four views – economic, passive, cognitive, and emotional – that form the foundation for setting and attaining goals. The decision making process then focuses on pre-purchase decisions (problem and needs recognition, information search, and evaluation of alternatives), decisions during the actual purchase, and post-purchase evaluation.

Sport marketers utilize opinion leadership in order to influence the sport consumer are opinion leadership. This concept focuses on the process by which sport marketers informally influence the consumption actions or attitudes of sport consumers. Opinion leadership seeks to pass marketing messages about the sport marketer to as many people as possible, creating the potential for exponential growth in the influence the sport marketer has, as well as exposure of the sport product. This type of marketing is commonly called viral marketing. The five major elements of viral marketing include giving away valuable products or services, providing for an effortless transfer of the marketing message to others, making it easy to scale the marketing efforts from small to very large, exploiting common motivations and behaviors, and taking advantage of the resources of others. Ultimately, sport marketers look at four key determinants of success: (1) did the marketing program influence sport consumers; (2) did the advertisements and other collateral materials stimulate sport consumer purchases; (3) was the spread of information about the sport product via word-of-mouth in an effective and controlled manner; and (4) was there a creation of a secondary level of opinion leader to further promote the sport product.

The message is spread to sport consumers through either the diffusion process or the adoption process. The diffusion process is where the acceptance of a sport product is spread through communication channels to sport consumers over a period of time. The four key elements within this process are the innovation of the sport product, the sport communication channels, the sport consumer social system, and the time period. The adoption process is made up of the stages (include awareness, interest, evaluation, trial, and adoption) sport consumer pass through when making a decision to try/continue or not to try/not continue using a sport product.

Ultimately, sport marketing professional utilizes the various processes in sport consumer behavior to influence the sport consumer into purchasing the sport product. Their overriding goal is to have the sport consumer believe that the sport product meets and satisfies their needs, which in turn results in the sport consumer purchasing and using the sport product.

FROM THEORY TO PRACTICE
Pamela Cheriton, President and CEO
Event Services International, Inc.

Fort Myers, Florida

When I graduated from Theatre School I never thought that I would make my living in the sporting world. And yet, thanks to the growing consumer desire that entertainment be both engaging and interactive, here I am with close to 20 years as a major league fan event manager. This experience includes 11 years as the Operational Staffing consultant for Major League Baseball's Events and Entertainment Department (MLB All-Star FanFest); 9 years with the National Hockey League (NHL All-Star FANtasy); and 6 years with the National Basketball Association (NBA All-Star Jam Session). In addition, I was involved with running the Super Bowl XXX Street Spectacular in Tempe, AZ, and the 2006 NCAA Hoop City at the Men's (Indianapolis) and Women's (Boston) Final Four.

Having both witnessed and participated in the FANomenon, I am a firm believer that fan fests are one of the most successful innovations of sport marketing and promotion: the perfect vehicle for fan appreciation, community relations, sport branding, and sponsor recognition. Celebrating and showcasing the best of the sport, these events have captured the market and set the standard for fan entertainment. As an ancillary event that accompanies an All-Star Game or the opening day activity in a team's parking lot, these types of events have become an excellent means of bringing the community in and getting the message out.

Most obviously the target audience for these events is the sports fan, and by extension, their family and friends. All of these events have been geared to appeal to fans of all ages and skill levels from the fanatic to arm-chair participant – they are truly a family affair. Exit surveys show that the majority of attendees are families with young children and adults in the 36+ range. In the early years, a participant would stay at the show for approximately 3 hours but over the past 5 years that time has expanded to an average of 5–7 hours! That is an excellent amount of "face" time for participating sponsors and

Continued

partners and also a goodly amount of time for snacking, drinking, and shopping for souvenirs and memorabilia.

Because the ticket price is comparable to the host city's other entertainment options, often less, exit surveys consistently show that event attendees consider them a FANtastic bargain. They most often respond that the appeal of these fan fests lies in the fact that they offer a "total" sport experience under one roof: interactive activities for the player participants, legacy and memorabilia displays for the history buffs, player/coach appearances with autographs and skill clinics for the die-hard fans; add the theatrical enhancement of the sounds, sights and "feel" of the sport and it is heaven on earth for the fan – a consumer's dream come true.

The other noteworthy (albeit quiet) consumers at these events are the volunteers who comprise 80% of the staffing of these shows. A fan fest can be as physically large as three football fields and can run for up to 12 hours a day, six plus days in a row – requiring a team of over 2500 people. Since it would be fiscally impossible to use the ticket or sponsor revenues to offset the salaries for such a large staff, these events are perforce required to rely on the willing participation of their most active and committed sports fans.

Traditionally these volunteers are people who have either a real love of the game or are motivated by their sense of civic pride – usually it is a healthy combination of both. A common characteristic is the active desire to share their enthusiasm with the event attendees. As the representative face of the hosting city, they come from a variety of backgrounds; usually range in age from 18 to 80, with the majority in the 18 to 25 and 35 to 55 range and are an equal mix of males and females. Almost all have high school education and many have post secondary degrees and while most are still working there are usually a good number of retirees and college students. In fact, at least a third of the total numbers are students who are pursuing their degrees in some kind of sports marketing or management or communications program.

For these students, volunteering at an event of the magnitude and caliber of a major league fan fest offers them the unique opportunity to get some valuable "mega-event" experience under their belts and the distinct possibility of being "discovered" by the professional event staff. I know of several cases where students have been able to parley their aptitude and attitude as a "star" volunteers (ever willing, ever able) into on-the-job interviews resulting in future employment.

Another strong motivation for volunteering at fan events is the social aspect of meeting like-minded individuals in a fun and productive environment. Having some longevity in this particular arena, I have been privileged to work with approximately 500 "return" volunteers who plan their vacations around the event in a new city. According to them, it is the perfect way to play: a few "structured" hours of enjoyable activity, an opportunity to meet the "locals" close up and then it is off to explore the new place – armed with the insider details they picked up during their shift.

Regardless of their reasons, these most excellent people are the life blood of any event and it is of the utmost importance that their valuable contribution be loudly recognized and appreciated. They are the ultimate grassroots marketers who, through enthusiastic word-of-mouth, can spread the "great event" reviews much further a field than even the media partners – and quite likely to a better, more receptive target audience: their fellow fans.

III

SPORT MARKETING
LOGISTICS

SPORT PRODUCT MANAGEMENT

CHAPTER OUTLINE

CHAPTER OBJECTIVES

The reader will be able to:

- Distinguish, identify, and classify the various elements of sport products and services.
- Identify and understand the stages of the sport product life cycle.

- Know the concepts involved with positioning and differentiating sport products and services, including branding, licensing, and intellectual properties.
- Understand product management and how this process is utilized as an integral part of the sport marketing process.

ELEMENTS OF SPORT PRODUCTS AND SERVICES

A sport product is something that is produced which is bought or sold in the sporting goods industry. Usually tangible products are referred to as "goods," while intangible products are called "services" or the "experience." A sport service is the process of providing quality, value, and satisfaction to the sport consumer. Intangible products also include "indirect goods," in which the customer has the opportunity to stylize tangible products as they wish. Intangible services involve providing a quality standard work, an offering, and/or duties generally expected by the sport consumer. These traditional services are provided to enhance the experience.

Tangible Sport Products and Services

In today's society, consumers want to touch the baseball and feel the jersey. Consumers want to customize their shoes and put their marks on hats. Examples of tangible products include the program that consumers purchase at the gate and the big "number one" foam finger they buy at the merchandise stand. Tangible services might include access to and use of a personal trainer, or ice-skate sharpening. Not only does tangible services help the consumer recognize or differentiate their specific product or service from others, but also it allows the consumer to show others their choice and in turn advertise by word-of-mouth.

The Central Illinois Collegiate League (CICL) was established in 1963. Since then the CICL has developed more than 150 Major League Baseball players. Some of which include Joe Girardi, Kirby Puckett, and Mike Schmidt. The CICL is one of three summer baseball leagues sanctioned by the National Collegiate Athletics Association (NCAA) and Major League Baseball. In order to be eligible to play you must have remaining collegiate eligibility. This league gives collegiate players an opportunity to develop their talents without jeopardizing their amateur status.

The cost to franchise a CICL baseball team is $25,000.00, Non-Affiliated team $500,000, and Minor League team $1–3 million. What does a franchise or sport produce have to sell in order to recoup the cost of entering a league? Tickets, stadium and team naming rights, concessions, radio or TV, signage, parking, and media guides are but a few of the tangible products. In order to create and keep fans, intangible products, such as customer service, must be practiced and perfected.

Intangible Sport Products and Services

Intangible sport products are the merchandise and extensions that we cannot touch or hold. For example, intangible sport products would be the appearance of the ball park, the usher that helped you to find your seat with a friendly smile, and the sights, sounds, smells, and euphoric feeling of your team's victory. Intangible sport services could be the customer service a fan receives when they purchase goods at the ball park, such as tickets, food, or memorabilia. In some ways, the intangible sport products and services, when negative, have a longer lasting effect as compared to the tangible products. Customers remember how a game was ruined for them because of foul language, inclement weather, or getting to the park late because it was difficult to find parking within a reasonable distance, more than they remember the great hot dog, exciting home run, or friendly ticket taker.

SPORT PRODUCT AND SERVICE MANAGEMENT

Sport product and service management focuses on the approach taken by sport marketers and organizations to define and market their products and services. There are a number of issues that a sport marketing professional must consider when managing products and services including the following:

- Choosing the appropriate sport products and services to produce and sell.
- Decide what new sport products and services to add or discontinue.
- How to introduce sport products or services to a market.
- Calculate the amount of time it will take for a sport product or service to penetrate the market.
- Ascertain the sport product and service life cycle considerations that need to be addressed.
- How to develop positioning and differentiation strategies for sport products and services.
- Establish the branding and licensing structures to be utilized for sport products and services.
- Determine the levels of protection (patents, marks, and copyrights) that needs to be implemented for sport products or services.

Sport product and service management usually starts as a function of the sport marketing planning process. This process involves the development of the sport organization's products and services marketing strategies, including the tactics and programs to be implemented during the lifespan of the plan. There are a series of functions that are undertaken during this planning process to determine the appropriate method for managing the specific sport product or service. First is defining the competitive set, which is the process of determining the direct competitors to a sport organization in the specific product or service area. Those organizations most closely defined as competitors are those who offer similar sport products and services, or are generic competitors in the marketplace.

Once the competitive set is defined, the company or organization engages in category attractiveness analysis. This involves developing a general understanding of the market segment category the organization operates in, and whether continued investment in that segment will yield an appropriate return. There are three main categories of concern in completing a category attractiveness analysis. First is the category of aggregate marketing factors, which are the indicators of the appeal of the sport product or service in the specific segment or category. These factors include category size, market growth potential, the sport product and service life cycle, the sales cycles and seasonality present in the segment, and profitability potential. The second category is the segment factors, which are the underlying opportunities and threats that affect the segment or category. This includes the threat of current competitors and new entrants to the segment, the bargaining power of buyers and suppliers, and the saturation of sport products and services within the category or segment. The final category is environmental factors that are beyond the control of the sport organization. These include technological innovations, politics, economic changes, legislative mandates, and changes in societal views.

In addition, there may be some businesses inside the trade radius offering similar products and services, but are not competitors because of differences in target market, class of product or services being offered, or target clientele. An example of this would be a pro shop at a hockey arena selling team merchandise and a "mom and pop" sporting goods store. The pro shop is targeting season ticket holders and fans on game day, while the sporting goods store is targeting the general public. Thus, the two are not of major concern to one another.

This analysis elicits some questions related to competitor analyses and consumer analyses. These questions include:

- How well is the sport organization doing as compared to the competition?
- Have our customers been pleased with our current sport products and/or services?
- Can we forecast the needs, wants, and desires of our customers going forward?
- What factors might cause customer behavior to change?

By collecting consumer-based research that is truthful, reliable, and valid answers to these questions will serve to help the sport organization move forward with confidence. The answers to these questions will also serve as a primer to develop the further management processes necessary in sport product and service management. This is especially important when determining market potential. By estimating the maximum possible sales of a sport product or service, a sport organization will gain valuable knowledge about the amount of sport product or service to make available. If an estimate is too low, it might result in a marketer determining that the segment or category has reach maturity too fast, and clouds his view on any untapped potential that may be present. If an estimate is too high, the sport organization may offer new sport products and services or extensions to current sport products or services which are not truly wanted, needed, or desired by the segment or category. The information about the market potential also serves to help the sport organization to make appropriate pricing, advertising, delivery, promotion, and publicity decisions (the sport marketing mix). It also helps the marketer focus on the continued development, introduction, and growth of particular products and services, as well as evaluates the products' eventual maturation and decline, through the sport product and service life cycle:

Marketing objectives

Pricing objectives

Examination of determinants (e.g. costs, demand, competition)

Decision on the role that pricing will play in the marketing mix

Development and evaluation of the effect of pricing strategies

ETHICS IN SPORT PRODUCT AND SERVICE MANAGEMENT

Ethics as a field of management has been slowly deteriorating for decades. Business ethics usually address the most outrageous violations generally dealing with human rights violations or extensive financial losses. The reality is that the so-called minor infractions happen on a daily basis. These infractions routinely go unpunished internally. The leading causes of many infractions are consumer dissatisfaction, employee turnover, and ineffective quality improvement and training efforts. This damages a corporations branding which intern cost the company its market share.

If this loss of market share for world-class organizations runs between 10% and 15% of total sales revenue, management ethics in the best world-class companies is costing companies billions annually. If the average were to continue or increase, it could pose an extraordinary opportunity for improvement or cause the collapse of the corporation.

Most quality improvement projects deal with visible processes such as customer service operations. It is entirely possible to address the processes but still have unresolved issues involving people. If people do not want to cooperate and work together, or if tensions are high, process improvement becomes increasingly difficult.

It is human tendency for management to seek single causes for failure when multiple, systematic causes are at work. In most cases blaming is placed on the failure of leadership. The common cause of sub-par performance can usually be traced to ethics patterns. The ability of corporations to manage ethics at this personal level will yield significant economic returns.

Ethical management, when done correctly, is a comprehensive program that continuously improves thinking and behavior patterns not just some high visibility issues and ethics policies. Many corporations spend millions on training and quality improvement initiatives without ever addressing the leading constraints to quality or performance improvement, which are ethics failures within the corporation.

Employees are more than just a collection of skills and capabilities. They are a system with a culture of their own. This culture is so powerful that it ultimately has more of an impact on what, where, and when decisions become reality than the decision makers themselves. The importance of hiring employees that share a similar core ethical belief to that of the corporation is monumental. This core of ethical beliefs is directly tied to the success or failure of the corporation.

Quality ethical management identifies the ethics needs before training or policy implementation ever begins. An ethics policy without regard to the specific needs of the organization is ineffective. An ethics policy addresses the underlying root causes of unethical behavior. Unethical behavior hinders organizational performance.

The speed at which we resolve ethical issues directly benefits performance. By focusing on the corporation's ethics, and not just policy, ethics management removes constraints to performance and reduces risks of large-scale ethics failures in the process.

ETHICS SURROUNDING THE MARKETING OF SPORT PRODUCTS: MARKETING TO CHILDREN AND ADOLESCENTS

Do you want strangers speaking to your kids without your permission?

Suppose a sports marketer followed your kids around practically everywhere. Suppose she was pitching products and services to them on soccer and baseball fields, in the school cafeteria, in magazines, newspapers, the Internet, radio, and TV.

Would you mind if she spent billions of dollars to teach your kids what to wear and eat and how to entertain themselves? Of course, she wants to sell them athletic equipment, cereal, CD players, and toys. But is it also OK with you if she sells them cars, cruise lines, antibiotics, and vacation destinations?

Apparently so, because according to the Judge Baker Children's Center, a children's interest group affiliated with Harvard Medical School, kids are subjected to 40,000 TV commercials a year that try to do all of the above. And that does not count radio, print, the Internet, movies, billboards, signage at athletic fields, school cafeterias, and many other points of contact.

Why pitch kids?
[Kids] exert a lot of influence over the $565 billion spent by them and their parents for the products kids want and need. Plus, children are more involved than ever with purchasing decisions regarding cars and vacations. Their devotion to the Internet has made many of them the key product researchers in their households.

Marketers are aware of this, and a gaggle of resources have leaped into the fray to help them.

Sports marketers acknowledge that kids influence brand preference and product purchase. And, of course, none of us believe that our products are harmful to children. As an industry we believe kids are fair targets. But is this ethical?

The answer is no, according to organizations such as Commercial Alert and to its executive director, Gary Ruskin. Headquartered in Portland, Commercial Alert was founded in 1998 by Ruskin and consumer activist Ralph Nader.

The organization has 2000 members from 50 states. Its mission statement says it "opposes the excesses of commercialism, advertising, and marketing."

According to Ruskin, one of the battlefields where sports marketers' interests clash with child welfare is school cafeterias.

He said companies such as Coca-Cola, Pepsi, and Burger King aggressively use sports marketing to reach kids, and they want the opportunity to sell their products to kids on-site at schools if possible.

Commercial Alert said that a growing number of public and private elementary and high schools (20.2%) sell high-fat fast foods from companies such as McDonald's and Pizza Hut. The organization also said that the number of overweight children ages 6–11 has increased 382% since 1974.

Commercial Alert reported that the likelihood of obesity for children increases 1.6 times for each sugar-sweetened drink they consume per day. In school districts that enable the sale of soft drinks, 43% allow brand signs on school property, including athletic facilities. And from 1977 to 1996, soft-drink consumption among 12–19-year-olds skyrocketed 40% among girls and 75% among boys.

Earlier this year Commercial Alert published its "Parents' Bill of Rights." The document's key points call for banning all advertising in TV programming

Continued

aimed at kids younger than 12, installing parental control over the marketing of their kids' mail and email addresses, making schools commercial-free, disclosing paid product placements in child-oriented TV shows and movies and nutritional labeling of junk foods.

It is tough to argue with the intent of Commercial Alert's "Parents' Bill of Rights." But there is no doubt that the sports marketing industry will continue to reach out to kids via their attraction to sports.

The only question is through what means will the industry continue to do so? And will we police ourselves before a regulatory authority does it for us? Where is a reasonable middle ground?

Perhaps a good start would be for us to pose this question to ourselves before launching any sports marketing campaign: Would I want this message communicating with my kids without my express consent?

Source: Taken from Poole, M. (2003). Before reaching out to kids, sports marketers should think of their own. *SportsBusiness Journal* 6(35): 10.

Suggested Discussion Topics

1. The goal of any sport marketer is to generate revenue for the organization they represent. Why should the sport marketer feel any less ethical in targeting young children with their advertisements, especially since they are so heavily involved in the decision making process? Explain the differences between marketing to young children as opposed to targeting other segments based on gender or origin, and why one may or may not be considered more ethically acceptable than another.

2. What is the importance of government involvement in "protecting" children from solicitations such as the ones described in the article? Should this responsibility lie solely with the parents, with the government, with the sport advertisers themselves, or some combination of the three? Explain your answer with specific examples.

THE SPORT PRODUCT AND SERVICE LIFE CYCLE

The sport product and service life cycle encompass six stages: internal development, introduction to market, growth, maturity, saturation, and decline. All stages are bound by the realities of competition, saturation, and change. A typical life cycle is similar to a bell curve as diagrammed in the next page.

No market is infinite. Competitors will always want to gain more market share, and someone will always think of a new twist to an old idea. Researching the products life cycle can provide the answer to the following questions. How

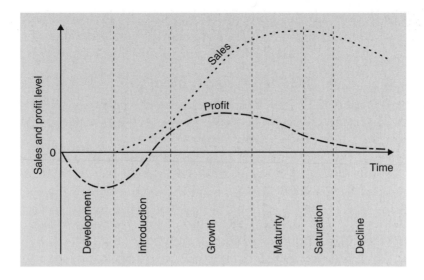

do I determine if my business is considered to be small, medium, or large? If I am small how do I compete against larger companies? How I figure it out and does it matter? How do I know when a product or service has reached a saturation point? What are the implications of this? When do I need to find something new to offer, when do I stay the course and do more advertising? These questions and more appear often these days. In the sports industry, the buying marketplace heats up for some and cooled for others quicker than other industries. Entrepreneurs and business owners need to realize and understand the success or failure is directly linked to the speed and accuracy in which we answer these questions. These questions can be addressed by market research. Marketing research can be desk or field based, can use face-to-face or telemarketing techniques, can use focus groups, and/or qualitative or quantitative research methods depending on the sport product or service.

Each stage of the sport product or service life cycle has attributes that will influence your decisions on weather this is the appropriate time for your business to grow. Continuous market research will help you avoid pitfalls such as not correctly anticipating demand, overhead expenses, and other variable factors.

Internal Development

The internal development stage begins with the idea of a new product or service or a new twist on an existing product or service. How does the company make the idea or invention a reality? This stage offers some of the largest most roadblocks. What material should the company use for the invention? Can the company's services be offered to anyone? What are the technological needs? Should this product or service be patented, branded, licensed, trademarked, or copy written? Who will lend the capital in order to mass produce the product? This stage is where the company develops a marketing plan. Has any company produced the same type of product and what were some of the problems they incurred?

A marketing plan for the sports product or service is a formal written statement of marketing intent that summary the key points of the operational sport marketing process. These steps include:

- *Marketing research* is defined as the organized methodical discovery of information about a marketplace. Market research can be desk or field based, can use face-to-face or telemarketing techniques, can use focus groups, and or qualitative or quantitative research methods.
- *Mission* is defined as an attempt by a corporation to encapsulate their purpose in a simple paragraph or phrase.
- *Marketing objectives* are defined as what the organization is trying to achieve through its marketing activities during a specified period. This is closely linked with corporate objectives.
- *Financial objectives* are defined as goals related to returns that a firm will strive to accomplish during the period covered by its financial plan.
- *Target markets* are defined as actively pursuing specific population segments for the purpose of research or sales.
- *Positioning* is defined as the work that a company may undertake to try to position their offering, brand, or service in a specific place relative to competing offerings in the minds of their target market.
- *Marketing mix* is defined as gathered information serves to help the sport organization to make appropriate pricing, advertising, delivery, promotion, and publicity decisions.

The marketing plan enables the company to understand which stage a product is entering, leaving, or passing through at any given time. Market data is available through print, media, and with the emergence of the Internet more information is at our finger tips than ever before. It is important to consider the source of the information. Just because it is the latest and greatest news, does not mean that the consumer cannot change their mind.

Some of the questions that your research should answer or address are:

- How many competitors are there?
- Who has the best idea and are they the leader?
- How strong is the business that is leading?
- How can I place my sport product or service competitively?
- How many suppliers are entering the market?
- What are potential buyers thinking about buying?
- How much research and development is being done by your competitors, relative to the current product or service, vs. new ones?
- What is the size of the market?
- How long is the life cycle of similar sport products or services?

Using desk, field based, face-to-face, telemarketing, focus groups, and/or qualitative or quantitative research methods will provide answers to the questions above in a quick, concise, and accurate manner. This research provides an organization with a sales forecast that is believable. This approach to internal development of a sport product or service, and the accompanying marketing plan should point out some of the problems encountered by sport organizations. These problems include not knowing what stage of the market the product is entering, a changing or poorly determined price point, and a higher-than-estimated number of competitors, all of which can lead to loss of capital investment.

Introduction to Market

Now that we have an answer for all of the questions from the marketing plan, it is time to put the plan into action. Through market research, the company has determined a price point that will be competitive. How does the company know the segment of the market it should enter? Having many competitors could indicate maturity or at least a large enough demand that could yield market share; having only a few competitors indicate either an early or late stage cycle. Ideally, a company should enter into the market before the growth stage.

The influx of competitors is a general indicator of the transition from stage one to stage two. When this second stage – introduction to market – begins, it is time for the organization to put its product or service into action and start capturing market share. When competitors begin dropping out of the market, the product is either in the maturity stage or passing maturity and heading to the consolidation and decline stages. This is the time for the company to launch additional products or services in order to reposition the product or service, or it is time to decrease inventory through a price cut and move on.

Growth

The growth stage of this cycle separates the competition. The company with the best product, price, and/or service rises to the top. The establishment of the sport product or service in the market results in an increase in sales and the need to spend money on building the brand. In general, sport services tend to have a longer period of growth as compared to sport products. This is because it is easier for competitors to react to sport products. As a result, the increase in sales and profits will eventually peak as a result of the increase competition. Rollerblades were like this. When they were first released, consumer demand spiked. Everyone had to have a pair – and the accessories that went with them – and sales and profits sky rocketed. Once more competitors entered the market, though, sales of rollerblades began to slow, profits dropped, and consequently, prices leveled out.

Maturity

Maturity refers to the time at which the sport product or service has maximized profits and is seeking to maintain a stable place in the market. Competitors have a direct influence on the sport organization's pricing practices, due to both new sport products and services entering the market, and alternative sport products and services being more popular. At this stage, the organization must decide whether to withdraw its product or service from the market, or to make modifications that will continue to maintain the product or service within the market.

If the company desires to maintain a presence in the chosen market, the sport marketing professional, in conjunction with the sport organization, must determine whether it is appropriate to take the risk of over-extending the company's reach. In the maturity stage of the life cycle, the marketer continuously reevaluates his marketing strategy and seeks to determine how much of the market the company can reasonably expect to control. This determination of appropriately choosing whether the sport organization should stay in the market for the long haul will ultimately define the destiny of the sport product or service.

Saturation

Eventually, the sport organization may come to the realization that it needs to reevaluate the sport product or service life cycle. When the gaining of market share begins to slow, it is usually a sign of market saturation. In turn, market saturation is the first sign that the sport product or service is going to be entering the decline stage. At this point, the product or service has little hope of future profits, either because there are too many competitors or because the popularity and interest in the product or service has significantly decreased. ESPN is a good example of this. For a number of years, ESPN was the only national service provider of its kind. Today, though, there are a number of competitors for ESPN's market share, such as Fox Sports Net, NESN, and CNNSI. ESPN has had to try to retake the market by creating other channels including ESPN2, ESPN News, and ESPNU in order to maintain its place in sports news and coverage.

Decline

The decline stage is the last stage before obsolescence. At this stage of the cycle, the business should have introduced new services or a next generation of the product. The business that finishes with the most market share gives the company name and brand recognition. With this recognition, it is easier to implement the next generation product or service. The company that gains the largest market share should have the stocks for replacement parts for your product if parts are required. This latter reason can dramatically increase the length of this stage.

The longer the life cycle, the longer a period the company has to acquire market share, make money, and continue research and development. The shorter life cycle requires more advertising to quickly position the product or service in the market. Sports products and services vary in the speed in which their life cycles are completed. In every case, however, there is no room for mistakes. Slower life cycles allow for traditional advertising and promotion such as print media. Quicker life cycles need an approach such as e-commerce or e-business, the advertising, buying and selling of goods and services through the Internet.

GLOBAL PRODUCT MANAGEMENT: THE RISE, FALL, AND REBIRTH OF DUNLOP

The Dunlop sports brand is more than just a textbook example of brand diversification – it also highlights the risks and benefits of licensing.

The Dunlop trademark grew from a humble tire brand into one of the world's most established sports brands. The revenues from the flourishing tire business and the expertise in rubber-based manufacturing at the beginning of the last century created a new challenge for the Dunlop brand – how could it broaden its activities by leveraging its expertise?

Rubber was used in hoses, pipes, belts, tennis balls, and golf balls, and over time Dunlop developed world-class business units in each of these categories. The sports ball business turned into a global sports business, which enjoyed an unrivalled international status. Throughout the 20th century, Dunlop was the most successful sports brand. The world's best golfers, including Arnold Palmer, used and promoted Dunlop equipment. By the 1980s, high-profile stars such as John McEnroe and Virginia Wade used Dunlop tennis racquets and, naturally, the company's global reputation was at an all-time high.

In 1985, the Dunlop business was divided up and BTR (now Invensys) bought its sports arm. However, despite steady licensing revenue the sports brand itself was neglected. According to Phil Parnell, then CEO:

> … the company stopped investing in players and operating at grass-roots level. It took 100 years to build the brand and 15 years to abandon most of the marketing support behind it.

In 1996, a private equity group purchased the company. The problem of rejuvenating the brand was exacerbated by serious financial issues – debt and cash-flow problems were damaging the brand and crippling the business. The key process for the business was to reestablish the credibility of the brand through the technical excellence of the products, and to highlight the consumer benefits that the purchaser of each product enjoyed.

On the legal side, the company focused on developing cost-effective and innovative strategies that protected valuable trademarks and existing licensing revenues. Review and amendment of the existing documentation and renegotiation of agreements placed greater emphasis on quality control, more frequent audits and reporting, tighter control of licensee activity, more detailed involvement in marketing plans, and the coordination of marketing execution.

Dunlop computerized its extensive trademark portfolio and rationalized it through brand and trademark sales. This created greater cost control and focus. The company appraised licensees and encouraged them to achieve closer alignment with the Group's product and brand values. This reemphasized the true origin and nature of the goods and ensured that new products fitted the brand profile, whether they were manufactured or sourced by the Group or by its licensees. Management of the portfolio ensured that brand equity

Continued

grew. This formed a key element of the Group's assets, upon which loans were secured.

Using these and other commercial and financial techniques, the Group successfully attracted a buyer. In 2004, Sports World bought the reinvigorated and highly profitable Dunlop brand.

The acquisition added Dunlop, Slazenger, and Carlton to Sports World's stable of brands. Since 2004, the company has consolidated the licensing revenues of these and several other brands, including Lonsdale, Karrimor, and Donnay. The licensing business is administered through International Brand Management Ltd., which is committed to brand management and choosing correct licensee partners. The business has had exceptional results in recent years, and is intent on taking the brand to places it has never been before in a controlled and well-managed manner, ensuring that its licensee partners buy into Dunlop's history as the longest-standing sports brand of modern times. Licensing revenue continues to grow rapidly as a result.

Dunlop is now sponsoring the likes of recent women's tennis world number one, Amelie Mauresmo, and licensing the brand into product categories such as clothing, cosmetics, inline skates, bicycles, games software, footwear, sunglasses, camping equipment, and inflatables on a global basis. Dunlop's tag line – "made of the right stuff" – not only epitomizes its brand, but also its approach to licensing.

Licensing should be taken very seriously. It is now an unavoidable part of big business and an invaluable tool for brand owners. And it is much more than simply borrowing a name and applying it to a product to increase sales. Each licensing opportunity must be assessed on its merits. A certain amount of risk is inevitable, of course, but the opportunities for building equity in the brand simply cannot be ignored. However, to borrow from Dunlop's philosophy, it is essential that license relationships are made of the right stuff!

Source: Adapted from Olivier, D. (2005). Dunlop Slazenger: a case study. In *Field Fisher Waterhouse*. Retrieved March 14, 2006 from http://www.legal500.com/.

Suggested Discussion Topics

1. As an international and global brand, the managers of the Dunlop brand need to repeatedly conduct a category attractiveness analysis on their various products. What is a category attractive analysis? If you were the Director of Product Marketing for Dunlop, what specific marketing factors would you analyze?

2. Let us assume you do a category attractiveness analysis for Dunlop tennis products. How would the answers to the following questions affect

market potential? Look at the answers from both the positive response and negative response perspectives:

- How well is the sport organization doing as compared to the competition?
- Have our customers been pleased with our current sport products and/or services?
- Can we forecast the needs, wants, and desires of our customers going forward?
- What factors might cause customer behavior to change?

POSITIONING AND DIFFERENTIATION

Positioning and differentiation are integral processes in the ultimate success or failure of marketing the sport product or service. Positioning is the process of influencing the perceptions of potential and current customers about the image of the company and its products and services. This is accomplished by applying the 4 P's of marketing – product, price, place (distribution), and promotion – with the goal of strategically placing the product or service firmly in the mind of the consumer.

Differentiation is creating or offering a like product or service with the intent to influence demand. This means that a company has developed a strategy of providing a similar product by a competing company to its customers with the claim that its product is better, stronger, faster, or last longer than its competitors' products or services. The company hopes that this different offering will better satisfy the needs of their particular customers. Using such a strategy may help to reduce the need to compete solely on price.

This strategy could allow the company to differentiate their offerings from larger players and allow you to gain market share and become more effective for its market share. An example of this would be the choice that Chicago baseball fans have. The sport consumer can choose to spend their money on the south side where the World Champions White Sox play or they can choose to spend their money on the north side where they have not won a World Series since 1918. The Cubs or "loveable losers," have less seats, no parking structure, and higher ticket prices. Yet, they have differentiated themselves in a city of nearly 3 million by selling the folklore and atmosphere of Wrigley Field the second oldest remaining baseball stadium, and surrounding neighborhoods.

To position and differentiate a sport product or service from others in the marketplace, sport organizations create branding strategies, implement licensing programs, and develop intellectual properties.

Branding

A brand is a name, term, design, symbol, or feature that identifies one sport product or services as being different from another. A brand can identify a single sport product or service (Celtics) or a group of sport products or services (Nike). Branding is what the consumer thinks of, positively or negatively, when they see or hear the name of a sport organization or business. By defining the brand, a foundation is created for all other components of the sport organization to build on. The Internet has allowed brand definition to serve as the measuring stick in evaluating the demands of customers by communicating directly with the consumer and pushing aside the middle man.

Sport organizations can begin to develop their brand or identity by answering some very simple questions:

- What products and/or services do you offer?
- What are the core values of your company, products and services?
- What is the mission of your company?
- Who is your target market?
- What is the essence of your company and what message do you think it sends to consumers?

By using the information gathered in sports marketing plan, a sport marketing professional can create a personality or essence for a sport organization that can exudes anything including innovation, creativity, energy, and sophistication. This can then be used to build a relationship with the chosen target market that the research has defined. The way in which the targeted sport consumers react to the personality or essence of the sport organization or its products and services will determine if the brand will be successful. Examples of this include footwear makers Nike and Timberland. Nike revamped its website so that the consumer could personalize his or her shoe in real-time on-screen, allowing customers to alter and/or approve the shoe design before confirming and purchasing the item. Timberland's website encourages each consumer to "build a boot as original as you are." Starting with a work boot silhouette, the consumer can select from a variety of colors and styles to create personalized footwear. This customization builds brand loyalty in today's marketplace.

Licensing

Licensing is a low-risk form of strategic alliance which involves the sale of a right to use certain proprietary knowledge (so-called intellectual property) in a defined way. The licensee usually makes a lump sum (front end) payment. Additionally, there is normally a royalty rate which tends to be around 5%, depending on the type of industry and rate of technological change. A minimum performance (payment) clause is considered essential and some firms allow the licensee a "period of grace" to get production and marketing started. There are also some companies that agree on a cross-licensing deal, whereby they just swap licenses instead of paying. Examples of this are regularly seen in NASCAR. The first was done in 1998 when the Action/DC Comic-designed Batman-themed car became the first motorsports cross-licensing merchandising program.

Licensing is often used where there is a barrier to trade or constraints on and risk in foreign investment. Licensing can open doors for a company to enter a foreign market where it otherwise might have been forbidden. On the other hand, problems with licensing include the potential for creating competitors. For this reason, licensing is often seen as a last-resort strategic alliance when other options are not available.

The Economic Espionage Act of 1996 (the EEA) for the first time makes trade secret theft a federal crime, subject to penalties including fines, forfeiture, and imprisonment, and greatly expands the federal government's power to investigate economic espionage cases. Trade secret theft is broadly defined to cover all acts of such as licensing, marks, patents, and intellectual property. The EEA was intended to fill gaps in the federal law and to create a national scheme to protect US proprietary business information.

Intellectual Properties

Intellectual property status is a protection that is granted by law to an individual or business providing it with the exclusive rights to something it has created. For sport products and services, the most common intellectual properties are patents, copyrights, trademarks, service marks, and collective marks.

Patent

Issued by the United States Patent and Trademark Office, patent grant property rights to an inventor for a particular invention. The term of a new patent is 20 years from the date on which the application for the patent was filed in the United States or, in special cases, from the date an earlier related application was filed, subject to the payment of maintenance fees. United States patent grants are effective only within the United States, United States territories, and United States possessions.

The right conferred by the patent grant is, in the language of the statute and of the grant itself, "the right to exclude others from making, using, offering for sale, or selling" the invention into the United States or "importing" the invention into the United States. What is granted is not the right to make, use, offer for sale, sell, or import, but the right to exclude others from making, using, offering for sale, selling, or importing the invention.

Copyright

According to the United State Copyright Office, a copyright is a form of protection provided by the laws of the United States (Title 17, US Code) to the authors of "original works of authorship," including literary, dramatic, musical, artistic, and certain other intellectual works. This protection is available to both published and unpublished works. Section 106 of the 1976 Copyright Act generally gives the owner of copyright the exclusive right to do and to authorize others to do the following:

- To reproduce the work in copies or phonorecords.
- To prepare derivative works based on the work.
- To distribute copies or phonorecords of the work to the public by sale or other transfer of ownership, or by rental, lease, or lending.
- To perform the work publicly, in the case of literary, musical, dramatic, and choreographic works, pantomimes, and motion pictures and other audiovisual works.
- To display the copyrighted work publicly, in the case of literary, musical, dramatic, and choreographic works, pantomimes, and pictorial, graphic, or sculptural works, including the individual images of a motion picture or other audiovisual work.
- In the case of sound recordings, to perform the work publicly by means of a digital audio transmission.

An example of a copyright can be seen in the broadcasting of most professional sporting events. A disclaimer is read during the broadcast protecting the sport organizations from illegal use of their copyright. For example, the Major League Baseball statement is as follows: "Any rebroadcast or retransmission of this telecast without the expressed written consent of Major League Baseball is strictly prohibited." If companies allowed their product to be used or duplicated at the discretion of the competition, those companies would lose market share. Without copyright laws, no company would spend the money to research and develop new products knowing that it would be duplicated immediately.

Trademark

According to the United States Patent and Trademark Office, a trademark is a word, name, symbol, or device which is used in trade with goods to indicate the source of the goods and to distinguish them from the goods of others. A service mark is the same as a trademark except that it identifies and distinguishes the source of a service rather than a product. A collective mark is used by members of a cooperative, association, or group.

The terms "trademark" and "mark" are commonly used to refer to trademarks, service marks, and collective marks. Rights to marks may be used to prevent others from using a confusingly similar mark, but not to prevent others from making the same goods or from selling the same products or services under a clearly different mark.

CONCLUSION

A sport product is something that is produced which is bought or sold in the sporting goods industry. Tangible products are referred to as goods, while intangible products are called services. Intangible products include indirect

EXAMPLES OF MARKS USED BY SPORT ORGANIZATIONS	
Trademark	
Service Mark	
Collective Mark	

goods, in which the customer has the opportunity to stylize tangible products as they wish. Intangible services involve providing a quality standard work, and are often provided to enhance the experience.

Sport product and service management focuses on the approach taken by sport marketers and organizations to define and market their products and services. Sport product and service management usually starts as a function of the sport marketing planning process. This process involves the development of the sport organization's products and services marketing strategies, including the tactics and programs to be implemented during the lifespan of the plan. It starts by defining the competitive set, which is the process of determining the direct competitors to a sport organization in the specific product or service area. Then the sport organization engages in category attractiveness analysis, in which aggregate marketing factors, segment factors, and environmental factors are considered. This is followed up with competitor and consumer analyses.

The sport product and service life cycle encompass six stages: internal development, introduction to market, growth, maturity, saturation, and decline. All stages are bound by the realities of competition, saturation, and change. The internal development stage begins with the idea of a new product or service or a new twist on an existing product or service. Introduction to market is the time when the sport organization puts its plan into action and start capturing market share by introducing products and services to the market. The growth stage is when the organization with the best product, price, and/or service rises to the top and separates itself from the competition. Maturity refers to the time at which the sport product or service has maximized profits and is seeking to maintain a stable place in the market. At the saturation point, the sport organization comes to the realization that it needs to reevaluate the sport product or service life cycle because they are no longer increasing their market share. The decline stage is the last stage before obsolescence, and either the sport organization should have introduced new services or a next generation of the product, or they need to exit the market.

Positioning and differentiation are integral processes in the ultimate success or failure of marketing the sport product or service. Positioning is the process of influencing the perceptions of potential and current customers about the image of the company and its products and services. Differentiation is creating or offering a like product or service with the intent to influence demand. To position and differentiate a sport product or service from others in the marketplace, sport organizations create branding strategies, implement licensing programs, and develop intellectual properties.

FROM THEORY TO PRACTICE

Tracy West, President

Hayson Sports Group, Inc.
Concord, Massachusetts

My undergraduate degree is in Finance and Economics and I have a M.B.A. in Marketing from Michigan State. Upon graduation in 1988, I held several positions in Marketing Research, Product Management and Forecasting and Research at a major insurance company and a major office furniture manufacturer.

My family instilled in me a strong sense of community and "giving back." While working at my "corporate" jobs, I became involved in the Grand Rapids Jaycees in Michigan volunteering for several community projects. One of those projects was the SENIOR PGA TOUR professional golf tournament which the Jaycees owned and operated. I had the privilege of volunteering for that tournament for 3 years in various corporate hospitality and media functions. The group of Jaycees that managed the event was a small, tight-knit group of friends. Each of those individuals had a successful career and was busy "climbing the corporate ladder," but also made the commitment to volunteer many hours per week in management of the tournament. The experience we each gained from doing so was invaluable. We were all fairly young but here we were running a multi-million dollar professional sporting event on our "off-time." The challenges we faced directly correlated into wonderful learning experiences which then had a direct impact on our careers moving forward. Many of us enjoyed managing the tournament more than our current jobs because by operating the tournament as a group, we were exposed to all facets of business management much quicker than in the limitations of a one-dimensional position in a large corporation.

Being talented does not always lead you to your perfect career in life ... many times it is all about timing. While working at the 1991 tournament in Grand Rapids, I had the great fortune of meeting the current Tournament

Director for a new SENIOR PGA TOUR event in Minneapolis. He was at our tournament reviewing the good things we did at that event and searching for an Assistant Tournament Director to help him begin the tournament in Minneapolis. Knowing he was coming to our tournament, I sent him my resume prior to his trip. We literally spent about 15 minutes together interviewing during event week in between all the normal event chaos. The following Monday morning he made me an offer to come to Minneapolis, which I promptly accepted. I knew that I was leaving a more financially rewarding and comfortable position at my Fortune 500 Company, but many times in life you need to take a step back financially to make a hopeful leap forward. In addition, to me it is more important to spend your life doing something that you enjoy ... you will hopefully never then think of yourself at a "job" but at a career. Also, by accepting the position in Minneapolis, I knew that I would be raising money for charity. What a better way to go through life!

The first tournament in Minneapolis was an operational and financial success. The SENIOR PGA TOUR staff was thrilled with our team's performance. Over a drink in the Rules Office on Sunday night after the tournament was over, one of the Rules Official remarked that he wished our team managed more of the events on the Tour. A light bulb went off and the Tournament Director and I, along with a few other partners, formed our first company, Pro Links Sports, within the next 2 months. A month after that, we landed the management contract for the 1996 US Senior Open. We went on to become the most successful management company on the SENIOR PGA TOUR (now PGA TOUR's Champions Tour) operating, at various times, eight Champions Tour events and three US Senior Opens. One of those tournaments was the Champions Tour event in Boston, which I specifically became Tournament Director in 1999.

In 2004, I formed my own professional golf and events management company, Hayson Sports Group, and continue to operate the Boston event while pursuing other professional golf management opportunities.

There are obviously a multitude of important skills necessary for success in the sport marketing and management field and in operating a professional sporting competition. However, the first and foremost thing to remember is that a professional sport is truly just a standard business. Just because it is a professional sport does not mean that you do not need to remember all your basic business skills and apply them appropriately to your unique setting. The other important item of note is not to have the fantasy that professional sport is always glamorous. The majority of people that work in this industry work long, hard hours in behind-the-scenes operations, and rarely have any direct contact with professional athletes.

A professional golf tournament is more unique than most other professional sports in the lack of control you really have over your final product. You have to recruit your product (the players) as they are independent

Continued

contractors, not part of a team. You have to recruit and retrain your "staff" each year (the volunteers). Your customers range from $20 (standard ticket holder) to multi-million dollars (Title Sponsors). You do not have a stadium in which to host your sport … you must rebuild your "arena" each year (bleachers, hospitality tents, restrooms, concessions, etc.) and your business is dramatically impacted by Mother Nature. All combined, it can be quite daunting to host a professional golf tournament.

The first message I would send to future sport marketing professional is to realize that ethical issues arise in professional sports management just as they do in all other industries. Buyers have the opportunity to take kick-backs. Accountants have the opportunity to cook the books. The key to remember is that, in the end, all you have is your good name and your word. These should be protected no matter what industry in which you work.

The second message is related to the importance of positioning and differentiation in the marketplace. One of the most important things you can do to have your business succeed is to be sure you have a tangible way to differentiate your product from that of your competitors. The Champions Tour is the most fan-friendly, interactive professional sport. Each Champions Tour event strives to provide opportunities for fans to interact with the pro golfers via clinics, autograph sessions, player panel discussions, and walking inside the ropes with pro groups. However, it is not only important to have these distinctions with your product; you must communicate them to your potential customers. At the Champions Tour event which we manage, this communication is a constant focus of our staff with our work through multiple media channels, our volunteers, and our corporate partners. We view our existing volunteers, fan, and corporate partners as our best spokespersons in the marketplace and work diligently with those groups to spread the good word about our tournament.

SALES MANAGEMENT IN SPORT

CHAPTER OUTLINE

CHAPTER OBJECTIVES

The reader will be able to:

- Understand the characteristics of sport sales, and the relationship between sport sales and sport marketing in sport.

- Appreciate the complexity of the sport organization, including design, management, and human capital.
- Recognize the stages of the buying and selling processes.
- Understand the steps involved with managing a sport sales force, and the complexity involved with training, determining sales territories, forecasting sales, budgeting and setting quotas, and motivating, leading, evaluating, and compensating the sales force within ethical and legal boundaries.
- Comprehend the distinctiveness of sport sales as related to advertising, naming rights, sponsorships, and ticket sales.

WHAT IS SPORT SALES MANAGEMENT?

Sport sales management is the process of directing and controlling those responsible for selling sport products and services (sales force), and achieving the desired level of exchanges between the sport organization and sport consumers. Integral to sport sales management is the ability to understanding multiple levels of the sales environment including the role of salespeople, the tasks of sales managers, and the complexity of the design, management, and human capital within the sport organization.

Sales involved the multiple stages of the buying process and the selling process. Sales management involves directing and controlling the sales force, including sales training, determining sales territories, forecasting sales, budgeting and setting quotas, and motivating, leading, evaluating, and compensating the sales force within ethical and legal boundaries. In sport sales management, there are distinctive inventories that are sold including advertising, naming rights, sponsorships, and ticket sales.

The relationship between sales management and sport marketing is significant in a number of ways. Within the sport marketing decision making process, the development of goals and objectives often center on sales processes. When targeting sport consumers, one of the components of the marketing mix to be considered is price – the price a sport product or service is to be sold for. By offering the desired sport product or service at the appropriate price through proper channels of distribution, and implementing promotional efforts that create positive image and increase awareness, the exchange process of sales will be enhanced and the likelihood of a customer going to a competitor to make a purchase diminished.

THE SPORT SALES ORGANIZATION

The sport sales organization is made up of three components. Organizational design in sport sales focuses on how the buying and selling process is implemented. The key in organizational design is to create a buying and selling process that take into consideration sport products and services available for sales, the most effective exchange process to entice the sport consumer to make a purchase, the most efficient methods for delivering the sport product or service to the sport consumer based on geographic location (local, regional, national, international, and global), and the integrate functional processes within the sport organization that allow for maximizing sales. These functional processes focus on the other two components of the sport sales organization – sales managers and salespersons.

Sales Managers

A sales manager is responsible for many functions within the sales organization. From a financial and economic standpoint, the sales manager develops sales plans and budgets, creates objectives and quotas, estimates demands, and develops sales forecasts. Managerially, the sales manager determines the number of salespersons needed, and then recruits, hires, trains, leads, and evaluates the sales force. The sales manger is also responsible for developing and administering compensation models, incentive programs, and bonus packages.

This interrelationship of planning, organizing, guiding, monitoring, administering, and staffing is integral to the sales manager's ability to effectively direct the day-to-day operations of the exchange function within a sport organization. The sales manager must have a broad view of the entire organization, and understand how each function directly affects sales. This is especially true with the sport marketing function, since it directly related to the communication process between the sport organization and sport consumers.

To accomplish this, the sport sales manager must develop a sales force that meets the goals and objectives of the sport organization. Since many goals are driven by profit, and sales are the primary revenue function of a sport organization, the effectiveness of the sales manager is of further importance. In addition, the increased revenue and success of the sales function is integral to moving the sport organization forward toward reaching the vision most sport organizations have – growth and maturity.

There are a number of skills and attributes that a sport sales manager must have to be successful. As with most positions within a sport organization, the ability to effectively communicate with all functional areas is crucial to success. If the sales force does not understand the goals and objectives of the sport organization, or does not know the sport product or service being sold, then the downward communication process from manager to employee is not working. Additionally, if the sales manager does not communicate with the other functions within the sport organization, or does not work with upper management to recognize what is important to the sport organization, the upward communication process is failing.

The best sales managers are also leaders of the organization. They influence the sales force to complete objectives, accomplish goals, and exceed expectations. Some of the attributes of a quality sales manager include being flexible as a result of the ever-changing sales environment, and remaining persistent and resilient to roadblock in the sales process. The sales manager also needs to show empathy toward the sales force and sport consumers in understanding problems, needs, desires, and wants. This will result in happier staff and customers. Finally, the sales manager must show integrity and honesty, both important in developing trust amongst all within the sales process.

Sport marketing is involved with the internal and external environments of a sport organization. Invariably, the sales function must also deal with both environments. The role of the sport sales manager is to be the intermediary between the two environments. Internally, the sport sales manager has to have a grasp on the organizational behavior present within the cultural, political, and social structures of the sport organization. The sport sales manager must also be able to scan and understand the multifaceted and complex external environment, including the competitive climate, political and legal influences, economic and sociodemographic situations, technological advances, and sport consumer behavior.

The sales manager serves as an integral part of sales system. They decipher the marketing strategies set by sport marketing professionals and organizational management based on the available marketing mix. The sales manager then translates those strategies in terms the sales force can utilize in making sales. The sales manager also directs and controls the sales force to maintain necessary levels of sales volume and mix. Ultimately, the sales manager is responsible for the financial performance of the sport organization, including maintaining positive levels of growth, market share, and net profits.

Salespersons

The goal of any sport sales manager is to recruit, train, and hire the most competent sales staff possible. But what makes a good salesperson? Intelligent and knowledgeable? Flexible, yet persistent? Self-motivated, disciplined, and dependable? Creative? Personable? It is all of these qualities and much more that make up a quality salesperson.

There have been many studies completed to determine the most predominant skills that successful salespersons have. In general, the skills are centered on five skills sets: communication, logic/critical thinking, organization, time management, and knowledge. Communication skills are the set of abilities that allows an individual to convey information that can be received and understood by another individual. This is crucial for a sport salesperson because the way they communicate can make the difference between making and sale (success) or not (failure). The first minute of an encounter between a salesperson and a potential customer is critical. The tone of voice, body signals, eye contact, and positive attitude are all vital to beginning the sales process. After that, being able to provide information in a concise yet complete manner educates the potential buyer of the attributes of the sport product or service. Finally, knowing when to stop talking, listen to the potential customer, answer questions, and eventually make the pitch to close the sale comes with experience and learning how to read the customer.

Analytical skills involve logical and critical thinking to understand the needs, wants, and desires of the sport consumer. Knowing the problem or issue at hand is only half of the process; knowing how to resolve the problem and answer the questions provides the sport consumer with the information they need to make an informed decision about purchasing the sport product or service.

Organizational skills apply to planning and managing the sport product and service information in an efficient and effective manner. Sport salesperson often deal with multiple sport products and services. For example, ticket inventory can range from individual game tickets to group tickets, to partial plans to season tickets, and vary in costs based on quantity or location. The sport salesperson must have the ability to keep this information organized by keeping it in an easy and useable format so they can service the customer quickly and accurately.

Time management skills refer to the ability control time. In general, the salesperson spends a limited amount of time with a customer. The way in which that time is used is crucial to the decision making process of the buyer. Earlier in the book we discussed the Pareto Principle, or the 80/20 rule, where 80% of a sport organization's business comes from 20% of its customers. Salespersons learn to spend more time with individuals to maintain the relationships, however they cannot forget about the other 80%, as they represent future potential sales.

Knowledge skills are the collection of gathering, organizing, and sharing information. The knowledgeable salesperson will be able to answer most of the questions of potential and existing sport customers. This knowledge includes knowing the sport product and service being sold, understanding the sport consumer, and having an intimate awareness of the industry, the competition, and the company itself.

Managing the Sport Sales Force

The managing of a sales force for a sport organization is an elaborate process that starts with the recruitment, selection, and training of salespersons. When training the salesperson, it is important that they have a significant knowledge about the company, their customers and products, the industry the company operates in, and the competition present. In addition, training should focus on selling skills. New salespersons may have a range of selling skills – from none at all to expertise from previous employment. Regardless, the sales manager is responsible for ensuring that the salesperson has the selling skills required for the individual organization. These skills are most often taught through on-the-job training and job shadowing. Some organizations will also utilize classroom training, role playing, case studies, and experiential exercises to articulate the desired selling skills to salespersons.

When working with salespersons, it is important that the sales manager communicates a clear purpose for the selling methods utilized, and motivates them to succeed. Practice and repetition are the most important methods for improvement, and reinforcement provided by the sales manager helps keep the salesperson on task. The sales manager may also use incentives to entice salespersons to reach predetermined levels of productivity. However, it is important to remember that those sales goals need to be realistic, as setting the bar too high is a recipe for disaster and failure.

As stated earlier, the sport manager is a crucial part of the evolution of the sales force by developing sales territories, forecasting the potential to sell sport products or services, and creating the resulting budgets and quota parameters for salespersons to work within. Throughout this process, the sales manager motivates and leads the sales force, and designs appropriate compensation programs based on their evaluation of salespersons.

Sales territories could be as small as a specific department within a retail operation, or a large as a section of the country or world. The main advantages for dividing the sales operation into territories are to focus marketing efforts, delineate the responsibilities of individual salespersons, and develop stronger tied with the customers. In turn, this helps the sport organization to minimize selling costs, increase market coverage, coordinate sales with other marketing functions more effectively, and most importantly improve the efficiency of the sales force as a result of their focus.

One of the most challenging jobs for the sport sales manager is forecasting. The prediction of how sport consumers will make purchases in the future (either tomorrow, next week, next month, or next year) is a function of a number of environmental factors. Obviously, changes in the level of competition within the target market will create change (either positive or negative) in sales opportunities (less competition = potential for increased sales; more competition = potential for a decrease in sales). The changes in the marketplace, both in consumer and industrial demand, will have a direct effect on sales. An increased demand has the potential to increase sales, while a decrease demand will probably result in a decrease in sales. In addition, there are leading business indicators published by the government and independent firms that state current market conditions, and estimate the future potential of that market. Examples of these business indicators used in sport business include reports published by the National Sporting Goods Association (www.nsga.org) and the Sport Business Research Network (www.sbrnet.com).

Planning, coordinating, and controlling the sales budget is also an important factor in managing a sales force. By estimating the costs of selling sport products and services, integrating that information with other important functions within the sport organization, and setting benchmarks that are achievable and cost effective; the sales force can maximize their efforts. These benchmarks are often reported to the sales force in terms of quotas. A quota is a number or percentage that constitutes an upper limit (such as maximum inventory available), or in most cases for sales, a targeted minimum. The sales quota is utilized to provide goals for salespersons, maintain control of sales activity and expenses, serve as an incentive for improved compensation for salespersons, and can also be utilized to evaluate the performance of salespersons. Sport sales quotas take many forms including sales volume, dollar vs. unit sales, financial, and activity quotas. Sales volume refers to the amount of inventory sold. Dollars vs. unit sales deals with how much money has been brought in compared to the number of unit of inventory that has gone out. This is often used in ticket sales where there is an inventory of seats in an arena, but have different prices based on location, type of purchase (individual vs. season), and quantity (group discounts). Financial quotas require reaching certain dollar levels of sales. Activity quotas require reaching certain volumes of sales such as minimum numbers of sales calls, services calls, advertisement sales, or new accounts established.

Regardless of the quota, it is important that the sales manager sets realistic quotas that salespersons can reach, and that the quotas are understood by all salespersons. If there is confusion, or if the quotas are perceived to be unachievable, the sales force will be resigned to failure.

This is where motivation and leadership become a crucial component of managing a sales force. Motivation is the influence that initiates the drive to satisfy wants and needs. Motivating a sales force involves inspiring individual salespersons to move to action. Motivation can be intangible (praise, recognition) or tangible (bonus, salary raises). Leadership is the ability to influence a follower. The sales manager serves an important role influencing salespersons to reach the specified goals. According to Sam Walton (Wal-Mart), "Outstanding leaders go out of their way to boost the self-esteem of their personnel. If people believe in themselves, it is amazing what they can accomplish."

In the American culture, compensation is the single most important motivator for salespersons. Financial compensation in sales can be salary based, commission based, or a combination of the two. Other types of compensation can be additional benefits including medical, dental, sick and vacation time, and retirement accounts. The sales manager has the most control over the financial compensation of the sales force. While it is the goal of the salesperson to reach quotas and secure incentives, it is the job of the sales manager to motivate, lead, and evaluate the salesperson. The evaluation process usually includes such factors as quantity of sales, relationship with customers and colleagues within the company, and the sales skills possessed and utilized by the salesperson. The better the salesperson, the more salary, commission, and other incentives they will receive. In a way, sales are very much like sports in general – competition and cooperation. While the entire sales force is cooperating to sell on behalf of the sport organization to improve their place in the market, they are competing against each other and toward the quotas set to make additional compensation, gain recognition as a top salesperson, and in some cases retain their jobs.

THE SPORT BUYING PROCESS

The roles of the sales manager, the salesperson, and their cooperation in operating as a sales force are vital to the sport buying and selling processes. Many sport sales managers focus solely on the selling process without consideration for the buying process. However, sport marketing professionals understand that in order to be successful in sales, one must understand how consumers buy their products. The sport buying process is the steps involved in making a decision to make a purchase – including identifying the need, searching for products or services that satisfied that need, evaluating options, making a decision, purchasing the product or service, and eventually reevaluating the decision to determine whether to make the same purchase again or to change:

Identify → Search → Evaluate → Decide → Purchase → Reevaluate

The way sport consumers make decisions was discussed in detail in Chapter 5 about sport consumer behavior. It is important to realize that the way in which the sport consumer makes a decision about a sport product or service will directly affect the way in which a sale is managed. For those decisions and needs that are simple in nature, all that needs to be accomplished by the salesperson is to make the sport consumer more aware of the sport product or service; build their confidence that the decision they are about to make is correct; supplement that with information that differentiate the sport product or service from others, and provides value to the sport consumer; and guide them through the purchase. For more complex decisions, the salesperson is increasing awareness, building relationships, educating the sport consumer, differentiating the product or service, resolving conflicts for the sport consumer, and customize the purchasing process to make it as easy as possible (and impossible for the potential sport consumer to refuse!!!).

To understand the type of decision that is being made by the sport consumer, the salesperson must recognize the four main types of customers. The first is the perfect sport customer who already knows the sport product or services they wish to purchase – right down to the features, brands, colors, and even model number. The job of the salesperson is to get that sport product or provide the sport service as quickly as possible because if it takes too long, the customer will move on to a competitor. Next is the sport shopper. They know that they need something, but are still in the process of narrowing their choices. The salesperson needs to provide important information about the sport product or service, articulate the benefits, and persuade them that this purchase is the logical choice. The sport browser is just looking around as the sport products and services available with no plan to purchase. However, these individuals tends to be impulse buyers – willing to make a purchase if they find something that interests them or are persuaded that they need the sport product or service. The salesperson needs to be more conversational and engaging, seeking to determine the interests of the customer, and finding those sport products and services that match the interest with the hopes of enticing that impulse purchase. The sport non-customer is lost or not interested in the sport products or services being offered. The salesperson needs to make an effort to engage this customer to determine if there is a possibility to convert them into a buyer. If not, the salesperson needs to move on to potential buyers. In understanding the customers, the salesperson gets a view of the world from the buyer's point of view. Through this understanding, the sport salesperson can learn how to address that point of view within the selling process.

THE SPORT SALES PROCESS

The sport sales process focuses on taking the sport products and services available for sale, and developing the best methods for luring the sport consumer to make a purchase. Sport sales is a six-step process that includes prospecting for customers, developing the method for communicating with the sport consumer, making actual contact, sending the message through a "sales presentation," closing the sale, and servicing after the sale is complete.

Prospecting for Customers

Prospecting is the process of identifying potential customers to purchase products and services. Probably the most difficult job for a salesperson is to find new customers. This is because it does not matter how well a salesperson knows their product or service, if they do not have a qualified prospect to sell it to, there is no sale. Prospecting involves two main components – identifying the needs and wants of potential customers, and determining those individuals who make the actual buying decisions. The second component is often more difficult as a result of individuals being in different life stages. Teenagers often influence and ultimately force the buying decisions of their parents, while in other family units the type of product or service will directly affect who makes the buying decision.

Prospecting requires practice. Those salespersons that prospect on a daily basis will get more leads. A good sports salesperson puts aside time every day to prospect via phone, email, and in-person. Part of that practice is to be prepared. This will include having a script and reviewing that information so it becomes second nature. Potential customers do not wish to hear a robot – speaking monotone and delivering what is exactly on the paper. Potential customers also do not want to hear a person who is unprepared and fumbling their message. A quality script that is practiced and delivered clearly will result in the ability of the salesperson to engage and gather information from the potential customer. It is also important to remember that the salesperson should also be organized and take good mental or written notes once they engage a potential customer. By showing more intimate knowledge of the sport consumer's needs, the salesperson will have a better chance of enticing them into a purchase.

Determining Communication Method

Once the customers have been identified, the salesperson must choose the type of communication method to use in order to build relationships with customers. Communication can be both verbal and non-verbal. Verbally, it can be part of asking open-ended questions, or part of stating a message about a sport product or service and seeking a response from the potential customer. Non-verbally, it can be the listening process, absorbing the feedback from customers and using that information to develop more effective plans for selling the sport product or service.

It is important that when communicating with a potential customer, the salesperson must recognize that purchases are made for emotional reasons as related to the benefits perceived or received by the customer. Therefore, it is conceivable that regardless of the sport products and services being sold, the manner in which salespersons sell themselves and the emotional reaction from the customer in relation to the salesperson is crucial in the communication process of sport sales management.

Therefore, a salesperson must be able to recognize the emotional needs of the sport consumer through this initial communication process. These emotional needs run the gambit, including saving money, saving time, increasing enjoyment, increasing social opportunities, satisfying a desire, or showing ones individualism and uniqueness. Through this filtering process, the salesperson must determine the emotional need that has to be addressed, and direct the consumer toward products and services that will meet the need.

Making Contact and the Pitch

Once the communication methods are understood, it is time to actually contact the potential customer. Prior to that contact, the salesperson should be establishing sales objectives that provide measurable, quantifiable, and understandable information to the potential customer. In conjunction with their prospecting efforts, the salesperson develops objectives that will offer the greatest benefit to the potential customer. The actual engagement of a potential customer centers on three main concepts – professionalism, goodwill, and confidence. The result of understanding and effectively utilizing tactics that enhance these three concepts are crucial to increasing the probability of a sale.

Once a plan for the initial contact with a sport consumer is completed, it is time to make the pitch. A sales pitch is where the salesperson outlines and explains the benefits of a product or service to a potential customer in order to stimulate interest and motivate them to make a purchase. There are numerous different approaches a salesperson can take when pitching a sale to a potential or returning customer. Here are some approaches used to entice an individual to purchase season tickets:

Approach	Example
Benefits	As a season ticket holder, you will also be eligible to attend special season ticket holder only events such as after game parties, team meet-and-greet sessions, and a preseason kickoff dinner.
Compliment	Let me tell you why a person of your stature in the community will benefit from being a season ticket holder …
Introductory	Hi, I am Bob Smith from the Merrimack Marauders football team here for my 3 p.m. appointment to discuss a potential partnership between our organizations.
Product/service	Let me give you a tour of the arena and show you exactly where you would be sitting if you were to purchase these season tickets.
Question	What are the benefits you feel are important in association with purchasing season tickets with our organization?
Reference	Your friend John Smith has season tickets; we can sit you right next to him.
Sample	Be our guest at today's game so you can experience the excitement.

The method of delivery of the pitch may differ – from email to phone to mail to television or in person. The focus of the pitch may also vary based on the type of sport product or service being sold, the knowledge of the consumer, the benefits being offered, and the sales objectives of the organization. However, the attitude when approaching the sport consumer must be the same regardless. There is an expression "you never get a second chance to make a first impression." This is especially true in sales management. A salesperson meeting a customer in person should be appropriately dressed, be neat and well-groomed, have an appearance of confidents without being cocky, and maintain eye contact. Those who communicate a sales pitch via telephone should speak clearly, use appropriate language that can be easily understood, and show confidence through practicing the pitch and delivering it in a conversational style. A sales pitch offered through email, mail, or other written means should be grammatically correct, without spelling errors, be concise, present pertinent information, and provide contact information so the potential customer can contact the organization for more information.

Closing the Sale

Once salespersons have made their pitch, their focus shifts to closing the sale. There are a number of factors that must be considered during this phase of the sales process. The potential customer will probably have questions and comments regarding the pitch and the product/service. The salesperson must learn to listen and read the individual, and often try to put their self in the shoes of the customer. Since most salespersons have high sales goals, they should learn not to accept the first "no" from the customer. Try to clarify points from the sales pitch and provide any additional information that might complete the picture for the customer and entice them to make a purchase. Regardless of the time this process takes or the resulting outcome, the salesperson must always maintain a positive attitude and be professional. Even if there is no sale, there is always the potential that the customer will return if they are not satisfied elsewhere, or if they have a need for another product or service offered by the organization.

As a result of the closing process, there are two main factors: handling objections, and the proper timing for closing the sale. Closing is when the customer has signed on the dotted line, or made a final decision to make the purchase. However, it is not always this straight forward. Another major factor a salesperson must deal with is handling objections. Some objections might include "I do not think this is right for me;" "I cannot afford this;" or "I am not familiar with that brand." The salesperson must not respond to objections too quickly. Providing misinformation, educated guesses, or too much information/too many answers can turn off the potential customer. In addition, the salesperson should not get frustrated by arguing with the customer or displaying a doubt that the sale will never be completed. Patience and precise information are the main concepts that can overcome objections to a sale.

When timing the closing of a sale, there are a number of subtle comments that might be made by the prospect that sends a signal to the salesperson that the customer is ready to make a decision one way or another. Some of these signals include the following:

- They make a positive comment such as "I really like this [product or service]!"
- They ask about the price.

- They ask about incentives.
- They physically handle the product, test or try the product, or ask for a pen when reading an order form for a product or service.
- They have a more positive tone than earlier in the conversation.

Servicing After the Sale

Many would argue that servicing after the sale is the most important stage in the selling process.

The concept of servicing involves providing work or a duty to a customer in response to a need or demand. Throughout the sales process, the salesperson is building a relationship and helping the buyer make a purchase decision. Once the purchase is made, the interaction is over unless there is adequate servicing after the sale. The majority of the sales process focuses on an individual sale. The servicing process seeks to persuade a repeat or additional purchase by those who did make a purchase. It also serves retain those who did not make an initial purchase in order to entice them into another purchase. Therefore, regardless of initial success or failure, the salesperson has a responsibility in servicing after the sale.

For those individuals who did make a purchase, there are a number of problems that can occur that are beyond the salespersons control, and could turn a good sales experience into a bad one. Some examples would include: if the price goes down shortly after purchase; the delivery of the product or service is late; for an installation of a product, it is done incorrectly or with damages caused; or frustration because there was insufficient training provided to operate the product. When handling such issues, the salesperson should encourage the customer to provide as much information about the issue as possible. Then, the salesperson often must weed through the information provided to find out what information is fact, and what information is extraneous to the problem. Then, the salesperson should attempt to find a solution to the problem. Solutions to the above mentioned problems could include: a store or company credit in the amount of the difference between the originally paid price and the new price (entices a repeat purchase); give a discount or credit back to the customer as an apology for the late delivery; pay for damage repairs and offer a discount on their next purchase; or provide the training they need on the sales floor.

The goal of servicing after the sale, and in fact throughout the sales process, is centered on overall customer service. Customer service is the behaviors exhibited by salespersons during their interaction with customers, including the general assistance provided before and after the sale. Salespersons that offer the best customer service do so because they:

- Know their products and services and can answer any question posed by the customer.
- Know their customers so that service can be customized based on their needs and wants.
- Have a commitment to offering quality service by creating a positive experience for the customer, under-promising and over-delivering.

- Have a positive attitude and treat people with courtesy and respect.
- Realize that the customer is the most important part of the selling process. Regardless of whether the salesperson feels that the customer is out of line or stretching the truth, they must never argue with the customer, ignore the customer, and assume they are telling the truth.
- Always provide what they promise, or offer compensation if unable to deliver on the promise.
- Work to make the sales process as easy as possible.
- Most importantly focus on building a relationship with the customer, not just making money.

NON-STORE-BASED INVENTORIES FOR SALES IN SPORT

Electronic Sport Sales

The Internet (or World Wide Web) is the fastest growing conduit for connecting consumers to retailers. The purpose of electronic sport retailing is to generate additional sales by expanding the geographic reach from local, regional, national, international, and global. The goal is also to create a presence and enhance the ever-increasing Internet market. This is accomplished by providing information to consumers in a user friendly manner through email and "point and click" links that are easy to follow.

The scope of electronic sales is growing exponentially around the globe, and sport retailing is right in the middle of that trend with the sale of merchandise, tickets, among many sport retail products. People use the Internet to search for information about products they might not otherwise find in the retail outlet. Often while searching for that information, sport consumers are attracted to the selection available. In turn, because of the lower price (which is often discounted on the Internet due to reduced infrastructure needed) and the convenience of ordering from their own home, the average person makes five Internet purchases per year. The major fear in electronic sport sales is an issue of trust and security, especially in the areas of inputting financial data on the Internet and shipping information not always being posted in the website. In general, these problems have been addressed adequately, but there are those who still will not purchase over the Internet because they want to talk to a salesperson and/or see/touch/feel the sport product in their hands.

Direct Sport Marketing

Direct sport marketing is a variety of sport retailing in which the sport consumer is first exposed to a sport product through a non-personal medium such as a catalog, television commercial or infomercial, then orders the sport product by mail, phone, fax, or Internet. As a result of this type of purchase behavior, direct sport marketers must initiate the contact with the sport consumer. Therefore, it is crucial that a comprehensive database be kept to collect relevant information about customers for use in future marketing efforts. The sport products offered through direct sport marketing may be specialized in nature, or may represent the entire gambit of sport product offerings.

Ticket Sales

Ticket sales is not only the most prominent entry level position for individuals entering the field of sport management, but it is the most important function within most professional sport organizations. The reason – it produces a significant percentage of revenue for the organization. Ticket prices are determined by a number of variables including: number of seats, socioeconomics, media revenue, facility demographics, sponsorships, fan base, and opponents to name a few. Offering a wide range of ticket prices and ticket packages will appeal to the greatest number of people.

While selling tickets is not in the spotlight as compared to other functions, the individual wishing to work their way up in sport marketing usually must start in ticket sales. This is because if the sales function is viewed as the most fundamental function of marketing. If an individual can sell the organization, then they understand how to communicate with the customer. As a result, sport organizations will often take individuals who have proven to be good salespersons, and move them into other aspects of sport marketing.

The unfortunate part of ticket sales is that there is often a negative connotation attached to the position. Some of the comments often made about tickets sales include "It is beneath me;" "I do not like rejection;" "Sales is not a prestigious position as compared to marketing, community relations, or media relations;" and "Ticket sales is the worst position in a sport organization." All of these perceptions are untrue. Ticket sales are not beneath anyone; it is a foundation of marketing. Rejection is part of all aspects of marketing – it just has the potential of happening more often because the ticket salesperson deals with a larger number of people. By percentage, it is probably no different that the rejection percentage of a marketing professional trying to sell advertisements, a sponsorship coordinator trying to secure a potential business partner, or even a general manager trying to negotiate with a player. The only reason ticket sales are not viewed as a prestigious position is because it is often done behind the scenes with little external recognition. And as far as it being the worst position within the organization, the truth is that it is one of the most important from a revenue standpoint.

The other important aspect of ticket sales is the diverse inventory available for sale. While the salesperson often has a cap on how many seats are available for sale (there are only so many in the facility), the inventory is made up of a number of categories. The most prevalent ticket inventory is season ticket equivalencies, which make up approximately 50% of tickets sold. These are the combination of season tickets sold and partial season ticket packages. Another 25% of sales come from advanced ticket sales – individuals who purchase tickets before the day of the event. The remaining tickets come from group sales, walk-up sales on the day of the event, and specialty seating. Specialty seating includes club seats with access to the private restaurant (e.g., Premium Club at the TDBankNorth Garden in Boston – premiumclub.dncinc.com), and executive suites and club box luxury seats with catered food service (e.g., FedEx Forum in Memphis – www.fedexforum.com/pages/buy_tickets/premium_seats.aspx).

There are four major strategies utilized in ticket sales management. The most basic is database management, where the ticket salesperson develops an organized collection of demographic, geographic, and other personal data (usually through a computerized program), and uses that information to maximize sales efforts. The sport salesperson uses this information to send direct mail and email, make phone calls, and during personal selling opportunities to generate sales.

Associated with database marketing is a concept called benefit sales. Often times data is collected that shows the reason why an individual does not wish to make a purchase. Benefit selling involves the creation of new opportunities, conditions, or perks that will counteract objections a potential customer may have about a product or service, and offer additional value to the consumer. An example of this is used in mini-ticket plans offered by most professional teams. There are always games that everyone wants to see because the opponent may be a rival or contender, or have a star player many want to see. There are other games where it would be difficult to sell out because of perceived inferior competition. So teams package a collection of "good games" and "bad games" to provide a benefit. So, the Boston Red Sox might package a Tampa Bay Devil Rays or Kansas City Royals game with a New York Yankees or Baltimore Orioles. The fan might not purchase the Devils Rays or Royals game on its own, but the benefit of also being able to go to a Yankees or Orioles game makes it a worthwhile purchase.

Upselling is directly associated with the "escalator concept" discussed earlier in the book. The goal is to move customers from less profitable products or services in a specific category to either a more profitable one in the same category, or into another, more profitable category. One example of movement within a category would be moving a single game ticket holder to a mini-plan of 5, 10, or 20 games, depending on the sport and interest of the customer. An example of moving an individual into another, more profitable category would be a mini-plan ticket holder who has an interest in moving up into a shared corporate box and spending some money in advertising with the team. The key is to create a market, a plan, or atmosphere for everyone from the $8.00 sun burnt bleacher bum to the $500,000.00 air conditioned corporate box. Everyone wants to feel special in some way shape or form.

Aftermarketing is a visionary sales process that encourages salespersons to communicate and service the sport ticket holders after the purchase is completed. Retaining a customer is significantly cheaper, easier, and less time consuming than starting from scratch. This is accomplished by the sport salesperson following consumer utilization and satisfaction periodically through regular communication. By addressing issues quickly, and showing genuine interest in the needs and wants of the consumer throughout their involvement, the likelihood of continued association with the sport organization is greatly increased.

Sport ticket sales is a unique aspect of sport sales management because aspects such as team performance and awareness, weather, problems with facilities, and the economy are beyond the control of the salesperson. However, the number of contacts made, networks created, and relationships built are controllable and will have a direct effect on the level of success of a ticket salesperson. Referrals are crucial to initiating relationships; renewals are equally vital to continued relationships.

Sport ticket sales are a volume business – therefore the more one sells, the more one makes, and the happier sales managers and sport organizations are. It is also a frustrating business that involves a lot of rejection. It is important that the sport ticket salesperson be persistent, send a consistent message to all potential customers, and maximize the opportunities available. It is also important to remember that salespersons who strive to survive on making the "one big sale" might make a lot of money from the sale, but it is only one relationship. Multiple relationships equal success in ticket sales.

ETHICS IN SALES MANAGEMENT

Shady practices may close more deals in the short run; however, relationships with customers and the bottom line of the corporation will suffer in the long run. Because sales representatives typically have personal interactions with clients and potential clients, their actions are more readily visible, and unethical behavior can have a profound effect on the branding of the company. Some would argue that the commission structure of compensation would encourage unethical behavior from sales representatives. Research has not been able to validate this belief. In other words, the sales representatives were no more likely to recommend a particular product when a high commission was associated with that product compared to the same product when a flat fee for sale was offered.

Salespeople tend to be excited over the products that they are selling and may use mild exaggeration in describing the product. The ethical question is how much is too much. Apparently there is a gray line between ethical business practices and unethical business practices. This topic is important because each day salespeople must make ethical decisions that can affect their family, corporate status, and their relationships with the clients, and the bottom line.

There are many variables that can influence one's ethical perspective. For example: personal or family life, job performance pressures, and competitive drive. These internal and external factors are for ever changing and the judgment or lack of judgment today does not guarantee repetition. Many people will allow minor ethical infractions to slide by without giving them a second thought. It is only in the major unethical acts that the salesperson begins to reflect on their own ethical decision making. Given these situational and personal lapses in judgment, it is not surprising that research has been inconclusive in its predictions of salesperson action in ethical and unethical situations.

Ideally, student athletes play sports for a free education and the love of the game.

But somehow that does not jibe with billion-dollar network contracts, celebrity coaches paid $1–2 million and football stadiums packed with fans paying Broadway show ticket prices.

The big money is in the National Collegiate Athletic Association's Division I-A men's football and basketball programs. Those sports make enough money to keep athletic departments solvent and university building projects going. Driving these programs are exceptionally athletic young men, many of them African Americans dreaming of becoming professional athletes.

Allen Sanderson, an economist with the University of Chicago who researches sports, calls the way money is shuffled from high-revenue sports to money-losing sports like tennis and cross-country running a "reverse Robin Hood effect." He notes that athletes in the low-revenue sports are whites from middle- or upper-income families, in contrast to black athletes from more modest backgrounds.

Sanderson calls college athletes "the most exploited workers in the United States economy," and argues that just about everyone in the system benefits more than the players. He believes they should be paid.

Scoffing at the romantic notion of the student-athlete, Sanderson argues that athletes have a job, and it is to produce heroics on the football field or basketball court.

"The colleges don't want them in the library," he says. "The kids don't want to be in the library. What they are there for is to play what amounts to minor-league football and basketball that they hope to turn into professional careers."

That argument strikes at the heart of what some say may be the most valuable lesson that workforce managers can learn from athletics, which is that it should not be about the money.

While investments in athletics are huge in dollar terms, the relationships between coaches and players are built on core values like trust and leadership. Management consultant Roger Herman, who writes about this subject in his book *How to Become an Employer of Choice*, says all companies should try to instill these core values in their workforces if they want to attract and keep top talent.

"Today's employees are not there for the money," Herman says. "They want meaningful work, they want to make a difference, and they want to feel like they belong."

Without those values, he says, coveted employees might walk out the door muttering, "You can't pay me enough to work here."

Herman says athletes represent the college community. Once they get paid, they would lose that role and become hired help.

Continued

SELLING COLLEGE ATHLETICS OR USING STUDENT ATHLETES? – *Continued*

Much of the debate hinges on graduation rates. The NCAA's report card on these rates in 2004 for Division I-A schools, the larger universities that generate the biggest crowds and television ratings, shows that students in general graduate at higher rates than student athletes, 64–62%.

But in men's Division I basketball, 44% of the players graduate. Football has a below-average 57% graduation rate, and for black athletes, the rates are much lower than they are for white athletes in both football and basketball.

Such statistics only bolster Sanderson's argument. He would like changes, but he is not holding his breath. "These kids have no bargaining power whatsoever," he says.

Source: Taken from Shuit, D. P. (2005). America's "Most Exploited Workers". *Workforce Management* 84(8): 35.

Suggested Discussion Topics

1. You are the Director of Marketing for a Division I institution. Your football team has a graduation rate of 50% and your basketball team is below that at 25%. However, the football team just played in the BCS Championship Series the past winter, and the basketball team just completed a run into the Final Four. Marketing the winning teams is the easy part, but marketing for an institution that does not graduate students poses some issues. How do you balance marketing the positive image of the winning athletic programs and the negative image of students not graduating?
2. Do you believe that the marketing and sale of an athletic contest where the college receives a disproportionate amount of money based on the cost of the program is fair? Why or why not?

CONCLUSION

Sales are the backbone of sport organizations. As a result of the increase in competition, the creativity involved in sales management in sport has been considerable. Sport sales management is the process of directing and controlling the sales force to sell sport products and services, resulting in achieving a desired level of exchanges between the sport organization and sport consumers. Sales involved the multiple stages of the buying process and the selling process, including directing and controlling the sales force, including sales training, determining sales territories, forecasting sales, budgeting and setting quotas, and motivating, leading, evaluating, and compensating the sales force within ethical and legal boundaries.

The sport sales organization is made up of three components. Organizational design in sport sales focuses on how the buying and selling process is implemented. The sport buying process is the steps involved in making a decision to make a purchase – including identifying the need, searching for products or services that satisfied that need, evaluating options, making a decision, purchasing the product or service, and eventually reevaluating the decision to determine whether to make the same purchase again or to change. The sport sales process focuses on taking the sport products and services available for sale, and developing the best methods for luring the sport consumer to make a purchase by prospecting for customers, communicating with the sport consumer, making contact and pitching the idea of a sale, closing the sale, and servicing after the sale is complete.

These functional processes focus on the other two components of the sport sales organization – sales managers and salespersons. A sales manager is responsible for many of the financial, economic, and managerial functions within the sales organization. Salespersons are the face of a sport organization, and must demonstrate excellent skills in communications, logic and critical thinking, organization, time management, and knowledge of sport products and services.

In sport, there are certain inventories, including advertising, naming rights, sponsorships, travel, and ticket sales that are unique because they do not adhere to the typical supply and demand model. There are only so many tickets to be sold, advertisement slots to be filled, naming rights to be applied, and sponsorship opportunities to be secured. Advertising inventories have evolved to include television, radio, and the Internet, but still have involvement with traditional print advertising through game programs, media guides, and on game tickets. Naming rights are often limited to that of the game facility, practice facility, or in some cases the team itself. Sponsorships require a lot of research, creativity, and time, as well as a significant financial commitment from the potential sponsor.

Ticket sales are the major revenue stream for a sport organization, and offer a diverse inventory available for sale. This includes season ticket equivalents (season tickets plus partial season ticket plans), advanced ticket sales, group sales, walkups, and specialty seating. The four main strategies utilized in ticket sales management include database management, benefit selling, upselling, and aftermarketing. While there are many factors that are beyond the sport salesperson control, the number of tickets sold is directly related to the number of contacts made, networks created, and relationships built through referrals and renewals.

FROM THEORY TO PRACTICE

Mark Rodrigues – Ticket Sales Representative

Orlando Magic (NBA) Basketball Club
Orlando, Florida

My role and experience in the sport industry has come a long way. I started my career in the sport industry as a sophomore in college in 2003 with the Nashua Pride (minor league baseball organization). My responsibilities with

Continued

the Nashua Pride focused on game day operations. The responsibilities ranged from on-field promotions to managing the game scoreboard. After a season with the organization I realized that I needed some additional experience in marketing and sales.

I then was informed by my advisor of a potential sales and marketing internship with the Manchester Wolves. I quickly applied and had the opportunity to become a sponge and absorb as much information as possible under one of the most intelligent marketing minds in minor league sports, Brady Sadler (see Chapter 2). My responsibilities during the internship with the Wolves ranged from running all of the on-field promotions during the game to some sales in the office during game weeks. During my internship I was able to tone my selling technique and see how marketing was applied and carried out in a professional setting. After the season concluded I was one of the top selling interns within the organization and for that reason I was offered the position as the Ticket Manager with the Wolves.

At that point in my career I was still only a junior in college and already the Ticket Manager for a professional team. Some of my major duties included, establishing the organizations record keeping system, the renewal process, and sales. Sales have played a critical role in why I have been so successful in this industry.

I have been able to be successful and move up in this industry in a short period of time because of my work ethic and my ability to sell. I was able to establish myself as a valuable player within the organization. I established myself as a key member of the Wolves through my sales efforts, which included $120,000+ in sales. I produced all of that revenue while taking six credit courses in college. I also provided a record keeping system that the organization became accustomed to and increased their renewal rate by 30% in 2005. I also came up with successful marketing and ticket campaigns that allowed the organization to establish a solid base for their future.

I then became the Director of Ticket Sales for the organization and I was also one of the key players in establishing the organizations future. My responsibilities included but were not limited to:

- Managing a sales staff of five people.
- Handling all ticket transactions within the organizations.
- Strategically planning out ticket promotions throughout the New Hampshire business area.
- Developing season ticket, group ticket, and premium sales programs.
- Established season, group, and individual ticket goals for organization.
- Responsible for all ticket sales efforts of the organization.
- Responsible for all ticket marketing efforts.

There is no secret on how to become successful in this industry. You must work hard, network, not be afraid to fail, and wait your turn. I have been attempting to break into the NBA, since 2002, when I was a freshman in college. After many unsuccessful attempts I recently was offered a position as a Ticket Sales Representative for the Orlando Magic.

The only reason for me getting this position was simply because of my past experience, my sales success, and my personality. I look forward to the new challenge and since getting this position my goals in life and in my career have changed. Make sure to establish short-, medium-, and long-term goals for yourself.

My advice to you moving forward in your career in the sport industry is to find your passion right away. Ask questions, job shadow, do internships, listen, and work HARD! By finding your passion and interest in a specific aspect of sport sooner than later you can begin building a solid foundation for yourself.

Once you get your foot in the door remember to establish yourself as a key player within the organization. One of the best ways to establish your worth to an organization is through sales.

"If you can sell, you will always have a job." This saying has been around for a while and it is true. Sales however can be more than just a job, it can be a career.

PURCHASING AND SUPPLY CHAIN MANAGEMENT IN SPORT

CHAPTER OUTLINE

CHAPTER OBJECTIVES

The reader will be able to:

- Recognize the characteristics of the numerous logistical functions a sport business must manage in purchasing and supply chain management (SCM).

- Understand the steps in the purchasing process and how those are applied to sport marketing, sourcing, and cost management.
- Identify and appreciate the importance of SCM as an integral function of logistics in sport marketing, including inventory management, team and equipment transportation, warehousing, order processing, and information systems.
- Have an awareness of the future trends in sport marketing logistics, including network design and global logistics, the integration of the various logistical systems, and the affects that integration has on the overall viability of the sport industry.

WHAT ARE LOGISTICS IN SPORT MARKETING?

The concept of "marketing logistics" is taken from a more traditional concept of marketing – identify your customers, identify their needs, and combine the company's resources to meet those needs. The lack of interest in logistics from senior management is over, and the time to become proactive is here. At today's business speed, logistical managers need to be quicker and more effective communicators and marketers.

Marketing logistics focuses upon the ways in which customer service can be used to gain a competitive advantage. It seeks to manage the relationship between the marketing and logistical concepts in order to unify their respective strategies within the context of the wider supply chain. Traditionally, marketing and logistics have been managed separately within most companies. The relationship between marketing and logistics has been poorly understood at best and the strategic importance of customer service was not always recognized. As markets and customers become more time and service sensitive, the importance of managing this convergence increases. If a company were to develop a marketing campaign based on a new synthetic basketball, and the marketing group had idea that there was insufficient stocks or labor strikes, the campaign may be successful, but the consumers would end up wanting a synthetic basketball that was not available.

From an ethical standpoint, company's can reverse this process. They can develop a marketing campaign designed to sell a synthetic basketball to the consumer at a greatly reduced price than that of a leather basketball. Because the company just entered into a new contract with a supplier that wants to offer this basketball at a lower price point than that of other name-brand basketballs, the company can take advantage of the supplier because of their eagerness to compete.

The model shown on next page indicates the three key areas that need to be strategically connected: the consumer franchise, customer value and the supply chain. In order for there to be a symbiotic relationship, all stakeholders must benefit.

An example of this concept would be two teams of industrial engineering students at North Carolina State University designing the logistics for supplying water, ice, soft drinks, snacks, and other materials to all of the sites at the 1999 Special Olympics World Games. This was a monumental task considering the

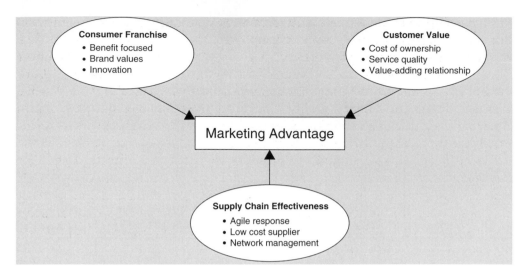

vast amount of supplies (40 truckloads of ice and more than 1 million bottles of water and soft drinks) that had to be distributed to 7000 athletes at more than 150 different sites. The team's challenge was to move hundreds of thousands of pounds of supplies from the central distribution area to strategically placed smaller distribution centers. The team spent hours driving around, measuring distances from the main distribution centers to each small holding center.

The job of the second team was to sort, store, and distribute these supplies to each of the five smaller compounds, which in turn supplied the 150 different sporting venues. A floor plan was designed for each compound to ensure there were adequate refrigeration units and storage bins, a delivery system to each venue, and a system to contain the flow of garbage and recyclables.

By designing this supply chain, the Special Olympics were able to put product into the athlete's hands when they need it most. Because of the design, they were able to replenish their stocks without interruption. All three stakeholders benefited from this venture. The athletes received their drinks when they needed them most. The two engineering team from North Carolina did a great job for themselves and North Carolina State University, and the Special Olympics produced a great event.

PURCHASING

The two general forms of purchasing arrangements are partnership sourcing and competitive sourcing. Partnership sourcing involves the commitment between customers and suppliers to create a long-term relationship based on understood and agreeable objectives that work toward maximizing capability and competitiveness. Competitive sourcing is where suppliers study the nature of the activity, and then determine the best performance for the given activity without input from customers. This performance may include eliminate an activity, modifying a product or service for greater efficiency, or outsourcing to another department, division, or company. Improvement of performance drives this type of sourcing, with competition driving the process.

Partnership sourcing is more preferable because it leads to long-term partnership based on trust between buyer and supplier. Once a level of mutual trust has been established, business partners usually give preferential treatment to its repeat customers in the form of price breaks. Partnership sourcing implies that both the buyer and the supplier have mutual reasons to be successful. Competitive sourcing is every company for themselves. Competitive sourcing in the short term is a more cost effective way to do business. However, this competition does not lend itself to building lasting supply chains.

Purchasing today is not about squeezing suppliers but rather strategic supplier management, which involves measuring supplier performance and risks as well as determining the optimum degree of profit. As logistics costs become an increasingly larger part of total costs, proactive SCM is the most important factor in keeping purchasing cost low. This supply chain is the link between the purchasing process, production, and logistics management.

Purchasing Process

In an era of global sourcing, the multinational company's success often hinges on the most appropriate selection of its foreign suppliers. International suppliers are very complicated and risky because of a variety of uncontrollable and unpredictable factors affecting the decision. These factors may include political situations, tariff barriers, cultural and communication barriers, trade regulations and agreements, currency exchange rates, cultural differences, ethical standards, and quality standards.

Sporting goods companies have been focused on providing the best possible quality for the lowest available price. Price is what the consumer equates to the value of a good or service. Value is what the consumer is willing to pay for a product. Both price and value are influenced by market trends, corporate climate and competition for suppliers. These purchasing objectives have forced companies to seek third world labor forces and partner themselves with long-term suppliers that have similar company values. Because of the high labor cost in the United States, it has been more economical to ship raw materials to the third world, have them produce the good, and then re-ship the finished product to its destination. This purchasing process stretches the supply chain and increases the number of logistical variables.

Purchasing in Sport Marketing

The single biggest cost saving measure to the sporting goods industry has been technology advances in the Internet. Electronic data interchange (EDI) has affected 100% of the supply chains. In only a matter of months, the change in the way supply chain partners move product from concept to point of sale (POS) resembled the difference between walking the basketball up the court and running the fast break.

The Internet continues to tear down communications barriers from geography to cost. This technology will be leveraged through new, web-based communities referred to in today's business world as e-business or as exchanges. The impact in purchasing will be on product cost, inventory, time-to-market, market responsiveness and market share.

With the standardization of sporting goods purchasing, exchanges on the web are popping up at an incredible pace, with leading industry companies, software vendors, venture capitalist, and dot com start-ups moving aggressively to capture early market share. With a 24 hours, 7 days a week venue that is not constrained by geographical location or time zones, the opportunity for cost cutting measures is endless. Computer companies have developed a web-based marketplace where industry-related businesses will conduct commerce. In return for providing this forum, owners may seek a subscription fee or a percentage of the business transactions made through the exchange. While this sounds like an ingenious way to create revenue for exchange owners, its potential value to consumers is even greater.

With the matching of inventory and/or qualified production capacity to demand, opportunities to lower overhead in the supply chain through bidding processes can be exploited. This model can be applied to raw materials and other supply chain services like transportation. Retailers and branded manufacturers will be able to go direct to source, significantly altering or eliminating the role of agents, brokers, and other middlemen in the process. This translates into retailers with a better bottom line and consumers with good-quality sporting goods at a lower price.

Sourcing

Should retailers concentrate most of its stock purchases in one wholesale supplier (single sourcing) or balance its purchases between two or more suppliers (balanced sourcing)? A concentrated purchasing strategy makes the retailer an important customer to its wholesaler, meriting preferential treatment, by ordering a larger volume. However, concentrated sourcing can also increase the retailer's dependence on the wholesaler. Reducing dependence, in turn, entails diversifying purchases, splitting them between at least two wholesalers, which, unfortunately, increases transaction costs and reduces the retailer's importance to either of its suppliers. The tradeoff is further complicated when retailers operate in a small or closed market with few suppliers and high barriers because genuine options are limited. In most cases, retailers tend use balanced sourcing, or to split their purchases more evenly between the two wholesalers as opposed to concentrating most of their purchases in a single wholesaler. Current trends suggest that over the long term retailers would prefer to move away from concentrated sourcing. One of reasons for this preference for balanced sourcing is a desire to avoid over dependence and opportunistic or unethical behavior on the part of wholesalers.

In 2005, quotas on imports of apparel products were eliminated from World Trade Organization (WTO) countries, including the United States. The new accord originates with what is known as the "Uruguay Round" of trade discussions, which were concluded in 1994 in Marrakech, Morocco. In that agreement, a 10-year tenure was established to progressively excise apparel and textile quotas.

Unlike the textile industry, which has systematically lost American-based jobs to overseas competitors, the elimination of quotas on apparel imports is generally viewed positively by sporting goods companies sourcing abroad. The lifting of quota restrictions affords US sporting goods vendors and retailers the ability to source apparel products indiscriminately; significantly cheaper which in turn offers a potential windfall. With the majority of apparel already being sourced offshore, American-based retailers and distributors will now be able to source an entire line, for example, from the country offering the least expensive manufacturing process.

China has emerged as the potential leader in sporting goods suppliers. The unanswered questions are whether China can produce high-quality product at a low price with consistency and on time. With those critical factors, many vendors and retailers sourcing their own branded or private label products are implementing a diversified balanced sourcing strategy. This strategy allows for the most competitive prices with the most reliable delivery.

Cost Management

Cost management considers competitive manufacturing and logistics costs, by optimizing the amount of stored materials, keeping capacities filled, achieving economical purchasing prices, and ensuring efficient transport and storage processes. Short processing times accomplish a high level of service and flexibility even in the case of short-term customer demands.

Web-based exchange technology providing a less constrained and more timely flow of information and fewer middlemen in the supply chain, it is possible to dramatically reduce overall lead times. Time-to-market and market responsiveness will have new lead time benchmarks recorded in days and weeks, eclipsing the current ones measured in months and years. These combined factors will allow for a faster flow of goods at a lower cost with lower supply chain inventories. As this trend continues, companies will have an opportunity to liquidate the slower moving competition.

Two areas with specific applications to the sporting goods supply chain are emerging. The first is the area of inventory liquidation. For example, Tradepac.com provides a place to post merchandise for liquidation, including a category specifically designated for sporting goods and apparel.

Another early exchange player with implications for the sporting goods industry is the transportation services category. An example is Celerix.com. Celerix's exchange goes beyond creating a community for transportation services buyers and sellers to meet. Celerix has also started to provide supply chain visibility through tracking components and alliances with other supply chain exchanges and software providers. Other sporting goods exchanges that provide more comprehensive services, including building and operating e-commerce networks between retailers and manufacturers, are EB2B.com and iCongo.com.

Sporting goods supply chain partners should be actively monitoring this market and swiftly determining how and when to get into the game. As this change to exchanges occurs, old organizational, process and information technology models will require major overhauls.

SUPPLY CHAIN MANAGEMENT

SCM is the combination of art and science that goes into improving the way your company finds the raw components it needs to make a product or service and deliver it to customers. The following are five basic components of SCM:

1. *Plan*: This is the strategic portion of SCM. You need a strategy for managing all the resources that go toward meeting customer demand for your product or service. A big piece of planning is developing a set of metrics to monitor the supply chain so that it is efficient, costs less, and delivers high quality and value to customers.
2. *Sourcing*: Choose the suppliers that will deliver the goods and services you need to create your product. Develop a set of pricing, delivery and payment processes with suppliers and create metrics for monitoring and improving the relationships. And put together processes for managing the inventory of goods and services you receive from suppliers, including receiving shipments, verifying them, transferring them to your manufacturing facilities and authorizing supplier payments.
3. *Production*: This is the manufacturing step. Schedule the activities necessary for production, testing, packaging, and preparation for delivery. As the most metric-intensive portion of the supply chain, measure quality levels, production output and worker productivity.
4. *Logistics*: Coordinate the receipt of orders from customers, develop a network of warehouses, pick carriers to get products to customers, and set up an invoicing system to receive payments.
5. *Returns*: The problem part of the supply chain. Create a network for receiving defective and excess products back from customers and supporting customers who have problems with delivered products.

Before the Internet, the aspirations of supply chain software devotees were limited to improving their ability to predict demand from customers and make their own supply chains run more smoothly. Now, companies can connect their supply chain with the supply chains of their suppliers and customers together in a single vast network that optimizes costs and opportunities for everyone involved. This was the reason for the business-to-business (B2B) explosion; the idea that everyone in the same business could be connected together.

Most companies share at least some data with their supply chain partners. The supply chain in most industries is like a big card game. The players do not want to show their cards because they do not trust anyone else with the information. But if they showed their hands they could all benefit. Suppliers would not have to guess how many raw materials to order, and manufacturers would not have to order more than they need from suppliers to make sure they have enough on hand if demand for their products unexpectedly goes up. And retailers would have fewer empty shelves if they shared the information they had about sales of a manufacturer's product in all their stores with the manufacturer. The Internet makes showing your hand to others possible, but centuries of distrust and lack of coordination within the industry makes it difficult.

The payoff of timely and accurate supply chain information is the ability to make or ship only as much of a product as there is a market for. This is the practice known as just-in-time manufacturing, and it allows companies to reduce the amount of inventory that they keep. This can cut costs substantially, since you no longer need to pay to produce and store excess goods.

Some of the roadblocks when installing supply chain automation are uniquely difficult because the company extends beyond the company's walls. Employees will need to change the way they work and so will the employees from each supplier that is added to the network. Only the largest and most powerful manufacturers can force such radical changes down suppliers' throats. Most companies have to sell outsiders on the system. Moreover, your goals in installing the system may be threatening to those suppliers. To get supply chain partners to agree to collaborate, all stakeholders have to be willing to compromise and help them achieve their own goals.

An extended supply chain is a clever way of describing everyone who contributes to a product. So if you make text books, then your extended supply chain would include the factories where the books are printed and bound, but also the company that sells you the paper, the mill where that supplier buys their stock, and so on. It is important to keep track of what is happening in your extended supply chain because with a supplier or a supplier's supplier could end up having an impact on you (as the old saying goes, a chain is only a strong as its weakest link). For example, a fire in a paper mill might cause the text book manufacturer's paper supplier to run out of inventory. If the text book company knows what is happening in its extended supply chain it can find another paper vendor.

Inventory Management

Retailers grow in different ways some, like Starbucks, plan their growth well in advance, do copious amounts of research on regional demographics, identify the best real estate, and stay away from new markets until they are fully prepared. Others, like many sporting goods retailers, have grown rapidly through expansion or gradually through the addition of new store locations or competitors' attrition.

As chains have grown, the logistics of managing multiple retail locations has created many new challenges. The knee-jerk reaction is to standardize everything we can. Of course, this is desirable when it comes to POS procedures or supply purchasing. But when applied to assortment planning, we have taken standardization too far. The quest for consistency, specifically in floor layouts and fixture types, is at odds with the need to tailor assortments to the demands and demographics of local consumers. Each market, with its distinct customer profile, geography, and local competition, can put a different spin on every store, even stores within the same trading area.

Inventory is usually a retailer's single largest asset; unless we dissect the way we assort and allocate merchandise to stores. A portion of eroding sales and profits can be attributed to what can only be described as misuse of inventory. Our automated information system gives huge amounts of data, most of which is after the fact. The automated system might show, for instance, that backpacks sell better in one location than another. In some case, we find the obvious answer that the store is near the University. Companies should not need detective work to find out why something sold better in one location than another. Companies should have planned, with all the information at their disposal, where their products would sell better, and stocked the store to maximize the opportunity.

Every day companies compile and store information that customers divulge. But when companies plan for the next season's products, where do we look? Why, to last year, of course, so they can perpetuate what they already know. The nuances of most of our customers' shopping habits and expectations are never built into the mix during the planning process.

Tailoring store assortments is not only desirable from an inventory management standpoint, but also critical if we are to retain our credibility. What can employees possibly be telling customers if they run out of youth soccer shin guards in August but always have them in stock in January? That we are a full-fine sporting goods store? No, it just confirms that the company has the right goods at the wrong time, or in the wrong place.

For large chains, standardization is just the easiest way to make a predictable presentation on a floor plan designed and can be easily executed. Senior management thinks it is great that the store in Montgomery, IL looks exactly like the store in Montgomery, AL. This gives management a warm fuzzy feeling that stores are following the corporate directives. But the benefit stops there. The local customer could not care less. In today's competitive environment, where the consumer can buy what they want through the Internet, companies need to manage inventory the smartest way they know how, not the easiest.

Certainly, it requires more skill to manage variable assortments and timing across multiple doors. But in Illinois, you had better have ice hockey equipment, and plenty of it, year-round in fact. In Alabama, the only hockey they are playing is on the streets, on wheels, and they need to look cool, not stay warm.

Transportation Methods

Transportation is one of America's largest industries. Its sectors range from automobiles and trucks to airplanes, trains, ships, barges, pipelines, and warehouses. Traditionally, the transportation industry accounts for about 10% of the GDP and employs nearly 22 million people or about 15% of all workers in the United States.

At a bit more than 10% of America's economic activity, transportation is remarkably efficient, considering the fact that it is a vital service to every other sector of the economy. In fact, thanks to increasing use of advanced information systems and such strategies as intermodal use of containers (sending freight via containers that are easily transferred from ship to rail car to truck as needed, without repacking), the transportation industry's productivity level is excellent. The ratio of ton-miles of freight shipped in the US per dollar of GDP declined by a remarkable 35.3% from 1970 through 2002. Meanwhile, transportation is growing rapidly.

The introduction of intergraded databases that can track inventory levels and shipments on a global basis has streamlined the supply chain. As a result, supply chain technology has been one of the fastest growing segments in the information field.

The rapid adoption of outsourcing has led many companies that find shipping to be vital to their business to turn to logistics services providers for all manner of shipping support, including warehousing and distribution services. The sectors of transport, SCM and logistics services are permanently intertwined creating efficiencies once undreamed of in the transportation arena.

The transportation, supply chain and logistics industry is going global, along with just about every other major industry. These companies, however, hold a unique position because they are the very entities that make globalization possible. This industry is made up of companies that supply the systems and software, run the warehouses, provide the consulting and operate the airplanes, boats, trucks, and trains that move raw materials, finished goods, packages, documents, and people throughout the world.

Offshoring (i.e., the transference of manufacturing, customer service centers and other labor-intensive work from nations like the US and UK to developing countries such as China and The Philippines) has been one of the biggest contributors to international commerce in recent years. To facilitate the offshoring of manufacturing work, it has become essential to ship cargo between distant locations, bringing the right goods to the right locations and doing it cheaply, efficiently and above all, on time.

The needs of modern business have spurred many transportation and logistics sectors to become technologically advanced and to build a truly global presence. This trend has forced many smaller companies to consolidate and merge into larger entities in order to compete effectively. The parcel delivery business is a prime example. Business demands have created courier giants such as UPS, FedEx, and DHL. Major enterprises have the ability to create global networks of offices and warehouses, purchase vast quantities of equipment such as trucks and aircraft, and invest in the expensive and complex information systems necessary to track shipments as they are moved around the world.

With the need to ship massive amounts of goods across long distances came the need to have vast supply chains monitored, organized, and controlled. This led to the advent of logistics companies, which specialize in handling goods on the way to market. Most products in today's marketplace are the result of a global effort. Raw materials for a product may be produced in one country, assembled in another and finally marketed to consumers in dozens of different nations at once. The key to making such manufacturing systems work is modern supply chain technology – the use of specialized software and networks in a coordinated effort to design, manufacture, ship, assemble, and distribute components and completed products.

The challenges faced by supply chains are multifaceted: coordinating the arrival of supplies in factories; bringing together all the necessary parts and assembling them into consumer-ready products; and distributing them across oceans, highways, and airways to arrive in the correct locations in the right quantities, colors, and styles to satisfy consumer demand, all at the lowest possible cost. Compounded by delays and mistakes that can be made along the way due to bad weather, communication breakdowns, accidents, inspections, or simple human error, these challenges can quickly become catastrophes. In order to prevent mishaps and manage day-to-day supply issues, companies hire supply chain managers and utilize advanced data systems. In some cases, supply chain services are outsourced altogether.

Third-party logistics companies (known as 3PLs) are quickly assuming a vital role in the supply chain. Logistics services are generally defined as services added onto regular transportation activities, including freight forwarding, which is the handling of freight from one form of transport to another (e.g., the movement of containers from ship to truck or railcar to truck). Transportation managers determine the most viable mode of transport (by train, truck, boat, plane, or a combination). Warehouses store the stock of other companies and ship the stock out as needed. SCM software makers specialize in software that can track or allow communication between the different parts of a supply chain.

Many freight and parcel shipping companies have jumped on the 3PL bandwagon to provide their customers with turn-key shipping services. Deutsche Post, UPS, and FedEx have all made logistics acquisitions as they battle for market share. British-based Exel plc, the largest provider of logistics services in the world, has made several strategic acquisitions in order to offer domestic and international SCM from beginning to end, with services including freight forwarding, warehouse management, multi-modal planning and powerful information technology. However, the industry has not consolidated to the point where there is no longer room for small or start-up companies. Many regional or specific service specialists have found a great deal of success in their own niche markets.

Use of Electronic Means for Delivery

Adidas had a press conference announcing their new branding position. There was nothing startling about that portion of the presentations. What was impressive was the company's willingness to set public performance goals for their supply chain system. The futures system answered retailers' needs in the 1970s, 1980s, and early 1990s. Lest we forget, Adidas' inability to ship product when it was needed was one of the main reasons Nike succeeded in the 1970s. It introduced futures. Now the industry needs shorter lead times from creation to the shelves. Nobody can be smart enough to predict fashion trends 18 months out, as is common today. Make the wrong color decision or overbuy a category, and there are closeouts for both the retailer and manufacturer, hurling margins.

Adidas is already working with certain retailers on pilot programs to reduce the supply chain time and auto-replenishment system. Adidas-America outlined the supply chain matrix used by all the major shoe companies. The creative portion of the process typically takes 12 months. The procurement function takes another six. Adidas' goal is to reduce that time period by 50% in 3 years. For a start, Adidas is closely linking its supply chain efforts to sales and marketing strategies. This may seem logical, but it is not SOP in the shoe industry. Adidas is also working with its factories to improve their operating performance and place their new products closer to the market. The company is investing in three-dimensional digital software that can reduce the timeline by at least 10 weeks. They also hope to lop a month off the delivery phase by shipping directly to retailers, bypassing the warehouses. The company is testing a labeling and special handling program with some of its factories now. Other retailers ought to demand to know what the other brands are doing to shorten the supply chain time cycle.

The sporting goods industry is not as easy a business on the Internet as many thought. There have been several examples of problems over the past years. Chipshot.com, filed for Chapter 11 bankruptcy protection. The site still operates, although it has been notifying customers who place orders that all items are on back order. There were 200 employees when the company flourished, and now there are seven. Chipshot.com allowed golfers to design clubs to their own specs. Investors include Sequoia Capital and Oracle Venture Fund.

SportsLine.com decided to sell its e-commerce to MVP.com because sporting goods offered lower margins than its other businesses and was not compatible with them. MVP appeared to be well-backed financially, having raised $75 million from Freeman Spogli and Benchmark. MVP was obligated to pay $120 million over 10 years as part of its SportsLine contract.

When the deal was consummated, there was every expectation that MVP could raise any additional capital through an initial public offering (IPO). However, the dot-com universe came apart making it virtually impossible for MVP to take that route. The resulting cash squeeze caused MVP to miss its fourth-quarter payment on October 1. This forced MVP to write off as worthless all its non-cash investment of more than $100 million. Before the announcement, The Forzani Group, Canada's largest specialty sporting goods retailer, decided to end the negotiations with MVP regarding its planned joint venture.

Gear.com was a pure-play sporting goods e-tailer. It had a special approach to the business. Buying closeouts from manufacturers, it sold the apparel, equipment and footwear at major savings direct to consumer. But over the past few months, there has been turmoil among the top managers. In addition, Gear.com laid off 30% of its employees. Gear.com raised $12 million in second-round funding and was able to keep their e-doors open until they were bought out.

Overstock.com bought Gear.com for an undisclosed amount of stock. The inventory consists of 3000 SKUs of name-brand closeouts from more than 550 manufacturers – including The North Face, Timberland, Pearl Izumi, Champion and Puma – at prices 25–75% below retail. Under the terms of the acquisition, Overstock.com will obtain Gear's entire inventory valued at an estimated $14 million retail, which will be added to Overstock.com's sporting goods department.

The use of the electronics industry is extremely competitive and highly volatile. A company's competitors can often turn on a dime. Outsourcing logistics is not always just a matter of saving money; often it is driven by the need to remain competitive. UPS, FedEx and other similar companies helps makers and marketers of sporting good products get their product to market quickly and successfully. Getting your product through the supply chain in a quick efficient manner is not enough. Great business plans are often like produce, they can be highly perishable.

Performance Metrics

Supply chain measurements or metrics such as inventory turns and backorders are used to track supply chain performance. Supply chain metrics can help the company to understand how it is operating over a given period of time. Inventory turns are the number of times that a company's inventory cycles or turns over per year. It is the most commonly used supply chain metric. Also used are backorders, which is defined as an unfilled customer order in demand (immediate or past due) against an item whose current stock level is insufficient to satisfy demand.

Supply chain measurements can cover many areas including procurement, production, distribution, warehousing, inventory, transportation, and customer service. However, a good performance in one part of the supply chain is not sufficient. Supply chains are only as strong as its weakest link. The solution is for the company to measure all key areas of your supply chain. Tracking the company's metrics allows them to view performance over time and guides them to optimize a supply chain. It allows management to identify problem areas, and to compare the company to other like companies through like industry benchmarking.

Measurements alone are not the solution to the company's weak areas. The solution lies in the corrective action that the company takes to improve the measure. The solution comes from process improvements. Using the correct set of metrics can lead the company to the solution of the question: Do we have the right balance between service and cost?

Tracking and measuring the performance of various supply chain functions is necessary but not sufficient for today's extended enterprise. Tying that performance to corporate strategic goals and closing the loop on execution to ensure continuous improvement are keys to effective performance management.

Establishing metrics to track supply chain performance seems, on its face, like a fairly simple and straightforward undertaking. If one is interested only in measuring individual functional performance, this perception is true. But most companies today need to understand performance in terms of the overall, inter-enterprise supply chain and be able to tie that overall performance to strategic corporate objectives – a far more complex task.

Breaking out of traditional metrics begins with top-level strategic planning. Companies need to ask, what is our strategy? Given that strategy, what does our supply chain need to excel at doing? May be it needs to be really fast, or really flexible or really inexpensive. Whatever it is, the company needs to pick metrics designed to measure that capability.

A strategic approach to supply chain performance also is being driven by the growing use of balanced scorecards at many large companies. At the beginning of the year these companies establish their most important financial goals as well as goals in other areas. Many of these top goals have supply chain components.

For example, if a company wants to improve its cash flow, supply chain managers and line employees may seek drive certain key performance indicators (KPIs) – those factors that influence the effectiveness of products and processes. In this situation, the KPIs to be driven may include speeding order processing and improving order accuracy and fill rates.

Establishing the proper KPIs, and targets for each, is an important next step and one that can be especially difficult when cross-functional or cross-enterprise agreement are required. Targets for each KPI capture the level of improvement desired. There is no point in setting very aggressive targets and having nothing to back it up, so the company must have initiatives that are going to move toward the goal.

The final step is actual implementation, where a company identifies data sources, starts collecting the data and creates an appropriate format for communicating it and commits to reviewing the information.

GLOBAL LOGISTICS: SKORPION SPORTS

Business Link West Yorkshire, part of The West Yorkshire Enterprise Partnership Limited whose head office is located in Millshaw, Leeds, and England, is the first choice for all small to medium-sized businesses in the region looking for advice and support on any aspect of their business. They are the gateway to a whole range of national services available to such businesses.

Business Link helps entrepreneurs to set up in business and encourage and support small businesses to grow and succeed. Services range from quick advice on business matters to in-depth consultancy. Their team of business advisers has specialist knowledge to help with issues such as information technology, human resources, and marketing.

They also work closely with other local organizations across West Yorkshire to bring their services within reach of all businesses in the area. Business Link is strong on quality and provides a high level of service to all their customers.

One such company is the Bradford-based sports goods manufacturer Skorpion Sports. They had the need for expanded publicity and a plan to create an expanded distribution system to support their growth into new markets. They also needed more cost-effective warehousing methods to deal with the necessary increase in storage space needed for products.

The reason for the growth is related to the sports goods manufacturer coming up with a product that has become popular and successful that it is now struggling to keep pace with the huge worldwide demand. The product is an innovative Indicator Glove for cyclists that contains flashing diodes to give greater visibility and safety especially at road junctions.

Mohammed Fiaz, Managing Director of Skorpion Sports, runs the design, marketing, and sales of the business from the United Kingdom while the manufacturing site is in Pakistan. Confident that the manufacturing operation meets European standards and is ready to respond to large scale orders, the

Continued

company now wants to bring the United Kingdom end up to speed and has sought the help of Business Link.

Mohammed Fiaz explains: "The market for this product is phenomenal and we know that the customers are out there. We've had excellent support from our Business Link Adviser who is working with us to open up new markets. Business Link has helped us to produce brochures and attend exhibitions and we recently won the Best Display Award at the Asian Business Convention which gave us good exposure to smaller businesses. We now need to manage the whole process including storage and distribution of products from the United States. A key issue for us is stockholding because to supply major retailers we must be able to store thousands of products. Business Link has helped us to source the best local warehousing. We are looking to develop more products and expand into markets in Europe and the USA. Our goal is to generate long-term business. The demand is there and we need to be there."

Source: Adapted from *Case Study – Business Link West Yorkshire* (n.d.). Retrieved March 13, 2006 from http://www.blwy.co.uk/newsite/case-studies/0106-skorpion-marketing-operations.php and http://www.blwy.co.uk/newsite/aboutus/index.php.

Suggested Discussion Topics

1. Skorpion Sports hires you as the Vice President of Marketing – United States Operations. Your first main job is to create an expanded distribution network in the United States market. Discuss how you would develop and implement an effective purchasing process, and efficiently manage the entire supply chain?
2. Explain the role purchasing plays in the management of costs, inventory, transportation, and delivery. What performance metrics would be most effective to determine successful implementation?

EMERGING TECHNOLOGY IN LOGISTICS: RADIO FREQUENCY IDENTIFICATION

An emerging technology that will affect the supply chain is radio frequency identification or RFID. RFID tags are essentially barcodes on steroids. Whereas barcodes only identify the product, RFID tags can tell what the product is, where it has been, when it expires, whatever information someone wishes to program it with. RFID technology is going to generate mountains of data about the location of pallets, cases, cartons, totes and individual products in the supply chain. It is going to produce oceans of information about when and where merchandise is manufactured, picked, packed, and shipped. It is going to create rivers of numbers telling retailers about the expiration dates of their perishable items – numbers that will have to be stored, transmitted in real-time and shared with warehouse management, inventory management, financial, and other enterprise systems. In other words, it is going to have a really big impact.

Another benefit of RFIDs is that, unlike barcodes, RFID tags can be read automatically by electronic readers. Imagine a truck carrying a container full of widgets entering a shipping terminal in China. If the container is equipped with an RFID tag, and the terminal has an RFID sensor network, that container's whereabouts can be automatically sent to Widget Co. without the truck ever slowing down. It has the potential to add a substantial amount of visibility into the extended supply chain. However, two of the biggest hurdles to widespread RFID adoption are the cost of building the infrastructure and the lack of agreed-upon industry standards.

RFID: RETAILER DREAM OR ETHICAL NIGHTMARE FOR CONSUMERS

For the past 35 years, barcodes have allowed retailers to keep track of products in the store and as they leave the checkout counter. The system works because each stock-keeping unit in the store has a unique barcode. But there is a new technology that stands to revolutionize product labeling – and personal privacy.

This technology, known as radio frequency identification (RFID), allows retailers – as well as manufacturers – to uniquely label each individual package with an identifying code. Although RFID has been around since World War II, the idea of using it to track consumer goods is relatively new.

The RFID tag is a tiny silicon chip with a number called the EPC (Electronic Product Code) on it. When an antenna (no larger than a postage stamp) is attached to the tag, the code can be scanned by a remote reading device up to 10 meters away. If equipped with a transmitter, the tag emits a signal that can be picked up at much greater distances – even by satellites.

It is still too expensive to place individualized tags on each item in the supermarket, so RFID is now chiefly used to identify shipping pallets and cargo containers. But near-term futurists see the day when it will be cost effective to label individual store items – perhaps no more than 5 or 10 years from now.

The positives of this technology is that it can be used to track shipments, aid in inventory control, help with forecasting for a retail outlet, and even deter stealing. However, it could also be used to gather personal information from the consumer, track where a consumer goes with the product, and determine its usage by the consumer. This issue is paramount in maintaining individual privacy. The RFID tool could be used as a tracking device – barcodes let the store know you purchased the product; RFID – if not removed from the product – continue collecting information and potentially track every move

Continued

that the consumer makes during the post-purchase period. The major fear is that this personal information could be then sold to other parties, including marketing firms and even the government. This could be the 21st century's version of mailing lists, but with so much more information about individuals. It is a marketing professional's dream, but potentially the consumer's worst nightmare.

Defenders of the technology have suggested that consumers worried about loss of privacy could simply tear the tags off their packages before leaving the store. However, there are reasons why this may not be practical. First, the technology will allow retailers to track where merchandise was bought, so the tags will have to be intact when processing customer returns. Second, the tags will almost certainly include warranty information that will have to be retained for the lifetime of covered products. With these constraints, it hardly seems likely that consumers will be completely free to remove the tags.

Here is one example. Imagine RFID tags on every can or bottle of beer. The RFID can track when the beer was opened, when the beer is empty, and even the time the beer was consumed. Now imagine that it could also cross-reference with your cable television system to see what you were watching on television, such as NASCAR or football. What marketing professional would not want that? However, what consumer would like to have someone keeping track of how much beer they consume?

It may come to a point where manufacturers might even be willing to negotiate with consumers for lower prices or even free product (incentives) in exchange for the marketing information. This concept still has a way to go. One of the websites that examined this possibility was www.priceline.com. Priceline.com offered the opportunity for the consumer to bid for products in order to get the best price. Due to the level of uncertainty of whether the consumer would "win" the bid, and the emotional issues attached to this concept, the idea did not work.

The problem was that the best way to sell products and services is by not having consumers think too much. Impulse buying is a significant part of sales. Another effort currently being extensively utilized is in store-discount and customer-loyalty cards. This is a precursor to RFID tags, but usually does not go beyond the checkout counter. However, it does collect a significant amount of data which allows retailers to target their incentive offerings and understand their consumers better.

RFIDs do also have some other uses. Barcodes have sped up the process of checking out. RFIDs could make this process even faster. Imagine being in a supermarket to grocery shop. As you put products into your shopping cart, the RFID tag is scanned into a mini-computer on the handle of the cart, and also into the computer system in the supermarket. On the cart you can instantly see how much your bill is as you are filling the cart. When you get to the checkout counter, your bill would be ready, and all you would have to do is pay and leave.

But is privacy really a legitimate bargaining chip for greater convenience? There are two sides to the story. One side is that individuals need to have the freedom to choose whatever they want, whether it is to protect privacy or put convenience first. On the other hand, allowing consumers to trade privacy for convenience would empower retailers and RFID users, and potentially lead to loss of privacy for all.

It seems quite possible the battle lines over RFID will end up being drawn at the checkout counter. Most of the benefits that manufacturers and retailers initially pointed to when they began thinking about RFID (lower costs to consumers, higher product availability, better tracking of inventory, and theft reduction) have yet to be realized. However, if it does come to the mainstream, will it become an ethical concern to even go shopping? Only time will tell.

Source: Adapted from Frost, R. (2005). *Beyond the Barcode*. Retrieved March 11, 2006 from http://www.brandchannel.com/features_effect.asp?pf_id=295.

Suggested Discussion Topics

1. The use of RFID tags is obviously a technological breakthrough that could be a great benefit for sport marketers, but also of great concern for consumers. How would you balance these two concepts to provide the best possible purchasing scenario for your consumers while maximizing the market research you can conduct using this technology?

2. One of the biggest issues with RFID technology is the exorbitant cost of building the infrastructure to implement such a system. You are the sport marketing manager for a sport manufacturer. The CEO has stated that the organization can have the RFID system, but you must prove the return on investment (ROI) for this system. You need to create and make a presentation to the board of the corporation to sell the concept of spending the money to implement the RFID system. Discuss what you would say to the board. In addition to including the benefits of the system, make sure to discuss how you plan on dealing with the pitfalls.

CONCLUSION

Sport marketing logistics involves identify your customers, identify their needs, and combine the company's resources to meet those needs through purchasing and SCM. The purchasing process involves offering products and services at a price customers are willing to pay (value), with the goal of creating a long-term relationship between the supplier and the customers.

Technology advances have significantly improved the purchasing process in sport marketing through EDI. Other innovations in sourcing and cost management have enhanced the purchasing process.

Effective SCM involves finding the best suppliers who can respond to needs through an efficient network. The major components of the SCM are the strategic plan, sourcing, production, logistics, and returns. One of the major advances in SCM for sport marketing is just-in-time manufacturing, where the payoff of timely and accurate supply chain information equals the ability to make or ship only as much of a product as there is a market for. This has allowed sport organizations to reduce the amount of inventory that they keep and cut costs substantially, since they no longer needed to pay to produce and store excess goods.

These advances in inventory management, combined with modern transportation methods and electronic delivery means has also provided modifications in performance metrics. It is much easier to track supply chain performance, especially inventory turns and backorders. This in turn allows the organization to better understand how efficiently and effectively it is operating over a given time.

The use of technology appears to be one of the strongest factors in determining the future of the logistics and the delivery of sport products. The evolution of barcodes to RFID tags has allowed the industry to lower overhead cost and improve tracking and distribution. However, it is important to remember that technology should not replace the individual relationships between customers, buyers, and suppliers.

FROM THEORY TO PRACTICE

Mary Pellegrino, Sales Manager of Canada

Buffalo Sabres (NHL) Hockey Club
Buffalo, New York/Hamilton, Ontario, Canada

I am currently employed with the Buffalo Sabres Hockey Club. The position I hold is Sales Manager of Canada. I am stationed out of my home in Hamilton, Ontario to better assist Sales efforts in Southern Ontario. My duties include: selling of signage, suite license sales, promotional sales, as well as majority of ticket sales.

Previously I was employed with the Hamilton Bulldogs Hockey Club. The position I held in the office was the Team Services Coordinator/Office Manager. My duties included: coordinating travel arrangements and itineraries for the hockey team and other staff travel; organizing all aspects of off-site meetings and events; dealing with the AHL communications and scheduling; as well as reporting directly to the CFO with the administrative support to Chairman and Executive Director of Operations.

Before the Bulldogs I was with the Atlanta Thrashers in the Marketing Department. As the Marketing Assistant my duties included: spearheading all college marketing; assisting with the Chevy MVP balloting, fan photo snap shot and many other in-game promotions; and assisting in data collection for our fan base, as well as working with the Kids Club.

Prior to working with the Atlanta Thrashers Hockey Organization I currently finished a spring internship at the NHL Enterprises Canada, L.P. in the Corporate Marketing Department. I would report every morning to Jeff Rockwell Sales and Marketing Manager. My duties as an intern included formulating a detailed summary of the NHL's partners' contractual obligations; responsible for an in-depth analysis of the Canadian sports and entertainment industry, with a focus on corporate partnerships; and assisted in developing PowerPoint's for future partner prospects.

In addition to the NHL internship, I have secured additional experience in the sports industry. In 2003, I worked at the NHL All-Star Game in Sunrise, Florida. In 2002, I worked NASCAR in Loudon, New Hampshire at the Square D Tent, also in 2002; I worked as "Floor Crew" with the American Hockey League's Manchester Monarchs. And in 2001, I volunteered at the Boston Marathon.

If it was not for the Sport Management Club at my college, and my professor caring about the students' hands-on experience in the sporting world, I do not think I would be where I am at today with the Buffalo Sabres. All of the above jobs and experiences I have had all started during a field trip in April of 2001 to the National Hockey League Offices in New York City. It was at this speaker series where we heard from a number of individuals including Claude Loiselle (Associate Director, Hockey Operations), Frank Supovitz (Vice President of Events and Entertainment) and Eustace King (Director of Corporate Sales and Marketing). After Eustace was done speaking with the students I followed him out of the conference room to let him know that I had an internship coming up in less than a year and that what he did was what I would be interested in pursuing as a career once I graduated college. Eustace and I kept in contact through out the summer and it lead to me getting a very rare internship with the NHL Offices in Toronto, Canada. After interning with the NHL in Toronto it opened up many doors for me in the hockey industry because I made many contacts that have helped me along the way.

From my experience with the NHL in Atlanta and now Buffalo, I cannot stress how important "Logistics in Sport Marketing" is important to the field of sport marketing.

Atlanta – One of my duties as the Marketing Assistant for the Atlanta Thrashers was to go around to local college and universities and teach the students in the South about Hockey 101 and also to let them know of the great college and university discount we had to offer every Thrashers home game.

What was expected of me was to take our HITS staff (Hockey in the Streets) with me to each and every college/university that I attended on a weekly

Continued

basis and we were to set up the inflatable slap shot machine so students could have some hand on experience in hockey. Once they were done they would come to the information table to grab a flyer that explained the college/university discount we had to offer of $10 for students w/I.D. in the 300 Level. They would also take with them a pocket schedule and some sticker, tattoo's as memorabilia. After each game our ticketing staff would be able to track how many students attended.

Buffalo – As Sales Manager of Canada my responsibility is to market the Buffalo Sabres in Canada. How this is done is that I would contact companies or companies would contact me asking if we had group discounts. What I than would do is prepare a specialty flyer with the companies logo and either go to the company and market right there with an information table or distribute through mass email. What this would allow companies to do is instead of them purchasing 20 tickets or more up front it allowed individual employers to purchase tickets at a discount price for family and friends at their convenience. We would than track sales through a computer system called CRM, which would allow us to enter the individual's personal details and the sale.

The recommendations that I would provide to a sport marketing student reading the book as they consider entering the field of sport marketing is to never let any students think that they are better than you and that you cannot do anything your heart desires. I remember when I was a freshman wanting to leave college because many sport management students thought that they were better than everyone else and would make it big with major sport leagues. However, I believe only two of us from my class moved on to major league teams. You need to present yourself in a professional manner and not with the attitude that you are great and should have the job. In the world today it is all about who you know to get a job and what you know to keep it.

The other piece of advice would be to go to as many career fairs as possible and network. In today's society it is all about networking. Having a college education is great – it will help you get a job. But it is also meeting people in the field that can be of great help as well. Go on character interviews, introduce yourself to people, and sell yourself.

PROMOTIONAL ASPECTS OF SPORT MARKETING

COMMUNICATION MANAGEMENT IN SPORT

CHAPTER OUTLINE

CHAPTER OBJECTIVES

The reader will be able to:

- Appreciate the role of communications in the sport marketing process.
- Identify the internal and external elements of organizational image in sport marketing including internal marketing communications, corporate image, logos, and publicity campaigns.

- Understand the various elements of the sport promotion mix, including public relations, licensing, personal contact, incentives, and atmospherics.
- Recognize the incorporation of sport promotion activities with integrated communication plans, event planning, pricing development, and location and distribution strategies.
- Identify the various elements for each of the promotion mix components.
- Know the various indirect (word-of-mouth) and direct (sales) promotional strategies in relationship to positioning, building brand equity, increasing credibility, and enhancing image transfer and association.

WHAT IS COMMUNICATION MANAGEMENT IN SPORT?

Communication management involves the planning, implementing, supervising, evaluation, and modification of the various methods of communication internal and external to a sport organization. Effective and efficient communication management is crucial to success in sport marketing because it is the conduit by which information between employees and organizations is exchanged, and ensures that parties have access to the same information. Communication management also seeks to created continuity in the decision making process by ensuring that all parties are involved in goals setting and attainment in a coordinated and organized manner.

The sport marketing professional is involved in a number of roles to make sure that effective and efficient communication takes place throughout the organization in terms of the marketing process. These include:

- Develop organizational communication strategies including the structure of the internal and external communication processes, the goals and objectives of organizational communication, and the policies and procedures to follow related to communication of information regarding the sport organization.
- Plan, implement, manage, and evaluate the flow of information in and out of the sport organization through verbal, written, and online communication methods.
- Manage all sport organizational images in terms of presentation to the public, the media, and the online environment.
- Develop, implement, manage, and evaluate the organizational crisis communication plan.
- Provide training to all staff of the organization about appropriate communication methodology.

In order to effectively and efficiently manage communication for a sport organization, the sport marketing professional must focus on having a full understanding of three main areas: the communication process, sport organization images, and sport promotions.

THE COMMUNICATION PROCESS

Communication is critical to the success of a sport marketing professional. Communication helps to establish and maintain relationships with the sport consumer by providing a conduit for listening and reacting to the sport consumer. The key components of the communication process are documented below:

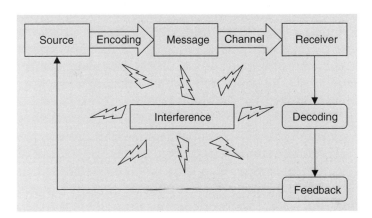

The source starts with an idea of how to communicate information about the sport product or organization. As the source continued developing the idea, it is encoded into a message. The encoding process involves giving the idea a personality. A representation of the idea and the sport entity is created in print, verbal, and/or visual form. This representation can range from a simple photograph to the use of sport personalities to endorse the sport product. Depending on the choice of representation, the message may be delivered as an autobiographical sketch, a narrative, or a drama. The autobiography is where the message about the sport product is directly from the sport entity to the sport consumer. The narrative is where a third party (such as an athlete endorsement) tells the sport consumer about the sport product. The goal is to entice the sport consumer to be involved with that product as a result of the reputation of the endorser. Sport products can also be advertised in a dramatic form, where "characters" act out events in front of an imaginary audience, and the act is reproduced in print, verbal, and/or visual form to persuade the sport consumer to purchase the specific sport product.

Once the message is encoded, it is then sent through marketing channels to the receiver. Marketing channels include many different forms of media, including print, radio, television, and Internet. The receiver then decodes the message and provides feedback to the source. The goal is to have effective and efficient communication between the source and the receiver. Effective communication occurs when the intended meaning of the sender is identical to the interpreted meaning of the receiver. One of the major reasons communication is not effective and efficient is due to interference with the process. This interference can come from a number of sources, including poor choices in communication channels, poor expression of the message, and environmental distractions.

SPORT ORGANIZATIONAL IMAGES

One of the most significant issues faced by sport marketing professionals in terms of communication management is the sport organization's image. Organizational image is the combination of how the internal organization believes others view the organization, and the beliefs and perceptions the external organization actually has of the organization. Based on these beliefs and perceptions, sport consumers either wish to be associated with or avoid the organization. It is a major role of the sport marketing professional to control communications to maximize the public image of the sport organization. One method used to control the outflow of information from the organization is through internal marketing communications. Internal marketing involves the perceptions of individuals from inside an organization about how they view that organization. As a result, the sport marketing professional treats individuals within the sport organization as customers, with the goal of using principles of leadership and motivation to help shape the organization's image.

Sport marketing professional also seek to control external organizational images, which involves the perceptions of individuals from outside an organization and how they view that sport organization. This is a significant challenge because external organizational images seek to control the beliefs and perceptions of potential customers – a challenge that is easier said than done.

There are a number of methods utilized by sport marketing professionals to articulate the organizational image to external constituencies, including brand image, publicity campaigns, crisis communications, and sport promotions. As discussed in Chapter 6, branding and brand image is one of the most powerful external organizational images. Branding involves using a name, term, design, symbol, or feature to identify one sport product, service, or organization as being different from another. The mixture of attributes can be tangible or intangible, are usually symbolized in a trademark, and if managed properly, creates value and influence for the sport organization.

Another method utilized to covey external organizational image is the publicity campaign. A publicity campaign is the use of communications, activities, and media coverage to convey specific information to a targeted market over a specific period of time. The development of this type of focused effort to communicate the sport organization's image involves a number of steps as listed below:

- *Internal audit*: The sport marketing professional must conduct an appraisal of the internal operations and systems of the sport organization to observe and evaluate their efficiency and effectiveness in quality delivery of products and services, appropriate risk management practices, and financial control.
- *Identification of weaknesses*: Identification of deficiencies within the sport organization and how they will adversely affect the sport organization's image.
- *External research*: An investigation of the opportunities and threats may result in a change to the sport organizational image.
- *Target audience*: The process of determining the best method for getting the sport organization's image into the minds of specific consumers.

- *Message structure*: Developing a specific communication that has a specific goal, is aimed at a specific group of individuals (target audience), and has a measurable component to determine effectiveness.
- *Methods for outreach*: A plan of action to communicate the message to the external environment.
- *Post-campaign evaluation*: An assessment of the overall campaign to determine whether the message was clear, understood, and was a positive influence on the organizational image.

Also integral to controlling the external organizational image is through crisis communications.

Crisis communications involve the development of a contingency plan that is based on existing communication resources and operational capabilities, and allow sport marketing professionals to effectively respond to a crisis related to the sport organization. This plan is crucial to maintaining a positive organizational image during times of public scrutiny. Crises can come in numerous forms for a sport organization, which required the sport marketing professional to forecast potential crisis and have a method of dealing with said crises from a communication point of view. This will often include having a plan for articulating the organization's response to all internal members of the sport organization, a policy for external communication regarding the situation (often by directing inquiries to a designated spokesperson) and a targeted channel for disseminating information regarding the crisis. By maintaining control of the information, the sport marketing professional can help to minimize the damage a crisis has on the organizational image of the sport entity.

The most extensive and significant methods for communicating external organizational image is through sport promotion. Sport promotion is defined as the procedure of communicating information about the sport product or service to consumers. The sport marketing professional entices consumers to make a purchase by managing the sport promotional mix. As a significant part of the sport marketing, because sport promotions is an integral part of the sport marketing mix, the remainder of this chapter will focus on the elements of sport promotions.

MULLET NIGHT

The Manchester Monarchs of the American Hockey League have administered a promotion called "Mullet Night." Prior to offering this promotion for the first time in 2003, the front office of the organization contemplated numerous promotions to offer during the season. According to Jeff Eisenberg, General Manager of the Manchester Monarchs, "The Monarchs have the same goals for other promotions: sell tickets, add value, and build brand. While the organization may have slightly different goals for individual promotions ... the ultimate goal is to use promotions to get to a sell-out." The organization's goals

Continued

are not to have promotions on the dates they call "dog dates" – those dates that will be low capacity due to a game being mid-week or on a holiday, or the game is against a non-rival opponent – as the promotion will do little to help attendance. The Monarchs gauge whether a promotion was successful or not by getting a game that was not going to be a sell-out to reach sell-out. The result of this will be that the more sell-outs, the "hotter" the ticket becomes.

According to Eisenberg, the Manchester Monarchs use promotions to "help keep the Monarchs on the minds of the fans," and that the promotions are used so "that the fans always have fun." They do this in a number of ways to maintain their visibility in the public eye. They begin this by being "promotion heavy" during first 20 games, which is traditionally the time of year where fans are not thinking about hockey yet – especially with the Major League Baseball post-season and the National Football League being in mid-season. As Jeff Eisenberg stated, "The goal with every promotion is to 'under promise and over deliver,' as this will enhance the experience of the fans, entice them to come back, and promote the team further through word of mouth."

To measure the success of the "Mullet Night" promotion, the Monarchs had three key benchmarks. The first would be an increase of ticket sales. Second is if the promotion enhanced the game experience. Finally, did the promotion create brand awareness and exposure, both before and after the event? In pre-event planning, the Manchester Monarchs felt that the promotion had a chance of success for a number of reasons. "Mullet Night" was unique, as it had never been done before by anyone. The number of people anticipated to participate in the promotion would be large (5000 wigs were to be given out). Not only is the hair style funny, but it also has a cult following in hockey. Finally, and most importantly, the promotion was geared to "make fun of themselves," hence not taking themselves too seriously.

For a promotion to work, the front office staff of the Manchester Monarchs had to get information out about the event. This was accomplished in a number of ways, including involving the media (including the largest radio and television media outlets in the state) by providing the media with material to "pre-sell." They also promoted a contest for the best mullet, and hyped the event as "a part of the American lifestyle …".

The first year, the event was a tremendous success. Why? According to Jeff Eisenberg, General Manager of the team, there were a number of reasons:

- Putting hair on people (5000) is funny.
- Players wore the hair during warm-ups.
- Kids wore the hair the entire game.
- There was a subculture that appeared at the game – people made their own T-shirts, wore fake teeth (ugly green teeth, buck teeth).
- The interviews conducted brought people into it – they became part of it. They took the interviews "seriously" and gave appropriate answers.

- They were able to get Barry Melrose involved, which gave the event credibility – he is a hockey icon, the "hockey guy" on ESPN – this also helped to get in on ESPN.
- "It was still funny in the third period."
- A certain "mood" had been created from the pre-event publicity. "You could feel the excitement."
- Fans were the ones who made the event so successful.
- Security wore mullets.
- Hall of Fame made it even more of an event – where famous people who had real-life mullet were "inducted" into the Mullet Hall of Fame.

In the case of "Mullet Night," all three benchmarks were achieved, and after 2 years the promotion exited in a "big" way, especially in the area of brand awareness and exposure. The promotion received coverage on ESPN (courtesy of Barry Melrose), CNN, TNN, and Hockey Night in Canada. In addition, over 80 local television and radio affiliates ran the story. Charlie Sherman, the Sport Director for WMUR TV in Manchester, New Hampshire, was critical in getting national exposure. Before the game was complete, Sherman went to the office and edited highlights, uploaded it to the satellite, and sent the corresponding satellite numbers for the networks to download. This allowed all media outlets to download footage and put it on TV. While the first mullet night received a short mention the first year and the second mullet night received approximately 4 minutes of coverage on ESPN. In expanding their reach nationally, the *Los Angeles Times* (the home city of the parent organization, the Los Angeles Kings) ran an article on the second page of the sports section that discussed the event. According to Eisenberg, "It was great to have the exposure in Los Angeles with the parent company, as it adds credibility to the Monarch's organization." From a local perspective, this exposure was well received and accepted by sponsors and fans. The ticket was the "hottest" ticket in town, with season ticket holders being "proud" to have a ticket to the game. The post-game coverage added to the "allure" of the event.

Source: Adapted from Schwarz, E. C. and D. Blais (2005). How to get a minor league promotion major league publicity. In *Where Sport Marketing Theory Meets Practice: Selected Papers from the Second Annual Conference of the Sport Marketing Association*, edited by B. G. Pitts, pp. 227–230. Morgantown, WV: Fitness Information Technology.

Suggested Discussion Topics

1. Is it ethical to use promotional techniques that might be deemed derogatory to a subcultural group? Why or why not?
2. Outside of specific promotions, one of the major ethical issues currently being dealt with in college athletics is the use of Native American names

Continued

as the namesake of their athletic teams (such as the Florida State Seminoles, the North Dakota Fighting Sioux, and the Utah Utes). You are the Director of Marketing for an athletic department whose team has a Native American name. You have two choices – prove to the NCAA that the use of the name is not derogatory; or start a plan for changing the name of the school's teams. In the interest of time, cost, and notoriety – you choose the first option. Outline the marketing efforts that will ensure that the Native American name is treated and used with respect, and is acceptable to all parties (the school, the NCAA, and the Native American community).

SPORT PROMOTIONS

The elements of sport promotions (also known as the sport promotional mix) include advertising, sponsorship, public relations, licensing, personal contact, incentives, and atmospherics. Advertising involves paid, non-personal communications about a sport product or service through the print, broadcast, or electronic media that are designed to attract public attention and subsequent purchase. In sport marketing, advertising may include broadcast commercials, direct mailings, facility signage, and manufactured media. Sponsorship refers to the relationship between a corporation and a sport organization as a tool to develop brand image and customer loyalty as a result of the association. Public relations is the collection of activities, communications, and media coverage that convey who the sport organization is and what they have to offer, all in the effort to enhance their image and prestige. Licensing is one of the fastest growing components of sport promotions, and involves the creation of a strategic alliance in which the manufacturer of a sport product gives permission to a second party to manufacture that product in return for specific royalties or payments. Personal contact involves one-on-one communication between a representative of the sport organization and the sport consumer that should result in achieving promotional objectives ranging from providing information about products and services, to generating sales. Incentives are the benefits or reduced costs that are offered to motivate a sport consumer to purchase the specified sport product or service. Atmospherics utilizes the design of visual communications in an environment, such as lighting, colors, music, to entice the sport consumer's perceptual and emotional responses to purchase the sport product or service.

There are a number of generalizations that can be made about promotion. Promotions temporarily increase sales substantially; promotion in one product category affect sales of brands in complementary and competitive categories; and promotions can result in increased traffic. Most of the generalizations are true; however, it is important to understand how to utilize these elements in order to ensure that the results are longer lasting, and lead to maintaining current and attracting new customers.

Advertising

Advertising is one of the primary elements of the promotional mix. It is the process of attracting public attention to a sport product or sport business through paid announcements in the print, broadcast, or electronic media. Sport advertising is the communication process utilized most often in sport marketing – sending paid messages through communication channels to the sport consumer with the goal of persuading them to make a purchase.

There are three distinctions within advertising: advertisements, advertising campaigns, and integrated brand promotion (IBP). Advertisements are paid public announcements about a product or service through the print, broadcast, or electronic media that are designed to attract public attention and subsequent purchase. Advertising campaigns are a series of advertisement messages with a single mission and theme that are promoted through a variety of media options during a specified time frame. IBP is the use of multiple promotional tools in a coordinated manner to build and maintain overall awareness, identify, and preference for sport products, services, and the associated brands. These methods, to be discussed in detail throughout the chapter, are crucial to getting the message out to the target audience. As a result, understanding the basic communication process is a natural first step in understanding the entire advertising process.

Sponsorship

Sport sponsorship involves acquiring the rights to be affiliated with a sport product or event in order to obtain benefits from that association. Sport sponsorship is another significant element of the promotional mix as the main goal is to promote a product or service through a third party (sport product or event). Sport sponsorship is seen at multiple levels within the sport business landscape, including with governing bodies, teams, athletes, facilities, events, and the broadcast media. Through the articulation of corporate and brand goals, the sport marketing professional creates various criteria for sport sponsorship, and then utilizes that criteria to choose the companies the sport organization should partner with. The sport marketing professional is involved at all levels from developing sport sponsorship packages to engaging in sponsorship negotiations.

Public Relations

In sport marketing, this element of promotions is so significant it is broken out into the fifth "P" of the sport marketing mix, and often referred to as publicity. Publicity focuses on the use of unpaid, non-personal promotion of a sport product or service through a third party that publishes print media or presents information through radio, television, or the Internet. The goal of any good publicity is that it is viewed as coming from an unbiased, neutral source.

As a sport marketing professional, understanding and utilizing public relations is critical to success, as it is the management function that helps to evaluate public attitudes, articulate policies and procedures of an organization that may be of public interest, and execute programs of action to acquire public understanding and approval. Three aspects of public relations utilized in sport marketing efforts are media relations, sports information, and sport journalism.

Media Relations

Media relations is the activity that involves working directly with individuals responsible for the production of mass media including news, features, public service announcements, and sponsored programming. Effective media relations maximize coverage and placement of messages and information in the mass media without paying for it directly through advertising.

Most media relations activities are designed to get free media coverage for programs and issues. The major advantage of this effort is in the appearance of neutrality. There is usually a significant level of cynicism toward paid advertising because it is viewed as a first person account of a message. Publicity through media outlets are viewed as second-party accounts, and therefore viewed in a more positive light.

Getting free media coverage is not easy because there is a lot of competition for limited amount of air time or print space. Therefore, in order to entice the media to cover your story, event, product, or service, it is imperative that the sport marketing department in coordination with the communications department cover the issues fully, and present an attractive and complete picture of what needs to be covered. This will entice the media to be more receptive to coverage, mainly because of the less work they must put into print or broadcast the information. However, it is important that the organization will have no control of the end result of the publicity – it is all in the hands of the media outlet. If your message is not clear to the media, they may interpret their own meaning, and this may result in the intent of the organizational message to become blurred or skewed.

From the internal sport organization, the sport marketing professional and/or separate sport media relations coordinator must provide to the mass media information that maximize the communication of ideas, images, and information that supports the philosophy, mission, and vision of the sport organization. At the same time, they seek to minimize the negative or incorrect impressions of the sport organization that appear in the mass media. While the latter is more difficult to control, building awareness through maximizing communication efforts is key to the successful integration of internal media relations efforts and external mass media production. This is most easily accomplished by knowing what the mass media is looking to cover and assisting the mass media present all information as clearly and fairly as possible.

The best media relations pieces include the following:

- Different, expanded, or new information about the organization or a product/service.
- The KISS (keep it simple, stupid) principle – state information in a simple and clear format that will be interesting to the reader.

- Include quotes or research from credible or well-respected sources.
- Have information that is relevant to the local community where the information will be published or broadcast.
- Provide information in a timely manner (in many cases, stories more than 24-hour old will not be covered).

Sports Information

A specialized area of media relations is sports information. Sports information involves gathering results and other pertinent sporting information on individuals, teams, departments, and leagues. Once the information has been gathered, it is the responsibility of the sports information director to shape the message and disseminate this information to all media outlets. This last aspect is where a sports information director or department differs from sports journalism.

The largest entity in sports information dissemination is ESPN. Now a subsidiary of ABC, ESPN started as an alternative to standard television news broadcasts and the information found in "Sports" sections of newspapers. It began as a fairly small operation and often had to broadcast unorthodox sporting events, such as the World's Strongest Man Competition; international sports relatively unknown in the United States, such as Australian Rules Football, as well as the short-lived United States Football League (USFL), to attract viewers. In 1987, ESPN landed a contract to show National Football League (NFL) games on Sunday evenings, an event which marked as a turning point in its development from a smaller cable television network to a marketing empire, a cornerstone to the enthusiastic "sports culture" it largely helped to create.

Sport Journalism

Sport journalism encompasses all types of reportage and media coverage of current events in the world of sport. All forms of media are included: press, magazines, television, radio, and electronic media. The various disciplines practiced include writing, commentary, reporting, interviewing, and photography. Sport journalism is highly specialized and requires specialist knowledge, but the disciplines and practices employed by a sport journalist do not differ greatly from those of a standard journalist.

Licensing

The licensing process gives sport organizations the opportunity to establish a presence in a specified marketplace while also creating a new source of revenue. This is most often accomplished through the creation of licensed merchandise, such as hats, shirts, uniforms, and other apparel. The goal of licensing is to enhance brand awareness and appeal, especially in new markets.

The licensing process involves protecting an intellectual property such as a logo or mark. The intellectual property may be registered publicly, for example in the form of a *patent* or *trademark*, as a means of establishing ownership rights.

It may also be retained within the firm. Commonly referred to as *know-how*, this intellectual property is commonly based on operational experience.

The licensee usually makes a lump sum (front end) payment. Additionally, there is normally a *royalty rate* which tends to vary around a "rule of thumb" of 5%, depending on the type of industry and rate of technological change. A minimum performance (payment) clause is considered essential and some firms allow the licensee a "period of grace" to get production and marketing started. There are also some companies that agree on a *cross-licensing* deal, whereby they just swap licenses instead of paying.

Royalty Management and Distribution

Licensing, as a promotional tool, is a business arrangement in which the manufacturer of a product (or a firm with proprietary rights over certain technology, trademarks, etc.) grants permission to some other group or individual to manufacture that product (or make use of that proprietary material) in return for specified royalties or other payment.

Royalties are a share of income, in accordance with the terms of a license agreement, paid by a licensor for the right to make, use, or sell a product or service. Royalty management and distribution of funds is usually handled by a third party who will advise and make recommendations during contract negotiations.

The benefits of a third-party royalty management firm are:

- An assessment of risks to the license portfolio.
- The development of strategies to manage, monitor, and control those portfolios.
- The establishment of compliance programs for licensing, distribution, pricing, and other contractual agreements.
- Forensic-based royalty examinations.
- Commercial reviews of royalty and financial provisions in agreements.
- Advice on royalty rates and licensing fees.
- Acting as expert witness.

Personal Contact

One of the most effective ways to promote products and services is through one-on-one communication between a representative of the sport organization and the sport consumer. The goal of personal contact is to provide additional information about products and services in a manner that is not sales based or visibly targeted. The sport marketing professional seeks to build awareness of the organization and its products and services through goodwill in the community, and social involvement with the members of the population. This is accomplished through community relations and "giving back" efforts through socialization.

Community Relations

Community relations is the process of the sport organization interacting and connecting with the target population within a specific area. Community relations is an integral part of any sports organization whether the relationship is player, team, or league initiated. The main goal of community relations and sport organization is to foster goodwill in the community and develop a long-term relationship with individuals and the community as a whole. This type of effort is a monumental and fragile undertaking, as it only takes one negative comment or action to erode years of goodwill.

There are a number of community relations projects in the sporting world. Community relations efforts can be league initiated, team initiated, player initiated, or event initiated. The NFL has a long-standing community relations effort (32 years) with the United Way to strengthen America's communities. Almost every professional team has a community relations department for involvement in their area. The Boston Red Sox work with an organization known as the Jimmy Fund. Since 1953, the Red Sox have worked to raise money and awareness in the fight against cancer in New England and around the world.

Individual players also engaged in their own community relations efforts. One example is Kansas City Chiefs wide receiver Eddie Kennison. He has set up a foundation called Quick Start – The Eddie Kennison Foundation (www.eddieken nisonfoundation.com). According to their website, the NFL player and his wife formed this foundation in 2003 to make a difference in the Kansas City area (where he plays) and his hometown of Lake Charles, Louisiana. The organization works to raise awareness and generate funds to find a cure for the autoimmune disease lupus, as well as to give back to the communities in the form of scholarships. They host a number of events to raise funds and build awareness, including a celebrity fashion show, celebrity golf tournaments, walks, decal sells, raffles, and more. In addition to his foundation, Kennison also is a part of the NFL's "Play It Smart" program by serving as a mentor to high school children, and regularly makes visits to hospitals to visit sick children.

As far as event community relations, one example would be the FedEx Orange Bowl Foundation (http://www.orangebowl.org/committee.php). The success of the Orange Bowl is accomplished by the hard work of more than 1000 community volunteers. In return, the Orange Bowl Foundation gives back to the Miami and South Florida communities. According to their mission [The Foundation's] organizes, sponsors, produces, promotes, and participates in athletic contests, educational opportunities, clinics, expositions, and other similar programs and projects for the youth of South Florida communities and to raise and receive funds from sponsors and the general public, and to use such funds to provide these benefits.

Socialization

Socialization is usually done by an individual or team to demonstrate their commitment to the community or city. This is a type of "giving back" to the community. Some players will not give their hard earned money to foster community relations; they prefer to give their time. A historic example that has been recounted in baseball lore for centuries is Babe Ruth, who regularly visited children's hospital to boost their spirits, telling one child that he was going to hit a homerun for him that afternoon … which he did. Today, professional athletes work soup kitchens on holidays, bring Thanksgiving or Christmas turkeys to homes of the needy, and even give free sports clinics, all in the name of giving back to the community.

During the 2005 season, the head coach of Notre Dame, Charlie Weis, visited a very sick child that was a huge Notre Dame Football fan. During their conversation, Coach Weis ask the child if their was anything that he could do for him, the child said he would like to call the first offensive play against the number one ranked University of Southern California. The child passed away the day before the game, but Coach Weis honored his request.

These acts of socialization are what solidify personal relationships and make differences in individual lives, as well as, the community. It also allows the viewing public to gain a glimpse into what they perceive to be the human side of being a celebrity in professional sports.

Incentives

Incentives are the benefits or reduced costs that are offered to motivate a sport consumer to purchase the specified sport product or service. This may include price deals, premiums, contests, free samples, and a number of other benefits that will encourage the sport consumer to purchase a product or service. Incentives are mainly used during the later stages of the promotional process, as the customer is already aware of the sport product or service, and often needs the extra push of an incentive to make a purchase. In sport marketing and promotions, there are three main categories of incentives: price-based incentives, sales incentives, and behavioral incentives.

Price-Based Incentives

Price-based incentives are benefits derived from lowering the retail price of a product or service. Some of the most common types of price-based incentives include discount pricing, coupon redemption, and free trials. While this method may be good to attract customers that would otherwise not purchase the product or service, the sport marketing professional and sport organization that becomes too reliant on such an effort is doomed for failure. Offering too many price breaks may decrease the image of the brand, and cause problems with those customers who had to pay full price for the product or service.

Sales Incentives

Sales incentives offer a premium to attract first time or bulk buyers of products and/or services, but more often are used to reward those repeat customers. It is important to make similar sales incentives available to all customers. An example would be the comparison between a season ticket holder who needs four extra tickets to a game, and an individual who is buying tickets for a group of 100. The season ticket holder has more revenue potential in the short term because of the price of the season ticket. Therefore, you may offer a 10% discount on the additional tickets. The group bringing 100 fans to the game is considered a solid customer who may repeat this buying behavior in the future, or any of the 100 fans might be a future customer. However, if that group leader did not get a discount equal to 10%, and they were to find out about the deal with the season ticket holder, they may be discouraged and not make this purchase or any future purchases. In turn, if the group gets a 20% discount on the 100 tickets and the season ticket holder finds out, he might be put off by the organization and potentially cancel their season ticket subscription.

Behavioral Incentives

Behavioral incentives are inducements made to consumers to entice them to purchase a product or service based on a perceptual relationship created between the consumer and the product or service. One of the most significant behavioral incentives is achievement. This achievement may be in the form of a participation opportunity, a desire to gain intellectual knowledge, or the desire to reach a certain level of recognition.

Another major behavioral incentive involves affiliation. Human beings in general have a sense of needing to belong. Sport products and services offer that opportunity of involvement. The singing and camaraderie seen at a home soccer match in England, where singing takes place during the game often with someone they have never met. Behavioral incentives also serve as an opportunity to be part of a group. In fact, studies have shown that less than 2% of Americans attend a sporting event by themselves. In Australia, they have taken this sense of belonging a step further by offering Australian Rules Football fans the opportunity to become a "member" of the club for a fee. This customer to organization affiliation is very strong and deep rooted, and can be utilized by sport marketers to offer additional products and services.

Atmospherics

Atmospherics is the intentional control and structure based on environmental cues. Sports business must direct considerable attention to way in which the atmosphere of their consumption environment can promote the desired relationship with clientele. Atmospherics represents the collection of all elements in a brand's marketing mix that facilitate exchanges by targeting the brand to a group of customers, positioning the brand as somehow distinct from other brands. Examples of this are sports drinks. Gatorade, Red Bull, PowerAde, SoBe, and Double Shot are all targeted primarily at teens. Companies have positioned the brand as standing for fun, exhilaration, and energy; and communicated the brand using a diversity of promotional media and sponsorships. By maintaining a consistent message over time the brands will achieve their goal.

Managing atmospherics starts with gaining an understanding of the target market. Once defined, the sport marketing professional will develop a theme

l be attractive to the market and meaningful to the sport consumer. This
s choosing those elements of the physical setting that the target market
able to relate to. To enhance the message, the delivery also will include
sensory elements to ensure the message is received and remembered.

rfect example of this process can be seen in Gatorade's commercials.

latest commercial depicts professional basketball player Minnesota's
Kevin Garnett bursting out of a basketball at center court of a fenced in black-
top basketball court, just like millions of recreational courts across America.
With sweat dripping off him, the first thing that he does is drink Gatorade.
Now, no one in the world is bursting out of a basketball, however, the notion
that arguably the best player in the game today attributes his success to drinking Gatorade all his life is plausible, and will result in fans around the globe
purchasing Gatorade.

Sport Promotion Strategies

The purpose of a sport promotional strategy is to build brand loyalty and product credibility, develop image, and position the brand. A promotional strategy is
similar to a marketing strategy, but the promotional strategy seeks short-term
objectives, both direct and indirect. Promotional objectives usually include
increased sales, stimulate impulse buying, raise customer traffic, and present and
reinforce image. It also provides information about products and services, pub-
licizes new stores or websites, and creates and enhances customer satisfaction.

A sport marketing professional must understand the various parts of promotional integration, which is usually viewed as one of the final stages of the entire
sport marketing process. Promotional integration is the actual creation and
delivery of the promotional message that involves defining how the message is
to reach the consumer, ensuring that the promotional message will be received
and understood, and that the promotional message will lead to the purchase of
a product or service. This process starts with building awareness, which is the
measurement of the percent of the target market that knows about the organization's products and/or services, including customer recall as related to brand
recognition, brand features, or brand positioning.

This is followed by a series of integrations that will lead to the overall strategic
promotional implementation. Image integration is the relationship of the opinion
of consumers and the sport product, service, and/or organization affects how it is
promoted. Functional integration is how the design or operations of the product,
service, and/or organization can be utilized to effectively promote it. Coordinated
integration is how all operational aspects of the organization work together to
promote the products, services, and/or the organization itself. Consumer-based
integration is the involvement of the buyers and users of product and services as an
integral part of the promotional process. Stakeholder-based integration is how the
ownership and employees of the organization have a vested interest in the efficient
promotion of the product, service, and/or organization. Relationship management
integration is how all aspects discussed above work cooperatively with each other
to effectively and efficiently promote the product, service, or organization.

Direct promotional strategy involves the actual process of identifying customers, connecting with them, increasing their awareness and interest in the product or service being offered, and persuading them to make a purchase. Direct promotional strategy is centered on the concept of sales management as previously discussed in Chapter 7. The promotional strategy employed by the sport marketer must involve initiating the contact with the sport consumer. This often involves creating exposure through a non-personal medium such as a catalog, television commercial, or infomercial. The sport consumer then enters into the decision making process, which may result in either ordering a sport product by mail, phone, fax, or Internet, or choosing to find out more information about the sport organization.

Indirect promotional strategy refers to all the methods an individual or organization can create, convey, and place messages in the mind of the prospective customer. There are four motives for an indirect promotional strategy:

1. Positioning the product
2. Enhancing the brand and building brand equity
3. Providing credibility
4. Using image transfer and association positioning

Unfortunately, with so much information provided, the promoter must be concise and clear in designing a message to win "space" in the consumer's mind. The consumer must believe that the product or service and in the company providing that product or service. The relationship between the company and the consumer must be based on the products: usefulness, prestige, durability, attractiveness, and/or perceived attributes.

The most common method of indirect promotions is word-of-mouth, defined as spoken communication that does not come from the primary party. Examples of this include testimonials, referrals, endorsements, and impressions through promotions. *Testimonials* consist of the words and experiences of past users of the products or services being promoted. Individuals who offer testimonials send a message to potential and repeats customers about the positive interaction they have had with the product, service, and/or organization, including the quality of customer service, and the plan to continue involvement with the product. Testimonials are often found on the websites or marketing materials of companies. While some testimonials come from famous people, the most beneficial often come from the general public since the potential consumer has a better chance of relating to that testimonial. The following are two examples of testimonials from Warrior Custom Golf (www.warriorcustomgolf.com), a custom golf club company:

> Thank you for inviting me to try your new golf clubs. After seventy years searching I have found the perfect golf clubs. The natural feel; the solid hit make the club feel like it is part of me. I am getting 10 to 20 yards more distance with the woods and the control with the irons in unbelievable. I LIKE THEM!!!

> These clubs and service meet and exceed my expectations … Thank you Warrior Custom Golf, your product speaks for itself, "outstanding"!

Referrals are recommendations made by one individual to another about a specific product, service, or organization. Most referral come from friends, but may also come from everyday people. Most referral programs are combined with incentives. If one individual refers another, and that person makes a purchase, then the referee would get a thank you gift, a discount on a future purchase, a gift certificate, or some other benefit as a reward.

Endorsements usually use high profile individuals such as athletes, actors, and prominent businesspersons to use their notoriety or position to assist an organization in promoting or selling their products or services, with the result being an increased image because of the association. One of the most popular endorsement efforts in the 1990s and 2000s is the Total Gym® (www.totalgymdirect.com). The Total Gym® is a single piece of exercise equipment that allows the user to do over 80 exercises in one's own home. To market this product on television, Total Gym® secured former supermodel Christie Brinkley, and actor and former karate champion Chuck Norris, to endorse the product. This association has been highly successful as the product now sells close to 100 countries worldwide and is not only regularly used by general consumers, but also sport medicine clinics, hospitals, and rehabilitation centers.

Impressions refer to the sport organization receiving third-party exposure through the media to create an association between the product or service being promoted and the reader (print or Internet), listener (radio and television), or viewer (television or live). Impressions are tracked by sport marketing professionals to determine whether the marketing effort being employed is beneficial and profitable to the organization.

CONCLUSION

Communication management involves the planning, implementing, supervising, evaluation, and modification of the various methods of communication internal and external to a sport organization. The sport marketing professional is involved in a number of roles to make sure that effective and efficient communication takes place throughout the organization in terms of the marketing process. These include developing organizational communication, control the flow of information in and out of the sport organization through various communication methods, managing sport organizational images, administering the organizational crisis communication plan, and providing communication training to all organizational staff.

In order to achieve total quality communication management, the sport marketing professional must focus on having a full understanding of the communication process, the sport organization's image, crisis sport communications, and sport promotions. Understanding the communication process helps to establish and maintain relationships with the sport consumer by providing a conduit for listening and reacting to the sport consumer. Managing the sport organization's images includes the role of the brand, the logo, and publicity play in communication information to the external environment. Crisis sport communication planning allows the sport organization to control the quantity, flow, and type of information being released to the public and the media.

Promotions is a very involved communications process that aids in providing information about the sport product, service, or organization to consumers through the promotional mix.

The elements of the sport promotional mix include advertising, sponsorship, public relations, licensing, personal contact, incentives, and atmospherics. Advertising involves paid, non-personal communications about a sport product or service through the print, broadcast, or electronic media that are designed to attract public attention and subsequent purchase. Sponsorship refers to the relationship between a corporation and a sport organization as a tool to develop brand image and customer loyalty as a result of the association. Public relations is the collection of activities, communications, and media coverage that convey what the sport organization is and what they have to offer, all in the effort to enhance their image and prestige. Media relations, sports information, and sport journalism are all significant components of public relations.

Licensing is the creation of a strategic alliance in which the manufacturer of a sport product gives permission to a second party to manufacture that product in return for specific royalties or payments. Personal contact involves one-on-one communication between a representative of the sport organization and the sport consumer that should result in achieving promotional objectives ranging from providing information about products and services, to generating sales. Community relations and giving back to the community through socialization efforts are critical elements of personal contact.

Incentives are the benefits or reduced costs that are offered to motivate a sport consumer to purchase the specified sport product or service. Incentives are categorized as price-based incentives, sales incentives, and behavioral incentives. Atmospherics utilizes the design of visual communications in an environment, such as lighting, colors, music, to entice the sport consumer's perceptual and emotional responses to purchase the sport product or service.

To coordinate the interaction between the elements of the sport promotional mix, a strategy must be developed that focuses on building brand loyalty and product credibility, developing image, and positioning the brand. The strategic process involves promotional integration, which is the actual creation and delivery of the promotional message that involves defining how the message is to reach the consumer, ensuring that the promotional message will be received and understood, and that the promotional message will lead to the purchase of a product or service.

This process starts with building awareness, and is then followed by a series of integrations (image, functional, coordinated, consumer-based, stakeholder-based, and relationship management) that will lead to the overall strategic promotional implementation. This implementation will either be indirect or direct in nature. Much of indirect promotional strategy focuses on word-of-mouth, including testimonials, referrals, endorsements, and impressions through promotions. In contrast, direct promotional strategy is centered on sales management, which involves the actual process of identifying customers, connecting with them, increasing their awareness and interest in the product or service being offered, and persuading them to make a purchase.

Opening Back Doors into the World of Sports Marketing

Sport marketing can be considered an umbrella term used loosely to describe behind-the-scenes elements of a sport, athlete, or game of some sort. From lawn mower racing to competitive eating, most events and the planning, publicity, and sponsorship efforts behind them can be classified as sport marketing.

So, if you are interested in pursuing a career in sport marketing, it is okay to dream big and go for that glamorous NFL job. Just do not forget to think out of the box and look for opportunities that may not be in your face, but can bring you invaluable experience to take to the big leagues, especially in the world of public relations.

As someone with more than 13-year experience in public relations, working on everything from food, hotels, and non-profit organizations to home repair and e-commerce, I am amazed at how almost every account I have worked on has had an element of sport marketing at some point. Why? Because sport is like music – a universal language that can bring out the passion in consumers and ultimately help with any purchasing decisions if it connects a product with the right audience.

Take, for instance, the launch of Post Oreo O's cereal (*do we need permission to mention brands? If so, then I would say "the national launch of a new cereal for kids"*). We knew that linking local professional NBA players with events in select target markets would add a cool factor for kids and make them interested in trying the new cereal and telling their friends.

There is also the idea of creating a sport to market your product. Lawn mower racing was created to market a fuel stabilizer and the public relations firm behind it became the national headquarters for the US Lawn Mower Racing Association, now the governing body of die-hard lawn mower racers everywhere. The sport gets bigger and bigger every year.

Working with non-profit organizations, especially those raising money to cure diseases, is a surefire way to gain experience working with professional athletes and teams. They are always looking for meaningful ways to get involved in their community and try to make a difference. Many athletes have personal connections to these causes, which can help in negotiating time commitment and help you gain experience with accommodating athletes.

Another thing to keep in mind is that while you may not be the person negotiating sponsorship deals, running an event, or representing an athlete, there are many details of those deals that need to be executed once an agreement is reached which can lead to opportunity. One of my clients is a national food commodity and a sponsor of the NFL. Because there are commitments each party has to keep with each other, public relations is usually the "go-to" discipline to help meet those commitments. Another client is a nationally known food brand and a NASCAR sponsor. They expect that relationship to be factored into public relations plans every year, thus providing their marketing and public relations folks some excellent exposure among the world of NASCAR.

Also keep in mind that many corporations that sponsor major sporting events, venues, or teams have marketing departments and staff solely devoted to handling those relationships or working with agencies.

There are many ways to gain entry-level experience for your resume and help it stand out to potential employers:

- Intern in the public relations or marketing department of a professional or amateur team – consider the minor leagues and arena football as well as the MLB and the NFL.
- Intern with a public relations firm or advertising agency with clients involved in sport marketing.
- Intern with a sport radio station.
- Volunteer with non-profit groups to work fundraising events like 5 K Runs.
- Get involved with staffing a local marathon, especially in a big market like New York, Chicago, or Boston.
- Intern or at least conduct an informational interview with a sport agent.
- Investigate resources such as IEG (International Events Group – sponsorship.com) or WorkInSports.com for leads.
- Be persistent.

You should know that most entry-level opportunities involve lots of hands-on grunt work, weekends and evenings. In other words, it is expected that you will be flexible with your schedule if you are really committed to doing well and having a career in sport marketing. It will pay off eventually.

Sidebar Ideas

Things you may not have considered when trying to embark on a sport marketing career:

- Do not always go for the glamour (knock on back doors too!) – there are opportunities way beyond pro teams or sport marketing agencies. Consider non-profit organizations, public relations and advertising agencies, or the actual sponsors.
- Think philanthropy – someone needs to be the liaison between a good cause and a pro athlete or sponsors, it might as well be you.

Continued

- Pursue sponsors – if you have a passion for NASCAR, then look at what kinds of products or companies sponsor NASCAR, not just the NASCAR organization itself.
- Do not let your dreams give you tunnel vision – be prepared to take your licks in the beginning and look beyond your No. 1 passion. You dream may be to work with major league baseball someday, but the rodeo just may be where the opportunities lie right now.

SPORT ADVERTISING

CHAPTER OBJECTIVES

The reader will be able to:

- Appreciate the role of sport advertising for sport team, sport retail business, and the overall business process.
- Know the structure of the sport advertising industry including advertisers, agencies, and support organizations.
- Recognize the various social, ethical, and regulatory aspects of sport advertising, including the role of consumer behavior, business ethics concepts, and ambush marketing.
- Realize the complexity of creating sport advertisements and commercials.

- Understand the integration of the field of sport and the engagement of inter-disciplinary thinking as it related to audio-visual communications, development communications, telecommunications, and mass communications.
- Be familiar with the relationship between sport marketing and integrated brand promotion (IBP).

WHAT IS SPORT ADVERTISING?

As discussed in the previous chapter, sport advertising is the process of attracting public attention to a sport product or sport business through paid announcements in the print, broadcast, or electronic media. Traditionally, advertising was viewed as an artistic profession that was simply used to articulate product benefits and image. However, advertising has evolved to become one of the critical elements of business. This is especially true in sport advertising, where these efforts are used as an integral tool of marketing as related to brand development and management, segmentation, differentiation, and positioning.

Consumers are increasingly "bombarded" with advertising messages and information. As a consequence of this information overkill, a brand has become the abbreviation of all of its positive and negative rational and emotional associations. The brand strategy has a direct impact on the brand's corporate value – success on the market, growth, market share, price, margins, and earnings – and thus on market capitalization and corporate value.

A brand strategy must result in a conclusive, focused, and efficient marketing mix, and must be economically viable. This strategy would involve looking at the following:

- What is the "actual" position of a brand from the consumer's perspective? What are the actual value perception (AVP), projected value proposition (PVP), actual consumer base, and competitive environment?
- What "ideal" target position should the brand take in the competitive environment? The target value proposition (TVP) should be strategically differentiated from the competition.
- What is the optimal brand strategy from the "actual" to the "ideal" brand position? A road map including milestones from actual to target position of a brand.
- What are the corresponding measurements for the entire marketing mix? Things such as an action plan, or future execution (FX), that are consistent across the entire marketing mix.
- What are the costs involved and what is the impact on the business plan? Cost of repositioning, consequences for turnover, margin, and profitability in the short, mid, and long term.

This strategy then flows into the branding process. The results of this process should provide the sport consumer with a clear understanding of the attributes and values of the brand. The process starts by completing an analysis of the target market, including identifying the brand audience, understanding the target consumers, determining key customer leverage points and behaviors, and monitoring the actions of direct and indirect competitors. Once this is enacted, the development of brand architecture should ensue. This involves managing the relationship structures between the various levels with the organization, as well as with sub-brands and other products and services being offered by the organization. As these relationships are solidified, communication with potential and existing consumers must be developed to provide a clear description of how they should view and value the product or service. This message not only be clear, but also articulate the quality and usefulness of the product or service, comes from a trustworthy source, and be consistent over time. The final step is the establishment of feedback systems, so that consumers have an avenue to response with their perceptions of the product or service. This is crucial to determine if whether the advertising and branding processes are working, and if there are other opportunities that could be targeted. It also provides significant information about problems with the entire process, which in turn requires the sport marketing professional to reevaluate and retool the entire advertising and branding process.

Today's markets are more volatile than before and possibly the traditional "mass media" advertising focus is no longer appropriate. One option is to focus on different niches of the market where we are able to satisfy their needs and wants. This is possible with market segmentation – dividing the market into groups of potential clients with similar needs and profiles and which present similar buying habits.

Market segmentation is the basis of other marketing actions. It will require a big management effort to direct the strategy to each market niche and also the necessary investigation, implementation, and control for realizing a correct segmentation. The main objective of the segmentation is to improve the position of the company and better serve the needs of the consumers. We will be able also to increase sales, improve our market share, and improve our image.

How many segments should we consider? The answer is logical; we should act in as many segments as our business capacity allows us. To get a product or service to the right person or company, a marketer would firstly segment the market, then target a single segment or series of segments, and finally position within the segment(s).

Segmentation is essentially the identification of subsets of buyers within a market who share similar needs and who demonstrate similar buyer behavior. The world is made up of many buyers with their own sets of needs and behavior. Segmentation aims to match groups of purchasers with the same set of needs and buyer behavior. Such a group is known as a "segment." Market segmentation allows product differentiation by preparing appropriate marketing mixes for each market segment, organized distribution according to buying characteristics, and more focused media advertising according to habits and lifestyles.

Targeting strategies usually can be categorized as concentrated, differentiated, product-specialized, market-specialized, or full coverage. Concentrated strategy is a single-segment strategy where one market segment is served with one marketing mix. A single-segment approach often is the strategy of choice for smaller companies with limited resources. Differentiated strategy is a selective specialization or multiple-segment strategy where different marketing mixes are offered to different segments. The product itself may or may not be different – in many cases only the promotional message or distribution channels vary. Product specialization involves an organization specializing in a particular product or service, and tailoring it to different market segments. Market specialization differs in that the organization specializes in serving a particular market segment, and offers that segment an array of different products. Full market coverage is the organization's attempt to serve the entire market. This coverage can be achieved by means of either a mass market strategy in which a single undifferentiated marketing mix is offered to the entire market or by a differentiated strategy in which a separate marketing mix is offered to each segment.

Positioning is the process of designing a company's offer and image so that it occupies a distinct and valued place in the mind of the consumer. Positioning a product consists gaining a benign meaning in the customer's mind as to where the product sits in the market segment to which it belongs. This may be achieved by the product's own attributes or through the influence of advertising. The objective of positioning a product is to make sure that it occupies a certain place in the mind of the consumer, differentiating it from the competition.

Positioning is about how the product or service is differentiated in the mind of a prospective customer. It is an organized system for finding a window in the mind of your prospect in order to position your product – merchandise, a service, a company, or a person – effectively against its main competitors. This system is based on the concept that communication can only take place at the right time and under the right circumstances. The mind accepts only that new information which matches its current state. It filters out everything else. In other words, positioning is a process by which a psychological "anchor" (any stimulus which evokes a consistent response) has been placed into the mind of prospects so that they come to choose one specific person or company over another.

ADVERTISING FOR SPORT TEAMS AND SPORT RETAIL BUSINESSES

The real lesson seems to be that the advertising rules that apply to most traditional consumer brands do not apply to sports teams. Consumers looking to purchase sporting goods, usually search for the best price and/or the quickest service. The get it and forget it attitude applies in most cases. But loyal fans have an emotional bond nearly impossible to break. The Cubs make a good counterpoint to the Yankees; the team's fans are just as true despite not having won a championship since 1908. You could argue that the Cubs are consistent losers, that they deliver on what has become an unfortunate brand promise. So ball clubs may have little to learn from brand marketers. But perhaps brands can learn from the sports teams' ability to develop ties with their consumers strong enough to withstand the toughest challenges.

In 2001, Manchester United, one of England's best-known soccer clubs, joined forces with Major League Baseball team the New York Yankees in a merger that sought to raise the profile of both clubs across the globe. Under the marketing alliance, Manchester United explored sponsorship, television, and other cross-promotional opportunities with YankeeNets LLC, the parent company of the New York Yankees, which also owned at that time the New Jersey Nets NBA (National Basketball Association) basketball team and the New Jersey Devils of the National Hockey League. The agreement resulted in Manchester United's own television channel, MUTV, broadcasting Yankee game highlights, for example, and Manchester United replica kits sharing boutique space with Yankee pinstripes.

In this example, the brand extensions for team loyalty and image sought to gain footholds in the American market for soccer, and in Great Britain, Asia, and the Far East for baseball. Both clubs hoped to use their fan base to promote each other's products. This marked a fundamental change in brand loyalty, with the introduction of cross-cultural marketing of unlike sports. The long-term benefits of mergers such as this could significantly distance the organizations from their peers financially, giving them another advantage on game day. While this partnership dissolved due in part to the break-up of YankeeNets LLC, the concept has now led to the discussion of similar partnerships between European Premier League Clubs and Major League Soccer (MLS) Clubs, including Arsenal and the Colorado Rapids, and Chelsea with DC United.

Is there too much promotion? More likely there is not enough. When it comes to the down time of professional sports, the "in-game entertainment" has become part of the show through various gimmicks, pyrotechnics, and promotions. These special events have blurred the line between sport and entertainment. Teams pay more attention to the food, free T-shirts being sling-shot into the crowd, blimps that circle over the crowd and drop items into the customers' laps, exotic laser light shows, and various events that take place at half-time or between the periods. It is all done with the intent to make games into events, and help the consumer justify the cost of the ticket.

Consumer communications are crucial for a retailer to position itself in customers' minds. Various physical and symbolic cues can be used, such as store location, merchandise assortment, price levels, physical facilities, mass advertising and public relations, personal selling, and sales promotion. A retail image requires a multifaceted, ongoing process. For chains, it is essential that there be a consistent image among branches.

The retailer's interior and exterior of a store encompasses its parking, display windows, flooring, colors, lighting, scents and sounds, temperature, width of aisles, dressing facilities, personnel, self-service, merchandise, price displays, cash register placement, technology and modernization, and cleanliness. All of these are designed to elicit a specific response while promoting the corporate message to consumers.

To persuade customers to devote more time in the store, some of the most common retail tactics include experiential merchandising, solutions selling, retailer co-branding, and wish list programs. Customers react favorably to retailers involved in such activities as establishing stores that are barrier-free for disabled persons, supporting charities, and running special sales for senior citizens. The more positive or pleasant feelings a retailer can provide the consumer, the more favorable feeling will be placed on the franchise or brand.

Advertising in pro shops can help a company, such as golf pro shops, transform their bottom lines in a number of different ways. Because the consumer has already entered the place of business, a company can focus their advertising dollars on making the consumers experience a pleasant and memorable one. The company can also solicit sponsorship because the pro shop has already created a target-rich environment in the golfing industry.

A pro shop can generate revenue by companies sponsoring a hole, tee box, fairway, green, club house, or naming rights for the course. Self-promotion in the pro shop can bolster corporate functions such as a golf tournament or inventory blow out. In some cases, golf pro shops offer touch screen GPS locators that helps their consumers range each green. In the down time for this technology, companies can advertise their products on the LCD screen or place an order at the snack bar to be picked up at the turn.

Brand loyalty is a consumer's preference to buy a particular brand in a product category. It occurs because consumers perceive that the brand offers the needed product features, images, or level of quality at the right price. This perception becomes the foundation for a new buying habit. Consumers initially will make a trial purchase of the brand and, after satisfaction, tend to form habits and continue purchasing the same brand because the product works well or is familiar.

Consumers must like the product in order to develop loyalty to it. In order to convert occasional purchasers into brand loyalists, habits must be reinforced. Consumers must be reminded of the value of their purchase and encouraged to continue purchasing the product in the future.

To encourage repeat purchases, advertisement before and after the sale is critical. In addition to creating awareness and promoting initial purchases, advertising shapes and reinforces consumer attitudes so these attitudes mature into beliefs, which need to be reinforced until they develop into loyalty.

SPORT ADVERTISING AND IMAGE

Sport is one of the most important social concepts. Many companies use sports as a tool to create brand loyalty. The companies using professional athletes produce the image that their equipment is the reason why the athlete is successful. As a result, the equipment produced by the company sells very well.

Advertisements make sports more popular. All the organizations hoping for profit use concepts like arts and sports to introduce or recreate themselves. This is the basic factor in sport image. Sport image can be used in various types in society. The basic objective of advertisements is to link the product with the success, and for the consumer to transfer that image of success to the product.

The case for advertising is traditionally based on its economic role. But a case can also be made for the psychological and social value of advertising. Advertising is everywhere, and people everywhere are united by it. Perhaps for the first time, young people of all ethnic and geographic origins share images and experiences, thanks in large measure to mass media and mass advertising.

More than 90% of the revenues from television advertising directed at children are reinvested into children's programs. Successful children's programs like Sesame Street rely upon advertising techniques to teach children all manner of things. Advertising has been doing this for years. Why, if a company can create brand loyalty at an early age, maintaining that loyalty is less costly as an adult. As stated earlier, it is more cost effective to foster the consumer–supplier relationship than it is to reinvent that relationship every time a purchase is made.

SOCIAL, ETHICAL, AND REGULATORY ASPECTS OF SPORT ADVERTISING

To identify and explain the economic, social, ethical, and legal issues, advertisers must consider that the basic economic principles that guided the evolution of advertising also have social and legal effects. When they are violated, social issues arise and the government may take corrective measures. Society determines what is offensive, excessive, and irresponsible; government bodies determine what is deceptive and unfair. To be law-abiding, ethical, and socially responsible, as well as economically effective, advertisers must understand these issues.

Since it is so visible, advertising gets criticized frequently, for both what it is and what it is not. Many of the criticisms focus on the style of advertising, saying it is deceptive or manipulative. Collectively it might refer to these as short-term manipulative arguments. Other criticisms focus on the social or environmental impact of advertising. These are long-term macro arguments. Discussion of the economic impact of advertising focuses primarily on the first two principles of free-market economics: self-interest and many buyers and sellers. The social aspect of advertising typically involves the last two principles: complete information and absence of externalities.

Social issue debates can be seen as instances where advertising tends to violate one or more of these basic economic principles. Some of the most important aspects of these principles are deception and manipulation in advertising, the effect of advertising on our value system, commercial clutter, stereotypes, and offensiveness. By examining these common criticisms of advertising, consumers can debunk some misconceptions, and examine the problems that do exist.

One of the most common short-term arguments about advertising is that it is so frequently deceptive. Anything that detracts from the satisfaction of the transaction produces a loss of activity that ultimately hurts both parties. If a product does not live up to its advertisements, dissatisfaction occurs – and in the long term that is as harmful to the advertiser as to the buyer.

For advertising to be effective, consumers must have confidence in it. So any kind of deception not only detracts from the complete information principle of free enterprise, but also risks being self-defeating. Even meaningless embellishment (puffery) might be taken literally and therefore become deceptive. Puffery refers to exaggerated, subjective claims that cannot be proven true or false, such as "the best," "premier," or "the only way to fly." Under current advertising law, the only product claims, explicit or implied, that are considered deceptive are those that are factually false or convey a false impression and therefore have the potential to deceive or mislead reasonable people. But puffery is excluded from this requirement because regulators maintain that reasonable people do not believe it anyway. Since advertisers regularly use puffery and non-product facts to enhance the image of their products, they must think consumers do believe it. Non-product facts are not about the brand but about the consumer or the social context in which the consumer uses the brand.

An example is "Pepsi – The choice of a new generation." The fact is that advertising, by its very nature, is not complete information. It is biased in favor of the advertiser and the brand. People expect advertisers to be proud of their products and probably do not mind if they puff them a little. But when advertisers cross the line between simply giving their point of view and creating false expectations, that is when people begin to object. One problem is the difficulty of seeing the line, which may be drawn differently by different people. These kinds of problems can be avoided if marketers simply improve the kind of information they give in their advertising. If companies required advertisers to have a reasonable basis for any claims they make, whether or not those claims are facts about the product. This would contribute positively to a free-market system.

Advertising to children presents different challenges. Kids are not sophisticated consumers. Their conceptions of self, time, and money are immature. As a result, they know very little about their desires, needs, and preference, or how to use economic resources rationally to satisfy them. The nature of children's conceptual ability makes it likely that child-oriented advertising can lead to false beliefs or highly improbable product expectations.

While most children and parents are still joint consumers, more and more children are becoming sole decision makers. To protect them, and their parents, both critics and defenders agree that advertisers should not intentionally deceive children. The central issue is how far advertisers should go to ensure that children are not misled by their advertisements. To promote responsible children's advertising and to respond to public concerns, the Council of Better Business Bureaus established the Children's Advertising Review Unit (CARU). CARU provides a general advisory service for advertisers and agencies, and also offers informational material for children, parents, and educators. For more than 20 years, CARU's Self-Regulatory Guidelines for Children's Advertising has guided marketers in the development of child-directed advertising for all traditional media.

In 1997, CARU published its updated Guidelines to include new directions for marketing to children via online media. The basic activity of CARU is the review and evaluation of child-directed advertising in all media. When children's advertising is found to be misleading, inaccurate, or inconsistent with the Guidelines, CARU seeks changes through voluntary cooperation of the advertisers.

In the developed world, other countries are far stricter than the United States about advertising to children. Sweden and Norway, for example, do not permit any television advertising to be directed toward children under 12, and no advertisements at all are allowed during children's programs. Germany and Holland prohibit sponsorship of children's shows, and the Flemish region of Belgium permits no advertisements 5 minutes before or after any programs for children.

In the area of television advertising, the government and consumer groups play an important role at both the national and international level to ensure that adequate consumer protection for children is maintained and strengthened where necessary.

One of the characteristics of the American political scene is our tripartite system of checks and balances. There are many laws that govern what advertisers can and cannot do. These laws are passed by legislatures, enforced by the executive branch, and interpreted by the judiciary. This system is repeated at the state and local levels.

On the national level, the president, cabinet departments, and various federal commissions are responsible for executing the laws passed by Congress. On the state level, the governor, attorney general, and state departments administer state laws. Locally, mayors, city managers, city attorneys, and police chiefs enforce the laws passed by city councils.

Similarly, local laws are interpreted by municipal courts, while the superior courts and state supreme courts interpret state laws. Federal laws are interpreted by federal district courts and the US Supreme Court. Every day, advertisers from the local mom and pop shop to international corporation marketers have to deal with the actions and decisions of all these branches of government.

In today's society, a major regulatory issue facing advertisers is privacy. Today, most advertisers know it is illegal to use a person's likeness in an advertisement without the individual's permission. Since 1987, even using a celebrity look alike or sound alike can violate that person's rights. The courts have also ruled that people's privacy rights continue even after their death.

Now, with the increased use of fax machines, cell phones, and the Internet, all of which can be used for advertising directly to prospects, the issue of privacy rights is again in the news. This time it is over people's right to protect their personal information. Privacy is an ethical issue as well as a legal one. It is also a practical issue: prospective customers who find advertising faxes, telemarketing calls, and emails annoying and intrusive are not likely to buy the offending company's products. Internet users worry about people they do not know, and even businesses they do know, getting personal information about them. This concern is not without reason since many websites create profiles of their visitors to get data such as email addresses, clothing sizes, or favorite books. Some sites also track users' hobbies, usually without their knowledge, to better target advertisements for products.

To create these user profiles, websites use tiny software programs, called cookies, that keep a log of where people click, allowing sites to track customers' web-surfing habits. The cookies are placed on people's computers when they first visit a site or use some feature like a personalized news service or a shopping cart. Internet companies argue that such tracking is not personal; it is typically performed anonymously and helps them customize sites and content to match users' interests.

Fortunately, consumers are not completely helpless. Consumers can disable the cookies on their computers. But this may limit their Internet access, because some websites actually require that cookies be implanted. Internet surfers also have the option to "opt-in." This feature allows users to set the terms for which they give personal information. Also available is the "opt-out" feature, which allows sites to continuously gather information about visitors unless they specifically inform the site not to by clicking on a button.

Business Ethics in Sport Advertising

Advertising helps to establish the corporate image or what the corporation wants as their image. The consumer interprets the advertising and promotional imprint and develops the corporate brand.

Advertising can announce a number of possibilities to the consumers. The "Truth in Advertising Creed" was developed because corporations wanted to gain market share. In the absence of information, consumers will listen and believe the loudest voice. If that voice is promoting fiction, or partial truths, how would the consumer know the difference? There are a number of non-governmental organizations that their sole purpose is to educate the consumer, such as the Better Business Bureau and Consumer Reports.

The Better Business Bureau keeps records of improprieties and of proper ethical standard on every business in the United States. While Consumer Reports continually tests products to provide the consumer with the most current, safest, quality products in the marketplace. Both of which can be accessed at no cost using the World Wide Web.

Some of the ethical issues in sport advertising include the following:

- *Truth*: Advertising shall tell the truth, and shall reveal significant facts, the omission of which would mislead the public.
- *Substantiation*: Advertising claims shall be substantiated by evidence in possession of the advertiser and advertising agency, prior to making such claims.
- *Comparisons*: Advertising shall refrain from making false, misleading, or unsubstantiated statements or claims about a competitor or his/her products or services.
- *Bait advertising*: Advertising shall not offer products or services for sale unless such offer constitutes a bona fide effort to sell the advertising products or services and is not a device to switch consumers to other goods or services, usually higher priced.
- *Guarantees and warranties*: Advertising of guarantees and warranties shall be explicit, with sufficient information to apprise consumers of their principal terms and limitations or, when space or time restrictions preclude such disclosures, the advertisement should clearly reveal where the full text of the guarantee or warranty can be examined before purchase.
- *Price claims*: Advertising shall avoid price claims which are false or misleading, or saving claims which do not offer provable savings.
- *Testimonials*: Advertising containing testimonials shall be limited to those of competent witnesses who are reflecting a real and honest opinion or experience.
- *Taste and decency*: Advertising shall be free of statements, illustrations, or implications which are offensive to good taste or public decency.

ETHICS IN ADVERTISING – SHOCK TREATMENT USING OFFENSIVE MARKETING

What is offensive marketing? Like pornography, it is hard to define, but we usually know it when we see it. In the race to grab audience's attention, some advertisers are willing to cross the line into blatantly sexist or even racist imagery. Yet there is little evidence to suggest this tactic is actually effective.

The reward centers in the human brain are activated by food, sex, drugs, money, and anything that feels pleasurable. A recent brain-imaging study at Massachusetts General Hospital found that the reward centers in the brains of young heterosexual males were activated by beautiful female faces. Dr. Nancy Etcoff, a leading author of the study, describes this as "a kind of visceral response to beauty." It is no wonder, then, that beautiful women are used to market everything from motorcycles to soft drinks.

The problems start when advertisers create images that denigrate or objectify women. Just ask the members of GraceNet (www.gracenet.net), a networking group of high-tech businesswomen who give DisGraceful awards for over-the-top sexist ads from technology firms. Founder Sylvia Paull says advertisers may depict women as prostitutes or make them appear stupid or trivial, ignoring the fact that women are a segment of the prospect group.

Sexist advertising does not just denigrate women. Advertisers increasingly depict men as incompetent or dumb jock, particularly in the areas of cooking or parenting, in a misguided attempt to appeal to women. And some advertisers even poke fun at ethnic groups.

The trend toward mainstreaming of pornography to sell products seems to be relentless. On the one hand, sports, fashion, and the music industry use deliberately suggestive images and symbols, not in themselves pornographic, but refer to sex in their marketing. On the other hand, pornography is treated as a serious issue which is then discussed in television documentaries and written about in papers and magazines.

Moral and ethical values differ from person to person, from culture to culture, and from continent to continent. New global communications technology allows more, often anonymous, access to pornography of all kinds, leading to a documented increase in the consumption of pornography. This advertising strategy usually focuses on male dominance and female submissiveness, a factor which some see as an element in the social oppression of women. These representations deviate significantly from the norms and values held in Nordic countries, where concern for welfare and gender equality translates into values such as reciprocity, equality, willingness, emotions, and a more equitable distribution of power in sexual relations. Thus, the sexualization of public space and the gender messages thus imparts raise deep questions about changes in values.

The portrayal of women in advertising may be backsliding, reports *The Wall Street Journal*. Some ad executives say the increasing acceptance of objectified

Continued

images of women may come from the highly sexualized and nearly nude images of women portrayed in sports and reality TV shows. Others say it is just a sign of companies trying to break through the clutter, and assuming that it is okay to use such sexual images of women when selling products (such as beer) that are primarily targeted to men. Female ad executives say they are working hard behind the scenes to expand the images of women beyond the stereotypical housewife or bikini-babe molds. Despite the increasing number of women in top agency roles, many creative departments are still dominated by men.

Source: Gordon, K. (2003). *Shock Treatment*. Reprinted with permission from *Entrepreneur Magazine*, April 2003, www.entrepreneur.com.

Suggested Discussion Topics

1. Is it ethical to use potentially offensive images to market a sport product if the target audience is presumed to be among those who will not be offended? For example, using scantily clad women in beer or sport advertisements aimed solely at men? Is it correct to still utilize such advertisements just because there may be some who are not offended, while fully aware that some (or many) others will be offended?
2. Has the United States desensitized its youth with the bombardment of sexual images in sport advertising? Even though these types of images may still offend some, is it still acceptable to use something that may be considered "less harmful" based on today's society?

Ambush Marketing in Sport Advertising

Ambush marketing is a method utilized by organizations to create an illusion that their products or services are associated with a specific sport endeavor. This association is without the permission of the sport endeavor or its official partner(s), and the desire is to deceive the sport consumer into believing that there is an official association.

Companies hire marketing firms to find creative ways to crash the event without having to pay the high sponsorship fees. They will do this in a number of ways, including signage near the event, buying television commercial time during the event, and offering promotions in conjunction with the sales of products that are related to the event. Four of the more classic advertising efforts that involved ambush marketing happened during the 1994 Winter Olympics in Lillehammer, Norway; the 1996 Summer Olympics in Atlanta, Georgia; the 1996 International Cricket Council (ICC) World Cup in India; and the 2002 Super Bowl in New Orleans, Louisiana.

In 1994, when *American Express* was replaced by Visa as the official credit card sponsor for the Winter Olympics, *American Express* came up with an advertising campaign centered on the slogan "If you are traveling to Lillehammer, you will need a passport but you do not need a Visa."

In 1996, at the height of the "cola wars," and the desire to be the most recognized soft drink company globally, Coca-Cola paid a significant amount of money to be the official soft drink of the Cricket World Cup. Pepsi, not to be outdone, countered with an advertising campaign centered on the slogan "Nothing Official About It." In addition, Pepsi sought to get further association with the event by flying hot air balloons near the venues with the Pepsi logo on them, and also encouraging players who had endorsement deals with Pepsi not to go near Coke drink carts.

Also in 1996, although Nike was not an official sponsor, they plastered their logo on billboard around the city, and on banners and merchandise handed out to people leaving public transportation headed to the Olympics. The images, captured in photographs and on worldwide television, created the impression that Nike was an official sponsor when it was not.

In 2002, Proctor and Gamble wanted to get its laundry detergent recognized in conjunction with the Super Bowl. Since they could not use the words "Super Bowl," they decided to have signage placed near the Louisiana Superdome that said "Because there are more than XXXVI (the roman numerals for that year's Super Bowl) ways to ruin your clothes. Enjoy the Big Game."

These ambush marketing efforts have resulted in many changes to laws and policies. One example in Detroit, Michigan is an anti-ambush marketing law that has created a no-ad zone around stadiums. While the original proposal was for 1 mile, the law was modified by the request of MLB and the NFL when bringing hallmark events to the city (the All-Star Game and Super Bowl, respectively). In response to the Pepsi scenario in 1996, the ICC has instituted ambush marketing protection contracts with sponsors, and has encouraged individual Board to have their players follow the approved agreement for tournaments. In addition, New Zealand, the host of the 2015 World Cup (and also host of the 2011 Rugby World Cup), is in the process of enacting laws to combat ambush marketing.

IS IT ADVERTISING OR AMBUSH MARKETING?

While football fans have been enjoying the World Cup, off the pitch FIFA has been cracking down on companies and individuals attempting to "ambush" the 2002 FIFA World Cup through various activities infringing its intellectual property rights.

Since the conclusion of the 1998 World Cup in France, FIFA has been using a specialized "anti-ambush" team, comprising trademark specialists, commercial lawyers, and sports marketing specialists. Their strategy for this World Cup began with a worldwide trademark registration program of "FIFA World Cup," the official mascots, the official emblem, and the FIFA World Cup Trophy. These measures were taken to ensure that FIFA is in strong

Continued

position to protect and enforce its intellectual property rights and the rights of the official partners, the official suppliers, and licensees.

One of the highest profile examples of FIFA's enforcement activities involves the soft drink manufacturer PepsiCo. Although Coca-Cola is one of the FIFA World Cup's official partners, rival PepsiCo has produced advertisements that suggest a sponsorship relationship between it and the FIFA World Cup.

On 5 June, an Argentinean court ordered PepsiCo to immediately cease the use of an advertisement. The court found that the prohibited advertisement would cause confusion among consumers as it suggested a "presumed sponsorship relationship" between the PepsiCo and the FIFA World Cup. The advertisement in question combined the use of the phrase "Tokyo 2002," famous footballers and other football imagery in association with the logo of PepsiCo. The court ordered PepsiCo not to use the advertisement on TV, in printed media, or by any other means. Had FIFA decided not to act, its inactivity would have diminished the value of its trademarks as well as the exclusivity of agreements with official partners such as Coca-Cola.

The Argentinean court order comes on the heels of PepsiCo's claims earlier the week that their advertising will not mention the FIFA World Cup. However, this is not the only promotion related to the FIFA World Cup which has caused PepsiCo to be in hot water with FIFA: in Ecuador, FIFA has also instructed counsel to initiate legal proceedings against PepsiCo as a result of similar TV commercials; and in Mexico, PepsiCo is in the midst of negotiations with FIFA to settle a case involving the unauthorized use of FIFA's trademark-protected emblem of "2002 FIFA World Cup."

Businesses spend considerable time and substantial sums of money devising brands and marketing their products or services. This investment should be protected whenever possible by registering trade names, logos, strap-lines, and other trademarks. If a trademark is registered, the registration gives the owner a monopoly right in that country to use the mark in respect of the goods or services in which it is registered and provides protection against infringement.

Source: Adapted from Meikle, E. (2002). *Lawless Branding – Recent Developments in Trademark Law … FIFA Defends World Cup Against Pepsi Ambush Marketing*. Retrieved March 3, 2006 from http://www.brandchannel.com/features_effect.asp?pf_id=103.

Suggested Discussion Topics

1. Even if PepsiCo does not use any official logos, player likenesses, or wording that implied direct association to the World Cup, can they create advertising that still could imply to the consumer that they are directly associated with the World Cup? Give at least three examples.
2. Come up with at least three examples of how you would use integrated brand promotions to advertise PepsiCo at the World Cup without fear of legal recourse from FIFA and Coca-Cola. Explain in detail how you would place these advertisements.

SPORT ADVERTISING AND CONSUMER BEHAVIOR

Marketing communicators direct their efforts toward influencing consumers' brand-related beliefs, attitudes, emotional reactions, and choices. Ultimately, the objective is to encourage consumers to choose their brand rather than the competitor. To accomplish this goal, marketers design advertising messages, promotions, packaging cues, brand names, sales presentations, and commercials.

Supply and demand makes the economic world go round, and creates the foundation for competition. Although the media usually portrays owners in pursuit of dollars, this is a two-way street. Just like any other product, sports fans demand team output and are willing to pay for it. What makes sports consumer demand team output? The answer is that all of the characteristics of the sports product – the beauty of athletic prowess, absolute and relative team quality, and the thrill of victory or the agony of defeat.

The quality of teams is a commodity that generates the competition that fans enjoy. In most cases the level of quality is directly related to the willingness of an organization to purchase high-quality players. In order for a league such as the NFL to gain dominance and maintain their consumer base, the league must ensure that none of the teams get too strong or too weak. The more the opportunity for parity, the more the consumer believes that their team will win, and the more the fan is willing to pay to see it happen.

Consumers are systematic decision makers. Consumers would not be responsive to advertising unless there was something in it for them, and there it. All advertising and promotions techniques provide consumers with rewards (benefits, incentives, or inducements) that encourage certain forms of behavior desired by brand managers. Consumers also obtain non-functional benefits when taking advantage of advertising and promotional offers, such as the sense of being a wish shopper, the stimulation of trying different brands, or in entertainment value.

When establishing symbolic relations, advertisers often use non-literal language. Nike has made famous the "swoosh" symbol to identify its brand and impart the notion of speed. This is a key in conveying a performance attribute, especially when this brand was introduced in the heyday of jogging and road-racing days.

Consumers are also an integral part of the overall decision making process for advertising. Once people have decided on what goods to consume, advertisements clearly present the array of possible choices for a particular good. Advertisements may help consumers make brand choices. The typical viewer of any sports is male between the ages of 25 and 52. It is not by coincidence that consumers are bombarded by beer, cars, and tools. Consumers identify with being in a particular consumer base such as Pepsi drinkers or Coke drinkers or Red Sox fans or Yankee fans. These advertisements solidify brand loyalty and once brand loyalty is solidified, it is very difficult to make a new first impression.

CREATING SPORT ADVERTISEMENTS AND COMMERCIALS

In the first ever televised World Series, Major League Baseball Commissioner Happy Chandler said, "It would not be good public relations for baseball to have the Series sponsored by the producer of an alcoholic beverage." Sport advertising has come so far since then. Advertising messages can be developed with little thought or in a systematic approach. To appreciate the role of an advertising plan, imagine a soccer team approaching an upcoming game without any idea of how it is going to execute its offense or defense. Without a game plan, the team would have to play in the same spontaneous fashion as do players in a pickup game. Advertising strategy is the formulation of an advertising message that communicates the brand's value proposition, its primary benefit, or how it can solve the consumer's problem.

A systematic approach to creative advertising makes sense in theory but ultimately the people who write the advertising copy must create a visually pleasing concept. Even though research has shown that advertising copy is based on copy writers' own implicit theories of how advertising works on consumers, they do not have the luxury to create for the mere sake of engaging in a creative pursuit.

In many advertising agencies, the work of copy writers is directed by a framework known as a creative brief. This is a document designed to inspire copy writers by channeling their creative efforts toward a solution that will serve the interest of the client. The creative brief represents an informal pact between client and advertising agency that represents agreement on what an advertising campaign is intended to accomplish. Once this agreement has been reached production can begin.

Advertising productions can take many paper forms such as newspapers, magazines, billboards, and direct and indirect mail. In addition to print, electronic and digital medium has opened many doors. The use of website banner advertisements, pop-ups, and site sponsorships have assisted the advertising world both locally and globally. Digital media has allowed different programming segments, syndication, networking, cable, and pay-per-view to reach more consumers than ever.

SPORT ADVERTISING AND IBP

As previously defined, IBP is the use of various promotional tools in a coordinated manner to build and maintain brand awareness, identity, and preference. The goal of IBP includes the coordination of all verbal and visual communication efforts for the purpose of reaching all members of the target market at a minimum, and with aspirations of reaching the entire population. In IBP, the sport organization incorporates their logo with advertising and other efforts that include support media, point-of-purchase (POP) displays, sales promotions, direct marketing, sponsorship, and promotions.

Support media is the use of non-traditional media efforts to connect with members of the target audience who have not been reached through traditional media (print, radio, television). The goal is to reinforce and support the original advertising messages. Examples of support media include aerial advertising (blimps, sky banners, sky writing), mobile billboards (trailers, truck, vans), transit advertising (buses, subways, taxicabs, trains), in-store media (kiosks, signs, video screens), promotional products, and the yellow pages.

POP displays are special exhibits involving a product or service at the point of sale. Examples of traditional POP displays include cardboard cut-outs, end caps, kiosks, and signage. As the digital age become more infused in all aspects of advertising, digital signage has become a very popular method for delivering messages to potential customers because it can be more easily customized for the target audience. These displays are considered one of the most important aspects of advertising (and merchandising) because of the concept of impulse buying, which is the act of making a spontaneous, unplanned purchase. POP displays helps to entice the consumer to make a purchase at the most critical point – when they are in the store and have money available.

Directly associated with this aspect is sales promotion. Sales promotion is a unique promotional method that is utilized to generate immediate interest in a product or service. Some of the most common methods utilized include contests and sweepstakes, and coupons and discounts. Direct marketing has some similarities to sales promotion, in that the goal is to generate immediate interest in a product or service. However, where sales promotion usually is directly connected to a store (whether retail or online), direct marketing seeks to deliver promotional materials such as brochures, catalogs, leaflets, or print advertisements straight to the current or potential consumer. Some of the most common methods are through direct mail, door-to-door selling, and telemarketing.

CONCLUSION

Sport advertising is the process of attracting public attention to a sport product or sport business through paid announcements in the print, broadcast, or electronic media. As a primary element of the sport promotions mix, it is the communication process utilized most often in sport marketing. Through advertisements, advertising campaigns, and IBP, advertising helps to establish and maintain relationships with the sport consumer by providing a conduit for listening and reacting to the sport consumer.

Advertising has evolved from being viewed simply as an artistic profession utilized to articulate product benefits and image to being one of the critical elements of business. This is especially true in sport advertising, where these efforts are used as an integral tool of marketing as related to brand development and management, segmentation, differentiation, and positioning. As a result, the sport advertising efforts need to be in congruence with the brand strategy and the branding process. The brand strategy has a direct impact on the brand's corporate value – success on the market, growth, market share, price, margins, and earnings – and thus on market capitalization and corporate value. The branding process provides the sport consumer with a clear understanding of the attributes and values of the brand. Regardless of whether sport advertising focuses on sport teams, sport retail businesses, or sport brand associations, advertising efforts will be unique to the products and services being offered. The two areas of continuity across all sport advertising efforts are creating brand loyalty and building image.

There are numerous social, ethical, and regulatory issues important to the sport advertising efforts. When violated, social and ethical issues arise, and the government may take corrective measures. Society determines what is offensive, excessive, and irresponsible; government bodies determine what is deceptive and unfair. Advertising gets criticized frequently, for both what it is and what it is not. Many of the criticisms and social debate focus on the style of advertising, saying it is deceptive or manipulative. This in turn brings about questions of the effect of advertising on our value system, commercial clutter, stereotypes, and offensiveness. This is especially true with advertising focused on children, where they are not yet sophisticate consumers who truly understand the decision making process. Therefore, creating sport advertising and commercials that stay within appropriate social, ethical, and legal constraints, and in conjunction with understanding the behaviors of sport consumers, sport marketing professionals can build the brand image and entice the sport consumer to be brand loyal.

This is most often accomplished through IBP, which is the use of various promotional tools in a coordinated manner to build and maintain brand awareness, identity, and preference. This is accomplished by incorporating the sport organization's logo with sponsorships and promotions, as well as with advertising efforts enacted through support media, POP displays, and sales promotions. Support media is the use of non-traditional media efforts to connect with members of the target audience who have not been reached through traditional media (print, radio, television). POP displays are special exhibits involving a product or service at the point of sale. Sales promotion is a unique promotional method that is utilized to generate immediate interest in a product or service. Some of the most common methods utilized include contests and sweepstakes, and coupons and discounts.

FROM THEORY TO PRACTICE

Matthew Lawrence, Director of Video Operations

Carolina Mudcats Baseball Club; Zebulon, North Carolina

Having a college degree in sport management has certainly complimented my career search, but it was what I took away from my business, marketing, and sports courses and applied in the sports world that got me to where I am today.

Experience, experience, experience; the three most important words one will hear when beginning a career search in the sports world. While a college degree helps, especially when compared with someone with no college experience, it does not put one significantly higher on the qualified applicant list. The fact that there are college grads everywhere looking for work, plus the fact that most people believe the sports world is full of money and great jobs, the applicant pool for jobs in sports becomes severely oversaturated.

Example I: I have attended three of the Professional Baseball Winter Meetings over the past 4 years, and each time I stepped onto the job fair floor, I found that there were more applicants and fewer openings than the year before.

Example II: When I interviewed with the Pawtucket Red Sox (AAA), I was informed that they had received over 500 resumes for their 13 internships, from which they chose to interview only 31. Since almost all of the resumes were from college applicants, what made my resume stand out?

Employers are looking for experience. Anyone can be a college student. The questions are then: who was more than just a student; and who exceeded what was asked or expected of them? This is where experience weighs in. Any experience in sports, no matter how trivial it may seem, is a major advantage.

Example III: During my first 2 years of college I worked as a volunteer at the NHL and NBA All-Star Events. I also worked at a couple of NASCAR races and the Boston Marathon, where I performed ushering and security duties. However, it was because of these experiences that helped me to land my first internship with the New Jersey Cardinals (A) as a sophomore.

The reason the experience in sports is so highly toted by employers is because the reality of working in sports is far from the idealistic view most college grads have of well-paid positions and a glamorous work environment. Employers know that those who have some experience in sports, no matter at what level, will have a more grounded idea of what it is like to work in the sports industry: long hours, low pay, and many responsibilities.

Experience does not have to come from sports. Granted I had many experiences in sports which led me to two internships and a part-time job with the Boston Red Sox, but it was that experience plus my college video production experience which led me to my first full-time job as the Director of Video Operations and Multimedia Productions for the Carolina Mudcats.

Example IV: The college I attended did not have a broadcasting department to compliment my interest in sports broadcasting and marketing, but I did not let this stop me. I took it upon myself to create a multimedia student organization to fill this void. I got several of my friends interested, mapped it out, and successfully

Continued

lobbied my school for money to buy cameras and other equipment. Before long the Media Broadcasting and Productions Organization was born. Everyone who joined did so to give themselves more experience. We self-taught ourselves how to use all the equipment and programs and soon we were having fun filming commercials, sports games, and covering other events on campus. Soon we were putting together videos and promotional pieces for private customers, the City of Nashua, NH, and eventually we did work for the State of New Hampshire. Needless-to-say, this little club gave me a unique experience that enabled me to become familiar with video and editing equipment and which ultimately gave me the experience I needed to be separated from the pack. Now, 22-year old and less than a year out of college, I am in a management position, and overseeing a game day staff of eight people.

My position is Director of Video Operations and Multimedia Productions, but like most minor league teams, my position covers more than one.

Directing Video Operations is my main priority during the season. Here I direct three live cameras during the game for our in-house cable feed (which is rare in minor league baseball) and I am in charge of running the videoboard (which is more common for minor league video operations). Also, I oversee the replays, stadium music, and the score lines and statistics for our scoreboards. Before games it is my responsibility to make sure that all of the computers and cameras are set up and functioning properly, to make sure that all imperative information is readily available for my staff members, and to make sure that all of the player and sponsor stills have been created and updated. If not, then I will have to put something together or go down to the field during batting practice and shoot the players' headshots myself. Another part of my Video Operations responsibilities is to write, direct, edit, and produce video segments for the team; whether it is creating an in-game commercial or putting together a highlight reel for the next home stand.

Directing Multimedia Productions was not something I was anticipating; however, thanks to my college experience in sports marketing, I was ready for the challenge. In this position I have the responsibilities of creating and producing almost anything the team puts into print; whether it is small projects like trading cards and pocket schedules or bigger projects such as stadium signs and the 64-page program. A lot of the smaller companies we do business with do not have an advertising department, so it commonly became my responsibility to create artwork and design ads. Another responsibility I have is to update the team website, which I knew nothing about before I came aboard, but have been able to pick up quite quickly.

Note: Matt is currently employed by the Video Productions Department of the Boston Red Sox as a videographer.

11

SPORT SPONSORSHIP

CHAPTER OUTLINE

CHAPTER OBJECTIVES

The reader will be able to:

- Gain an appreciation of the significant role sponsorship plays in the sport promotional mix.
- Understand the history and growth of sport sponsorship over the past 20 years.
- Recognize the various areas of sport sponsorship, including governing body sponsorship, team sponsorship, athlete sponsorship, broadcast sponsorship, facility sponsorship and event sponsorship.
- Appreciate the corporate and brand goals of sport sponsorship.
- Understand the various criteria for sponsorship, and how they are utilized in choosing the companies to partner with, developing sponsorship agreements, and engaging in sponsorship negotiations.
- Know how to identify components within the sport organization that are available for sponsorship.
- Recognize the role advanced research plays in sponsorship acquisition, including the corporate decision making process regarding sponsorship spending.
- Understand the processes for developing, selling, managing, and evaluating sport sponsorships.

HISTORY OF SPORT SPONSORSHIP

Sponsorship has been a significant part of sport promotions for well over 2700 years. The first sport sponsorships have been recorded back to the period of Antiquity. This period of history ran from 3000 BC until the fall of the Roman Empire around 476 (this is the period prior to the Middle Ages). Classical Antiquity started during the 7th century BC, during the time of growth in Europe, the Middle East and North Africa, starting with the poetry of Homer, running through the rise of Christianity, and ending at the fall of the Roman Empire. During the early days of classical Antiquity, the Ancient Greeks developed a concept called "ekecheiria," which roughly translated means "Olympic Truce." In 776 BC, the first celebration of the "Olympic Games" took place as a celebration of the achievements of the human body. It was during this and subsequent events that the first sport sponsorships were seen. Prominent Greek citizens and the local governments gave financial support to the organization of the Olympics. This desire to improve standing and reputation (awareness and image) for their cities made the Olympics a commercial event. These sport sponsorships ranged from minor financial contributions to show involvement and improve political aspirations; to the level of sponsorship on one Irodis Attikos, who individually incurred the entire expense of the Kalimarmaro stadium.

Over the years, sport sponsorship has ebbed and flowed. However, there is a marked event in sports that changed the way sport sponsorship would be conducted forever. The 1984 Olympics in Los Angeles was an interesting time in the world for sport. The end of the 1970s and the early 1980s were some tumultuous times. The former Soviet Union has invaded Afghanistan in 1979, and the United States in protest boycotted the 1980 Summer Olympics held in Moscow. In response, the Soviet Union almost decided not to show up at the 1980 Winter Olympics in Lake Placid (which would have resulted in no "Miracle on Ice"). Many countries followed suit in the boycott of the Summer Games in Moscow. In 1984, with the Summer Games coming to the United States, the Soviet Union among 14 other countries including East Germany and Cuba boycotted the Games. There were significant concerns that a number of events (especially boxing and track and field) would be a lesser quality, and hence that people might not come. There were also concerns that this would yet again create a situation where the Olympic Games would be a losing business venture, as no Olympics has turned a profit with the exception of the 1932 Summer Olympics in Los Angeles (however, this was during the Great Depression, no other city in the world even bid on the Games, and less than half the usual number of athletes and nations competed because they could not afford the trip to Los Angeles).

Enter Peter Ueberroth, President of the Los Angeles Olympic Committee, who had anticipated the possibility of a boycott, and at the same time viewed the Olympics as an event that should be profitable. He had a vision of creating a financially successful Olympic Games that would be in total contrast to the deficit spending most host cities engaged in. He worked with the USOC and IOC to allow use of the Olympic symbols by corporations in their advertisements in exchange for financial support. A total of 43 major sponsors stepped forward for the opportunity to be the official Olympic sponsor. Sponsorships at the time cost a minimum of $4 each, with the television network ABC (American Broadcasting Company) paying slightly over $200 million. This first effort into sport sponsorship was successful, with the Olympic Games making a profit of $225 million dollars.

This subsequently led to the International Olympic Committee's (IOC) creation of The Olympic Partner (TOP) Program. As the only sponsorship vehicle that offers exclusive worldwide marketing rights to both the Winter and Summer Olympics Games, TOP also provides technical and product support for the International Olympic Committee (IOC), Organizing Committees (OCOGs), and National Olympic Committees (NOCs). This in turn trickles down to provide benefits to athletes, coaches, and spectators. As the most successful brand name in worldwide sports, the Olympics and the TOP Program provides the most exclusive global sport marketing platform in the world.

Peter Ueberroth was also a key figure in increasing the amount of sponsorship for professional sport leagues. Ueberroth succeeded Bowie Kuhn as Commissioner of Major League Baseball (MLB) in 1984. In the subsequent 5 years, he was the driving force behind increasing owners' revenues through television contract sponsorship negotiations, as well as sport marketing programs that enticed large corporations, so spend significant amounts of money of promotional opportunities and sponsorships. This model serves as a framework not only for MLB, but moving forward to all sport organizations in the future.

The growth across the board, both domestically and globally, is historic. The growth of commercialization of sport through sponsorship has reached a projected value of $9 billion per year in the United States, and according to International Events Group (IEG), the leading sponsorship research and consulting company in the world, the value of worldwide global sponsorship reached $30.5 billion in 2005. It is also projected that with as a result of upcoming worldwide events including the Winter Olympics in Torino, Italy (2006) and Vancouver, Canada (2010); the Summer Olympics in Beijing, China (2008), and London, England (2012); the Commonwealth Games in Melbourne, Australia (2006) and Delhi, India (2010); and the FIFA World Cup in Germany (2006) and South Africa (2010), the probability of substantial growth in that total is inevitable.

The chart below shows the top 15 sport sponsors in the United States (IEG, 2006), all of whom spend a minimum of $100 million per year.

2006 Rank	Company	Amount (millions)
1	Anheuser-Busch Cos.	$330–$335
2	PepsiCo, Inc	$305–$310
3	General Motors Corp.	$230–$235
4	The Coca-Cola Co.	$225–$230
5	Nike, Inc.	$225–$230
6	Miller Brewing Co.	$175–$180
7	DaimlerChrysler Corp.	$150–$155
8	Ford Motor Co.	$140–$145
9	Sprint Nextel Corp.	$135–$140
10	Visa	$120–$125
11	McDonald's Corp.	$115–$120
12	MasterCard Int'l, Inc.	$110–$115
13	The Proctor & Gamble Co.	$110–$115
14	FedEx Corp.	$105–$110
15	Bank of America Corp.	$100–$105

AREAS OF SPORT SPONSORSHIP

Sport sponsorship has grown for a number of reasons ranging from the increased media attention in sport to the desire for companies to target consumers through the sport lifestyle through non-advertising efforts. In contrast to other industries, the majority of sport sponsors are not sport corporations. In fact, only one of the top ten corporations engaged in sport sponsorship is from the sport industry (Nike at approximately $162 million per year in 2005). Most sponsorship comes from the food and beverage industry (PepsiCo, Anheuser-Busch, Coca-Cola, Miller Brewing, and McDonalds), as well as the automotive industry (General Motors, DaimlerChrysler, and Ford Motor).

As alluded to earlier, sport sponsorship is divided into six categories: sport governing body sponsorship, sport ream sponsorship, athlete sponsorship, broadcast and media sponsorship, sport facility sponsorship, and sport event sponsorship. Each of these distinct areas makes up the majority of a $9 billion dollar sport sponsorship industry in the United States.

Sport Governing Body Sponsorship

Sport governing bodies are sport organizations that are responsible for developing the rule structure for the specific activity as well as organize competitions at levels from local youth to international. At various levels, the sport governing body is also responsible for selecting teams, raising and distributing funding, providing coaching and other administrative and technical services, and promoting and developing the individual sport.

All sport activities have governing bodies. They range from national governing bodies such as the National Football League (NFL) and the National Collegiate Athletics Association (NCAA); to international governing bodies such as the International Olympic Committee (IOC) and the Fédération Internationale de Football Association (FIFA).

From a sponsorship standpoint, these associations between corporations and sport organizations tend to result in receiving "official sponsor" status. "Official sponsor" status refers to the sport organization's public acknowledgment of the association between the sponsor and the organization. Often official sponsors are guaranteed exclusivity, which is the guarantee that the products or services of the sponsoring organization will be the only type in that category to have an association with the sport organization. Official sponsors also receive additional benefits as a result of the sponsorship, including inclusion in all sport organization marketing efforts, the ability to use the sport organization's logo in their own marketing efforts, and hospitality opportunities to entertain subsidiaries, clients, and customers.

The corporations that tend to enter into sponsorship with governing bodies tend to be larger, national, or multinational companies, mainly due to the large financial investment required with these sponsorships. An example of a national governing body sponsorship would be Nextel/Sprint's sponsorship agreement with NASCAR. On June 19, 2003, NASCAR ended its 33-year relationship with RJ Reynolds (RJR) Tobacco Company to take on Nextel as its title sponsor. The 10-year contract was the largest sponsorship deal in the history of professional sports, at a staggering cost of over $700 million.

Many wondered how Nextel could expect to turn a profit with such a high-priced sponsorship affecting its bottom line. Nextel countered by stating that if it were to secure 1% of the NASCAR viewing market per year, which is estimated to be near 75 million fans, the 750,000 new customers would translate to $600 million in revenue. Nextel also hedge its bets on NASCAR continuing to be the number one spectator sport in the United States. It also recognized that a number of other factors would also be a positive to their bottom line:

- It is only second behind the NFL in television viewership.
- Approximately, 15% of Forbes 500 companies are involved in NASCAR.
- NASCAR fans are the most loyal of any sport fan when it comes to purchasing products and services from companies that sponsor NASCAR. More than twice the rate of baseball and basketball fans; more than three times the level of football fans; and five times more likely than fans of the Olympics.

An international governing body with significant sponsorship partnerships is the FIFA. Their sponsorship opportunities range from grassroots initiatives to signage at World Cup events. Their partners, called commercial affiliates, originally fell under three categories. Official sponsors have global marketing rights. Official suppliers have marketing rights in the host country of the individual event only. They also have licensees who have association, but are not able to associate their corporate brand with licensed products. In 2006 during the year of the World Cup in Germany, the official sponsors and suppliers are listed below:

- *Official partners*: Adidas, Anheuser-Busch, Avaya, Coca-Cola, Continental, Deutsche Telekom, Emirates, Fujifilm, Gillette, Hyundai, MasterCard, McDonald's, Philips, Toshiba, and Yahoo!
- *Official suppliers*: Energie Baden-Württemberg AG (EnBW), OBI, Hamburg-Mannheimer Versicherung, Postbank, ODDSET, and Deutsche Bahn AG.

However in 2007, their sponsorship program changed to create three new levels of sponsorship. A FIFA Partner enjoys full association with all that FIFA operates, including competitions, special events, development programs, and exclusive marketing assets. The first company to become a FIFA Partner was Adidas, followed shortly thereafter by Hyundai, Sony, and Coca-Cola. A FIFA World Cup sponsor received global rights to category exclusivity, brand association, specific marketing assets, and secondary media exposure for the 2010 and 2014 World Cups. A National Supporter allows local companies to promote their category exclusivity, association, local marketing opportunities, and domestic media exposure within the host country of the 2010 (South Africa) and 2014 (undecided at press time) World Cups.

Sport Team Sponsorship

Traditional team sponsorships are usually more appropriate for local or regional companies that have smaller marketing budget but have a desire to become the official sponsor of a team. Team sponsorship often serves as a loophole for ambush marketing, as a team sponsor may be contradictory to the sponsorship of the governing body. For example, Burger King is an official sponsor of the Read to Achieve community literacy initiative, but the NBA is sponsored by McDonald's.

The goal of most team sponsorships is to create long term and mutually beneficial relationships between the team and a corporation. The resulting objectives include building awareness of the company's products and services; enhancing opportunities for new customer relationships; ability to offer internal benefit programs such as employee rewards, hospitality areas, and sales incentive programs; and brand association with the sport team. Sponsorship opportunities range from signage on the field/court or boundaries in association with special events (home team introductions, halftime/intermission/time out contests). It might also include other opportunities including sponsorships of the cheerleading and dance team, or on promotional package given away on game days.

However, large corporations will be involved with team sponsorship based on the market or the ability to significantly expand awareness. Some of the most prominent team sponsorship deals take place in soccer, especially in Europe. Some of the current examples of team sponsorship deals for corporate names to appear on the front of game uniforms are shown below (in equivalent US dollars in 2006):

Team	Sponsor	Sponsorship Agreement (per year)
AC Milan (Italy)	Opel (car company)	$10.72 million
Arsenal (England)	O2 (mobile phone company)	$17.25 million
Bayern Munich (Germany)	T-Mobile (mobile company)	$19.68 million
Chelsea (England)	Samsung (electronics/mobile)	$17.25 million
Juventes (Italy)	Tamoil (oil company)	$26.20 million
Manchester United (England)	Vodafone (mobile)	$15.53 million
Real Madrid (Spain)	Siemens (mobile)	$16.67 million

Another example of team sponsorship that includes both national and multinational corporations, as well as local and regional companies, is with individual NASCAR teams. Teams can bring in anywhere between $15 and $40 million, and in some cases more, just from sponsorship of the car. The picture below illustrates the price breakdown of NASCAR team sponsorship of automobiles per season:

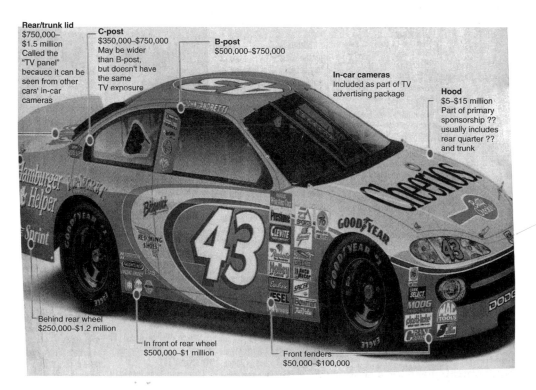

Rear/trunk lid
$750,000–$1.5 million
Called the "TV panel" because it can be seen from other cars' in-car cameras

C-post
$350,000–$750,000
May be wider than B-post, but doesn't have the same TV exposure

B-post
$500,000–$750,000

In-car cameras
Included as part of TV advertising package

Hood
$5–$15 million
Part of primary sponsorship ?? usually includes rear quarter ?? and trunk

Behind rear wheel
$250,000–$1.2 million

In front of rear wheel
$500,000–$1 million

Front fenders
$50,000–$100,000

Athlete Sponsorship

There is often confusion between athlete sponsorships and athlete endorsements. They are often used as interchangeable terms, but they are two different concepts. An athlete sponsorship is where a corporation seeks to become affiliated with an athlete to secure the rights to market their association and reap the benefits of that association. An athlete endorsement is a type of athlete sponsorship where the athlete is describing their personal association with the product or service.

Athlete sponsorship tends to work better in individual sports than in team sports, simply because the sponsor can focus their efforts and generate significant numbers of visible impressions for the consumer. For example, golf and tennis players can have logos on hats or shirts, and can easily be focused on.

The superstar athlete in most team sports can overcome this desire of corporations to focus their athlete sponsorships on individual athletes. Some of the most prominent athletes who currently have significant sponsorship deals are basketball players in the NBA. This is mainly because of the "Michael Jordan" effect. In 1997, Michael Jordan earned $47 million from sponsorships with companies ranging from Nike to McDonald's to Gatorade to Wheaties. After his retirement, a number of NBA players have reaped the benefits left behind by Michael Jordan. Examples include LeBron James' 7-year, $90 million deal with Nike, and Allen Iverson's $5 million per year for life sponsorship agreement.

In light of this, if an athlete is a superstar in an individual sport, the sponsorship dollars come rolling in. Such an athlete is Tiger Woods. The chart below reflects a sampling of the $80+ million in endorsement and sponsorship agreements in effect for 2006:

Sponsor	Value of Sponsorship (per year)
Accenture (global management consulting/ technology/outsourcing company	$8 million
American Express (financial services)	$7 million
Buick (automobile)	$8 million
Electronic Arts (video games)	$7.5 million
Nike (athletic apparel)	$20 million plus bonuses and profit sharing
TAG Heuer (sport watches)	$2 million per year
TLC Laser Eye Centers	$3 million per year
Upper Deck (sport collectibles)	$7 million per year

Broadcast and Media Sponsorship

Broadcast sponsorships involve corporations that purchase an association with specific sport programming either via the radio or television. Broadcast sponsorships can range from a basic sponsorship of a local radio broadcast to being some of the most lucrative associations in all of sport sponsorship.

Before broadcast sponsorships can even be considered, there must be an association between a sport organization and the media outlet. This usually involves a broadcasting rights contract. These broadcasting rights contracts are the single largest revenue source for sport organizations. These contracts happen at two levels: local and national. Local broadcasting contracts usually cover events of and game played by the individual sport organization. Local agreements are usually for multiple years, and may include such additional broadcasts as pre-game and post-game shows. Many local broadcasting contracts also include team sponsorship in the form of "the official team station" or the "official broadcasting partner of the sport organization." For example, WEEI in Boston is in the final year (2006) of their contract as "official radio station of the Boston Red Sox." WEEI pays the Boston Red Sox a fee for the right to broadcast their games, and then attempt to make up the difference by selling advertising. The rights fees for the Boston Red Sox are substantial with the team being regional in nature (New England) and interest being at a high level (especially after winning the World Series in 2004). The current contract has WEEI paying somewhere between $8–12 million per season.

National broadcasting contracts are usually multiple year deals with a series of local radio or television networks to broadcast the games of leagues. Usually, the broadcasting dollars are split evenly across all teams within a league. For example, as a result of the National Hockey League (NHL) strike of 2004–2005, they lost a lucrative $60 million agreement with ESPN. After the strike, Comcast took a chance to improve their status as a national sport broadcaster and signed a 3-year, $200 million contract to have games broadcast on upstart television station Outdoor Life Network (OLN). This broadcasting contract is relatively small in comparison with more stable and established events and leagues. These include the following:

League	Network	Event	Agreement
NASCAR	Fox	First half of season and Busch Series	$1.6 billion (2001–2008)
	NBC/TBS	Split second half of the season	$1.2 billion (2001–2006)
NBA	ESPN	Selected games during the season	$2.4 billion (2002–2008)
	TNT/TBS	Selected games during the season	$2.2 billion (2002–2008)
NCAA	CBS	Men's Basketball Tournament	$6.2 billion (2003–2014)
	ABC	Football BCS (four games)	$80 million (2007–2010)
NFL	CBS	AFC Games/Super Bowl in 2008 and 2011	$4.27 billion (2006–2011)
	ESPN	Monday Night Football and NFL Draft	$8.8 billion (2006–2013)
	Fox	NFC Games/Super Bowl in 2007 and 2010	$3.73 billion (2006–2011)
	NBC	Thursday night opener; Sunday nights; Super Bowl in 2007 and 2010	$3.6 billion (2006–2011)
	DirecTV	Sunday Ticket Package (pay per view)	$3.5 billion (2006–2010)
Olympics	NBC	2006 Winter Olympics (Torino, Italy)	$613 million

Continued

League	Network	Event	Agreement
		2008 Summer Olympics (Beijing, China)	$894 million
		2010 Winter Olympics (Vancouver, Canada)	$820 million
		2012 Summer Olympics (London, England)	$1.18 billion

Once the broadcast agreements have been signed, then the broadcasted attempts to recoup some of that expense by selling broadcast sponsorship agreements. Examples currently seen on television includes ESPN College (Football) Gameday "Built by Home Depot"; "College Football Saturday" on FoxSportsNet sponsored by Kyocera; the T-Mobile Halftime Show on TNT (NBA); and Cingular at the Half on CBS (College Basketball). Also, these broadcast sponsorships have expanded to online viewing of games. In 2006, NCAA March Madness on Demand presented by Courtyard by Marriott and Dell will provide free coverage of all 63 NCAA College Basketball Tournament Games through www.sportsline.com/cbssports.

Sport Facility Sponsorship

Facility sponsorships are naming rights agreements for stadiums, arenas, and other sport facilities. Since 2000, this is the fastest growing area of sport sponsorship, as many sport facilities across the country have sold their naming rights to sport corporations. These deals are usually long term and significant in value. Also, the value of the sponsorship will vary with the size of the market, the level of competition playing, and the assorted of events scheduled by the facility. Some of the current deals in place in 2006 include the following:

Name of Facility	Location	Sponsor	Terms of Agreement
Major professionals sport facilities			
Reliant Stadium	Houston, TX	Reliant Energy	$300 million for 32 years
FedEx Field	Washington, DC	Federal Express	$205 million for 27 years
American Airlines Center	Dallas, TX	American Airlines	$195 million for 30 years
Philips Arena	Atlanta, GA	Royal Philips Electronics	$182 million for 20 years
Minute Maid Park	Houston, TX	Minute Maid OJ	$178 million for 28 years
Independent, minor league and minor professional sport facilities			
Raley Field	Sacramento, CA	Raley's and Bel-Air Markets	$15 million for 20 years
Wells Fargo Arena	Des Moines, IA	Wells Fargo Financial	$11.5 million for 20 years
Verizon Wireless Arena	Manchester, NH	Verizon Wireless	$11.4 million for 15 years
Keyspan Park	Brooklyn, NY	Keyspan Energy	$10 million for 20 years
Ricoh Coliseum	Toronto, ON	Ricoh Electronics	$10 million for 20 years

One benefit of the sport organization or the sport facility owner is the out clause for the sponsorship. Should the corporate sponsor go out of business or miss a required payment, the facility reacquires the naming rights of the facility and may resell the sponsorship. Some of the prominent facilities where this has happened include the following:

Location	Former Name of Facility	Current Name of Facility	Reason for Change
Foxboro, MA	CMGI Field	Gillette Stadium	Rights bought by Gillette as a result of the dot.com bust that started in 2001
Houston, TX	Enron Field	Minute Maid Park	Bankruptcy of Enron
Nashville, TN	Adelphia Coliseum	The Coliseum	Missed payment by Adelphia

Sport Event Sponsorship

Sport event sponsorship provides a way for corporations to create an association with a sport event. Most relationships of this type are with hallmark events, such as tournaments (golf and tennis), championships (college football bowl games), and others including ranging from the Visa Triple Crown (made up of horse racing's three major events in the United States – the Kentucky Derby, the Preakness, and the Belmont States) to the ING New York City Marathon.

However, there are questions of whether sponsorship of an event is beneficial to the corporate sponsor as compared to those sponsorships that offer more impressions over a longer period of time, such as naming rights being on a facility 365 days a year, or being associated with a league or sport that promotes the association over the numerous months of prime operations. The answer is yes, event sponsorship is lucrative as a result of the significant media and advertising exposure related to the hallmark event. The chart below is representative of the profitability of being a sponsor of one of the four Bowl Championship Series games in 2005, simply from the media image exposure during the television broadcasts of those games. These figures are as reported by the ABC, the media outlet who broadcast all four games. The information was compiled by Image Impact, Inc. (www.imageimpact.tv):

Sponsor	Event	Location	Total Estimate Value (by ABC)
Federal Express	Orange Bowl	Miami, FL	$29,599,506
Nokia	Sugar Bowl	Atlanta, GA*	$20,911,958
Tostitos	Fiesta Bowl	Tempe, AZ	$30,376,683
Citi	Rose Bowl	Pasadena, CA	$25,466,643
TOTAL			$106,354,790

*The Sugar Bowl is usually hosted in New Orleans, LA, but after the devastation of Hurricane Katrina in 2005, the game was moved for 2005 to Atlanta, GA.

ETHICAL ISSUES IN SPORT SPONSORSHIP

Two of the biggest ethical challenges in sport marketing today are popular athletes being toted as role models and ambush marketing.

The Use of Sport Personalities as Role Models

Right or wrong, children see the success of professional athletes and equate specific sports talent as someone to emulate. The use of popular athletes in advertising has existed in North America for many years. Baseball players such as Babe Ruth, or Ty Cobb were some of the first to allow their names and likeness to be mass produced for the sale of candy and tobacco products. Many athletes have appeared to represent a higher physical ideal and their superb individual performances, whether as Olympians or as professionals. These accomplishments make athletes commercially attractive to corporations for the purpose of endorsing a product or a brand.

In 1969, Joe Namath shattered the idea of the clean cut speak only when spoken too image. Namath was cocky, opinionated, anti-establishment, but good looking and a winner. Namath ushered in the notion of a young hero who was ready to replace traditional sport icons.

In the last 30 years, a new dimension has been added to the use of sports celebrity role model. Many companies, Nike, Reebok, and AND 1 in particular, have taken deliberate action to recruit the not so nice athlete. Nike was the first to promote a non-conventional athlete (Steve Prefontaine). Nike also changed their marketing approach to have athletes who stood out to promote their products. Non-traditional, controversial athletes such as tennis players John McEnroe, Andre Agassi and basketball player Charles Barkley became Nike advertising icons.

Celebrity endorsers are influential as role models because of their ability to attract attention to a commercial, product/service or organization. However, the use of sport endorsers benefits the product or brand in many more complex ways.

Role models change with the passing of time. Active sport athletes become retired sport athletes and younger athletes are there to take their place. An active athlete can be viewed in a number of different and unpredictable performance contexts. These contexts include winning, losing, honor, good sportsmanship, dirty play, and or emotional outbursts. Any of these can be used in a commercial format. These athletes are placed on a pedestal made of gold. Children only see the end product and equate this type of promotion with success. If I want to be like Mike, I have to wear Nike shoes, Hanes underwear, eat at McDonald, and drink Gatorade.

Marketing firms and corporations are not focusing on making future leaders of the world or even future Michael Jordan's. Their focus is on getting children to purchase these products for the rest of their lives. Hopefully there is a true role model in their lives to explain the difference.

The Ethics of Ambush Marketing at Sporting Events

Ambush marketing is one of the newest ways to attach a corporation's products or services to an entity without the permission of that entity. The rapid growth of sponsorships has resulted in a number of opportunities designed to maximize profits. However, while this outburst of sponsorship opportunities has ensured that companies can purchase rights to any aspects of an event, it has also created some difficulties. As the number of sponsorship possibilities increases, the loopholes in contracts and potential litigation over rights of sponsorship. Because there is so much money at stake and so many facets of a game or event, the potential for many sponsors create conflicts of interest.

Ambush marketing first appeared at the 1984 Los Angeles Olympic Games because of the exclusivity within product sponsorship categories. Competitors were explicitly excluded from obtaining sponsorship rights; some sought alternative means implying an association with the Olympic Games. This illegal practice reduces the effectiveness of the sponsor's message while devaluing the sponsorship opportunity.

This tactic is used to attribute good will to company who may not deserve it and who has definitely paid for it. Some ambush tactics included activities such as sponsoring the broadcast of an event sponsored by a competitor, or sponsoring sub-categories of the same event. Other tactics include purchasing advertising spots during a broadcast, then placing the alleged ambusher's brand with the event. More recently, some companies have developed images that are similar to those used by official sponsors and have allegedly ambushed an event, many of which have been dealt with by the courts.

Ambush marketing usually falls into two categories: flagrant and ambiguous. Flagrant infringements would include breach of copyright or unlicensed use of trademarks. Ambiguous infringements exploit the so-called gray area of contract law.

The law provides limited support, sponsors need to create a climate in which companies engaging in this unethical behavior are exposed and held accountable. The IOC has attempted to shame alleged ambushers into discontinuing their tactics by producing and running advertising that describes the companies as cheats. This serves to educate the public about the existence of ambush marketing. Increasing emphasis is thus now placed on the legal aspect of contract and trademark law and the coordination between event owners and broadcasters has reduced the likelihood that naming rights and the broadcast rights to the same event would be divided. Given the global nature of sponsorships, and differences in trademark registration, event owners need to register the images they use in every market they currently trade in, or in which they may wish to trade.

Ambush marketing is the attempt by a third party to create a direct or indirect association of a sport event or its participants without their approval, hence denying official sponsors, suppliers, and partners parts of the commercial value derived from the "official" designation. Some of the various reasons that entities engage in ambush marketing is because of their desire to be associated with an effect. One major reason is because they cannot afford to pay the sponsorship fees. Another reason is because they are prevented from entering into an association with sport event due to a contract of exclusivity or long-term association with a competitor.

Sport marketing professionals, in coordination with the event organizers need to be proactive and reactive toward ambush marketing to protect the integrity and financial viability of the event; to build the event "brand" and goodwill in it for the future; and to fulfill contractual obligations to sponsors. If this is not guaranteed, sponsors will have uncertainty about the value of their association.

Australian has been at the forefront of controlling ambush marketing. With the 2000 Summer Olympics coming to Sydney, the government passed the Olympic Arrangements Act 2000, which put into place a series of measures including:

- The creation of a law where it would be an offense to sell unauthorized articles during the period of the Olympic Games within a certain geographical radius of sensitive venues – also enabled offending articles to be seized and forfeited.
- A temporary restriction on the airspace over competition venues – an idea successfully translated from the Atlanta 1996 Olympics when the Federal Aviation Authority banned unauthorized flights within the city limits.

There are four main areas of concern when it comes to ambush marketing: the facility; the participants; the teams; and the media. Using the 2000 Summer Olympics in Sydney, and the 2003 Rugby World Cup in Australia as examples, here are some examples of how ambush marketing can affect sporting events, and can often lead to some drastic actions:

Facility Nightmare: New Zealand Loses 2003 Rugby World Cup

The 2003 Rugby World Cup was scheduled to be held as a joint venture between Australia and New Zealand. The International Rugby Board and Rugby World Cup Ltd., who are the organizers of the event, needed to guarantee control of the event, especially as it came to advertising, sponsorship, and ticketing. The New Zealand Rugby Football Union could not provide what is known as "clean stadia," or facilities clear of all sponsorship and advertising. As a result, the organizers took away New Zealand's right to co-host the event, and held the World Cup entirely in Australia.

But They Are My Sponsor: Participants Revolt

At the same Rugby World Cup, a number of nations including the host country Australia, England, France, Ireland, and South Africa, balked at signing an agreement giving up their "image rights" for the tournament. They were fearful of personal sponsor backlash if their images were used by official sponsors of the World Cup that were in contradiction to that sponsorship. They also were not keen that they could not be allowed to advertise their own sponsors during the event (other than the makers of their uniforms).

I Paid For My Ticket: Leave Me Alone

The 2000 Sydney Olympics was a landmark event for controlling ambush marketing. They instituted within their ticket policy the following statement:

"… engage in ambush marketing … display commercial or offensive signage … sell any goods or services … wear or give away political, advertising, or promotional materials … [or] engage in any other activities which [the Sydney Organizing Committee for the Olympic Games] considers dangerous or otherwise inappropriate."

At the aforementioned World Cup, this was significantly tested at Telstra Stadium in Sydney. Telstra is a large mobile phone conglomerate, whose main competition is Vodafone. Vodafone stood outside the stadium and gave fans Vodafone flags to wave at the opening match. The stewards in the stadium spent a lot of time confiscating those flags so that Telstra would be guaranteed their exclusivity in the stadium.

Freedom of the Press … Sort Of

In general, broadcast partners must give the right of first refusal to official sponsors when it comes to advertising airtime. With the introduction of many new technologies, one such is "virtual advertisements," when the broadcaster can superimpose an advertisement, image, or logo that would be seen by the viewing public. In Australia where this use of computer generation is a regular practice, there are limitations placed on broadcasters from utilizing this technology when the advertisement is in contradiction to a title sponsor, or place over what is intended to "clean stadia."

Source: Adapted from Harbottle and Lewis (December 2003/January 2004). *Ambush Marketing*. Retrieved March 3, 2006 from http://www.legal500.com/devs/uk/en/uken_065.htm.

Continued

Suggested Discussion Topics

1. Assume you have been hired as a consultant by the Government of South Africa to work with the South African Football Association to develop and implement a plan to prevent ambush marketing at the 2010 FIFA World Cup. What recommendations would you make?
2. Assume you are the marketing director of a large multinational corporation that has just secured "official sponsor" status for the 2010 Winter Olympic Games in Vancouver, Canada. What would your plan be to ensure that your competitors do not reduce the value of your association through ambush marketing?

CORPORATE AND BRAND GOALS FOR SPORT SPONSORSHIP

The reason for entering into a sport sponsorship agreement varies from organization to organization. It also differs from whether it is the corporation becoming involved with a sport entity, or the desire of the sport brand to engage in a partnership with specified corporate entities. Regardless, it is important that any entity determine what they desire to achieve through the sponsorship. This will involve the sport marketing professionals and management from each entity creating a list of desired outcomes that will serve as a framework for determining the appropriateness of the partnership.

Corporations have numerous goals as a result of sport sponsorship. The most logical are increase public awareness and enhancing their company image. Most promotional efforts do that. From a business standpoint, corporations use sport sponsorship to build business and trade relationships with other sponsoring organizations. In the public relations area, corporations use sport sponsorship to change or improve public perception of their company. They can use the usually positive relationship to alter the opinion of the consumer as related to the corporation. This is also accomplished through community relations, where the sport sponsorship can be used to increase community involvement in that target area. This is often achieved through goodwill efforts. Finally, corporations often use sport sponsorship to enhance personnel relations by offering opportunities for employees to attend sponsored events, including attendance at hospitality areas. The company hopes to use the relationship created through the sport sponsorships, especially when significantly positive, to increase the morale of employees through the perceived association with that brand.

Sport brands also have numerous goals as a result of sponsorship other than the obvious ones of taking in additional revenue from the agreement, and increasing target market awareness and image. The sport brand is also seeking to use the relationship with the corporation to increase their own sales. Associations often bring about more interest from the general public, and especially from those connected with the sponsoring corporation. The goal is to market this new association to get more people in the seats. As a result, there is a hope that the sponsorship will increase the market share for the brand, which in turn will prevent competition from getting the upper hand in the marketplace.

SPORT SPONSORSHIP ETHICS: TOBACCO, ALCOHOL, AND NOW … DRUGS

First the tobacco magnates had their day in the world of professional sport sponsorship. Next it was beer companies and now liquor. Next up to bat on the sport sponsorship bandwagon – the pharmaceutical companies are ready to move in. Direct to consumer (DTC) advertising of prescription drugs has become big business. There are more adverts for medicines on primetime TV now than for new cars, and pharmaceutical marketing departments are always on the lookout for new promotional channels. Sport sponsorship seems to be the latest craze.

Of course, like the athletes themselves, only the elite make it to the top. Only the blockbuster products can successfully compete for the finite sponsorship packages up for grabs. The big names in the sporting world at present include Viagra (MLB and NASCAR), Levitra (NFL), and Cialis (PGA Tour).

The deal between GSK and Bayer (co-marketers in the United States for Levitra) and the NFL is football's first sponsorship agreement with pharmaceutical companies. It allows GSK and Bayer to run men's health awareness and education advertisements to the NFL audience, which totals around 120 million people on an average weekend.

In the past the NFL avoided sponsorship deals with medical products, but in 2003 changed their stance because of the success in other professional sports. The NFL permits sponsorship from therapeutic products in eight categories: allergies, cholesterol, dermatology, diabetes, gastrointestinal, hair renewal, prostate, and erectile dysfunction.

Sport sponsorship is especially attractive to drugs in the field of men's health; the MLB, the NFL, the NBA, and the NASCAR all have a dedicated, loyal – and largely male – fan base. However, the success of the sponsorship will depend on the type of drug being promoted. If the sponsorship can be related directly to sport, then it would make sense. If not, then the purpose of the sponsorship is to simply increase awareness in the marketplace.

However, one of the dangers is that the drug and the sport become inextricably linked. Could Cialis, for example, become "the PGA drug"? This endorsement might work for golf fans, but would possibly turn off other

Continued

target populations. Companies must consider the possible dangers of high profile brand associations. Links with sports are great when everything is going well, but what happens when things go bad? However, these possibilities are small as long as the companies stick to sponsorship at the governing body level instead of with individual teams. Most drug companies have done that, while others have taken a chance and entered the team sport realm (e.g., Mark Martin #6 Viagra car in NASCAR).

The biggest concern for potential sponsors is getting mesmerized by being involved with professional sports and not ensuring a proper return on investment (ROI), which is extremely difficult to accurately measure in relationship to sponsorship. As a result, most pharmaceutical companies have been satisfied that sponsorship simply means increasing their brand visibility. Certainly more pharmaceutical sponsorship deals should be expected in the near future, although only in the United States. The rules in most other countries currently prohibit DTC advertising of pharmaceuticals.

In conclusion, even if the millions of devoted sports fans vehemently resist the influence of sponsors' marketing, at least these sponsorship deals should begin building a rapport between the pharmaceutical industry and the general public. This is because research has shown that a company that supports sport is a company with significant credibility.

Source: Adapted from Colyer, E. (2004). *Drug Makers Get in the Game*. Retrieved March 11, 2006 from http://www.brandchannel.com/features_effect.asp?pf_id=194.

Suggested Discussion Topics

1. Drugs such as Viagra, Cialis, and Levitra have had early success with their sport sponsorships. In 2006, the NFL did not renew its sponsorship with Levitra, and has decided to end its relationship in the erectile dysfunction category. Other sports have started to follow suit and are limiting their sponsorships to over-the-counter medications. What were the potential ethical issues present that may have lead to the decision to eliminate these types of sponsorships?
2. Another category of sponsorship that has been of great concern over many years is alcohol sponsorship. Beer commercials, advertising, and sponsorship have been a staple in American sport for centuries. However in 2005, NASCAR took it one step further and now allows hard alcohol companies such as Jack Daniels and Jim Beam. On the other hand, tobacco companies have now been banned from sport sponsorship – one of the most prominent examples is the NASCAR Winston Cup needing to change its association and becoming the NEXTEL Cup.

SPORT SPONSORSHIP AGREEMENTS

Sport sponsorship relationships offer the corporate sponsor and the sport brand to project their image, increase their audience, and amplify the number and quality of media opportunities. With this in mind, the potential corporate sponsor and the sport organization should have similar target markets, and have a mutual understanding about the mission, goals, objectives, and vision for each other. This information is then utilized to develop sport sponsorship proposals and negotiate sport sponsorship agreements. Sport sponsorships are designed to articulate the benefits derived from the agreement for all parties involved.

In a sport sponsorship, the corporation is referred to as the "sponsor," and the sport brand is called the "sponsee." One of the main benefits that a sponsor will often pay a premium for in exclusivity, to guarantee that all other competitors, their products, and their services will be prohibited from entering into sponsorship agreement with the sponsee. Other benefits derived from the sponsorship usually will include the right to use the logo of the sponsee, advertising support, signage and announcements at events, and tickets to events. Other than the rights fee, the sponsee benefits from an agreement with a corporate sponsor due to the guaranteed advertising and promotional commitments that are a part of the sponsorship. In addition, sponsees seek to have multiple year commitment to ensure continuity in those advertising and promotional efforts.

Identifying Components Available for Sponsorship

The process of developing sponsorship agreements involves a number of stages. The initial stage is for a sport organization to identify every element that could be available for sponsorship. While a sport organization could maximize revenue by putting sponsorship on everything they own, this would be unwise as the organization will become a walking billboard for other corporations, and will most likely overshadow the sport organization's brand and purpose. As a result, sport organizations seek to optimize its sponsorship program by determining what components are sponsorable without adversely affecting the visibility of the sport organization.

In identifying those components available for sponsorship, the sport organization must fully detail the extent of benefits that can be offered for each individual element. This information is crucial to the overall sponsorship process, as it would be unwise to develop sponsorship agreements without knowing what is to be offered. Benefits can range from building brand awareness from the association between the sport organization and the sponsor, to perks such as free tickets, merchandise, and other promotional opportunities.

The Role of Advanced Research in Sponsorship Acquisition

Once the sport organization understands what they have to offer, they must conduct significant research to match potential sponsors to the sponsorship opportunity. This research starts with an internal evaluation of the strengths and weaknesses of the sport organization, as this information will be crucial in articulating benefits to sponsors. Information that is important to understand for the sport organizations include the consumer demographics, psychographics, and geographics; the successes and failures of the organization; the growth or decline in popularity, participation, and/or attendance; current and past sponsors; relevant public relations/media relations/community relations; and financial status.

Once this information is collected and disseminated, the research process moves to an analysis of potential sponsors. There are two major stages in this research process: prospecting for sponsors and determining the needs of the potential sponsors.

Prospecting for Sponsors

The prospecting process involves identifying potential sponsors and investigating whether a partnership would be mutually beneficial. If both the sport organization and the potential sponsor cannot reap rewards from a relationship, then the sponsorship should not be pursued. However, the information should be kept on file for future sponsorship opportunities where a relationship has the potential to be mutually beneficial.

When identifying potential sponsors, the following should be considered:

- List the potential sponsors that have a similar target markets and demographics of the sport organization. Also identify sponsors of competitors, and find direct competitors of those sponsors.
- Divide the list based on the category of product offered by the potential sponsors.

- Establish whether the potential sponsor has an interest or the financial ability to enter into a sport sponsorship agreement.
- Determine if there are any natural links with the potential sponsor – including but not limited to geographic region; similar demographic and psychographic target markets; historical associations; similarities in values, beliefs, and/or vision; products and/or services of mutual benefit; etc.
- Evaluate the status of the potential sponsor in their industry segment, including the success of their marketing approaches; their success in their industry segment as compared to direct competitors; and their previous involvement with sport organizations, including positive and negative experiences.
- Determine the value of a potential sponsorship and the projected results.
- Prioritize and determine the needs of the potential sponsors from top down.
- Finalize a list of those potential sponsors that offer the best probability of mutual success through a sponsorship partnership.

Determining the Needs of Sponsors

Prior to finalizing a list of potential sponsors to approach, a crucial stage of research is to determine the needs of the sponsor. All the advanced research may point to a partnership that has the potential of being mutually beneficial. However, when further detailed research into the needs of the potential sponsor is conducted, the sponsorship may no longer be mutually beneficial.

Major corporate goals for sponsorship agreements may include some or all of the following:

- Increase the market awareness of the corporation and their products and services.
- Either improve image (usually when the corporation is viewed in a positive light) or modify perceptions (usually when the corporation is viewed in a negative light).
- Position products and services in a manner that will result in increased sales and market share.
- The desire to increase visibility in a community by building relationships, developing programs of goodwill, and other avenues to become more involved with the community.
- The overall performance of the sponsorship agreement should result in a profit for the corporation – considering both tangible and intangible benefits.

Developing Sponsorship Proposals

In developing a sport sponsorship proposal, there are four main features that should be considered as a framework for the agreement: goals and objectives; characteristics of the sport organization; compatibility between the potential sponsor and the sport organization; and maximizing exposure for the potential sponsor.

Goals and Objectives

The first feature is the goals and objectives of the parties entering into the sponsorship agreement. This provides an opening mechanism to present the values, beliefs, and position of the sport organization. It also allows the sport organization to articulate what they would like to accomplish as a result of the sponsorship, and how they propose to do it. In addition, by articulating the perceived benefits to the sponsor in terms of the advanced research, the sport organization can convey an understanding of the needs of the potential sponsor (provided the research conducted was reliable, valid, and evaluated properly).

Characteristics of the Sport Organization

The second feature of the sponsorship proposal should include the characteristics of the sport organization. This section includes three main components: a full description of the sport organization; a description of the specific aspect to be sponsored; and an overview of the sponsor's industry in terms of sport sponsorships in place. A sport marketing professional cannot make the assumption that a potential sponsor knows about the sport organization or about sport in general. So the initial task is to provide a complete overview of the sport organization to educate the potential sponsor. Once this overview is complete, then the proposal should target the specific aspect of the sponsorship. This section is often the meat of the proposal, as it will serve as the introduction to the remaining structure of the sponsorship proposal. Included here will include the components of the agreement, the products or services to be sponsored, and the major people to be involved in implementing and managing the sponsorship. Finally, the sport marketing professional will provide an overview of the potential sponsor's industry in terms of similar sponsorship agreement in place. The goal here is to show the potential sponsor that there is already competitors using this type of promotion for their company, or that there is an opportunity to be the leader in their industry in becoming involved in sport sponsorship.

Compatibility

The third feature involves showing the compatibility between the sport organization and the potential sponsor. This often starts with a comparison of goals and objectives from the initial research to show the similarities in mission between the two organizations. The most important factors to be analyzed in this comparison are as follows:

- The correlation between corporate images.
- The similarities in target markets and customers.
- The likelihood of a successful relationship between brands, associated products and services, and related activities in terms of building awareness and increasing sales.

- The ability of the relationship to offer additional perks to the sponsor that will increase employee motivation (e.g., free tickets, merchandise, and priority seating) and customer importance (hospitality opportunities).

At the end of this section needs to be an illustration of how the price being paid for the sponsorship translates into value for the potential sponsor. The goal of the sport organization is to prove that although the cost of a sport sponsorship may be high, the value received in return has the potential of being significantly higher. This is especially important to communicate to the potential sponsor as one of their main goals is to determine if the overall performance of the sponsorship agreement will be a profitable venture.

Exposure

The final feature of the sponsorship proposal is an explanation of how the sponsorship will maximize exposure for the potential sponsor. There is a wide range of opportunities for increasing exposure for a potential sponsor, but usually falls into one of two categories: attendance and participation, and exposure. Attendance and participation involves individuals from outside the sport organization utilizing the offerings that have been made available. These offerings include membership in a club, attending an event at a facility, and a player for a team. Exposure would include signage, product sampling, announcements through public address systems, and any other method utilized to increase visibility.

A second area important for increasing exposure for the potential sponsor is through the media. There are two distinct areas media exposure can come from: broadcasting and media coverage. Broadcasting allows the sport organization to control the level of exposure a sponsor receives. Whether it is television, radio, or the Internet, the sport organization has greater control of promoting their loyalty to sponsors by maximizing sponsor exposure within the broadcast. This can be as simple as a mention at the beginning or end of the broadcast of the list of sponsors, to maximum exposure via the exclusive sponsorship of a segment during the broadcast. On the other hand, media coverage is independent of the sport organization and hence cannot be controlled. However, the sport organization will attempt to maximize exposure for sponsors through public relations, media relations, and communication relations efforts (as discussed in Chapter 9).

The final area utilized to offer exposure for the potential sponsor is through promotions (Chapter 9) and advertising (Chapter 10). While these areas are different than the sponsorship itself, they are utilized in conjunction with the sponsorship to increase value.

Selling Sponsorship Opportunities

Now that the proposal has been designed, it is time to approach the potential sponsor. As discussed in the sales management chapter (Chapter 7), the sales process involves five stages: prospecting for customers (as discussed in the previous section), determining communication methods, making contact and the pitch, closing the sale, and servicing after the sale. This process is slightly modified for the sport sponsorship process, but generally follows the same methodology.

Communication and the Corporate Decision Making Process

Corporations receive many sponsorship proposals over the course of a fiscal year, and have to make shrew decisions regarding which would be most beneficial to them. In order to have the greatest chance of the sponsorship proposal being read, the sport organization must create two very important documents: the cover letter and the executive summary.

The cover letter is the introduction to the sport organization and the proposal. It will cover the essential elements of the sponsorship proposal and the enthusiasm the sport organization has for the potential partnership. The letter needs to be well-written, grammatically correct, and professional. If not, there is very little chance that the sponsorship proposal being read. In addition, the letter should be personalized to target the special relationship that is possible, and hopefully create enough interest for the reader to continue reading.

The executive summary is placed at the beginning of the sponsorship proposal, although it is the last document created as part of the sponsorship proposal development process. This short document (usually fewer than two pages), would include everything that would be covered if the potential sponsor conducted a 5-minute interview with the sport organization. Covered in the executive summary would include the fundamentals of sponsorship opportunities with the sport organization, the specific aspect of the sponsorship to be considered in the proposal, the anticipated benefits from the partnership, the major people to be involved with the sponsorship, and a vision for what the sponsorship can bring to the business in the future. Again, this document should be professional and enthusiastic, but also complete and concise. The executive summary serves as an introduction to the sponsorship proposal, and if written correctly will encourage the corporate sponsorship decision makers to continue reading into the details of the proposal.

At this point, the sport organization has done all it can to get the sponsorship proposal into the hands of a potential sponsor. Should the sponsorship proposal get through the cover letter and executive summary phases, it will then be reviewed by the major decision makers within the marketing or sponsorship department of the corporation. During the decision making process, the potential sponsor will balance the sponsorship proposal against their benchmarks and goals to determine a level of best fit. They will also determine how the sponsorship can be amalgamated within their overall integrated marketing communications plan. Ultimately, regardless of best fit, the potential sponsors will determine whether their investment into the sponsorship agreement would bring about a positive ROI. Should the results of these issues be viewed as positive to the corporation, usually the proposal will be moved forward for further consideration.

Presentation, Modification, and Closing the Deal

Should the sponsorship proposal move forward for further consideration, the sport organization will be brought in for a presentation and discussion about the potential partnership. The presentation should not only include verbal discussion; it should also include visual aides including a PowerPoint presentation, copies of all relevant documentation, and related merchandise and collateral materials as applicable. As a result, it is important to know how many people are going to be at the presentation, and bring more than the required quantity of materials (some for important people who could not be at the presentation, and/or people who show up unplanned).

During this presentation, the sport organization is effectively making a sales pitch to the potential sponsor. As previously discussed in sales management (Chapter 7), the focus of the pitch should be on the sponsorship proposal, especially targeting the benefits to the corporation. The attitude of the presentation is crucial during this stage, and they become the face of the sport organization. In this sense, you will not get a second chance to make a first impression. Therefore, the presenter should be appropriately dressed, be neat and well groomed, have an appearance of confidents without being cocky, and maintain eye contact.

After the presentation, there will often be a question and answer session to clarify points from the presentation or proposal, and to ask ancillary questions that may be of interest to the corporation. During this time, the representatives from the sport organization must listen and read the individuals asking the questions. They must make every effort to clarify points from the proposal and/or presentation, and provide any additional information that might complete the picture for the potential sponsor and entice them to enter into an agreement. This process may take a long time, and a number of meetings. Regardless, the sport organization must always maintain a positive attitude and be professional. Even if there is no agreement, it is important to leave the door open for possible future sponsorship agreement.

Assuming that the presentation goes well and there is interest in creating this mutual agreement, the tactics change to closing the sale. This is often conducted through negotiations, which is a type of alternative dispute resolution utilized by two parties to complete transactions. Prior to entering the negotiation forum, the sport organization usually will review their initial meeting with the potential sponsor, determine if any modification needs to be made to the sponsorship proposal based on feedback received, and modify and resend the updated proposal prior to the negotiation session.

While negotiations may differ slightly because of cultural issues, the type of discussions to be negotiated, or the parties involved, the generic process is as follows:

- *Non-task sounding*: Where the first 5–10 minutes is used to introduce all the participants and briefly talk about topics other than the business at hand, including family, sports, news, and the economy.
- *Information exchange*: This is the point when all the cards are laid out on the table and information is provided by both parties and feedback exchanged.

- *The first offer*: This is the offer made by the sport organization, and is usually fairly close to what they want to get for the sponsorship agreement.
- *Consideration*: The sponsor mulls over the offer, asks additional questions, and considers tactics to discuss modifications.
- *Counter offer*: This is where the potential sponsor articulates what they want and/or are willing to pay for the sponsorship.
- *Persuasion stage*: Each side is seeking to gain some ground on issues, answer questions, clarify positions, and often argue over points.
- *Making concessions*: Each side will make concessions in order to reach a mutually beneficial and agreeable point. It is important to realize that this point is not always reached, and without agreement, the partnership opportunity may terminate at this point.
- *Reaching an agreement*: However, should there be agreement on the terms of the proposal, they are laid out in contracts. The contracts will spell out the terms of the contract including the rights of each party, the parameters of the sponsorship (broadcasting, signage, advertising, promotions, collaterals, merchandise, hospitality, public relations, community relations, etc.), the price to be paid and over what time period, whether this is a contract of exclusivity, the liability of all parties, the protection of intellectual properties for both parties, confidentiality statements, contingencies, termination clauses, and any additional errors and omissions. These contracts are then read over by legal counsels, and signed by the proper authorities for each organization.

Managing the Sponsorship

In addition to ensuring that the terms and conditions of the sponsorship contract have been met, the sport marketing professional has additional responsibilities regarding the management of the sponsorship. First and foremost is the creation of a yearly sponsorship report. This document is effectively an annual report on how the sponsorship was implemented, and details the tangible and intangible benefits that the sponsor received. This report often includes a sample of advertising and promotional materials, PowerPoint slides with pictures and/or CDs/DVDs with videos showing commercials, broadcasts, and game action which incorporated elements of the sponsorship agreement. The goal is to list all of the contractual elements, describe how they were fulfilled, and provide a measure for the sponsor to determine whether they received value and a result on investment for their sponsorship dollars.

Evaluation of the Effectiveness of Sport Sponsorships

The evaluation process involves investigating the performance of the sponsorship and determining whether the marketing efforts associated with the sponsorship are working. This evaluation process is also crucial as a part of the sport marketing professional's responsibility for entering into renegotiations and renewals of sponsorship agreements.

Many of the qualitative and quantitative research methods discussed in the sport marketing research chapter (Chapter 3) are effective means to evaluate sponsorships. Focus groups, interviews, and surveys can be used to collect primary data regarding sponsor awareness and association to the sport organization. Secondary data including sales reports, advertising effectiveness report through media outlets, and sponsorship effectiveness reports from companies such as IEG also serve an integral role in evaluating sponsorships.

When sponsors evaluate the effectiveness of their sponsorship contracts, they are specifically looking at measurable increases in exposure, awareness, media coverage, and sales. In addition, the sponsor also evaluates whether the goals of the sponsorship and an acceptable level of ROI were met. Should the results show that objectives were not met, value or an appropriate level of ROI was not attained, or other concerns arose (direction of sport organization or company, budgetary issues, increase in costs, insufficient execution of contracts, or other conflicts), the marketing professionals from the sport organization need to work to rectify those issues and assure the sponsors that terms will be met in the future.

CONCLUSION

Sport sponsorship involves acquiring the rights to be affiliated with a sport product or event in order to obtain benefits from that association. Sport sponsorships play a significant role in the sport promotional mix, and take place at multiple levels of the sport business landscape. The history of sport sponsorships has its roots in Ancient Greece during the Olympic Games, but entered the modern era of sport business during the 1984 Summer Olympics in Los Angeles. The profitability of these Olympic Games as a result of significant corporate sponsorship, and the subsequent move of Los Angles Olympic Committee President Peter Ueberroth to MLB, has led to an age of growth and prosperity in sport created by these partnerships. The growth since pre-2004 levels ($300 million) to a projected value of $9 billion per year in the United States, and $30.5 billion worldwide in 2005 is astronomical.

Sport sponsorship is a global multi-industry concept. In fact, only one out of top ten corporations engaged in sport sponsorship in the United States in 2005 was Nike. Other industries such as food and beverage, automotive, electronics and mobile industries are engaged in sport sponsorship. These companies have options in six main sport sponsorship categories: sport governing body sponsorship, sport ream sponsorship, athlete sponsorship, broadcast and media sponsorship, sport facility sponsorship, and sport event sponsorship.

Sport sponsorship agreements are usually documented within a sponsorship proposal. These packages are designed to articulate the benefits derived from the agreement for all parties involved. The reason for entering into a sport sponsorship agreement varies from organization to organization. Corporations have numerous goals as a result of sport sponsorship, including increasing public awareness, enhancing their company image, building business and trade relationships with other sponsoring organizations, changing or improving public perception of their company, increasing community involvement in the target area, and enhancing personnel relations by offering opportunities for employees to attend sponsored events, including attendance at hospitality areas. The goals of sport brands as a result of sponsorship include taking in additional revenue from the agreement, and increasing target market awareness, image sales, and market share.

FROM THEORY TO PRACTICE
Dean Bonham, Chairman and CEO
The Bonham Group, Denver, Colorado

As President of the Denver Nuggets in the late 1980s, I was charged with putting a price on the team's sponsorship inventory at McNichols Arena. Ownership's approach to this valuation process was "need-based": they needed a certain amount of money to meet their financial obligations, so I was told to charge that amount for the team's sponsorships. I disagreed with this approach and, instead, formulated a "value-based" approach linked to empirical criteria that included the location of sponsorship exposure, the number of impressions it would generate on an annual basis and its integration with other sponsorship elements. The result was a revenue figure that was substantially higher than the one initially requested.

After leaving the Nuggets, I formed The Bonham Group in 1988, offering sponsorship-evaluation services, as well as advice on the sale and negotiation of sponsorships. The goal from the beginning was to provide properties with a defensible basis for marketing their sponsorship inventory. This led to the development of the TBG Property Analysis®, a document designed to identify all of a property's relevant sponsorship benefits; to calculate the total number of impressions and value that would be generated through these benefits; and to create sponsorship packages based on the benefits. Because it involved proprietary methods of valuation, the process for arriving at these values would later be trademarked. Early users of this service were colleges (Syracuse), national governing bodies (USA Wrestling) and entertainment entities (House of Blues, Motown).

As the era of accountability in sponsorship activity gained steam in the early 1990s, corporations became enamored with "media analyses," the quantification and evaluation of their in-broadcast corporate exposure (logos, signage, and audio mentions). Other agencies enjoyed success in marketing this service, despite their simplistic methodologies that led to inflated valuations. Sensing a desire for a more conservative and "real world" approach, we began offering media analyses. Early clients were IBM and FedEx.

It also became clear that a sophisticated method of identifying a property's sponsorship value, such as that used in the TBG Property Analysis®, would also be useful to corporations who wanted to evaluate existing or potential sponsorship relationships. This led to the development of The Bonham Group's Sponsorship Analysis. Although this service could be used by either corporations or properties, it was particularly favored by the former who were looking for ammunition during renewal negotiations or a tool to help them justify their investment.

A variant of this service, the TBG Naming Rights Analysis, was developed in 1996, when The Bonham Group was retained by PNC Bank to analyze its potential naming rights sponsorship of the Pittsburgh Pirates new stadium. This service has since become the foundation for all our naming rights projects. By April 2006, The Bonham Group had evaluated 91 naming rights agreements in 38 US markets, two European markets (Turin, Italy and London, England) and three Canadian markets (Toronto, Calgary, and Ottawa). Additionally, we have negotiated 10 naming rights agreements on behalf of corporate and property clients.

In the mid-1990s, The Bonham Group ventured into two new sponsorship arenas: shopping centers and casinos. The shopping center activity began with analysis work for The Taubman Company and developed into multiple projects for a consortium of mall developers that included Taubman, The Rouse Company, and Urban Retail Properties. This work gave The Bonham Group a background and expertise that would be applied in projects for several other developers in subsequent years. The casino activity started with analysis work for Harrah's and later Caesars World, who were exploring the sponsorship potential at their respective properties. This subsequently expanded into additional analysis work for several other resort/gaming properties.

For those interested in getting into the business of sports, here is a formula that has worked for many:

- *Network*: Most successful job searches in this industry are a direct result of knowing someone either already in the business or with a connection to it.
- *Be willing to pay your dues*: The pay in the first few years very seldom matches what you can make in corporate America.
- *Be persistent*: The competition is enormous, but there is no substitute for the power of persistence.
- *When you get your shot at an interview, prepare, prepare, prepare*: You should know everything from the challenges the agency or team faces to how you can immediately contribute to its ability to meet its objectives.

If you are still interested, keep your expectations in check, your eyes wide open and go for it.

SPECIALIZED CONCEPTS IN SPORT MARKETING

SPORT RETAIL MANAGEMENT

CHAPTER OUTLINE

CHAPTER OBJECTIVES

The reader will be able to:

- Gain an understanding of sport retailing and sport retail management through a presentation of various retail strategies and a strategic approach to retailing in the sport field.
- Understand the concepts of strategic retail management; the factors and skills associated with situation analysis; the manners to target customers and gathering information; the concepts associated with choosing a retail location; the concepts related to managing a retail business; the concepts related to merchandise management and pricing; and the various ways of communicating with the customer.

WHAT IS SPORT RETAIL MANAGEMENT?

Sport retail management is the process of directing and controlling the business activities related to the sale of the sport product to consumers for their personal consumption. Sport retail management, as the end result of the distribution process, becomes an integral part of the entire sport marketing process – if there is no sale of the sport product then the previous sport marketing methods implemented have been useless. With the increased opportunities for sport product sales through the Internet, and the growth of global sport marketing efforts, it would seem that sport retail sales in general are on an upward swing. However, the challenges faced by sport retailers are great due to a number of factors including the general population having less discretionary time and income, oversaturation in the competitive market leading to lower profit margins due to cost cutting, the high level of customer service expected in society, and the lack of knowledge by many sport retailers as to the proper use of the Internet as a tool.

Retail in the United States is a significant part of the economy. As reported in January 2005 by one of the world's largest marketing information companies – AC Nielsen – annual retail sales in the United States topped $4 trillion (US) for the first time last year. Total sales of $4.1 trillion in 2004 were up 8% from 2003, the biggest annual increase since 1999. The leisure goods sector of the retail industry, of which sport retail falls under, grew almost 1% last year. Included in this sector are companies such as Sports Authority, Decathlon, Olympia Sports, and Dick's Sporting Goods.

As the last stage in the distribution process, sport retailers play an integral role as the primary contact between manufacturers and sport consumers. Sport retailers utilize the sorting process, whereby they assemble a variety of goods and services from various suppliers, buy them in large quantities, and sell them to consumers. The goal is to maximize manufacturer efficiency while allowing consumers to have a choice when shopping at the sport retail outlet. In general, the goods and services sold by sport retail outlets are not owned and operated by the manufacturers. This allows manufacturers to reach a wide range of consumers, while focusing on its area of expertise. The result of this is often reduced costs of producing the good and services, which in turn will improve cash flow and increase sales.

Sport retail management can be quite a challenge because the average amount of a sales transaction for sport retailers is much less than for manufacturers. As a result, the sport retailer must control costs and inventory, while at the same time utilizing advertising and special promotions to maximize the number of customers coming through the door. Once the consumer is in the door, the sport retailer must increase the number of impulse sales by utilizing a very aggressive selling style. The reason for this is that final consumers often make many unplanned purchases. They may walk through the door to buy a T-shirt, but you as the sport retailer want the consumer to walk out the door with that T-shirt, along with a pennant and a ball. Therefore, a major part of the aggressive selling style includes effective use of in-store displays, catalogs, and websites. In addition, stores must have an organized layout and be appealing to the consumer's eye. With the wide variety of sport retail outlets, the sport retailer must be able to draw consumers to their store location. Factors such as location, transportation, store hours, proximity of competitors, product selection, parking, and advertising need to be considered.

To make the process less challenging, it is important that a sport retail manager develop and utilize an effective sport retail strategic plan to guide the organization. All retailers should utilize the following six steps when developing a retail strategic plan:

1. Define the type of business based on the goods or service category and the company's specific orientation.
2. Set short-term and long-term goals and objectives.
3. Determine the customer market on the basis of its characteristics, wants, and needs.
4. Devise an overall, long-run plan that provides a vision for the sport organization and its employees.
5. Implement an integrated strategy that combines store location, product diversity, pricing, and advertising to achieve goals and accomplish objectives.
6. Regularly evaluate performance, maintain or enhance strengths, and correct weaknesses and problems observed.

RETAIL VALUE AND RELATIONSHIP BUILDING

A sport retailer must understand and effectively apply the concepts of value and relationship from the perspective of the consumer, the manufacturer, and itself. The resulting goal is to have consumers believe that the sport retailer offers good values for the money being spent by the sport consumer, and to have a positive relationship between the sport retailer and the sport consumer.

Value

Value is an amount of goods, services, or money that is a fair price or return for something of an equivalent amount. In sport retail management, the manufacturer and retailer represent value as a series of activities, exchanges, and processes that provide a set value for the consumer. These series of activities, exchanges, and processes are known as a value chain. The goal of a value chain is to create a perception in the mind of the consumer as to the benefit of the sport product, and that the price being paid is worthwhile. Consumers must always believe they got their money's worth. Sport retailers must understand that price is not the only consideration for value. Other considerations including location, parking, level of customer service, the variety of products, the quality of products, availability of products, and retailer's image are a significant part of value in the mind of the consumer.

The goal for the sport retail management is to ensure they are offering an optimal level of value to their consumers and hence maximizing the number of consumers entering their retail outlet. There are three levels of a value-oriented sport retail strategy. First, there are minimal expectations that all consumers desire. These expected value chain essentials include convenient hours, educated employees, quality service, a clean store, ample parking, having desired products in stock, and an acceptable return policy. Second is an expanded value chain, which is a sport retail strategy that offers additional elements to differentiate themselves from other sport retailers. These elements include offering exclusive brands, frequent shopper programs, delivery options, and superior salespeople and service. The third level is known as a niche sport retail strategy. At this level, the sport retail outlet encompasses value chain elements that have not yet been addressed or refined by the competition.

Those sport retail outlets that encompass multiple levels of a value-oriented retail strategy have a greater likelihood of success. However, sport retail managers must ensure that they remember that value is more than just price, and enhanced elements do not always create value. Sport retailers must provide value-enhancing services that customers want or are willing to pay extra for. In addition, sport retailers must make certain that they are competing in the appropriate value and price segment. If not, sales will either be greatly reduced (low value/high price) or less profitable (high value/low price). Finally, sport retailers must realize that the most important element of a value-oriented sport retail strategy is a high level of customer service. Regardless of all other things, poor customer service will result in failure, regardless of the level of value or price.

Price/Quality Matrix

This relationship between price and value is often articulated in terms of the price–quality matrix, which articulated the relationship between price and quality in positioning the sport product as compared to others. The following chart diagrams the four quadrants of the price–quality matrix:

Successful sport retail businesses operate in as many quadrants as possible. The high-price/low-quality quadrant is one in which all sport retailers avoid, as

	QUALITY	
P R I C E	High price, low quality	High price, high quality
	Low price, high quality	Low price, low quality

in most cases sport consumers will not pay top dollars for inferior products. However, the other three quadrants do offer opportunities for profitability albeit at different levels. Of the remaining quadrants, the least desirable for the sport retailer is the low-price/high-quality quadrant because of minimal profits (high cost to produce product vs. low selling price). However, most sport retailers must target this quadrant with many of their product because this is the most desirable for the sport consumer (getting the most for their money). High price/high quality is an advantageous quadrant for sport retailers because consumers are paying the most for the best, and there is always room to maximize profits. Low price/low quality does have its benefits, but it often requires large volumes of product to be in stock and sold to maximize profitability.

From the standpoint of specialized sport products, and based on the ever-changing perceptions of the sport consumer, price is often a more powerful tool than quality. With these types of sport products, the level of quality is often similar. Consumers often perceive products differently based on the price charged by the sport retailer. Therefore, sport products with a higher price often increase sales significantly as sport consumers may perceive the product to be better because it costs more. This concept only works if the sport retailer understands their customers and can effectively determine whether their sport product fits in this category.

Relationships

This leads into the importance of building relationships with sport consumers. There are four critical factors to take into account when building those relationships – the market, customer service, customer satisfaction levels, and customer perks.

The Market

The market is the fundamental concept of retail management. The market is what provides the opportunity to buy and sell based on the demand for goods and services. Inclusive of the market is the customer base, which is targeted based on the needs of segments such as population and lifestyle trends; reasons for shopping; the level of loyalty; and what kind of customer mix is desired between new and old customers? According to statistics from the United States

Census Bureau, the population is aging, a fourth of all households have only one person, and a sixth of the population moves annually. Most people live in urban or suburban areas. The number of working women continues to grow. Household income has been rather stable for the past 25 years. In addition, minority and immigrant populations are expanding. Research shows that gender roles are changing, shoppers are more demanding, and market segments are more diverse in today's marketplace. In addition, there is less interest in shopping, and time-saving goods and services are desirable.

Therefore, in building consumer relationships, there are three major consumer-oriented factors that contribute to the success of sport retail businesses: (a) saving customer's time and energy; (b) the service and assortments offered; and (c) the uniqueness of the shopping experience. In addition, the sport retail business owner must realize that not all customers are equal. There are those who are worth cultivating long-term relationships with as they represent the core of the sport retailer's customers (80/20 rule). To maximize how a sport retailer fosters these relationships, they should analyze their customer base from three standpoints. First, the sport retailer should determine which customers are the most profitable and most loyal. This will define the customers who spend the most money and seem to prefer stable long-term relationships. Second, analyze which customers place the greatest value on what they have to offer. As stated earlier in the chapter, consumers must always believe that they are getting their money's worth. Third, an evaluation must be completed by the sport retail manager to determine which customers are worth more to them than to their competitors. A sport retail outlet cannot be everything to all people, but consumers who are worth more to a competitor will eventually go over to them.

Customer Service

Customer service refers to the retail activities that increase the value consumers receive when they purchase goods and services. To service consumers in an effective manner, a sport retail firm must first understand how to take care of the consumer then outline a service strategy and plan for specific individual services.

To start, the sport retail firm must determine the most effective way to communicate with consumers about their goods and services. Once the consumer is "in the door," the sport retailer must get to know their customers so they can predict their needs, wants, and desires. This knowledge differs based on the type of customer. For repeat and loyal customers, it is remaining trustworthy in the eyes of the consumer, and continuing to offer the products, services, and value essential to the consumer. For new customers, it starts by reading the consumer to determine not only what they need, want, and desire, but also what impulse items they might be apt to purchase. As the relationship grows, there is a shift to enhancing value and building trust, with the eventual goal of the new customer moving up the escalator to become a repeat or even loyal customer.

In all cases, the sport retailer needs to have a high level of product knowledge to better service the consumers. Often in mass merchandise stores such as Wal-Mart and Target, the individuals working in the sport department do not understand the products they are selling. In sport retail outlets, the consumer should know that employees have been trained to understand the products and services, and how to deal with a very knowledgeable customer – which many specialized product consumers are. When a customer believes that the retailer cares about the individual and the product, they tend to continue their patronage of the retail firm.

In devising a strategy to take care of the consumer, a number of questions need to be answered. What customer services are expected? Do customers have a choice of services? Do we charge a fee for customer services (cost–benefit analysis)? What is the relationship of customer service to the sport retail firm's image? How long is customer service offered after the sale, and at what level?

Once these questions are answered, the sport retailer must choose the services they will offer. Some are basic such as credit. Will you accept all major credit cards? Personal checks? Will you have your own credit card? Will you allow for corporate accounts that pay on a revolving basis? Other services might include delivery, installation and assembly, gift wrapping, gift certificates, return policies, special sales for repeat and loyal customers, and outside sales (orders via catalog, mail, phone, and/or web).

Customer Satisfaction Levels

Customer satisfaction takes place when the value and customer service provided through a sport retail firm meet or exceed consumer expectations. As discussed in detail in the consumer behavior (Chapter 5), this is one of the most difficult areas for a sport retailer to understand because most consumers do not complain when they are dissatisfied. They just leave and go to purchase their goods and services at a competitor. Therefore, one of the most important tasks a sport retailer must perform to maintain a solid relationship is to make it easier for consumers to provide feedback. This can be done in simple ways by providing customer feedback opportunities at the register, or via the web. A more detailed manner is to subsidize ongoing customer satisfaction surveys and track the ebbs and flows. Whatever methodology is utilized, one thing is abundantly clear: if the consumer does not believe that their concerns are being met, they will no longer be customers. To retain customers, sport marketing professionals involved in retail management must utilize the marketing concept, which is a consumer-oriented philosophy that suggests that satisfaction of consumer needs provide the focus for product development and marketing strategy, to enable the retail operation to meet its own organizational goals.

Customer Perks

Customer perks reward those repeat and loyal customers for their long-term relationship with the sport retail outlet. Sport retailers spend time with these loyalty programs because of the Pareto Principle (or 80/20 Rule) – which states that 80% of business come from the top 20% of customers. To implement a program, a sport retail firm must first have a manner in which to track shopping behavior – usually through a database created in conjunction with some type of buying card or tag. The sport retail firm must then find a way to personalize communications with those frequent consumers to make them feel special and to articulate the participation rules. Most importantly, the rewards have to be useful and appealing to the consumer. They must be reasonably attainable, have features unique to the retailer, and offer a range of rewards for short-term and long-term participation. An example of this is both Sports Authority and Dick's Sporting Goods email special offers and notification of sales to frequent shoppers. Retail operations also offer perks to their best customers in conjunction with the corporate sponsorship of sporting events, such as hospitality and participation opportunities at golf tournaments and auto races.

Channel Relationships

Relationship building must also take place with other members of the distribution channel, specifically manufacturers, wholesalers, and potentially other retail outlets within a franchise. Each channel member is dependent on the other. However, due to contradictory goals, some channel members become difficult to deal with. The goal is to create positive relationships between the members of the sport retailer's channel so that they can better serve each other and the final consumer. This is often accomplished through category management – where all parts of the channel manage products in categories rather than individually. Category management allows all members of the channel to maximize their profit from the mix of brands in the category. This is often accomplished by allocating funds and marketing efforts according to the profit potential of each brand in the mix while deleting weak brands and adding new brands with higher profit potential.

Category management requires cooperation between all members of the channel. Sport retailers listen to customers and stock what they want. Profitability is improved because inventory follows demand closely. By being better focused, each department can become more desirable for shoppers. This data is then shared, usually through computerized means, to all levels of the channel so they can have efficient inventory management and stock what the customer wants. If the suppliers stock what the retailer needs, their profitability will also be maximized.

Relationship Building Differences Between Goods and Service Retailers

The move to the 21st century has seen a greater shift to service-based retailing. Therefore, sport retail firms must not only understand the differences between goods retailing and service retailing, but also whether they are engaged in one, the other, or both. Goods retailing focuses on the sale of tangible products such as hockey pucks, sticks, helmets, and uniforms. Service retailing involves transactions in which consumers do not purchase or acquire ownership of tangible products, such as personal services, facility and equipment rental, and recreational services. An example of this for the sport of hockey would be renting a hockey rink for practice or a birthday party, and hiring a coach for goalkeeper lessons.

Service retailing in the United States and worldwide continues to grow at a consistent rate, and represents a significant portion of overall retail trade. In the United States alone, consumers spend almost 2/3 of their income on services. Almost 80% of the labor force works in the services sector. A significant percentage of these services are in the fields of sport and recreation.

Service retailing is much more dependent on personal interactions and word-of-mouth communication than goods retailing. Therefore, the intangible nature of many services makes it more difficult for a sport retail firm to develop a clear consumer-oriented strategy because of three main factors. First is the inseparability of the service provider from their services, which makes that individual indispensable. If the service provider cease operations or no longer offers the required services, the sport retailer is left without the ability to service their customers. Second is the short life span of many services. This is especially true with technology-based products and services, where the average turnover is approximately 6 months. Third, the variability of services creates a situation where service quality may differ for each purchase, retail outlet, or service provider.

RETAIL STRATEGY

One of the major concepts discussed in the development of value and relationships is the development of a sport retail strategy. A sport retail strategy is the overall plan of action utilized to guide a sport retailer. This plan includes a situation analysis, goals and objectives of the organization, and an identification of customer's needs, wants, and desires. The creation of the overall strategy will include the specific tasks to be completed, how the work is to be controlled, and how feedback on the retail strategy will be collected and evaluated.

A well-implemented strategy results in the coordination of all aspects of the business, and helps the firm complete tasks and avoid disasters in a more efficient and effective manner. This involves variables the sport retail manager can control, such as store location, organizational structure, human resource management, operational management, merchandise management, and the ability to communicate directly with sport consumers to determine their needs, wants, and desires. In addition, there are other variables that cannot be controlled by the sport retail manager, which therefore requires a modification to the retail strategy. These variables include the sport consumer itself, threats caused by competitive situations, and changes in economic, technological, and legal conditions.

To succeed, the sport retail strategy must be integrated throughout the organization. From an internal viewpoint, work is controlled via a sport retail audit. This periodical review involves analyzing the performance of the sport retailer with the goal of revealing the strengths and weaknesses of the organization. The goal is then to maintain and build on strengths, while improving upon and eliminating weaknesses. From an external standpoint, sport retailers must utilize tactical decisions to be responsive to the external aspects of the business – taking advantage of opportunities and avoiding threats to the organization. This is usually accomplished through a variety of retail tactics that are the basis of daily and short-term retail operations including: (1) the location of the sport retail outlet; (2) the efficient and effective operating procedures; (3) efficient product management and pricing; (4) effective communication with customers/pleasant retail outlet atmosphere; (5) knowledge of sport retail products and services; and (6) implementation of effective promotional programs.

These elements of a strategic sport retail mix are utilized to help a sport firm become a destination retailer – one that sport consumers view as unique to the point of becoming loyal to the company and being willing to go out of their way to shop there. The largest sport destination retailer is Bass Pro Shops. Bass Pro Shops has built an enterprise that serves the needs of millions of outdoor enthusiasts around the globe. They are the world's leading outdoor retailer with over 75 million visitors to their 26 stores annually (six of which only opened in 2004); 100 million catalog and sale circulars mailed per year, 2 million website hits per month, and sales in 2004 of $1.98 billion. According to Sporting Goods Business, their plans are to open another six locations in 2005 and seven locations in 2006. In addition, they are rumored to be readying for an initial public offering (IPO) late in 2006 or early 2007.

So how did they become the most successful sport destination retailers? According to www.basspro.com:

> Few businesses have had the opportunity to grow an entire industry where none existed before. In 1971, top anglers were continually frustrated by the lack of a consistent source for the specialized gear they needed to compete in the growing sport of tournament fishing. Starting with just 8 feet of retail space in a Springfield, Missouri store, Bass Pro Shops began by offering a crude selection of the latest gear from the tournament trail. The rest, as they say, is history…
>
> Bass Pro Shops has established itself as a prime destination for the outdoor enthusiast. Almost invariably, Bass Pro Shops retail stores rank among the top tourist attractions in their respective states. Customers actually plan getaways and even honeymoons around a visit to a Bass Pro Shops superstore because of the one-of-a-kind experience it offers. Impressive indoor waterfalls, glass aquariums, wildlife mounts, delicious food and more make each Bass Pro Shops store a must-see attraction for the sporting family.

Data to determine the level of success of each element of the sport retail strategy mix must be collected and evaluated. This feedback involves relating the results to two main areas: goals and objectives; and the situation analysis.

Goals and Objectives

The goals and objectives of a sport retail organization reflect the short- and long-term targets a sport retailer hopes to reach. These goals and objectives must be clearly stated without ambiguity to ensure that the mission can be put into action. In sport retail management, goals and objectives are usually centered on sales, profit margin, customer satisfaction, and company image. Sales objectives focus on reaching specified volume goals such as increasing revenues, maintaining sales levels, maximizing percentage share in market, and attaining specified levels of units sold. Profit goals include dollars earned and increased operating efficiency (decrease operating expenses while increasing sales). Other profit goals may include reaching a specific level of return on investment (ROI) or return on equity (ROE), both of which are profitability measures which tells how effective investments and resources are utilized by the organization to make profits.

Customer satisfaction objectives go beyond meeting the needs, wants, and desires of valued constituents, but also maintaining good relations with them. Company image goals relate to the proper positioning of the sport retail organization so that they are perceived in the best light as compared to competitors. This image differentiation varies based on the type of retail outlet. Mass merchandise sport retail outlets strive to offer value, a maximal level of merchandise offerings, and substantial retail facilities, whereas niche retailers focus on specific segments and address the necessities of those segments.

If the goals and objectives can be achieved, the sport retail operation has a better opportunity to succeed. However, it is impossible to succeed without understanding and identifying the needs, wants, and desires of the sport consumer. A sport retailer utilizes three methods to reach their target market. Mass sport marketing is where goods and services are available for sale to an extensive group of sport consumers, such as Sports Authority, Modell's, or Dick's Sporting Goods. Concentrated sport marketing, or niche marketing, is concentrating on one specific group of sport consumers, such as Nevada Bob's Pro Shops (world's largest chain of retail golf stores), Eastern Mountain Sports (focuses on hardcore, edgy outdoor enthusiasts), and Pacific Sunwear (action sports lifestyle retailer of casual fashion apparel, footwear, and accessories for the chain's target customers – men and women ages 12–24). Differentiated sport marketing focuses on two or more different sport consumer groups with divergent retailing approaches for each group. Examples include Aldila (high-performance graphite golf club shaft maker who also manufactures hockey sticks and hockey blades); Ski Market (New England regional ski shop in the winter; bicycles/kayak/surf shop in the summer); and Brunswick (bowling and billiards products; fitness equipment including Life Fitness, ParaBody, and Hammer Strength; pleasure boats including SeaRay, Bayliner, Boston Whaler and Hatteras, and marine engines including Mercury and Mariner).

Situation Analysis

A situation analysis looks at the current status of a business and examines which direction the business should head. In order to accomplish this, the sport retailer must complete a detailed evaluation of the opportunities available to capitalize on, and the threats facing the business from competitors and the environment. This becomes difficult, especially in retail operations, as the firm strives to identify trends at an early stage to satisfy customer wants and needs and stay ahead of their competitors. However, if the retailer enters a new market too quickly, customers may not be ready for the change.

Mission

A situation analysis requires a comprehensive appraisal of the retail operation. This usually starts with an analysis of the organization's mission, which encompasses the goals and objectives of the firm. This mission should be in congruence with the firm's desired area of business, and the unique placement within the desired marketplace. The analysis of the organization mission includes: (1) evaluating the attitude of the business as related to their constituents; (2) the level to which consumers identify with the business entity; (3) how the retail business differentiates itself from its competitors; (4) whether business should be based on the goods and/or services sold by the entity, or based on consumers needs, wants, and desires; (5) whether the sport retail outlet is to be an industry leader or follower; and (6) what the scope of the sport retail operation should be. As a result of this continual review, the organizational mission is often adjusted to reflect changes in the marketplace.

Ownership Structure

There are numerous structures of ownership for a sport retail outlet depending on the marketplace niche. Some statistical background regarding the sport retail industry needs to be understood prior to discussing the structures. Currently, over 75% of all sport retailers own and manage a single retail outlet, and more than half employ two or fewer paid employees. On the other hand, according to a study conducted by Sporting Goods Business, the top two sporting good retailers are Wal-Mart ($17.1 billion in year 2004 sales for sporting goods and toys) and Target ($2.6 billion in year 2004 for athletic sales). In the direct sport retail industry itself, the top five companies (Sports Authority, Dick's Sporting Goods, Bass Pro Shops, Foot Locker, and Cabela's) accounted for nearly $10 billion in sales for year 2004.

The most basic of ownership structures is the independent sport retailer – your local small town sporting goods store. The independent sport retailer usually owns only one outlet, and hence requires a limited investment to start. This type of ownership offers great flexibility as a result of the outlet's independent nature. Hence, the sport retailer can focus their offerings, have control of their own retail strategy, and project the image they desire for the organization. While this type of entrepreneurship does provide for consistency, it does create a significant reliance of the ownership which often results in a decreased amount of time and resources to put into planning. Additionally, an independent contractor has limited bargaining power due to the limited quantities they purchase from manufacturers and wholesalers, which results in few economies of scale.

A sport retail chain runs multiple stores under one ownership group – such as Sports Authority and Dick's Sporting Goods. In this type of ownership, purchasing and decision making are not made at the retail store level – it is usually centralized within the ownership. This centralized ownership often results in efficient levels of management throughout the organization because of multiple locations being run in the same manner. Another advantage of chains lie in bargaining power and cost efficiency, increasing the number of economies of scale. While this reduction in costs is beneficial, it is often is at the expense of flexibility, control, and independence at the local store level.

Additionally, from the corporate level, it requires purchasing large quantities of product that needs to be delivered locally, regionally, nationally, and even internationally. These increased investments require high levels of cash flows and credit lines.

Many chains seek to reduce their liability while returning some levels of flexibility, control, and independence to the local retail store through franchising. Franchising involves a chain granting authority to an individual or business to distribute and sell products and service under the chain's established name. An example of this would be Golf USA (www.golfusa.com), where a individual who desires to open their own golf store would pay a fee and a percentage of sales to Golf USA in exchange for any number of benefits including exclusive selling rights, startup practices and management training, negotiated buying programs, special buying opportunities, proprietary equipment, marketing and promotional programs, and business support. A franchisee is a middle ground in the retailer landscape – allowing an individual who may not have the ability to be an independent contractor due to a lack of resources to take advantage of the benefits of a chain.

Another option for a potential sport retail operation is to be a leased department. This is where a sport retail operator rents out a section of a larger store such as a department or specialty store. Usually rent is in the form of a negotiated monthly payment or a percentage of sales, whichever is more. An example of this would be a company like Ticketmaster having a retail location in places such as Filene's, Foley's, Coconuts, and Tower Records.

A final method of ownership structure is a consumer cooperative. One of most successful sport retail consumer cooperative is Recreational Equipment, Inc. (REI). According to www.rei.com:

> In 1938 mountain climbers Lloyd and Mary Anderson joined with 21 fellow Northwest climbers to found Recreational Equipment, Inc. (REI). The group structured REI as a consumer cooperative to purchase high-quality ice axes and climbing equipment from Europe because such gear could not be purchased locally. The word quickly spread, and soon many other outdoors people joined the co-op. As REI grew, so too did the range of outdoor gear available to the co-op members.
>
> During the past six decades, REI has grown into a renowned supplier of specialty outdoor gear and clothing. We serve the needs of outdoors people through 78 retail stores in the U.S. and by direct sales via the Internet (REI.com and REI-OUTLET.com), telephone and mail. Today, REI is the nation's largest consumer cooperative with more than 2 million members.

Although the gear sold by REI looks much different now than it did in 1938, being a cooperative business remains central to REI. While non-members are welcome to shop at REI, only members enjoy special benefits, including an annual member refund on eligible purchases. REI's business success allowed the co-op to return member refunds to its active members in 2003 totaling $41 million, and provide nearly $2 million in donations in support of the outdoors and outdoor recreation.

ETHICS IN SPORT RETAIL MANAGEMENT: SELLING SPORT PRODUCTS MANUFACTURED BY CHILD LABOR

Children working in the Pakistani soccer ball industry and in the garment sector of Bangladesh received much attention because they were working in industries that produced goods destined for export to the United States. But children in export manufacturing industries represent only a tiny share of all child labor.

About 120 million children 5–14 years of age work full-time in the developing world. If part-time work is included, the number of children working grows to 250 million. Even this figure is probably an underestimate because it excludes unpaid work that does not make its way into the market, such as the work of children – particularly girls – who stay home to do household chores or watch over younger siblings. Probably less than 5% of all child workers are employed in export industries in manufacturing and mining, according to the US Department of Labor. The vast majority of children who work – over 70% – do so in agriculture.

The best predictor of the incidence of child labor is poverty. Child labor declines steeply as one moves from low-income to high-income countries, notes Princeton economist Alan Krueger. Asia, the most densely populated region of the world, has the largest number of child workers, but it is in poverty-stricken Africa where highest proportion of children work. About 20% of African children aged 5–14 work full-time – a little under 40 million children. Eighty million children work if part-time work is included. In countries where 1990 income per capita exceeded $5000, the employment of children was negligible, says Krueger.

The relationship between poverty and child labor is also true within countries. A range of studies in settings as varied as contemporary Côte d'Ivoire and 19th century Philadelphia have found that the incidence of child labor decreases as family income rises. Because of this, many believe that economic growth – if evenly distributed – is a key factor in reducing child labor.

Yet, the issue is not just poverty. Cultural factors also play an important role. In many instances, whether a child works or not depends on such factors as gender, religion, or social caste. In his work on child labor in India, MIT political scientist Myron Weiner pointed out that India's incidence of child labor was higher than that of some countries with lower income per capita. He speculated that religious beliefs and India's hierarchical caste system have prevented education from playing an equalizing role in society. "Those who control the education system are remarkably indifferent to the low enrollment and high dropout rate among the lowest social classes," he writes. "The result is one of the highest child labor rates in the world."

In terms of work hazards, children are more susceptible to injuries or work-related illnesses than adults doing the same type of work. The greatest number of illnesses and injuries occur in agriculture, not surprisingly, given the number of children working in that sector. But the likelihood of injury is by far the greatest for children who work in construction and mining, sectors that employ about 3% of working children.

Children also tend to work very long hours, leaving little time for school even when it is available. In surveys of 20 countries, the ILO found that in some countries more than half of the children who worked were doing so for 9 or more hours per day and up to four-fifths of them did it 7 days a week. But evidence on the relationship between school and work is mixed. In a study of child labor in Côte d'Ivoire, World Bank economist Christian Grootaeert found that working actually allowed many children to attend (afford) school.

Just as the importance of different forces varies across individual industries and regions of the United States, there is a consensus in the field that no one solution to the child labor problem can be applied to all countries. What can be done to eliminate child labor will vary, depending on the level and distribution of income, the availability of education, and the cultural factors that influence child labor.

For the poorest of countries, it maybe impossible to really eliminate child labor without income growth or some form of international aid. But for countries with relatively more resources, a range of policy alternatives can help bring about change. "Government can intervene in the market to create a variety of incentives, such as providing better and more schools, giving school meals, and improving conditions in the adult labor market, which result in a reduction of child labor," says Cornell economist Kaushik Basu.

What is to be done depends on the educational infrastructure in place. The American example clearly showed that education played a key role. Better educated workers in the United States were more productive and thus were better able to provide for their own children, reducing the need for child labor. However, for the permanent elimination of child labor, a cultural change ultimately has to come from within developing countries.

Source: Adapted from Wasserman, M. (2000). Eliminating child labor. *Regional Review* 10(2): 8–17.

Suggested Discussion Topics

You are the Director of Marketing for a sport retail chain. You are sitting in an office with the CEO of the company with a major dilemma. In an effort to cut costs, the CEO is considering changing to a new manufacturer who gets their products from Bangladesh, Pakistan, and Cambodia. If costs are not cut, there is a chance that the company could suffer, and possibly go into bankruptcy. If costs are cut, the potential for consumer backlash because of stocking products made by children living in third work economies may also result in a decline in traffic, which in turn may negatively affect sales and revenue, and may result in the possible same bottom line – bankruptcy.

Continued

The CEO wants to hear their options from a marketing standpoint as far as potentially being able to control the damage:

1. Assume that the CEO chooses to change manufacturers, and that the anticipated consumer backlash will be negative. How would you market the products and the company in a positive light in spite of the ethical issues present?
2. Would you have a problem marketing products, services, and an organization that is engaged in an ethically questionable practice of selling items manufactured by child labor in third-world countries? Why or why not?"

METHODS OF PLANNING A SPORT RETAIL MIX

To plan a sport retail strategy mix, one of three methodologies is used: the Sport Retail Life Cycle; Scrambled Sport Merchandising; and the Wheel of Sport Retailing.

Sport Retail Life Cycle

This concept is similar to the product life cycle. The first stage is the development stage, which determines the best techniques for entering the new sport retail organization into the marketplace. Inclusive of this stage is the initial maintenance of the sport retail operation in an environment of controlled costs, limited but quality human resources, and selective product and service offering that the sport consumer desires. The goal is to provide optimal conditions for future growth and development of the business.

During the introduction stage of the sport retail life cycle, the goal is to find a niche in the marketplace and build a customer base. At this point the doors are open and the need is to attract customers. Therefore, advertising costs are often high to increase customer awareness. At the same time, sales are low in the beginning – at least until the sport retail outlet is accepted by the general public. As a result, the introductory stage is a time of negative profit at the beginning.

The goal of the growth stage is for sales and profits to increase as the business becomes more established. During this time, a sport retail firm expands their operations regionally, nationally, and perhaps even internationally. In turn, new retail firms enter the marketplace striving to take a percentage of the market. To remain in a strong market position, the costs of business to the sport retail firm often increase. The result is a negative effect to profit, either because the increase costs affect the bottom line, or a decrease in sales resulting from an increase in price to absorb the increase expenses.

If the result is a decrease in sales, this signals that the sport retail firm is entering the maturity stage. The sport retail firm must reduce their profit margins to promote an increase in sales. Some of the reasons for the decrease in sales may also include a significant increase in competition, changes in the psychographic composition of the market, or the leadership of the sport retail firm may not be able to lead the sport retail organization to higher levels of profitability.

If changes are not made, the result for the sport retail firm will be the decline stage. This is where sales and profits continue to decline, and no matter what the sport retail manager does, they cannot recover from the tailspin. There are two decisions to me made: either reinvent the sport retail brand to encourage new growth, or have your "going out of business" clearance:

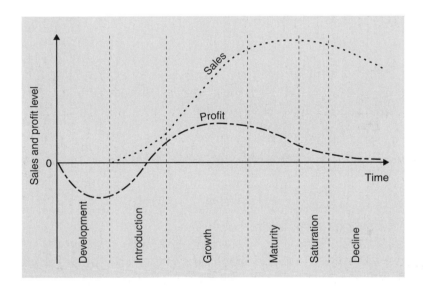

Scrambled Sport Merchandising

Scrambled sport merchandising is where a sport retailer offers goods and services that are dissimilar to the primary area of expertise of the firm. An example of this would be a golf store selling sunglasses. Although the expertise of the sport retailer is in golf products, they add this item because golfers may need sunglasses, and may make an impulsive purchase while in the store. These additional items are usually highly sought after by customers, and can provide a high profit margin because of the convenience factor. Many consider superstores such as Sports Authority and Decathlon to be scrambled merchandisers as they offer a wide variety of products, with limited expertise in the specific products. The goal of this is to reach a wider variety of target markets by attracting customers to this one-stop shopping opportunity. Also, by offering a wide variety of products that change seasonally, the sport retail outlet becomes a year-round operation, and hence reduces the effects of targeted competitors and seasonality.

The Wheel of Sport Retailing

In the wheel of sport retailing, the sport retail landscape is viewed as an ever-evolving system. Most sport retailers start as low-price options for the sport consumer. The sport retailer is strictly concerned with establishing themselves in the market – they are less concerned with low profit, and make every effort to keep their costs down. As the sport retail outlet becomes more established in the marketplace, the sport retailer will upgrade the quality of the products offered; improve the facilities housing the sport retail operation; and offer additional services. All of this should work to increase sales, and if costs have been controlled, increase profit margin.

Since the wheel of sport retailing is based on the availability of discretionary income by the public, consumer who only care about price will not be loyal to the sport retail outlet. This provides an opportunity for competition to enter the market and fill in the void left in the market.

The wheel of sport retailing has three levels: low end/discount; middle of the road/general; and high end/luxury. Sport retailers must be careful when moving from one level to another, as the move will affect sales, the target market, and the image of the organization. The goal is to obviously improve on all levels. However, the sport retail firm must have a solid strategy to accomplish their goals.

STORE-BASED SPORT RETAIL STRATEGY MIX

As we enter the 21st century, sport retail firms have needed to modify their store-based strategies to as more convenient purchase options have become available. These include the Internet, direct marketing efforts, and satellite outlets (video kiosks, mall kiosks, airports). These store-based strategies are focused on increasing profit margin by more adequately controlling internal costs, promoting higher margin goods and services, and doing away with items that yield little or no profit.

There are two methods that are being utilized by sport retailers to sustain sales growth in the ever increasing competitive marketplace: mergers and diversification. Mergers involve the union of two or more separately owned business entities. Examples of this would be when the Gart Sports Company merged with Sports Authority in 2003, and when Galyan's Trading Company merged with Dick's Sporting Goods in 2004. The goal of mergers is to maximize the resources available through both companies, increase customer base, improve on productivity and bargaining power, and control weaknesses by increasing competitive advantage.

Diversification involves spreading out business activities and investments. While diversification creates a larger number of competitors with which to contend, it does allow for increased leverage whereas if one market segment shows a decrease in sales, other market segments can pick up the slack. In the sport retail business, an example of a company who has been engaged in significant diversification is Reebok. In the early years, Reebok was strictly dependent on a few lines of sneakers. To stay afloat, Reebok diversified into international markets and numerous product niches. Originally, it was into the new and unexplored product segment of women's aerobic shoes. Reebok branched out further by entering the walking and casual footwear market through the acquisition of Rockport. Since then, Reebok has further diversified through increasing brand image (Avia), new footwear product lines (John A. Frye Company – high-quality leather boots; Ralph Lauren – footwear); new sportswear product lines (Ellesse International of Italy; the Greg Norman Collection); new sports product line (The Hockey Company with their subsidiaries CCM, JOFA, and KOHO); and leisure product line (CMI Boston Whaler – power boats).

If sales growth cannot be maintained, a company may have to downsize. This is where unprofitable stores are closed or sold due to their lack of productivity. This could be caused by sport retailers overextending themselves, choosing a poor location for the outlet, being swallowed up by superstores, or the increasing reliance by consumers on shopping via the Internet.

TARGETING CUSTOMERS AND GATHERING INFORMATION

Once a sport retail strategy has been established, the sport retailer must develop a plan for targeting customers. The purpose of this is to identify the characteristics, needs, attitudes, and purchase behavior of sport consumers. Characteristics include demographics (the unique qualities representative of human populations and population segments) and lifestyles (a manner of living that reflects the person's values and attitudes). Needs are an individual's basic shopping requirements. These needs often have a direct correlation to retail desire, which are the shopping goals that impact attitude and behavior. Attitude and purchase behaviors focus on the state of mind of the sport consumer. This state of mind often affects the way people shop, where they shop, how decisions are made, how purchases are made, and whether there will be repeat purchases.

With this target plan in mind, the sport retailer must then gather the information necessary to make informed retail decisions. Gathering data to make decisions is crucial to the decision making process, and while this information gathering should be an ongoing process, it should also be constantly evaluated to determine whether the research is yielding information needed.

A successful sport retail information gathering operation involves not only the sport retailer, but also their suppliers and consumers. This coordinated effort keeps all parties on the same page. Sport retailers learn from suppliers about new models, sales forecasts, and reasons for price adjustments, while at the same time they learn about attitudes about styles and models, the extent of brand loyalty, and the willingness to pay a given price from customers. Suppliers and consumers gather similar information from this collaborative process.

Unfortunately, many sport retailers feel that this cooperation will actually be used against them in favor of competitors. As a result, the sport retailer often uses non-systematic research to make retail decisions. Other reasons for using this methodology include lack of time, resources, and the ability to conduct solid research. While many feel this is an easy way out, having inadequate information may cause a sport retailer to implement a bad strategy.

In order to avoid this, sport retailers must implement a sport retail information system. This system, if implemented in an effective manner, will foresee the information needs of sport retail managers, store important data on an ongoing basis, and create a flow of information that will allow the sport retailer to make efficient operational decisions. Technology is a powerful tool that can be utilized as a framework for a sport retail information system. The two major technologies include database management and universal product codes (UPC) and electronic data interchange (EDI) technologies.

Database management is the process of gathering and organizing information in a manner that allows the sport retailer to integrate and apply that data into the sport retail strategy. It also allows for storing the information for future evaluation and use. Database management can be internal or outsourced. Internal database management allows for better control of the information and instant access, while outsourcing to a database management company saves time and energy that could be utilized in other aspects of the sport retail operation.

The other technologies available to sport retailers are through information compiled through UPC and EDI. Through UPC codes, the bar identification codes found on most retail products, sport retailers can record data on a number of product characteristics, including size, color, model, and brand. This also can help with inventory management, sales analyses, and purchase behaviors of consumers. As far as EDI, this process allows retailers and suppliers to share basic information with regard to inventory, delivery time, and unit sales, to name a few. In turn, this collaboration between supplier and retailer enhances the sport retailer's ability to make more effective decisions, control inventory more efficiently, and be responsive to sport consumer demand at a higher level.

In general, a sport retailer must understand their company, their consumers, and their competitors to appropriately target customers and utilize information. This also involves understanding the internal strengths and weaknesses of the sport retail operation, as well as its external opportunities and threats. This is then put into a plan that allows the sport retailer to select their target markets; identify the characteristics, needs, and attitudes of sport consumers; gain an understanding of the purchase decision making process of sport consumers; and implement an action plan for the sport retail operation.

LOCATION, LOCATION, LOCATION

Another significant part of the action and strategic plan is location. The placement of the store, whether as a traditional infrastructure or an e-store, is crucial to the success of the sport retail business. This is because a good location can often overcome shortcomings in strategy. In turn, no matter how good the strategy, a poor location cannot succeed.

The first step to choosing a location is completing a geographic trade-area analysis to determine the most appropriate place to set up the sport retail location. This trade-area analysis looks at the geographic and socioeconomic characteristics of the proposed site. The major characteristic to look at is the size and shape of the trade area. The best location has a primary trading area that encompasses the majority of the potential customers to the sport retail firm (75–80%). Another key feature of the trade area is the trend analysis, which involves projections for the future in an area (housing, population change, infrastructure) based on past data. This information can usually be obtained from governmental agencies or the local chamber of commerce.

Once a trade area has been determined, then the sport retailer must examine the current attributes to determine minimum standards for moving forward with the chosen location. The major attributes to examine are population, economic base, and competition. For population, general demographics that can be obtained through the United States Census Bureau (www.census.gov) are important. However, more important is using the data to determine effective buying power in a trade area. This disposable income represents 50% of a formula called the buying power index (BPI). The formula, which takes into account retail sales and population size in a trade area, is used to determine the retail sales potential of an area. The formula is as follows:

$$BPI = 0.5 \, (DI) + 0.3 \, (\%USRS) + 0.2 \, (\%USP)$$

where
DI = disposable income for the area
%USRS = percent of US retail sales for the trade area
%USP = percent of US population representative of the trade area.

For the economic base of a trade area, the sport retailer is seeking one that offers the most stability and is not detrimentally affected by environmental changes. This is assessed by analyzing the labor force available in the trade area; the infrastructure available including transportation, banking, and facilities; the stability of the economy in the trade area; and the growth potential of the trade area. Again much of this information can be obtained through local chamber of commerce offices, or via the Internet.

As far as competition, the most important factor to consider within the trade area is the level of saturation within the industry. If a trade area is undersaturated, then there are not enough sport retail firms selling goods and services to satisfy the needs of the consumers. When a trade area is oversaturated, then there are too many sport retail outlets, which in turn will lower the potential profit of the sport retailer due to the need to lower prices to compete. The ultimate for a sport retailer is a moderately saturated market where the addition of your firm will provide just enough sport retail operations to satisfy customers and maximize profit.

Once the trade-area analysis has been completed, the sport retail professional must determine the type of location. The three major types are as an isolated store, within a business district, or as a part of a planned shopping center. An isolated store is a sport retail outlet standing alone. This is usually reserved for large sport retail outlets or discount stores. A business district may take numerous forms. A central business district (CBD) is the main retailing area of a city (downtown). A secondary business district (SBD) is located in a city or town at the intersection of two main streets. A neighborhood business district (NBD) serves the goods and service needs of a single residential area. A planned shopping center can take the form of a strip mall (groups of a limited number of stores), a shopping mall (a larger group of store with diverse offerings), or an outlet mall (group of stores offering discounted shopping).

Once the general location has been determined, an exhaustive analysis of the specific site must be completed. This rating is individual to each sport retail firm, as each outlet has its own needs based on their philosophy, mission, and vision. Some of the general areas of analysis include pedestrian and vehicular traffic, availability of parking and mass transportation, access of the facility to major highways to aid in smooth delivery of inventory and customers, and the quality and quantity of competition. Specific areas of analysis include visibility, store placement (corner vs. "middle of the block"), and infrastructural esthetics including size and shape of the lot and building, and the condition and age of the building.

Another important consideration for location choice is whether the sport retailer plans on owning or leasing the facility. Most small operations are owned, and the major decision is whether to build from scratch or to buy an existing building. Sport retail outlets who lease usually have five options. A straight lease is the most simple as the sport retailer pays a fixed amount per month for the life of the lease. A percentage lease is where a minimum and maximum rent is set, and a sliding scale per month is charged based on a percentage of sales. A graduated lease is variable, with rent going up over a specified period of time during the life of the lease. A maintenance-increase-recoupment lease states that rent will go up if the expenses of the landlord rise beyond a predetermined point. A net lease is where the sport retailer pays rent plus all maintenance and utility costs.

ORGANIZATIONAL STRUCTURE

In the previous sections we have discussed sport consumer relationships, the development of sport retail strategy, and the location of the business. Now to the people of the sport retail organization ... in order to meet the needs, wants, and desires of the market, a sport retail firm must design an organizational structure that effectively and efficiently allocates tasks, resources, authority, and responsibilities. This is set in motion by creating a list of the tasks to be performed throughout the sport retail management process. The list below represents some of the typical tasks to be completed by a sport retail firm:

- Purchasing merchandise from suppliers and wholesalers to be sold
- Delivery of merchandise to the retailer
- Receiving and checking incoming merchandise shipments

- Setting prices and marking merchandise
- Inventory management, including control and storage
- Developing merchandise and window displays
- Store maintenance (clean, working condition)
- Marketing and market research
- Creating ease of flow for shoppers
- Handling of complaints
- Human resources management
- Merchandise alterations, repairs, and returns
- Billing customers
- Maintaining financial records and credit operations
- Sales forecasting and budgeting
- Gift wrapping and other customer perks

Once the list is developed, tasks are divided amongst organizational structure members. In dividing these tasks up, it is important to remember that a task only should be carried out if it is determined that the target market needs, wants, or desires it. If this is true, then management must choose the individual or group with the greatest competence to complete the task, and in a manner that is most economical to the sport retail firm. This is often accomplished by grouping the tasks within specific job responsibilities. These responsibilities are usually classified as functional tasks or product-based tasks, and are documented within the organizational chart. Usually within a small sport retail operation, there are few employees and limited specialization. This requires most employees to carry out multiple job requirements. In larger retail operations, the organization is usually divided between four tasks: publicity, financial control, store management, and merchandising. Publicity deals with the majority of the marketing function. Financial control deals with accounting, profit planning, asset management, and resource allocation. Store management deals with human resource management and operations management. Human resource management focuses on the recruitment, application process, interviewing, hiring training, and retention of employees, as well as recurring evaluation of job descriptions, evaluation processes for jobs and employees, and compensation issues (salary, benefits, perks). Operations management focuses on setting goals and objectives, maintaining policies and procedures, space allocation in the store, scheduling of personnel, maintenance of the facility, security and crisis management, and inventory management. Merchandising deals with buying and selling of merchandise.

MERCHANDISE MANAGEMENT

The buying and selling of merchandise focuses on having the proper assortment of inventory and selling those products in conjunction with the sport retail strategy. To be an effective merchandiser, sport retail managers must understand the planning aspects of merchandising, the manner in which merchandising is implemented, the maintenance of financial integrity, and the resulting development of merchandise pricing.

Merchandise Planning

The planning aspect of merchandising centers on the development of a merchandise philosophy; defining the procedures for buying and selling; the creation of merchandise plans; and the establishment of a management process for brand categories. A merchandise philosophy is the sport retail firm's values and beliefs. This philosophy centers on both buying and selling activities, and may be looked at as a collective pursuit or two separate efforts. Regardless of the focus, the philosophy acts as the framework for the organizational mission, goals, and objectives. In turn, the mission, goals, and objectives serve as a basis for the managerial processes of the sport retail organization. These processes include the level of formality, the degree of centralization, the scope of offerings of the sport retail organization, the manner in which personnel and resources are utilized, and the method by which general sport retail functions are performed.

The processes are utilized to develop the sport merchandising plan. This plan articulates the intended selection of merchandise, the management process of product categories and brands, the distinctiveness and innovativeness of the merchandise offered for sale, the timing of when merchandise is to be kept in inventory, the determination of how much inventory will be kept on the sales floor, and the resulting forecast of expected retail sales.

Implementation of Merchandising

To implement the plan involves an eight step process. First, the sport retail manager obtains information about the target market and potential suppliers by researching sources including consumers, suppliers, competitors, governmental agencies, commercial data, and the media. Next, the sport retailer will select multiple sources of merchandise and start a dialog with them. During this discussion the sport retailer will be evaluating merchandise via inspection, sampling, and description buying – which is ordering in quantity based on the description of the product. At this point, the sport retailer will negotiate a purchasing contract with the supplier. Upon completion of the negotiation phase and signing of contracts, the ordering process is created. For larger sport retail operations, purchases are usually made through a computerized system. Smaller firms that do not have this capability usually process orders manually.

After orders are placed, the sport retail manager must plan for receiving and stocking the merchandise. This coordination of the movement of merchandise from the supplier to retailer, and ultimately to the consumer is called logistics. Logistics, as previously discussed in Chapter 6, has external and internal aspects. Externally, logistics deals with supply chain management, order processing and fulfillment, transportation systems, and warehousing. Internally, the sport retailer deals with logistics related to customer transactions and customer service. This is when the sport retailer takes control of the merchandise and is responsible for inventory management, including receiving and stocking merchandise, paying the supplier for the merchandise, pricing the merchandise, setting up displays, completing sales, and processing returns and damaged goods.

Throughout this implementation process, reordering merchandise takes place to ensure that the sport retail outlet does not run out of stock. The process for this reordering involves understanding the process and time needed for ordering and delivering, the level of turnover for the specific inventory, the amount of money that must be paid, and ultimately whether keeping the merchandise in stock or ordering as needed is most effective and efficient.

Also throughout this implementation process is the constant evaluation of the entire merchandising process. The purpose of this is to see what is working, what aspects can be improved, and what should be eliminated. The conclusions collected as a result of this evaluation process will be utilized as the entire merchandising implementation process is ongoing and cyclical.

Merchandising and Financial Integrity

In order for the previously discussed implementation process to go smoothly, there must be financial integrity within the sport retail organization. This involves controlling the products to be purchased, when they are to be purchased, and the quantity to be purchased. To maintain financial integrity within the merchandising function of the sport retail organization, there must be precise inventory control, accounting methodologies, and controlling monetary outflows.

Inventory Control

The two main inventory control systems utilized in sport retail management are perpetual inventory systems and physical inventory systems. The method utilized depends on the size of the sport retail firm and the desired outcomes of tracking inventory.

Perpetual inventory, also known as continuous inventory, is where the book inventory is always kept in agreement to the actual inventory through daily bookkeeping. Therefore, cost of goods sold is determined each time inventory is sold. This inventory can be accomplished by hand, but this is extremely time consuming and would only be appropriate for sport retail operations with low inventory turnover. Most often, a point-of-sale system is used to process information via scanning of barcodes. This information is immediately processed internally to tabulate profit, track inventory, and in some cases order new inventory from suppliers when stock on-hand reaches a specific preset level.

In a physical inventory system, the cost of goods sold is determined at the end of the accounting period. The most effective means of managing a physical inventory system is by a stock-counting system. This involves the actual counting of units of merchandise, sometimes as often as on a daily basis. This system not only counts inventory in stock, but also purchases, sales volume, and shortages. This method requires a lot of clerical work to maintain, and is not significantly effective unless the items are low value and whose sales are predictable.

Accounting Methodologies

Sport retail inventory accounting systems help the sport retail manager keep track of sales, purchases, inventory value, quantity of merchandise, and the need to reorder merchandise. There are two major methods utilized in tracking these methods – the cost method and the retail method.

The cost accounting method involves measuring, classifying, and recording costs of all merchandise. This method is used to identify and segment various production costs in terms of the actual total cost of the merchandise purchased and the value of the inventory on hand. This information is used to assist the sport retail firm in making prudent operating decisions. This method is also most effective when utilized by a sport retail firm that have low inventory turnover (speedboats), limited assortment (a specific piece of workout equipment such as Bowflex), and high average prices (season tickets to the Boston Red Sox).

The retail method is more of an end-result method of accounting, and is utilized by most retailers in all industries because it is easier to use with larger and physical inventories. This retail accounting method is a three step process. First, the cost complement is determined by computing a ratio of the relationship between actual total cost and total retail value (CC + ATC/TRV). This is accomplished by putting a value on beginning inventory, determining net purchases, and adding shipping and handling costs from both an inventory valuation and retail valuation standpoint. Also included in retail valuation is the projected retail markup.

Next, the adjusted ending retail value (AERV) is determined by examining the value of ending inventory and deducting markdowns and discounts. The sport retailer then estimates their inventory shortages or overages, since physical inventory is taken infrequently due to the quantity of inventory and variation of products (however once inventory is taken, retail book value is corrected).

Finally, the cost of the ending inventory is estimated by multiplying the AERV by the CC. This cost of ending inventory is also known as gross profit. While this method is very cumbersome and requires a lot of bookkeeping, and the numbers are not 100% accurate because it is based on average costs instead of actual costs, it does provide an average relationship between costs and selling price. This can then be used in general across the sport retail operation to make adjustments to increase profit on a total scale.

Controlling Monetary Outflows

Ultimately, all inventory control and accounting methodologies are utilized to develop the budget for the sport retail organization, as well as to forecast future financial operations. The combined functions of budgeting and forecasting are called the dollar-control process. The four steps of this process are selecting merchandise classification units, inventory and purchase planning, planning for profit margins, and forecasting for future sales.

Classification units for sport merchandise serve the purpose of categorizing selected sport products in order to control the inventory, target opportunities to sell more sport merchandise, and determine problems with any sport product lines. The most common ways to categorize sport retail units is by department (golf, tennis, basketball, etc.) or price (budget items, general retail stock, high end and specialized merchandise).

Inventory planning takes two forms – level planning and reduction planning. Level planning strives to ensure that inventory on hand will be sufficient to meet sales projections. This can be accomplished in a number of ways such as stockpiling inventory and utilizing comparative ratios. The comparative ratios typically utilized in sport retail management differ depending on the classification unit, and can be researched via the National Sporting Goods Association (www.nsga.org) or the Sport Business Research Network (www.sbrnet.com). Reduction planning is represented by the following formula:

$$\text{(Beginning inventory + Planned purchases)} - \text{(Projected sales + Ending inventory)}$$

Profit margin planning is determining the percentage of earnings the sport retail firm would like to make collectively and on individual products. To determine this profit margin, an analysis is conducted on net sales, operating expenses, actual profit, and the aforementioned reductions. While profit margin may be generalized across the retail firm, individual items may be marked up further based on demand.

Sales forecasting is a sport retailer's projection for future revenues. Usually these forecasts are estimated across the sport retail organization, and then broken down for specific divisions or individual sport products. In general, sales forecasts for small sport retail firms are made by "best guess," whereas larger sport retailers will incorporate multiple types of statistical analyses, including consumer trends, time series factors, and regressions.

Development of Merchandise Pricing

As mentioned earlier, profit margin is a primary concern resulting from controlling monetary outflows. Sport retail products and services must be priced in a way that maximizes profitability for the retailer and satisfies customers. At the same time, the strategy employed to develop prices must be in congruence with the sport retailer's overall image, sales, profit, and ROI.

As defined earlier in the chapter, the wheel of sport retailing has three levels: low end/discount; middle of the road/general; and high end/luxury. The level at which a sport retail firm targets its customers will directly influence their place on the wheel, and hence direct its pricing options. For a low end/discount sport retail organization such as Play It Again Sports, prices will be low, especially since most of the merchandise sold is used. A middle of the road/general sport retail such as Sports Authority or Decathlon will price sport products at typical market price as determined by the overall industry. High end/luxury sport retailers tend to be specialty stores where the upscale client would shop and pay premium prices. An example of this would be a country club pro shop.

Pricing can be affected by a number of external sources, the most important of which is the consumer. From the point of view of a sport retail organization, elasticity of demand is the biggest influence on pricing. Elasticity of demand is the sensitivity sport consumers have to pricing changes, and the relationship to the quantity of sport product they will buy. When there is inelastic demand, changes in price do not significantly affect purchases. Elastic demand is where the percentage of change in purchases is significantly and inversely correlated to the change in price ($\uparrow$ price $=$ $\downarrow$ sales; $\downarrow$ price $=$ $\uparrow$ sales).

Other external factors ranging from manufacturers and suppliers to competitors and the government can directly affect a sport retailer's pricing strategy. Manufacturers and suppliers would prefer to control prices because they want to maintain their image, regardless of whether it is at the expense of the profit of the sport retailer. They try to control the eventual retail price by charging their selected price to the sport retailer. However, as the end point of the sport retail channel, and the part of the channel most influenced by the sport consumer, the sport retailer will usually set the prices based on their own goals, vision, and image.

Competition has a significant effect on pricing. When there are a large number of similar retailers in a target market, sport retailers have little control over price because consumers can shop around. As a result, market pricing occurs, which is very susceptible to elasticity of demand and competitive reactions. As a result, some retail firms try to utilize administered pricing. This is when sport retailers seek to attract customers based on image, assortment, convenience, and service, thereby taking price out of the consideration process for the sport consumer.

The government also has a direct effect on pricing strategy. There are regulations set forth at the local, state, and federal level to control price fixing. Horizontal price fixing involves agreements between sport retailers and suppliers to set certain prices. This practice is against the law by way of the Federal Trade Commission Act and the Sherman Antitrust Act. Vertical price fixing occurs when suppliers seek to control the retail prices of their goods and services. As per the Consumer Goods Pricing Act, sport retailers cannot be forced to stick to retail prices guidelines set by suppliers. The goal of this is to support competition in the marketplace.

Sport Retail Pricing Strategy

In order to develop a sport retail pricing strategy, the sport retailer must look back to the philosophy, mission, and goals of the organization. The sport retailer then uses this information to develop pricing objectives that support sales, profit, and ROI. Depending on the type of sport retail firm, either a market penetration or a market skimming strategy will be employed. A market penetration strategy is used when a sport retail firm seeks to gain greater market share in their existing market. This is accomplished by lowering prices to a point where profit is ultimately increased by the resulting increase in sales volume. This can only work if total retail costs do not significantly rise as a result of the increased volume. With a market skimming pricing strategy, a sport retail firm sets premium prices and attracts sport consumers whom are less concerned with price. These individuals are influenced by service, assortment, and prestige. This strategy is appropriate when new competitors are unlikely to enter the market, and added sales will greatly increase retail cost.

Once the objectives have been set, a pricing policy must be implemented. This policy serves as the framework for applying the pricing objective within the sport retail organization. In general, sport retail firms employ a broad pricing policy so that short- and long-term objectives can be met. In addition, the sport retail firm must coordinate the pricing policy with the sport retail firm's image, the composition of the target market, and the elements of the sport retail mix discussed earlier in this chapter. Examples of pricing policies include: (a) discount pricing vs. market pricing vs. luxury pricing; (b) pricing leader in the market segment or price follower; and (c) consistent pricing or changing pricing based on costs.

The creation of a pricing strategy comes as a result of the pricing policies, as well as from the understanding that the sport industry is demand oriented. As a result, the sport retailer starts developing their strategy by attempting to determine the maximum price the sport consumer will pay for a given sport product. The pricing is then adjusted based on the quantities purchased and feedback from sport consumers. This adjustment is referred to as markup pricing (which includes markdowns). However, a major external factor may create an additional alteration to pricing. Competitor-oriented pricing is set in equivalence to that of a competitor to maintain an average market price, and allow the sport retailer to concentrate on other factors to differentiate their organization, including service, image, and convenience.

After the strategy is set, a plan for implementation must be instituted. The most common ways to implement a pricing strategy are via customary pricing or variable pricing. Customary pricing is when the sport retailer sets prices for goods and services and seeks to maintain them for an extended period. The most common practice of customary pricing is "everyday low prices." Variable pricing is when a sport retailer changes their prices as a result of changes in costs or demand. This is especially true in the sport and recreational travel industry, where changes in costs and demand change based on environmental trends (seasons, weather, politics, societal issues).

There are a number of other implementations of pricing policies and strategies. A one-price policy is where all products are the same price ($1 store). A flexible pricing policy is where consumers bargain over prices of products (eBay, Boston Whaler Boats). An odd-pricing strategy is a psychological pricing strategy where all products are priced slightly below the even dollar. For example, a person will spend $44.99 for sneakers at one store more likely than $45.00 at another. A multiple-unit pricing strategy is where a sport consumer will receive a discount for purchasing in bulk. An example would be a camp director could buy one basketball off the shelf for $24.99, but will only pay $22.49 for buying 100 basketballs (10% discount saves almost $250).

GETTING THE MESSAGE OUT:
SPORT RETAILER COMMUNICATIONS

Earlier in the book, promotional tools utilized in sport marketing have been discussed, including advertising, sales management, and public relations, to name a few. These principles also apply to sport retail management – however a major focus for sport retailers is image. Part of this image involves how the sport retail organization interacts with the community in which they are located. However, the sport retail firm does not have control of how those marketing and community relations efforts are viewed by the potential sport consumers. The one aspect that a sport retailer has total control over is atmosphere.

The sport retail atmosphere refers to the physical characteristics that projects an image, attracts customers, and keeps them shopping. There is an expression that states "you never get a second chance at a first impression." This is true in sport retail management – many customers form impressions of a retailer either just before or right after entering a store. Therefore, a sport retail manager must consider four major components of the sport retail atmosphere: the exterior, the interior, the layout, and the displays.

The exterior of the sport retail facility is the physical exterior of the store, including signage, entrances, windows, lighting, and parking areas. Signage including marquees and billboards, should display the name of the sport retail firm, advertise important information, and attract attention. The major issues regarding entrances include how many, what type (automatic, push–pull, revolving), and ease of flow. Windows serve three functions – to display merchandise, to show the interior of the store, and brighten the interior with natural light. Abundant exterior lighting provides for ease of ingress and egress to and from the store. Parking facilities should be well lit, convenient, and uncongested.

The interior of a store will directly affect the mood of the customer and be a significant factor in the purchase decision making process. Some of the most important factors to consider include the cleanliness of the store, adequate but non-distractive lighting, and store fixtures and shelving that are appropriate and easy for the customer to access. The interior also needs to be esthetically pleasing, including the color of walls and ceiling and comfortable floors to walk on. If the sport retail outlet is more than one floor, there must be adequate transportation via elevators, escalators, and stairs.

The layout of the store should be in an organized manner with wide aisles, easy ingress and egress, and appropriate amenities such as restrooms and customer service areas. The typical floor space for a sport retail outlet is divided into selling space (displays, registers), merchandise space (storerooms), personnel space (break areas), and customer space (aisles, vending areas, wide aisles, vertical transportation). Throughout the design, easy traffic flow is crucial to a quality layout. A straight traffic flow has displays and aisles in a grid pattern, whereas a curving traffic pattern places displays and aisles in a free flowing manner.

Displays are the interior point-of-purchase efforts that provide the sport consumer with product information and promotional offerings. A traditional open display allows the sport consumer to look at, pick up, touch, feel, and even try out or on the sport product. A closed display is usually behind locked glass due to its higher value. However, the sport consumer can often touch and feel the sport product with the assistance of a customer representative. An ensemble display is utilized when products from different but associated product lines can be displayed together to complement each other and entice multiple purchases. A rack display is often used for sport clothing because it is hung and displayed on racks. The hardest problem with this type of display is to keep items from being cluttered and misplaced. Regardless of the display, there are usually promotional peripherals such as posters, signs, and product description cards, which are used to further tempt the sport consumer to purchase the product.

Of course, these concepts differ if the sport retailer does not have a physical store, such as a company whose sales are mainly based on mail orders, catalogs, and on the web. The exterior is the front page of the advertising pieces, catalogs, and web pages. The interior is the ease in which the sport retailer can navigate through the catalog or website. The layout aids with this ease, using indexes, tables of contents, forms, and links. The displays can be unlimited, but must avoid clutter and confusion.

One of the major difficulties for non-store retailers has to do with checkout. Customers do not get the product immediately in exchange for payment – they have to go through a longer process. Mail order goes as fast as mail service moves, and orders are processed. Catalog orders are often made over the phone and are faster, but again the time to receive the product is not instantaneous. The same can be said for online orders, but there are still concerns regarding the security and privacy of orders as compared to in person. In addition for all of these non-store options, there are often additional fees incurred for shipping and handling. Therefore, in order to entice the sport consumer to purchase sport products, the non-store based organization must create both a positive tangible and intangible atmosphere.

CONCLUSION

In sport retail management, success is often measured by the amount of profit. Sometimes numbers lie. It is equally important to coordinate policies and strategies, and assess performance, to work toward reaching the goals of the sport retail organization. By incorporating and evaluating the overall organization, sport retail firms of any size or format can create a high-quality retail experience for the sport consumer.

As sport retail management continues to grow, its future is evolving into new areas. The sport industry continues to grow globally, which has opened new international and global markets to sport retailers. Changes in sport consumer lifestyles as a result of new sport segments (i.e., alternative sports) and the acceptance of marketing toward underrepresented markets (women, gay/lesbian) has opened up new market opportunities to sport retailers. As technology continues to grow, sport retail firms must decide whether they are going to become a multi-channeled retailer. This may become mandatory as competition among and between channel formats continues to be more prevalent.

Sport retail management is the end result of the distribution process, and is the focal point for the sale of the sport product to consumers for their personal consumption. Without sport retailers, there is no sale of the sport product, and sport marketing becomes useless. While there are many challenges, success in sport retail management is probable if a sport retail firm has a solid retail strategy, strong organization, sound application of the sport retail mix, and effective and efficient merchandise management.

FROM THEORY TO PRACTICE

Mandy Cormier, Merchandise Manager

Norfolk Tides Baseball Club, Norfolk, Virginia

When I started in working in retail in 1998 for Lady Foot Locker I just considered it a job to make some money while in High School. After I decided where I was going to go to college my current manager wanted me to stay with the company and transferred me to the Pheasant Lane Mall in Nashua, New Hampshire. I continued to work throughout college and they were always understanding about basketball and schoolwork. I became a Shift Manager, which allowed me to be the manager on duty if the Manager was not in the store. Soon after graduation in May I became the Assistant Manager for the Nashua store, I still could not believe that I was still with the company. After only being an Assistant Manager for 2 months I got a promotion to Manager in Cambridge, Massachusetts. This was an enormous step and big accomplishment. Even though I was excited to be close to home the Boston cliental is completely different than New Hampshire.

My first week as manager was really difficult the staff at Cambridge were already set in there ways and most of my employees were the same age if not older. It was definitely a big change for me even though I had grown up right outside of Boston because there needs were different than what I was used to. In Nashua most of the customers were looking for technical sneakers for performance, whereas in Cambridge they were more looking for fashion styles. Since Lady Foot Locker is a corporate company I really did not have a say in what product I would receive. I could always give my input, but we (the managers) did not get to actually choose the items we would sell. With that said we would make the best of it by contacting other managers to either send them a style that has been sitting in the stockroom in our store, but they could have sold out of it. By doing this they in turn would send an item that we may have sold really well to replenish our stock. Basically the idea was to produce as much money at the end of the say as we could. We would be unable to do so if the trend remained that we are out of stock or sizes that had been repeatedly asked for.

In a corporate environment and for such a big company you have to listen to your customers. At Lady Foot Locker customer service was a big part of ones training, as a manager we would constantly train our employees on customer service. I believe this to be an integral part of running a successful business, especially in the retail world. Up until that customer walks out that door you are there to provide them with your knowledge that is why you work for a certain company. When that customer leaves you want to put an impression on them to want to come back to your store and tell their friends to shop there too. Throughout this time as manager I realized that I had been with the company for almost 7 years and it was a great company to work for, but I felt as though I needed to move on.

A few months after I left Lady Foot Locker I had sent my resume to the Norfolk Tides Baseball Club in Norfolk, Virginia. At this time they were looking for a Director of Merchandise and considering I had plenty of retail experience I was confident that I could do a good job. After only about 2 days after I sent my resume in the General Manager called and asked to do a phone interview. We concluded our conversation after about an hour and he asked for a reference at Lady Foot Locker considering that was all of my retail experience. About a week went by and he called me to ask if he could fly me down for a day to meet the front office, see the area, and to make sure I could see myself living there. This was all happening so fast that I could barely even talk to my parents about it; they just knew that they were dropping me off at the airport.

When I arrived in Virginia the General Manager was there waiting for me. We headed back to the stadium where the office was and everyone was very welcoming and was hoping that I was going to join their staff. They had taken me out to lunch just to get a little background and what I thought I could bring to their novelty store. They must have been impressed because soon after we got back from lunch I was offered the position. I waited about 4 days to discuss it over with my family; to me this was a pretty big move. After finally moving all of my stuff from New Hampshire to Virginia, I was ready to start work. This is what I had been waiting for since I graduated college.

Working for a sports team's novelty store is much different than the corporate world. Here at the Tides I actually get to decide which items to sell in the store. Part of this is that I also get to work with the art designers to figure out designs and colors to put on the items. One of the first things I had to do when I arrived here was trying to figure out the style that people dressed and figure out what my cliental was going to be like. Seeing as though it is my first season here it was kind of difficult figuring out what was going to sell or not. By asking the office and doing my own research I tried to incorporate

Continued

mainstream styles into the store. Once I can see the trends that come in and out I will be able to get more of a variety. The main goal is to have little inventory at the end of the season; you want to keep some because on your Internet orders but you do not want to have a full stockroom. In a corporate environment if you are sitting on a certain item for a long period of time you can have sales or send the items back to the vendor. In a novelty store you are stuck with the leftovers and having a sale will sell some of the items but not as many as you would think.

When you are thinking of what items to put into a store another main thing is you want to make it look colorful and change displays. Most minor league baseball fans are regulars or season ticket holders, so you do not want them to walk into the same store every home stand. At the beginning of the season you want to put your cold weather items toward the front of the store, blankets are a big seller at this time of year. Then you gradually want to push your T-shirts and tank tops toward the front. One thing that I instill in my game day employees is customer service, that is very important whether you work in corporate or not. After working the first exhibition game sales were really good and so far all of the methods I learned from Lady Foot Locker have worked here at the Tides. I learn something new everyday here as far as paperwork and talking with the vendors.

Overall this has been a great experience and I have learned a great deal about the retail industry. There are major differences as far as preparation, paperwork, and ordering items between corporate and sports novelty. Once all that is figured out it is the same as working at Lady Foot Locker and shining through with customer service. When working for a Professional Sports team you have to know the general cliental and how much you think the average baseball fan is going to spend. It is very important to watch the cost of items and realize what you can actually sell the item for. Of course you are going to have to take some risks with certain items or you will never know the outcome. In general keep the risks low and minimal, if a new idea sells then the organization will be more open to new ideas. One of the most important things to also look for throughout the season is your inventory. Know what you have in stock and keep track of what was sold for two reasons; you never want to run out of a hot selling item and you will know what trends to go with next season. Working in retail has been a great experience and I have met many people. There are many different aspects of retail other than just working in a mall, which most people do not know. The important thing is to get in the right environment like professional sports and let your ideas be heard. With that you can go so many more places than you ever imagined.

13

SPORT E-BUSINESS AND E-COMMERCE

CHAPTER OUTLINE

CHAPTER OBJECTIVES

The reader will be able to:

- Understand the prevalence, importance, and continued growth of e-business and e-commerce in sport marketing and sport business.
- Know the categories of e-business and e-commerce, including business-to-business (B2B), business-to-consumer (B2C), consumer-to-business (C2B), and consumer-to-consumer (C2C).
- Appreciate the growth in digital technologies used to manage sport e-businesses, including the Internet, the World Wide Web, Intranets, and recent introductions of new technologies.
- Understand the factors that drive sport e-business in the new economy.
- Recognize how sport businesses utilize electronic means to overcome barriers of geographic boundaries to market, produce, and deliver sport products and services.
- Be cognizant of the latest technologies being utilized in the sport marketplace.

WHAT IS "E"?

In the 21st century, the use of electronic technologies to conduct business domestically, internationally, and globally is integral for growth and success. When we talk about the concept of "e," we are referring to electronic networks, including the Internet, World Wide Web, and Intranet. These digital technologies make sport products and sport services more easily accessible to more people than ever. The two major areas that facilitate this accessibility are e-business and e-commerce.

Sport E-Business

Sport e-business is an all-encompassing term that covers the internal information technology processes of a sport organization including human resources, finance, inventory management, product development, and risk management. The purpose of the e-business strategy is to streamline operations, reduce costs, and make productivity more efficient. This is accomplished by integrating business processes, information technology applications, and the infrastructure of the sport organization to facilitate business and marketing functions including communications, sales, and services.

A sport organization engaged in e-business will find numerous challenges when seeking to integrate with traditional business operations. Usually, a combination of the following four strategies is employed to integrate the systems: horizontal integration involves a number of the internal processes needed to bring sport products and services to market through an e-business structure. Sport consumer relationship management (to be discussed in greater detail later in Chapter 15) involves the use of various methodologies, information technologies, and Internet capabilities that help sport entities organize and manage sport consumer relationships by developing a system that all members of the sport marketing effort can utilize to access information about sport products and strive toward meeting the needs and wants of sport consumers. Knowledge management involves the methods utilized by a sport organization to create, gather, classify, modify, and apply knowledge about sport consumer's values and beliefs to achieve goals and objectives. Sport organization resource planning involves assimilating all functions of the sport organization through information technology methods to become more efficient and effective in planning, manufacturing, marketing, and selling sport products and services. Supply chain management (Chapter 8) is the process of coordination of the movement of sport products, sport services, and other pertinent information from raw materials to manufacturer to wholesaler to retailer and eventually to the sport consumer.

Vertical integration is the speed in which information is delivered through internal and external information technology processes. Internal information technology includes the in-house servers and other automation utilized to take, process, and deliver orders, as well as track feedback from the sport consumers. External information technologies are those utilized by the sport consumer where the sport consumer can view the sport product, possibly in some cases individually design the sport product, order the product, and track the order process.

Downward integration is the movement of information throughout the entire sport organization using information technologies. Lateral integration is the movement of information between a sport organization and the sport consumer or business partners. All of these sport e-business integration strategies are difficult to implement because of the complexity and need for significant knowledge of information technology. However, sport e-business has a greater possibility of revenues and profits as a result of more efficient and effective processes, and the overall lower costs of conducting business.

Sport E-Commerce

Sport e-commerce entails the external information technology processes of a sport organization including the marketing and sales functions. More specifically, sport e-commerce involves the buying and selling of sport products and services through the World Wide Web (www) and the Internet. It also involves Intranet functions such as electronic funds transfers (EFT) and smart cards (card with a chip that holds customer information and money available), and fan-loyalty reward programs. Sport e-commerce also includes the internal function of the organization that facilitates these external exchanges.

E-commerce is a function of e-business, but is the area most sport marketers work as a part of because the functions are outward facing and involves interaction between the sport consumer and the sport organization. From an integration standpoint, e-commerce specifically coordinates with the vertical integration function of e-business. E-commerce also integrates with traditional sport business operations in two additional ways. First, there is cross-business integration where the sport organization must coordinate with the information technologies of suppliers, sport consumers (personal websites), and web-based marketplaces (such as eBay). Second, there is technology integration. This involves modifying the traditional processes of order handling, purchasing, and customer services with the specific needs of the sport consumers and the unique abilities of the sport organization in mind.

In the 21st century, sport marketers must understand e-commerce strategy if they are to be successful. Most organizations, especially as a result of the expansion from domestic markets to international and global markets, are engaged in e-commerce, and utilize this function as a primary method for interacting with sport consumers, suppliers, and distributors. The major challenge for the sport marketing professional is that the electronic environment changes even more rapidly than the traditional marketplace. Therefore, the ability to shift resources, update content, and modify revenue models is crucial to success in sport e-commerce.

There are two major strategies that are utilized by sport marketing professionals to react to this quickly changing electronic environment. The KISS (keep it simple, stupid) approach is just that – have simple rules within the sport marketing strategy to allow for easy reactions to changes in the environment. This makes it easy for the sport marketing professional to adapt to change, which will help the overall organization reduce overall time in creating and/or modifying products and services desired by the sport consumer, and in turn will reduce overall costs in the long term.

The sense and respond approach is another method utilized to quickly respond to changes in the sport market. The premise is that strategic thinking is intuitive, reactionary, and simple. This adaptive sport marketing approach means that the sport marketing professional must utilize the e-commerce structure to allow the sport consumer to tell who they are, what they value, why they have an interest in a sport product or service, and how they want to consume it.

This approach is a significant departure from traditional market approaches where there is a collection of information, the information being overanalyzed, coming up with a number of options, further analyzing the pros and cons of each solution, and eventually choosing a course of action. By the time this entire process is completed, the e-commerce environment may have changed again and the sport organization missed out. The sense and respond approach encourages sport marketing professionals and sport organization management to be more proactive in their decision making and problem solving processes. This is accomplished by taking the information collected, realizing that those who take their time providing feedback via e-commerce communication methods are most likely those with a vested interest in the sport product or service, and reacting to that information by experimenting with solutions that will satisfy the needs, wants, and desires of the sport consumer.

In general, the evolution of sport e-commerce has introduced two significant concepts into the sport marketing vocabulary. Individualization takes personalizing and customizing sport products and services to another level by allowing for personalized communications between the sport consumer and the company (usually via a website). The sport consumer can also customize the interface with the sport organization to suit their needs. An example of this ability to customize is the website www.trophycentral.com. On this website, a customer can start with a basic uniform or trophy and customize that order by designing the product to their specifications. The customer can choose color, style, graphics (either uploaded by the customer or selected from a catalog), text (font and size), material, and much more. The customer can then review the order, make changes as necessary, select quantity, delivery and payment methods, and complete the order.

The other main concept that has evolved as a result of sport e-commerce is interactivity. This is the ability for the sport consumer to have more two-way communication with sport organizations and sport marketers. In traditional marketing, most marketing communication is one way through television, radio, and print advertising. There are also sport marketing communication efforts that are one-to-one, where methods such as direct mail and telemarketing created one-time, one-way contact. In interactive marketing communications, these efforts can be in real time (instant feedback via email) or asynchronous (discussion and message boards). This allows the customer to be in control of the communication, and increases the likelihood of a positive interaction between the sport organization and the consumer.

The sport marketing professional who manages an e-commerce strategy must be able to coordinate technology, capital, media, political, and legal issues. Therefore, the sport marketer must take a cross-discipline, integrative position to be able to make strategic decisions quickly and with the proper authority. As a result, the sport marketing professional must be able to create a vision for e-commerce, develop the methods for setting objectives and accomplishing goals, be the central figure in driving the implementation of processes, and be ultimately accountable for the performance of the strategy.

Sport e-commerce is a relatively new concept that requires the sport marketing professional to understand the evolution of consumer behavior and technology, balance the changes that are inevitable in the sport marketplace, and integrate traditional business operations with online activities. The sport marketer who can effectively integrate these concepts can design plans that will react to environmental changes, maintain a competitive advantage, and create new value chains in the sport marketplace.

CATEGORIES OF E-BUSINESS AND E-COMMERCE IN SPORT MARKETING

The concepts of sport e-business and sport e-commerce involve the various interactions between businesses and consumers through digital communications. In the traditional communication process, the sender uses a channel to send a message to a receiver, who then provides a response and feedback. In the digital communication process, the type of interaction is directly related to who the sender is and who the receiver is. For sport e-business and e-commerce, there are four categories: B2B, B2C, C2B, and C2C.

B2B refers to the transactions, collaborations, and business interactions that occur between two organizations. For sport organizations, this can include a multitude of functions including management of inventory, channels, and sales, as well as service and support operations. In the sporting goods industry, Sport Supply Group (www.sportsupplygroup.com) is one of the leading B2B e-commerce suppliers of equipment for institutions and the youth sports marketplace. Sport Supply Group acts as an intermediary in online sales of sports equipment from selected manufacturers to primary and secondary schools, colleges and universities, camps, youth organizations, and governmental agencies.

B2C focuses on the transactions between businesses and consumers. For the sport organization, these transactions are usually plentiful, but smaller in scope than those transacted through B2B. Ticketmaster (www.ticketmaster.com) is one of the most popular B2C websites, offering to the consumer tickets to sport events, concerts, shows, and other leisure activities across the United States and the world.

C2B is where the consumer initiates the transaction process by soliciting organizations to compete for the individual's business. While this is not widely used directly in sport business, an example of C2B would be www.priceline.com. Priceline.com is a travel service that allows the consumer to name their own price, and airlines, hotels, travel packages, and rental car agencies will respond to the consumer and potentially meet their demand.

Consumer-to-consumer (C2C) involves transactions between customers. Many of these transactions will involve an online third-party business, such as eBay (www.ebay.com). One customer can sell directly to another customer an assortment items ranging from sport memorabilia to event tickets.

DIGITAL TECHNOLOGIES UTILIZED TO MANAGE SPORT E-BUSINESS AND E-COMMERCE

Digital technologies are the centerpiece of sport e-business and e-commerce, as they are used to manage the exchange of sport products and services. The two major digital technologies utilized are the Internet and the World Wide Web, and Intranets. One of the common misconceptions is that the Internet and the World Wide Web (www) are one and the same. This is not true. The Internet is a worldwide system of publicly accessible computer networks that transmit data by a process called packet switching to standardized Internet Protocol (IP) addresses. Computer networks are the system of data processing points that are interconnected to communicate data between and through the network, most often with the endpoint being a computer. Packet switching is the method of moving data through computer networks in the most efficient and effective manner possible by splitting the data up into smaller units (called packets), each labeled with the destination address, sent individually, and reassembled at the destination. IP addresses are the unique identifiers of a computer. It is very similar to addressing a letter and mailing it through the post office. The return address is the sender's IP address; the letter is addressed to another person (receiver's IP address), and the United States Postal Service sorts the mail (packet switching) and delivers (computer network) the mail.

The Internet is the collection of computer networks interconnected by wires, fiber optics, and cables. This is very different from the World Wide Web (www), which is a collection of interconnected documents that are connected by uniform resource locators (URLs) and hyperlinks. URLs, more commonly known as main web addresses, are the actual location of an Internet item that an individual would like to see, such as www.atomicdog.com. Every page on the web has a unique URL. Hyperlinks refer to text or graphics placed on a web page to provide cross-referenced materials for the user. For example, www.oursports-central.com is one of the leading minor league and independent league news websites. It would be impossible for them to put every bit of news onto one page, therefore they create separate pages for each news item, and put hyperlinks on the main page to connect with each story.

As far as the exchange of sport products and services via e-business and e-commerce, the main method is through sport company websites. This allows for interaction between the buyer and the sport company 24 hours a day, 7 days a week, 365 days a year, regardless of the location of the company.

In addition, there are three other types of websites that are utilized for the exchange of sport products and services. Brokering sites act as an intermediary between one sport business wanting a sport product or service and another sport business seeking to provide such a product (see Sport Supply Group under B2B).

Infomediaries publish trade and industry standards about an industry for those who operate in that industry. An example for the sport industry is F+W Publishing (www.fwpublishing.com), who publishes special interest magazines and books for a variety of consumer enthusiast categories, including sport collectibles. Some of their publications include "Sports Collectors Digest" and "Card Trade."

E-procurement, also known as product supply and procurement exchanges, is when the purchasing function is often outsourced to a third party. That company acts as an agent to shop for supplies, request proposals, and bid on making purchases on behalf of their client. It is also used for storage of items occasionally, as the e-business rarely pays for that kind of storage space. An example of an e-procurement site would be www.bidnet.com, where buyers can streamline their purchasing processes and vendors are connected with the ability to bid on government contracts. Specifically, their e-procurement department was established to create and manage website so that purchasing agencies could register their vendors and deliver bid information directly to them.

CONDUCTING SPORT E-BUSINESS AND E-COMMERCE

Operating in sport e-business and e-commerce has some similarities to traditional sport retail management. While a traditional sport retail store is a physical setting, a sport e-business or e-commerce store is virtual. While the e-business or e-commerce manager will be mainly focused on functions related to payment collection, delivery of orders, and security issues, the sport marketing professional will be concerned with three main areas: placement, size of "location," and presentation.

Placement

Placement refers to the actual location from where sales will be conducted. In traditional sport retail management, the major concerns regarding location include the competition in the area, the geographic attractiveness, adequate floor space, and a convenient locale for customers. For those sport organizations involved in e-business and e-commerce, location is in terms of a highly visible website that is easily found. Traffic to an e-commerce website is determined by the placement of links in prominent locations, or the placement of advertisements on the websites of business partners or collaborators. On the website of the organization, hyperlinks need to be clear and easy to find, and cannot require the user to go to more than three additional hyperlinks to find information. In addition, organizations will pay search engines such as Google and Yahoo to make sure that when a search is done on their category, their organization comes up early in the search.

Size of Location

The size of the location is traditionally dependent on how much inventory and merchandise needs to be kept on hand, and the potential number of customers that will enter the establishment. Size of the location also includes associated facility needs, including adequate parking, restrooms, and entrances/exits. A sport organization engaged in e-business and e-commerce are concerned with digital size in the forms of bandwidth, data storage capacity, and processing power.

Bandwidth is the amount of information that can be passed through a communication channel at one time. General standards in e-business and e-commerce state that average bandwidth utilization should not exceed 30% of maximum available and during peak usage should not exceed 70%. It is also important to realize that if a sport organization needs a website that requires high-resolution graphics, streaming audio or video, or provides downloadable files, they must spend more on digital infrastructure to accommodate larger servers. If not, the website will provide information at a significantly slower rate, which in turn will likely result in lost sales.

Processing power is the amount of information that can be handled by a website at any given time. This includes being able to show the breadth of sport products and services available, handle the number of transaction in proportion to the size of the sport business, and the level of interactivity the sport organization plans to have with customers – including email, discussion boards, and real-time assistance.

Data storage capacity is also important to sport e-business and e-commerce. Working in an online environment provides the sport organization with the ability to collect large amounts of information, including demographics, billing and payment histories, and customer purchase patterns. In addition, a valuable tool for sport marketing professional is click streams, which tracks the sequence of pages visited by a customer after the initial interaction.

Presentation

Presentation involves how the sport product or service is viewed by consumers. In traditional sport retail management, as well as e-business and e-commerce, the two main concerns about presentation are store layout and customer service.

Store layout in a traditional sport retail management operation focuses on the image a store wants to portray for itself, in addition to the type of customers they wish to retain. In e-business and e-commerce, the store layout is better known as user interface. User interface involves the ability to create a digital representation of the theme of the store, the ease in which the consumer can navigate around the website, and provide a pleasurable experience for the consumer. This requires the sport marketing professional to work with the information technology specialists to ensure that the sport consumers are seeing everything that the sport organization wants them to see. This goes back to the earlier discussion of having the appropriate size of bandwidth, processors, and data storage capacity. It also means having the appropriate hardware and software to maintain the desired effect.

Customer service in a physical setting involves creating a positive image for the sport organization and offering a significant positive experience for the consumer. This includes physical interactions between salespeople and the customer, as well as intangible interaction created by advertising, promotions, and publicity. Online customer service differs because there is no direct physical interaction with the customers, and the customers do not experience the purchasing environment. This requires the sport marketing professional to be savvy when it comes to being able to communicate with customers via the World Wide Web and Internet, especially utilizing tools including email, chat rooms, and discussion boards.

ETHICS IN SPORT E-BUSINESS AND E-COMMERCE

Technology has allowed a number of things that were never possible to become reality. Many of those things may be illegal, immoral, or unethical and still quite easy to do. The legal system has not been able to catch up with the technological growth of new business models. This opportunity has led some corporations down a somewhat dark path with the lure of an impressive boost to the bottom line. E-business technology allows both employees and consumers to be watched and profiled in ways never before imaginable. Employees have at their finger tips, the means of using the Internet for personal transactions and/or ethically and morally provocative sites. There are allegations that companies make against employees, such as invasion of privacy. There are also allegations of companies against consumers through invasion of privacy, unauthorized data collection, price fixing, or sale of personal information. Unethical uses of the Internet to steal identity, vandalize, and corporate espionage are all possible from an employee's desk.

The potential for a corporation to run into financial and legal difficulties due to unethical decisions is staggering. In many cases, because of greed, executives tried to make the company look more successful than it really was. The need to raise capital, trying to increase stock price, wanting to borrow capital from the banks, desire to earn personal performance bonuses are all potential reasons for unethical management. Whatever the reasons, it seems that there had been an epidemic of such behavior in the years leading up to the MCI WorldCom and Enron's collapse.

The cloud of suspicion moved beyond the companies to those who provide audits, analysis, or research upon which investors rely. Arthur Anderson was completely destroyed by their work with Enron and other companies with suspect accounting practices. Merrill Lynch and other brokerage firms were forced to settle with clients who felt that the analysts had given falsely positive reports on companies in order to win their business. In some cases firms were found to have given positive public reports while privately downplaying their own research to selected customers.

Although these legal and ethical lapses were of monumental impact, many companies have used the government's lapse in positive ways. E-business has allowed large corporations to expand their market share by offering individualization of their products. An example of this is Nike's customization program for their licensed apparel. This customization has allowed large corporations to gain market share with the mom and pop shops who were providing after sale services. E-business has also allowed the mom and pop shops to compete globally with their products with the touch of the keyboard. With little overhead cost, small business can gain market share and compete in markets that were never before open.

ETHICS IN E-BUSINESS: SUSTAINABLE KNOWLEDGE

In the 1950s, retail automation was exemplified by polished copper containers and an elegant system of vacuum tubes into which any salesperson could insert a copper container from anywhere on the sales floor. The copper containers traveled quickly to the accounting department upstairs, to be returned just as quickly with the correct change, and the sales receipt. I particularly remember the customer gossip when the new system was installed as everyone in our neighborhood heralded "a new age in retail sales."

Fast-forward 40 years to the late 1990s and into the early 2000s, the rise and fall of the dot.coms was the focal point of business in the media. Regardless, it is to recognize the long-lasting benefits of the technology that was created and implemented during that decade. Major corporations discovered new revenue channels and new ways of reaching existing customers. Hundreds of new technologies emerged to assist in the transformation. For example, as the Director of Internet Applications in 1996, I [the author Robbins] was responsible for building a single method for searching all corporate information. The cost, in staffing and software licenses, exceeded

$1 million and required 10 months to implement. Today one can purchase the Google Server for under $50,000 and it requires only 6 minutes to install. This is the contribution afforded to everyone during that technology boom, benefits that are only now coming to light.

Now into the 21st century (2005), every type of American business is now dependent on some form of information technology: credit card transactions, supply chain, inventory control, etc. Most adults conduct some manner of transactions via the Internet for travel, hotels, little league registration, birthday wishes, and charitable donations. It has recently been suggested that eBay has become the largest employer in the world, with its ecosystem of buyers and sellers providing products via that portal.

With the ubiquity of technology enabling business transactions for even the smallest stores and markets, when all business has become an e-business, how can we specifically distinguish the term "e-business" today? The term remains useful to help us understand our evolving information economy by means of a more distinct definition: in an information economy, e-business is that form of financially related exchange that is accompanied by aggregated information – information about the customer, the supplier, and the product. For example, according to this definition, a small site providing handcrafted stationary via an online Web form may not be an e-business. It may simply be a modern version of retail automation reminiscent of the vacuum tubes – a more efficient method for buying and selling product. To be an "e-business" by the above definition, the transaction must also be founded upon a secure gathering of pertinent information that can be usefully reviewed and utilized to further understand the exchange. In other words, as a part of the financial transaction, there must be a transfer of knowledge.

In its simplest form, it may be the provision of basic contact information, so that the next time the customer visits the site, their shipping address and billing information are already provided by the underlying system. In more complex transactional systems, this information becomes a valuable repository of customer preferences, allowing for additional sales – of similar items, additional software licenses, etc. Value increases (to the buyer and the seller) as our knowledge of the transactions increases, allowing for in-depth analysis of patterns and trends.

A basic diagram (Figure 1) demonstrates this definition of e-business. This circular aspect of successful e-business ventures is wholly dependent on the capability of the provider to capture, analyze, and utilize knowledge about the interaction for the benefit of all parties involved. This sustainable knowledge becomes an essential component of an institution's ability to leverage a single event's information in multiple dimensions; indeed, the knowledge about the initial transaction may prove to the more valuable than the actual profit margin of that transaction over time.

Continued

FIGURE 1

DEFINITION OF E-BUSINESS

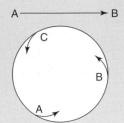

The straight line, moving from A to B, is the old way of doing things. The circle, encompassing A through B to C and back to A, is the "new way."

The circle epitomizes an exchange of value in an information-based economy, wherein each transaction adds value, provides new opportunities, increases understanding, and creates a sustaining advantage for both the customer and the supplier.

Source: Robbins, S. (1996). The System Is a Mirror, AGM-SIGDOC Proceedings.

As with previous historical phases when we were challenged to adjust to the influence of new technologies, we are once again faced with the obligation to reconsider aspects of our institutional cultures.

There is an explicit responsibility, as we gather knowledge about ourselves and others in our business systems, to review our use of this information, and that remains the challenge of e-business in the coming decade: to not only capture and utilize the knowledge that adds value to our businesses, but to intelligently consider the broader social consequences and their impact on our industry, to ask and to answer the difficult questions about ethics and intellectual property and, in doing so, to elevate the discussion beyond the simple equations of profit and loss.

Source: Adapted from Robbins, S. (2005). In e-business, the value of every transaction increase. *Information Systems Management* 22(3): 85–86.

Suggested Discussion Topics

1. By definition, e-business is that form of financially related exchange that is accompanied by aggregated information – information about the customer, the supplier, and the product. An e-business customer is often willing to transmit valuable personal information (address, credit card number, social security number, etc.) over the Internet to purchase the product or service being offered by a sport organization. From an ethical standpoint, what types of issues could arise to create an aura of distrust for the sport consumer? What steps would you take, as the Director of Sport Marketing for an online sporting goods firm, to ensure that these issues are prevented, and the image of the sport e-business organization is maintained at the highest level possible?

2. From an ethical standpoint, how much information should a sport e-business be allowed to collect? What types of information gathering would be considered ethically correct? What types would not?

SPORT E-BUSINESS AND E-COMMERCE IN THE NEW ECONOMY

The concept of the new economy has changed over years. In its original form, it referred to an economy without business cycles or inflations. It evolved during the dot.com era into an industry that produced computers and other related products and services, and an industry of accelerated rate of productivity and growth. After the crash of many Internet-based businesses, the definition has been modified to reflect the influx of e-business and e-commerce throughout all industries. For the purpose of this chapter, the new economy is the use of information, communication, and digital technologies for manufacturing, selling, and distributing products and services.

The new economy as related to the sport industry is continuing to grow at a rapid pace. As a result, the sport marketing professional must understand the effects of the new economy on the sport organization as a whole, and more specifically how to utilize sport e-business and e-commerce to enhance sport marketing efforts. In assessing the strengths and weaknesses of the sport organization when it comes to e-business and e-commerce, they will look to the digital technology infrastructure discussed earlier in this chapter. From an external standpoint, the sport marketing professional must evaluate the sport marketing opportunities available as a result of the e-business and e-commerce infrastructure. In addition, sport marketers must be concerned with sport business development, sport consumer relations, integrated sport communications, sport marketing metrics, and strategic sport management, through e-business and e-commerce.

Sport Market Opportunities

There are numerous marketing opportunities that are unique to sport e-business and e-commerce. This is especially true when it comes to dealing with competition. First, competition moves beyond industry boundaries as a result of products and services being offered virtually. As a result, sport organizations can create value based on the perspectives of a wider range of sport consumers. Second, competition is not one-on-one in sport e-business and e-commerce; it is team-on-team. There is significant reliance on additional complementary products (computers, servers, operating systems software, etc.). Therefore, sport marketing professionals and the management of the sport organization must evaluate those collaborators in business in order to determine the feasibility of accomplishing specified goals and compete in the marketplace. Finally, competition in sport e-business and e-commerce changes rapidly due to the speed in which changes in trends, events, and opportunities can be addressed. This requires the sport marketing professional to continually assess the environment and effectively react with speed and efficiency.

In addition to competition, the manner in which consumer behavior is evaluated has changed significantly with the introduction of e-business and e-commerce. Sport marketing professionals must listen even closer to the needs, wants, and desires of the sport consumer. This is because the opportunity to meet those needs will be short-lived, and those sport organizations that try to meet only sport consumer expectations will be ignored as a result of more choice. As a result, the sport marketing professional must be visionary, determining the experiences that sport customers will want in the future as a result of their actions now.

Involvement in sport e-business and e-commerce also creates a need for sport organizations to reorganize their value chain – those activities that add value directly to the consumer while adding indirect value through the support of other organizational operations. There is more direct contact between sport consumers and sport organizations through e-business and e-commerce as a result of the increased amount of information that can be made available at lower costs through e-value chains.

The sport market opportunity analysis framework is utilized by sport marketers to identify and evaluate the attractiveness of an opportunity in the sport marketplace. The premise of this framework centers on four environmental factors: the sport consumer, the sport organization (and its collaborators), the technology available, and the competition within the marketplace. The diagram below identified the steps a sport marketing professional would follow in assessing the sport market opportunity:

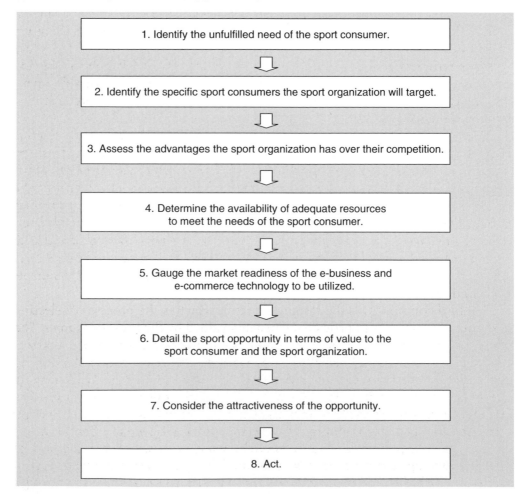

1. Identify the unfulfilled need of the sport consumer.

2. Identify the specific sport consumers the sport organization will target.

3. Assess the advantages the sport organization has over their competition.

4. Determine the availability of adequate resources to meet the needs of the sport consumer.

5. Gauge the market readiness of the e-business and e-commerce technology to be utilized.

6. Detail the sport opportunity in terms of value to the sport consumer and the sport organization.

7. Consider the attractiveness of the opportunity.

8. Act.

Sport Business Development

As with any business, a sport organization engaged in e-business and e-commerce must have a business model. There are four components that are necessary in the development, implementation, and management of such a business model. The first are value propositions, which describes how a sport organization will differentiate itself to sport consumers in terms of the value to be offered. Value propositions require choosing the appropriate target segments, customer benefits, and resources.

The choice of the sport consumer target segment focuses on the attractiveness of the market chosen, and the ability of the sport organization to compete in that chosen market segment. This attempt for operational excellence is a function of a number of variables including market size, growth rate of the market, needs of the sport consumer in the segment, and the level of competition within the segment.

The choice of customer benefits to be delivered to the target segment requires an understanding of digital supply and demand. From the supply standpoint, the sport organization must employ the appropriate digital systems to deliver those benefits. From the demand end, the sport organization must ensure the message is clear and singular, as multiple messages will often confuse the sport consumer.

The choice of unique, differentiated resources is what separates one sport organization from another. By becoming a leader in the specific sport product or service market, the sport marketer seeks to show that the benefits of association with their sport organization are more beneficial than that of a competitor. Leadership in the marketplace comes from having better core abilities, business strengths, and unique capabilities.

The second component of the business model is the online offering, which is the determination of the sport products, services, or information that will be placed on the Internet and World Wide Web. To accomplish this, the sport organization must first decide on the scope of the categories of sport products or services to be offered online, and whether they will be offering within their specific category, or across multiple categories. Next is to identify the decision making process of the sport consumer, from pre-purchase through the actual purchase and afterwards into post-purchase. Once this process in understood, the sport marketing professional will design a plan to enter into the purchase cycle and return often.

The third component is the resource system, which is the process of selecting and utilizing resources to provide the benefits valued by the sport consumer. The activities involved with a digital resource system involves utilizing virtual assets to offer a wide number of benefits through strategic alliances with collaborators based on the demand of the sport consumer. This is accomplished by identifying the most important benefits valued by the sport consumer, determine the resources that can be used to offer the benefit, establish a plan for delivering those benefits, and secure strategic partnerships that will help to offer them.

The final component is revenue models, which focuses on the method of securing earnings for the sport organization. The sport marketing professional will work with the e-business and e-commerce staff to secure revenue through advertising, sport product and service sales, subscriptions to website content, and the licensing of content on the website.

Sport Consumer Relations

Sport consumer relations in e-business and e-commerce focuses on the use of various methodologies, information technologies, and Internet capabilities that help sport entities organize and manage the interaction between the sport consumer and the sport organization. Sport marketing professionals need to manage these relationships very differently in the virtual world through their involvement in designing an effective website. The framework of this online relationship with sport consumers can be articulated using the following diagram:

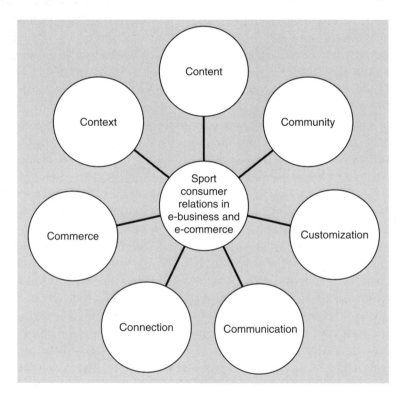

Content is the actual text, pictures, graphics, audio and video found on a website that provides information to the user. Context refers to functionality and esthetically pleasing look of a website, including the ease of navigation, and the use of appropriate graphics, colors, and design features. Commerce involves an organization's ability to sell products and services using their website, including the collecting of items in a "shopping cart," and payments through secure websites. Communication involves an ongoing dialog between users and the website (the organization managing the website), including customer service requests, email notifications of specials and opportunities, and instant messaging. Community is the ability to interact with other users including email, chatrooms, and discussion boards. Connection is the ability for websites to link to other websites. Customization is the ability for a website to adapt and modify itself based on the wants, needs, and desires of the user.

Integrated Sport Communications

Integrated communications in sport e-business and e-commerce, as in traditional marketing communication, focuses on branding. However, the importance of integrated sport communications to the online medium cannot be understated. It is integral to the interaction between sport consumers and sport organizations, utilizing general online communications (banner advertisements, emails, and online transactions); personalized online communications (building individual relationships through specialized services); traditional mass media communications (utilizing radio, print, and television advertising to market online capabilities); and direct communications (using sales representatives, direct marketers, and telecommunications to market online capabilities).

Branding, just as in traditional sport marketing efforts, is the process of seeking to provide a clear message to the sport consumer for the purpose of building organizational image. The sport organization seeks to build this brand equity by increasing brand awareness to, and brand association with, the sport consumer. This is not only an internal process conducted by the sport marketing professional, but it is also accomplished by partnering with collaborating organizations that aid in the delivery of the sport product or service. In sport e-business and e-commerce, the process of branding has evolved. In the introductory phase of the Internet and World Wide Web, brands were categorized as either offline or online. Offline brands were traditional brick and mortar stores such as Foot Locker, Sports Authority, and the merchandise stand or pro shop at an arena or stadium. Early online brands focused on the sport industry, such as Online Sports (www.onlinesports.com). With the growth of the online environment, and the opportunity to grow into other markets, most traditional offline sport organizations now brand themselves in both mediums.

Therefore, these sport organizations have had to learn to re-brand themselves utilizing these new digital technologies. The five methods utilized for e-branding an offline product in the online environment includes brand reinforcement, e-brand creation, virtual sport product and service trials, sales leads, and e-store traffic. Brand reinforcement is using the online environment to strengthen a brand that is already in the traditional sport marketplace. E-brand creation is the development and introduction of a new brand via the online environment. Usually this focuses more on building awareness rather than loyalty, as the digital environment changes rapidly. Virtual sport product and service trials through online branding provide the sport consumer with an opportunity for free access to the sport product and service. The goal of the sport organization is to entice the sport consumer to become a new and eventually repeat customer. Sales leads via e-business and e-commerce involve the sport marketing professional deciding that the online environment will be utilized to attract new customers. E-store traffic is used to determine whether the online sport marketing efforts are working. These are measured through e-business and e-commerce sport marketing metrics.

Active Marketing Group and Road Runner Sports Team Up

Road Runner Sports (www.roadrunnersports.com), is a multi-channel retailer with over two decades of history providing top quality running products at competitive prices through several branded running and fitness catalogs, corresponding shopping websites, and retail stores located on the West Coast of the United States. In September 2005, they implemented an online marketing program that included display ads, customized emails and a Shoe Blog – all strictly targeted to an athletic audience and more specifically to recreational runners. As a result, the running gear superstore had increased its new customer base substantially and is well on its way to achieving desired conversion rates.

With a go-to-market plan focused on getting runners into the right gear to run injury free, Director of E-commerce Peter Taylor and his team sought an agency's expertise to align Road Runner Sports more closely with its target customer. The team turned to Active Marketing Group (www.activemarketinggroup.com), who is a full-service promotion agency division that helps brands develop authentic relationships with active customers. The agency offers access to millions of active Americans involved in sports and activities, an understanding of consumer behavior, and a portfolio of consumer promotional services.

A four-step plan was implemented – identify the target market, choose the appropriate media channel, drive sales conversions, and engaging customers. An initial challenge was identifying the true target market, especially since it was very diverse due to a marketing mix that included catalog and web marketing. Road Runner Sports wanted its online effort to drive new customers and increase brand presence. The result was a monthly online advertising program that drove direct sales by serving online display ads and customized emails to a very specific targeted audience. The main reason for this move – new customers (especially younger ones) use e-commerce more often to make purchase decisions, rather than through print catalogs and other traditional means. The premise behind this decision was that display ads provide a good foundation for building the brand; however, the added email component was critical to driving conversion percentages and sales.

Next was the choosing of appropriate media channels to reach the active customers. Active Marketing Group chose Active.com as the online medium for the display ads, placing ads on the running and triathlon pages of http://www.active.com/. The site is an online community for active lifestyle consumers and one of two active consumer media channels the agency has direct access to. Active.com attracts active consumers involved in multiple sports and activities, offering activity-specific content and services such as online event search via a database of more than 100,000 events and activities in more than 5000 cities, and online event registration. Active.com also offers specialized web pages dedicated to individual sports with local event calendars, health and fitness information, and training tools.

Active Marketing developed custom Road Runner Sports emails promoting free shipping offers and product discounts. For the email component, the agency tapped Active.com's audience of registered members, specifically active consumers, ages 25–55, who participate in running activities 3–5 days a week and have a history of online registration transactions for community events and activities. The site has signed up over 6 million members – 1.5 million of those have opted-in to receive a variety of e-newsletters specific to their participation interests – offering database segmentation opportunities by gender, age, income, and sport or activity to reach a number of direct marketing goals. In addition, as part of its database marketing services, Active Marketing Group also provides demographic targeting, matching specific product offers with a specific audience.

To drive sales conversions, which is the number of visitors (in this case to the website) that actually make a purchase, the challenge was leveraging opportunities within the media channel to make meaningful connections with active consumers and drive conversion percentages. Throughout the email program, the agency team continued to experiment with creative and messaging, looking at the consumer experience on certain web pages and ensuring the message was clear.

Results have shown that this e-commerce effort has worked to engage new and returning customers, and conversion rates have soared. With the continued innovations in e-business and e-commerce, more and more individuals will use this medium for sales and purchases. Sport marketing professional needs to embrace the online medium quickly and learn as much as they can to leverage it. If they have the right components in place and the goals set to take advantage of it, it can be very successful.

Source: Adapted from Johnson, J. (2005). *Case Study: Road Runner Sports*. Retrieved March 17, 2006 from http://www.imediaconnection.com/content/7544.asp.

Permission granted for reprint by copyright holder iMedia Communications, Inc.; a trade publisher and event producer serving interactive media and marketing industries.

Suggested Discussion Topics

1. You are the Assistant Director of Marketing for Road Runner Sports, and your main job was to work with the Director to implement this new e-commerce effort. You get hundreds of email and phone calls related to this successful initiative, and you are now being asked to consult many of these companies in implementing such an effort with their organization. You decide to leave Road Runner Sports and work for yourself as a Consultant. Your first job is working with a company who

Continued

wishes to expand their e-commerce efforts on a global level to Australia, Asia, and Europe, but is unsure of their capability to succeed on a global level.

One of the toughest issues you encounter is not in the intricate development of such a program, but in determining whether implementing an e-commerce component on a global scale is appropriate for this company. What are the major considerations that you would recommend an organization to bear in mind when they are deciding the appropriateness of engagement in a global e-commerce strategy? Assuming that you recommend to the company they would not be well served entering into the global marketplace, how would you explain to the company that they should either remain a domestic company, or reduce their plan to more of an international strategy.

2. You are the owner of a domestic sporting goods business that has a distribution network across the United States. Your sales have plummeted over the past few years because of sporting goods superstores such as Sports Authority and Dick's. In addition, you have severe reservations in entering into the digital age and using e-commerce efforts to retain old customers and connect with new customers. You have always had success dealing personally with customers, and selling products through your catalog and via a very basic website where customers can view products, but must still call in orders.

After completing some research, you determine that even if you expand your e-commerce effort, you probably will still lag behind sporting goods superstores. You determine that the only way to save your business is to expand internationally. What would you develop in a plan to expand your visibility internationally in the marketplace utilizing e-commerce efforts?

Sport Marketing Metrics

Sport marketing metrics are the indicators that a sport marketing professional utilizes to evaluate the sport organization's impact on the environment, and the sport organization's level of progress and success. Metrics are used for a range of activities including determining financial success, the level of relationships with sport consumers, the quality of internal operations, and the growth potential of the sport organization. The sport marketer focuses on metrics that will evaluate market opportunities, enhance marketing communications, and build brand awareness.

In sport e-business and e-commerce, metrics would normally change on an ongoing basis in conjunction with rapid changes in strategy. However, this change can be very costly to a sport organization because change requires a significant strain on resources.

The most basic of metrics used is the number of hits on a website. Hits are the number of times an individual goes to a web page. Eventually this metrics was deemed to be unreliable because pages that had graphics with multiple elements registered a hit for each elements, hence providing an inaccurate count. As a result, sport marketers could not easily track whether a page with all text (one hit) was truly more popular than one with graphics that registered multiple hit.

Metrics evolved to utilize a counter to determine the number of times a web page was viewed within a specific period of time. While better than hits, this method was also deemed imperfect because it did not account for individuals who came back to the page multiple times. For example, every time a screen refreshed while an individual is watching the scoreboard during a game on nfl.com was marked as a page viewed. There was no way to truly determine how many individuals were viewing the web page.

Then, a metric called conversion rates was developed. Conversion rates are measurement utilized to calculate how many viewers of a web page actually do what the organization wants. This is a two-step process. It starts with micro-conversions, which is tracking the specific behavior a sport marketer would like the sport consumer to do to become more involved with the sport product or service being offered. Examples include going to a selected number of different pages on the website, signing up for an e-newsletter, or providing feedback on a question provided on the web page. This is followed by the main conversion, which is enticing the sport consumer to take action, including making a purchase or contacting the sport organization for more information. A metric utilized in conjunction with conversion rates are impressions. An impression is the number of times a banner or static advertisement is viewed on the web. The goal of the sport marketing professional is that a specific number of impressions will translate to a set amount of sales.

Strategic E-Management

Sport marketing professionals must have an appropriate e-strategy when working in an e-business and e-commerce setting. This sport marketing strategy focuses on three areas: technology, the media, and resources. Technology drives e-business and e-commerce, and the sport marketing professional must understand how the Internet and websites drive change for the sport organization. This not only includes understanding the methods that are most effective to communicate through technology, it includes understanding the infrastructure, the available software and programs, and how to make the appropriate choices to drive awareness, loyalty, and eventual growth about the specific sport products, services, and organization.

Since the online environment is a convergence of mass communication, the media plays a crucial role in the marketing of sport products and services, as well as the awareness and image of the sport organization. The external media still provides a third-party presentation about the sport organization and its products and services. However, since there are thousands of opportunities to place information external to the website of the sport organization, a major task of the sport marketing professional in e-business and e-commerce is as a publisher of information. The sport marketer must basically also become an e-journalist – including deciding on what design programs to use, styles to use, where to publish editorial pieces, and especially what content to include or exclude.

Managing the resources available to the sport marketing professional is another crucial factor in the implementation of a sport e-business and e-commerce strategy. Building a resources system that will endure the ebbs and flows of sport e-business and e-commerce will be an important step to make certain online sport marketing efforts successful. The resource system starts with quality leadership, including the management structure of the sport organization, and especially the sport marketing manager. It involves all aspects of the sport organization, including organization structure, human capital, efficient processes for task accomplishment, and a culture that provides a sense of meaning and belonging to its employees. The resource system also needs quality internal systems including supply chain management and technological infrastructure, as well as effective external partnerships and collaborations to create, promote and sell the sport products and services.

The implementation of the sport e-business and e-commerce strategy brings a new set of challenges upon the sport marketer and the management of the sport organization. A primary concern is the high visibility of errors as a result of the expanded number of potential customers that can view the sport organization through digital technologies. In addition, with the ever increasing number of services and websites that provide a forum for customer feedback on sport products and services, the effect of any error may be multiplied. It is also important to remember that errors may decrease the customer base because the cost of switching to another company is nil for the sport consumer. In the offline world, if a person is not happy with sport products and services, it is not as easy to switch because there may be additional costs associated with the switch including more travel time, costs (gas, wear and tear on a vehicle), and learning about a new company. In the online world, it is as quick as a click of the mouse!

Another challenge to implementing a sport e-business and e-commerce strategy comes from the complexity of transactions. With the need for partnerships and collaborations, the communication processes that need to take place between all parties involved can be difficult and messages can be misinterpreted more easily. The result is that the boundaries dividing the sport organization and partners/collaborators become more blurred, which in turn may cause confusion in the marketplace.

CONCLUSION

The use of electronic networks for mass communication is an integral part of sport marketing in the 21st century. Sport e-business, the internal information technology processes, focuses on integrating all the systems within the sport organization to ensure that the business functions of communications, sales, and service can be offered in an online environment. This is accomplished through a combination of horizontal, vertical, downward, and lateral integration. Sport e-commerce focuses on the external information processes through the World Wide Web and the Internet. Sport marketers today most often work in this area of digital technology, working to conduct cross-business and technology integration with traditional marketing functions to build brand equity, image, and awareness. The goal is to provide individualization and interactivity for the potential and returning sport consumer.

E-business and e-commerce have four major types of relationships. B2B refers to the transactions, collaborations, and business interactions that occur between two organizations. B2C focuses on the transactions between businesses and consumers. C2B is where the consumer initiates the transaction process by soliciting organizations to compete for the individual's business. C2C involves transactions between customers, many of which will involve an online third-party business.

Digital technologies are the centerpiece of sport e-business and e-commerce, as they are used to manage the exchange of sport products and services. The two major digital technologies utilized are the Internet and the World Wide Web. The Internet is a worldwide system of publicly accessible computer networks that transmit data by a process called packet switching to standardized IP addresses. The World Wide Web is a collection of interconnected documents that are connected by URLs and hyperlinks. The sport product and service exchanges take place through sport company websites, brokering sites, infomediaries, and e-procurement.

When conducting sport e-business and e-commerce, the store is virtual – no bricks and mortar. The sport marketing professional must focus on the actual locations where sales will be conducted from (placement); the size of the virtual location in terms of bandwidth, processing power, and data capacity; and how the sport product or service will be viewed by the sport consumer online (presentation).

In the 21st century, the sport business is operating in the new economy – where information, communication, and digital technologies are widely used in the manufacturing, selling, and distributing of sport products and services. This has a direct effect on how a sport marketing professional manages sport marketing opportunities, sport business development, sport consumer relations, integrated sport communications, sport marketing metrics, and strategic sport management, through e-business and e-commerce.

The sport e-business and e-commerce marketplace is a dynamic, changing, and competitive environment that places a sizeable set of responsibilities on sport marketers and the management of sport organizations. However, those firms who choose to ignore the online environment are sure to be left in the dust. With the complexity of the online marketplace, sport marketing professional must take a hands-on approach to ensuring quality and success. They must hold all members of the sport marketing team accountable for reaching goals in line with the metrics set, and that the guidelines, processes, and rules are followed. In addition, because the online environment is continuously changing, there is always a need for constant improvement. Finally, as with all types of marketing, it is important to remember that regardless of whatever strategic plan is decided upon, the customer is still the most important factor. Everything to be accomplished must be completed with building image and awareness in the mind of the sport consumer at the forefront of the sport e-business and e-commerce strategy.

FROM THEORY TO PRACTICE
Bruce Lerch, VIP Relations Manager
XpressBet, Inc., Washington, Pennsylvania

My start with an e-commerce business began as a result of my desire to get involved in the sport industry. I was able to procure a job with a company in the horse racing industry called XpressBet, Inc. XpressBet is an online/telephone wagering company that process wagers on horse races from racetracks all over the world. I got my start as a Welcome Center Manager, and my role was one of recruiting customers to use the service and processing financial transactions for those customers at a booth located inside of Suffolk Downs Race Course in East Boston, Massachusetts.

Over the course of the next year, I spent a majority of my time traveling from my home base at Suffolk Downs to racetracks around the United States, including Maryland's Pimlico and Laurel Park racetracks, California's Santa Anita, Golden Gate Fields, and Bay Meadows racetracks, The Meadows Harness Course located in Western Pennsylvania, and Cleveland's Thistledown Race Course. In addition to my role as a Welcome Center Manager, I was fortunate to be involved with live events such as The Preakness Stakes, Sunshine Millions, and numerous other events at each of these tracks.

I was fortunate to have my career coincide with my decision to further my education by taking sport management classes. I was able to take everything I learned in my classes each morning with me to the racetrack in the afternoon, giving me a real-world opportunity to use and better understand the principles of sport management. This combination of real-world experience combined with my education helped me earn a role as the VIP Relations Manager for XpressBet.

In this role, I was responsible for managing a select group of customers who were deemed highly valuable to the business. This is also the time period in which I became greatly familiar with the "e" side of the company. Due to the management structure of the company, I was reporting directly to Vice President of Technology, who filled a dual role as head of marketing. Not only was I managing a select group of customers, I was actively participating in the marketing initiatives of the company, as well as getting the opportunity to gain a better understanding of the technology side of the business as well.

Originally, my role was one that leaned heavily toward customer service. I dealt with our customers in a face-to-face setting at the racetracks, as well as with the various employees at each individual track, working to enhance both of those relationships for XpressBet. I was able to coordinate contests that sent some of our customers as our guests to our larger events, which required a great deal of cooperation with each host track: securing event tickets, gifts, travel accommodations, parking passes, along with numerous other details that went along with these events.

As I continued my upward progress with the company, I retained my heavy accent on customer service while joining the executive management team. I became more involved with national marketing programs designed to promote XpressBet within the horse racing industry: special deposit bonus programs; bonuses for wagering activity; and working together with our partner, HorseRacing Television.

My primary role, however, remained with the group of VIP customers. We chose to develop a more personalized approach in dealing with this valued group of customers, and I spent a great deal of my time in contact with these individuals on a regular basis, either via email or telephone, as well as in person when the occasion dictated. I was able to institute a series of monthly programs designed to reward these customers for increasing their activity, which, in turn, helped XpressBet increase profitability.

I was fortunate to get involved with XpressBet in the early stages of development. The e-commerce world was relatively new to the horse racing industry when I started, and XpressBet itself was barely a year old when I joined the company. I was able to watch and partake as a new business rose through the ranks of the e-business world to establish its place as a force in the industry.

14

INTERNATIONAL AND GLOBAL MARKETING IN SPORT

CHAPTER OUTLINE

CHAPTER OBJECTIVES

The reader will be able to:

- Understand the ever-growing and ever-changing internationalization and globalization of marketing in and through sport.
- Appreciate the historical, cultural, political, and legal dynamics that are evident in international and global sport marketing and cultural environments.
- Understand the complexity of negotiation, mediation, and arbitration with international and global sport markets.
- Identify the numerous international and global sport marketing opportunities available in established and emerging sport markets.
- Gain an insight into the differences between international strategic sport marketing strategies and global strategic sport marketing strategies.

INTRODUCTION TO INTERNATIONAL AND GLOBAL SPORT MARKETING

Many have seen the documentary "Do You Believe in Miracles" and the movie "Miracle," the story of the 1980 US Olympic Hockey Team who against all odds beat the mighty Russians and eventually went on to win the gold medal. The time was very different – fear as a result of the Cold War, a hostage crisis in Iran, and an overall turbulent political and social environment. Business and sport was a very competitive arena, but generally focuses domestically.

How things have changed in a quarter century. While there are still many issues facing the world today, including terrorism and assorted political and social issues, the world has fundamentally changed. It is a smaller place because of innovations in travel and technology. Changes in trade agreements have made the movement of goods and services easier on an international and global scale.

This growth is not lost on the continuous growth of sport marketing and management. Numerous companies have overseas offices and factories to conduct business in emerging markets. The training and recruiting of athletes from other countries is increasingly evident in the United States. More international sport figures want to play in the United States – examples include David Beckham's recently signing a contract to finish his career in Major League Soccer (MLS); and the 2005 NBA Champions San Antonio Spurs having five players from outside the United States (two from Argentina, two from Slovenia, and one from France). The internationalization and globalization of sport is an integral part of the growth of sport business, and hence is a crucial aspect of sport marketing. But what is international and global sport marketing?

International and Global Sport Marketing Defined

To understand the implementation and existence of sport marketing outside of a domestic context opens a new door to significant opportunities for sport businesses. International refers to those efforts that extend beyond national boundaries and involve two or more nations. In the 21st century, opportunities in sport cross international borders on a regular basis, and it requires sport marketing professional to capitalize on this opportunities, especially as a result of advances in technologies. As this growth has continued, another term, "global" has become important to sport marketing. Global is a more comprehensive term that refers to worldwide involvement. As a result, the definition of international has been modified, and for the purpose of this text the following definitions will apply:

- *Domestic*: Sport marketing efforts focused internally (one country).
- *International*: Sport marketing efforts that involves at least two countries to a maximum of 10. Usually the countries are within one or two continents.
- *Global*: Sport marketing efforts that involves more than 10 countries and usually a minimum of three continents.

These definitions are generic in nature, and may have some fluctuation based on the makeup of the association. For example, if a sporting goods distributor focuses their business on the United States, Canada, Australia, and England, by definition they would be global. However, since the business effort is not truly global (North America, one country in Europe, and a country that is for the most part a continent unto itself), this business would most likely be referred to as an international company. However, if this company were to expand their business efforts to China and France, they would most likely be referred to as a global company since even though they only operate in five countries, they operate on more than 50% of the continents in the world.

Determinants of International and/or Global Sport Business Involvement

A sport business can be involved in sport marketing efforts in one of five stages. The most basic of stages is where a sport organization is not involved in marketing efforts outside their own country, or no direct foreign sport marketing. For those sport organizations that dabble in foreign markets as a result of a surplus of products or a temporary increase in demand, it is referred to as infrequent foreign sport marketing. Regular foreign sport marketing is where a sport organization has a permanent presence outside national borders, but their primary market (50% or above) is domestic. This level of involvement necessitates a domestic sport market extension orientation, where domestic business is the priority, and that the manner in which business is oriented at home will work anywhere in the world. If it works – great; if not – minimal effort will be made to make adjustments, or else the sport marketing mix of these products and services will be modified to entice purchases domestically.

International sport marketing, in addition to the definition discussed above, actively engage in marketing in the various markets. Those sport firms involved in international sport marketing will develop a multi-domestic sport market orientation. In this model, the sport marketing professional develops an individual sport marketing strategy and program for each country.

Global sport marketing takes the international distribution of products and services to more of a worldwide level. This global sport market orientation differs in the fact that countries are usually grouped into marketing units based on similar economics, political environments, legal structures, or cultural compositions, and sport marketing strategies and plans are developed for each unit. This is done especially with sport organizations that are involved in a significant number of countries. For example, it would be almost impossible to manage 50 different marketing strategies and plans for a sport organization involved with that many countries. They instead might have 10 plans that encompass 5 countries each.

Therefore, the major difference between international and global is the scope and spread of the sport business. As a result the terms will be used concurrently throughout the remainder of this chapter.

The Mission of International and Global Sport Marketing

A mission for a sport marketing effort involves understanding the philosophy of the sport organization (its values and beliefs) and developing appropriate goals and objectives to operate under. As we have defined earlier in Chapter 1, sport marketers segment, target, position, and deliver to the chosen market. Our decision factors regarding product, price, place, promotion, and publicity (the five P's) are generally internally based and are able to be controlled. The difficulty in domestic sport marketing as generally discussed in this text comes from opportunities and threats within the environment. Those major opportunities and threats come as a result of competition, political and governmental policies, and the economy. International sport marketing is even more complicated because there are additional situations that directly affect the ability to effective market the sport product or service. These situations are even greater when a global sport marketing effort is undertaken.

Competition is greater simply from the expanded sport business operations. Political and governmental policies will differ because not all countries in the world are a constitutionally based federal republic with democratic and capitalistic traditions like the United States is. Economics will also differ because of the numerous currencies around the world with variable values. The level of technology is not the same in all countries – while some are more technologically advanced that the United States, most are less. This is also true with the ability to distribute sport products and services. Often this is as a result of the geographic terrain of a country, and the infrastructure present. Most of the understanding of these opportunities and threats stem from one key aspect that all international and global sport marketing professional must understand – culture.

THE RELATIONSHIP BETWEEN CULTURE AND THE INTERNATIONAL/GLOBAL SPORT MARKETPLACE

As defined earlier in the text, culture is the principal attitudes, behaviors, values, beliefs, and customs that typify the functioning of a society. The difficulty for the sport marketing professional is that when working in an international or global context, they must be able to comprehend how culture will affect the desired outcomes of the sport marketing effort. To understand the international and global sport market, sport marketers must understand the principle of marketing relativism. This principle focuses on the realization that the sport marketing efforts are usually based on strategies, values, and beliefs formulated from experiences. The result is that sport marketing professionals develop their plans and outcomes as a result of their own past experiences and knowledge. When entering an international or global market, the sport marketing professional often must ignore a significant part of this relativistic thinking, and enter the marketplace with an open mind willing to learn and understand about the culture they will be marketing toward.

So how does the sport marketing professional avoid making decisions based on their self-reference criterion? First, the sport marketing professional must define the marketing goals in terms based on their own experiences. Next, the sport marketer must also define the marketing goals in terms of the culture of the place in which the effort will be applied. This requires a clear understanding of the cultural habits, norms, and values. Once the two definitions are made, the sport marketing professional must compare the two "lists" to gain an understanding of the similarities and differences between the two marketplaces. The sport marketer may be able to use past experiences to reach outcomes in the area of the similarities. On the other hand, the sport marketing professional will have to understand the differences, redefine the problem statement in terms of the cultural differences, and create a plan to accomplish the goals in consideration of the different culture.

In order to success in accomplishing goals and reaching outcomes, the sport marketing professional must be able to work under three guiding principles. First, when working outside cultural norms, the sport marketing professional must be unbiased. This objectivity will allow the sport marketing professional to assess the opportunities within the international or global market. Second, the sport marketer must be open-minded. One of the most difficult concepts for humans is respect for individual differences. The sport marketing professional must especially have tolerance for and acceptance of cultural differences if they wish to succeed. Third, sport marketers must be educated and well verse about the various markets they will be working with. In addition to understanding the history of the culture, sport marketing professionals engaged in international and global sport marketing must also be able to assess the international and global sport marketplace in terms of worldwide market opportunities, international and global economic conditions, and the variations in international and global business customs, politics, and the law.

Understanding and Assessing Cultures

Culture is a significant part of all part of human existence. As such, the sport marketing professional must understand all aspects of that culture when trying to communicate information to that culture. Culture is a philosophical based concept that directly relates to their individual value and belief systems. These value and belief systems are often centered on religious beliefs, but often go much deeper into social tradition. The most basic of these is language. The ability to communicate appropriately with members of different cultures is central to the entire sport marketing effort. By communicating in their language, the sport marketer can get messages across more clearly, and it often shows the members of that culture that the sport organization has respect for their individual culture by making the effort to communicate with them in their language. Too often sport marketing professionals assume that the English language is universal. This is untrue. Understanding and appropriately using language allows sport marketers to show respect for the culture and the individual within it.

In addition, understanding the history and social makeup of a culture is integral to success in sport marketing. Knowledge regarding the humanities and social sciences of a culture allows the sport marketing professional a deeper understanding of symbols, meanings, and practices within the culture. Awareness of the social makeup, including education, politics, legal issues, and social organization allows the sport marketer an insight into how the population interacts with each other. Additionally, the technological and economic structures and abilities are instruments utilized to determine the extent of engagement in specific sport marketing efforts, and the likelihood of success or failure.

To gain knowledge about a culture, one must be very careful to understand the difference between factual knowledge and interpretive knowledge. Factual knowledge is information that can be easily researched through secondary resources – an example would be that the most popular sport in England is soccer, and that can be found through any number of websites, periodicals, and literature. Interpretive knowledge is the meaning of those facts with the society. In the scenario listed above, one cannot get a true flavor of the popularity of soccer, especially how fans live and die with their teams, without being immersed in the culture (primary research). This is why so many leagues, teams, and marketing organizations have offices across the globe – to place individuals in the culture to better understand how to communicate with them through sport marketing efforts. This immersion also serves to gain greater cultural sensitivity, as well as provides an opportunity to articulate that information to the domestic public with the goal of increasing cultural tolerance.

International and Global Sport Business Customs

Culture also serves as framework for the business customs within that country. Therefore, the sport marketing professional must understand how culture affects sport business practices, attitudes, and motivation. An example of this was when Yao Ming was to become the #1 pick in the National Basketball

Association (NBA) draft in 2002 for the Houston Rockets. Usually when a player is drafted, a team would be negotiating with the player's agent, the player, and potentially the parents. However, in China, it is done very differently. First, the Houston Rockets must deal with an intermediary between them and China. That person was Erick Zhang, a distance cousin of Yao Ming, and two professors from the University of Chicago who have family ties. This is because personal relationships are very important in Chinese culture and business. In addition, negotiations not only took place between the agents and team, but the Houston Rockets also negotiated with the Shanghai Sharks (Yao Ming's team in China), the Chinese Basketball Association, the Chinese National Team, and the Chinese Government (who asked for half his salary and endorsement contract money to be sent to them).

In general, there are four main concepts that a sport marketing professional must keep in mind when entering a foreign market. The first is the ability to adapt. Adaptation (the ability to make change or modification) may in some cases be imperative to maintain successful relationships. For example, in the scenario with Yao Ming, if at any time the Houston Rockets or the NBA created a situation where the Chinese "lost face," Yao Ming would not be in the NBA today because negotiations would have ended.

At other times, adaptation may offer the option of involvement – if the action is not engaged in, it will not hurt the relationship ... however involvement might enhance the relationship. For example, if an American does not bow when meeting a Japanese businessperson, it will not hamper negotiations. However, if the American does bow, it is a sign of respect and goodwill, and will often go far to enhance negotiations.

It is also important to remember that there are certain practices that are exclusive to a culture, and involvement may be unacceptable or a sign of disrespect. For example, it would be inappropriate and disrespectful to act like a Muslim by bowing and praying to Mecca if undertaken by an Arab businessman during negotiations.

Second, the sport marketing professional must realize the various methods of doing business in different countries. People in each country have different goals and objectives as related to the purpose of business. Some make decisions based on their own personal goals (Arab countries), while others make decisions that will offer them additional security or mobility (industrialized European Union countries such as England, France, and Italy). In Japan, personal life is business life, and the decisions made often must correlate with either business identity or social acceptance. In other countries, especially those in South America, social and political power is directly related with any business decision.

It is also important to remember that concepts such as methods of communication, formality, time, gender biases, and speed of decisions will vary greatly from country to country. In addition, the sport marketing professional must understand business ethics in each country they deal with, as what is right in one country may be very wrong in another.

Third is the effect of politics on international and global sport marketing efforts. There are arguments that sports and politics should not mix. Whether that is true or not, business and politics always have had a relationship. In fact, the structure of the political environment in a country will have a direct effect on the success or failure of sport marketing efforts. Issues including the stability of the government, the political parties and structure in power, and the relationship of nationalism to the sport marketing effort must be understood by sport marketing professional prior to engaging in business with foreign lands.

Fourth are the legal issues affecting international and global sport marketing. International and global sport marketing can bring about conflicts of law as a result to the differences in law between the home country of the company and the place of business. There are four manners for determining what law should be applied:

Center of gravity approach	The law of the country that has the most significant relationship to a given situation has jurisdiction.
Grouping of contacts approach	The law of the country that is most concerned with the outcome of the case has jurisdiction.
Lex Fori theory (law of the forum)	The law of the court in which a situation is brought to has jurisdiction.
Renvoi	Where a court utilizes its own laws, and has the option of adopting the center of gravity laws from another country.

Alternative Dispute Resolution in the International and Global Sport Marketplace

As in the United States, many countries around the world utilized alternative dispute resolution, which is the collection of methods utilized to hear disagreements and determine an appropriate ruling about a situation. Negotiations are utilized by two parties to resolve disputes or to complete transactions. If the two parties cannot agree, they bring in an independent person to hear both sides. The independent person is a mediator, and the process is mediation. The mediator is neutral, and has no legal standing to make a decision on behalf of the facts. The mediator simply assists the parties to reaching a mutually agreeable solution. If the parties still cannot agree, the process moves to arbitration. This is where an arbitrator oversees a hearing to determine the facts of the situation. The arbitrator is authorized and given the power by all parties involved to make a decision that is final and binding.

Challenges to Alternative Dispute Resolutions

Alternative dispute resolution takes on a challenging role in international and global sport marketing. The most basic of these challenges is the ability to communicate – both verbally and non-verbally. Research shows that Americans lack multiple language skills and prefer to do all business in English. This has a direct effect on alternative dispute resolution in two ways. First, there is room for misinterpretation. For example, if you were doing business on the Dutch island of Aruba and you suggested in English to go out to lunch for sushi, an English speaking person would think lunch was raw fish. However, a native of Aruba who may only speak Dutch or Papiamento (although most do also speak English and Spanish) would ask why you were going to eat garbage for lunch (sushi=garbage in Aruba). Second, during negotiations, often people will have side conversations in their native tongue to clarify points or explain a concept further. However, the message often comes across to the other party much differently. Some of the assumptions that are often made include "they are talking behind our back;" "they are plotting something;" "they are keeping something from us;" or "how disrespectful is that."

Communication issues are also non-verbal in nature. Depending on the culture, there are certain tactics that are used as a normal function of bargaining behavior. Silent periods of 10 seconds or more are commonly used in Japanese and Russian cultures to think about what has been said, attempt to draw out additional information, and seek to control the room. Conversational overlap, or the number of times conversations are interrupted because of hand or facial gestures, is a tactic used by the Germans, French, and Spanish to control a conversation. These cultures also are adept in using facial glazing, which is extend time looking directly into the face of a speaker. In Latin and South American culture, touching during negotiations (pat of the hand, tap on the shoulder) is commonplace.

A more serious challenge regarding the effectiveness of alternative dispute resolution in both international and global sport marketing is the significant differences in values and beliefs. Concepts including competitiveness, equality, objectivity, and time vary widely from culture to culture. The American business culture tends to make decision based on facts, what will make the most money for the organization, and the notion that "business is business." However, in most countries around the world (with the exception of some European Union countries), these notions will not work. This is especially true with the concept of time, where in many cultures the time to complete negotiations often is slower, either because they have a "just make them wait" attitude (typical in Russian negotiations), or that time just tends to go slower because of the pace of life in those cultures (typical in Latin and South American cultures).

The most significant challenge to alternative dispute resolution in international and global sport marketing is the considerable difference in decision making processes. We understand in American culture that each individual or group has a different thought process as a result of their education, experiences, and environment. Now multiply that by thousands of different culture around the world that a sport marketing professional might engage with as a result of their involvement in international and global sport marketing efforts. This is a challenge, and requires the sport marketing professional to take a holistic approach to negotiations. This approach includes being prepared to discuss multiple concepts simultaneously, and must often defer to an unorganized, disorderly process. This is as a result of negotiations not taking place in the step-by-step process that Americans are usually accustomed to.

There are a number of telltale signs that can help the sport marketing professional to recognize whether negotiations are progressing, and decisions are nearing their conclusion. In most foreign countries, as more high-level executives join the conversations, a decision is closer to being reached. As a result, questions about the situation become more direct, whereas most questions at the beginning of negotiations tend to be broad and generic in nature. Another sign of success in negotiations is that attitudes become softer and more reasonable, and often results in the parties taking more time to study the issues at hand. A final sign that the decision making process is nearing conclusion is that the language used becomes less formal and more personable.

Succeeding in Alternative Dispute Resolutions

To succeed in alternative dispute resolutions on the international and global stage takes a lot of preparation and patience. To start, the sport organization must select the most appropriate individuals to be on the negotiating team. While this often does include members of the sport marketing department, there is often a need to secure outside consultants experienced in negotiations with the specific country or region.

After the team is selected, negotiation preliminaries must be addressed. From an internal sport organization standpoint, this includes assessing the situation and individuals involved in the negotiation, and reviewing the facts involved in the negotiation and creating an agenda. In addition, the sport organization must consider alternative solutions and concessions willing to be made. From an external view, there are a number of aspects that must be agreed upon prior to the start of the negotiations. They include the location and physical arrangements, the number of individuals or groups to be involved, whether the meeting will be open to the public or closed door, the level of confidentiality required, and limitations on time per session.

Once all the rules have been put into place, the time has come to "sit at the table." One can think of the negotiation table like a football game – four quarters. The first quarter involves non-task sounding, where the first 5–10 minutes is used to welcome the participants and briefly talk about topics other than the business at hand, including family, sports, news, and the economy. It is important to understand the background of the other parties involved in case certain topics would be inappropriate because of their culture. Also important is the time spent on non-task discussions as the time Americans spend in this area domestically is considered very short as compared to most places around the world. In fact, in cultures ranging from Japan to Brazil, the time spent on non-task sounding is crucial to the overall success of the negotiation, and these cultures will not do business with a salesperson – they want to do business with someone they know, feel comfortable with, and may even consider to be a friend at the end of the negotiation.

The end of the first quarter, depending on the culture, could be a significant amount of time. In American time, this may seem to be wasted time. However from an international and global perspective, it is often viewed as being time well spent. At an appropriate time that can only be judged being at the negotiation table, the second quarter would start with information exchange. This is the point when all the cards are laid out on the table. Information is provided by both parties and feedback exchanged. One thing to remember is that negative feedback is usually impossible to gauge during this process, as most cultures view this as being inappropriate during the initial stages of negotiation. Therefore, it is important for the sport marketing professional to view the material presented in a neutral manner, not make negative comments or connotations when not in agreement, and do not expect to get much information back.

At the 2-minute warning (near the end of this segment of negotiation), a first offer is usually made. It is important to remember that the first offer made by an American negotiator tends to be pretty close to what they want. In most international and global cultures, the first offer is usually significantly inflated to encourage longer periods of bargaining. Halftime comes with the initial offer being considered and tactics being modified and recreated.

The third quarter of the negotiation game is a true persuasion stage. Each side is seeking to gain some ground on issues, answer questions, clarify positions, and often argue over points. In the American culture, we often seek to get objections out on the table, provide more information, and handle the situation. When the negotiation does not go the direction desired, frustration and anger enters the equation. This often results in making threats and ultimatum, and even sometimes leaving the table ("taking their ball and going home"). While these tactics may word domestically, internationally, and globally is a different study. Many cultures will just let you walk out the door and never open that door again. This is true in Japan and China, where threats and ultimatums may be viewed as creating a loss of face. In France and Germany, it will elicit an attitude of "typical Americans," and they will make the negotiations even more difficult. In other countries, the tactics may be viewed as being childish, taunting, or barbaric.

We finally reach the fourth quarter of the negotiation game – making concessions and coming to an agreement. Americans tend to make concessions during the negotiation process and expect reciprocation from the other party. However, in most international and global negotiations, concessions are not made until the persuasion process is complete. Again this is very frustrating as it is a different way of thinking to the American way of negotiating.

Probably the most important stage happens once negotiations are finished and an agreement is reached. It is important to understand how the agreement will be viewed by the other culture. For example, American companies have no problem sending contracts through the mail for signatures, or signing contract behind closed doors. Other countries often require much "pomp and circumstance" with a formal signing ceremony including the highest level of authority from the organization (usually the CEO). Another difference is the way in which the contract is viewed. While in America a contract is a legal and binding agreement, in China it is viewed as a guideline for business operations, and is renegotiable at any time. In all cases, follow-up communications and the continued building of personal relationships will allow continued success in the sport marketing efforts agreed upon in the negotiation process.

INTERNATIONAL AND GLOBAL SPORT MARKET OPPORTUNITIES

Developing relationships with international and global sport markets serves as a foundation for entry into those markets. With the continued growth of international and global trade as a result of improvements in technology and transportation, sport organizations must create a vision for this involvement. This vision will differ depending on whether the sport organization wishes to enter an existing sport market or try their hand at entry into an emerging sport market.

International and Global Trade in Sport Business

As stated above, the continued development of digital, satellite, and Internet technologies have been an integral part of the evolution of international and global trade. This, combined with the decrease of barriers to international and global trade, many corporations have started to develop an international and global marketing strategy. This has not been lost on the sport industry. The ability to transmit visual images related to sport has broadened the scope in which fans can view sport across the globe. This has also increased the ability to market products, services, and related peripherals around the world, with the eventual goal of generating the same demand as in the domestic market.

International and global sports used to be exclusively associated with the Olympics, international federations, and continental tournaments. Now, professional sports leagues from the United States and corporate involvement in sport on an international and global stage has evolved at an astronomical rate, especially due to the aforementioned development of technologies and reduction in trade barriers.

There are a number of reasons sport firms, and indeed non-sport firms, have become involved in the international and global marketplace. One is that there has become an oversaturation of products and services in the American market. Much of this has been caused by the relationship of too much competition in comparison to the maximum level of discretionary income being spent by Americans on sport products and services. Therefore, many corporations have sought to extend their product and service distribution to an international and global audience. Therefore, the sport marketing professionals must seek way to understand those foreign markets, and communicate with those markets about the image and components of the sport products and services. Just as with traditional sport marketing domestically, the goal is to increase awareness and sales in the international and global market. The most common method utilized by sport businesses to expand the awareness, and hopefully resulting sales, in international and global markets is by sponsoring non-American athletes in their home countries, marketing popular American athletes on a global scale, and enhancing their sponsorships of prominent events such as the Olympics and World Championships.

Aside from sport corporations, professional sport organizations such as Major League Baseball (MLB), the National Basketball Association (NBA), and the

National Football League (NFL) have sought to increase their popularity around the world. All three of these leagues have created international divisions to guide sport marketing efforts and manage offices overseas. The international and global sport marketing efforts have focused on the marketing of foreign athletes, broadcasting and multimedia efforts, licensing and merchandising, and the growth of sports through various grassroots efforts.

The chart below shows how these three leagues have expanded their offices in order to effectively market their leagues on an international and global basis:

League	Offices in
MLB International	Central Office in New York City Japan Office in Tokyo Europe, Middle East, and Africa Office in London Australia Office in Sydney
NBA Global	Central Office in New York; other offices in: ■ Barcelona ■ Hong Kong ■ London ■ Melbourne ■ Mexico City ■ Paris ■ Singapore ■ Taiwan ■ Tokyo ■ Toronto
NFL	Central Office in New York NFL Europe Offices in New York and London

Some examples that show the expansion of these international and global efforts:

- Major League Baseball has co-sponsored the first World Baseball Championship in 2006; with 16 countries playing games in the United States, Puerto Rico, and Japan. Teams represent all six continents where baseball is played (no Antarctica).
- The National Basketball Association has regularly sent teams to play in Europe since 1988. They also have played exhibition games in Russia, China, and Japan.
- NBA.com has separate websites for Brazil, Canada, China, France, Germany, Japan, Taiwan, and the United Kingdom. In addition, they have NBA.com Español for Spanish speaking countries.
- The National Football League, in addition to having a pre-season game outside the United States every year since 1986, they had their first regular season game outside the United States in 2005 (Arizona Cardinals vs. San Francisco 49ers in Mexico City). They now plan to have up to two regular season games per year outside the United States.
- The National Football League has run NFL Europe every season since 1991. Teams have played in England, Germany, the Netherlands, Scotland, and Spain.

- International and global grassroots efforts focused on increasing participation and educating people about the specifics of the individual sport are offered by MLB (Pitch, Hit, and Run; Play Ball!; Envoy Program; Elite Baseball Development); the NBA (Basketball without Borders); and the NFL (play-football.net and the NFL Global Youth Football Championships).

THE EFFECT OF THE INTERNATIONAL AND GLOBAL MEDIA

Sport has become an international and global culture unto itself to link people around the world. As the sport marketplace becomes more technologically and industrially developed, the actions of those who operate within this marketplace become undifferentiated. Uniqueness is abandoned in favor of the rationalized world, in which the need to maximize production in the most efficient manner reigns supreme. Athletes, event managers, sponsors, and sport organizations have taken what they have learned from domestic (local, regional, and national) competition and participation, and have expanded across the world.

Internationalization and globalization efforts are only be possible with the aid of the global media. Throughout the history of sports, children have evolved in their interest in sports, much of which has been controlled by media influences. In the era prior to significant media influences, children generally participated in cultural and primitive games tied to their homelands. These activities were considered tradition by the citizens of their country. As the influx of media began through first print, then radio, and eventually television, there was a growth in interest in American games such as baseball and basketball, and European sports such as soccer.

As the digital technology age has evolved over the past 10–15 years, children tend to be more individualistic. As a result, another evolutionary process has taken place from traditional sports to alternative sports. This change has occurred for three reasons. First, alternative sports are more individual based, so the participant can take part without the limitations placed on an activity that required teammates. Second, these games are events that are relatively inexpensive to replicate. Sport activities that are very affordable to the middle and lower class citizens of various countries have a better chance of succeeding. Third, many alternative sports were at one point in time introduced into these various countries by some kind of source originating outside of the country's border (Wenner, 1998). In most cases this outside influence came by the way of the media.

The global media is mainly responsible for bringing these alternative sporting events from all over the world into the living rooms of citizens of all social classes worldwide. By the 1990s the American based ESPN sports network was being seen in across the globe. In fact, according to ESPN.com,

Continued

through ESPN, ESPN2, ABC Sports, and ESPN International, alternative sports programming such as the X Games are broadcast to over 110 million homes, in more than 145 countries and territories worldwide.

Continued growth in the international market has resulted in positive feedback. Richard Young, Vice-President of Event Management Group stated in a July 18, 2000 article: "The popularity of extreme sports is on the rise in Asia. We first brought the event to Asia in 1998 as a qualified for the premier sporting event of this genre, the US summer X Games. It quickly established itself as the ultimate goal for Asia's extreme athletes. Since then sponsors have been quick to see the potential of these events. Whether they are looking at an on-ground sponsorship or advertising on-air, they understand the X Games' power to capture the imagination of people of all ages" (*SportBusiness Journal*, 2000).

In 2000, ESPN announced it was going to organize and televise a new global sports event. The X Games Global Challenge will take place at different locations outside of the US every other year beginning in 2002. It is the latest step in ESPN's major worldwide expansion of the X Games franchise. Said ESPN vice president, programming, event creation, and management: "Different from our annual X Games, the Global Challenge will focus on a format with worldwide bragging rights, as well as medals and money on the line" (*SportBusiness Journal*, 2000). As a result of this, the popularity of action sports continues to grow.

ESPN now claims that the X Games has achieved truly global appeal (Wallace, 2002). They, along with other alternative sports activities including the Gravity Games, the Mountain Dew Free Flow Tour, and the various events produced by Red Bull, have realized that these sports can succeed on a global level, and are becoming increasing a part of the mainstream. However, to maintain that success, the key is in the ability to continue to attract the younger demographic known as Generation Y (Wallace, 2002).

Source: Adapted from Schwarz, E. C. and D. Blais (2005). Marketing and the globalization of alternative sports. *Presented at the 2nd Annual Sport Marketing Association Conference*, Memphis, TN.

Suggested Discussion Topics

1. With the continued growth of alternative sports on the global stage, there is a distinct possibility that similar growth is taking place with traditional sports? Currently, there is a significant influx of athletes from overseas come to play in traditional sports in the United States, and the explicit interest of the MLB, the NFL, and the NBA to expand internationally.

Do you think the next step will be MLB, MFL, and NBA teams playing regularly overseas, and perhaps eventually teams having homes in Europe or Asia? Depending on your agreement or disagreement with the previous question, what effects will this decision have on domestic, international, and global marketing efforts?

2. While the growth of American sports outside the United States continues to grow, there is also an expansion on non-American sports into the domestic sport landscape. Some of those include the California Australian Football League, and the continued growth of USA Rugby. If you were working as the Director of Marketing for either of these, how would you market the organization to increase brand awareness in the United States sports landscape?

Creating a Vision for the International and Global Sport Marketplace

The concept of developing a vision for the international and global marketplace is a significantly more difficult task as the scope of the vision is greater because of the expansiveness of the research needed to be undertaken. In domestic sport marketing, the scope usually focuses on developing a marketing plan that addresses the elements of the sport marketing mix – product, price, place, promotion, and publicity. In international and global sport marketing, the research necessary for establishing an appropriate vision also includes collecting information about the country, the region, and the foreign market. In addition, the sport marketing researcher must have a grasp on the trends apparent in the overseas marketplace, and how to forecast the needs of that marketplace in terms of the sport consumers, potential economic growth, sport industry trends, the political and sociological climates, and growth opportunities in technology.

While many of the same domestic sport marketing research tactics (discussed in Chapter 3) are utilized in completing international and global sport marketing research, one of the unique challenges involves multicultural research. Multicultural research is dealing international or global sport markets that have different attitudes and beliefs, economic and social structures, and language. There is a challenge, as a result of these differences, in being able to compare data across cultures, and therefore it is difficult to find correlations between results. It is also difficult to guarantee reliability and validity in the research, as research design of surveys and questionnaire will vary from culture to culture. For example, the Japanese culture usually will not respond to mail surveys – they usually need to be distributed from a known source and face-to-face.

Existing International and Global Sport Markets

The manner in which the aforementioned research is utilized will serve to develop a vision for entering, maintaining, and creating growth in international and global sport markets. Many of the partnerships being forged are with existing markets in the North and South America, Europe, Asia, and Australia. The following are some examples of partnerships between sport in the United States and sport in other countries. The continued growth of these partnerships is sure to increase the number of sport marketing opportunities internationally and globally.

North America

One of the most recognized soccer teams in Mexico, Las Chivas Reyadas de Guadalajara (Chivas), has expanded their operations to Chivas USA – the first and only Hispanic-based team in the United States, playing in MLS. The majority of the roster is comprised of players of Mexican heritage or former Mexican league stars. The goal is to bring a Mexican style of soccer to the MLS, which consists of style, technique, and grace. This is in stark contrast to traditional American soccer, which is based more on strength, power, and speed.

The sport marketing opportunities have been endless, especially to target the primary niche market of Mexican-Americans, and a secondary niche market of Hispanic-Americans. One such grassroots effort is called "Sangre Nueva," which is translated to New Blood. This involves inviting young Hispanic players to attend a tryout camp for a spot on the team. Some of the marketing efforts linking Mexico and the team include:

- A register to vote program for the Mexican elections that took place in Los Angeles in coordination with the Mexican government and the Instituto Federal Electoral.
- The development of "Sí se Puede," a documentary which describes the behind-the-scenes story of the formation of Chivas USA. The film was introduced in the Los Angeles Latino International Film Festival in 2005.
- For Hurricane Katrina relief in 2005, Chivas USA partnered with Chivas Guadalajara to field a select team (players from both the US and Mexican team) to face Mexican First Division team Santos Laguna in Santa Barbara, California.

As a result of this initial partnership, there have been rumors that someday in the future the Mexican League (who has high scoring and not as much defense) and the MLS (lower scoring and very defensive) might merge to create an international soccer league between the two countries.

Central and South America

Traffic Sports Marketing is one of the largest sport marketing firms in the world. Based in São Paulo, Brazil, this company develops, manages and markets transmission rights, sponsorships and promotions of major intercontinental events of soccer clubs and national teams. In addition, Traffic Sports Marketing also develops sports events and promotional actions according to the needs of its clients, manages the image of athletes and sport personalities, and develops communication plans and promotional actions abroad to increase and expand Brazilian exports. They have also expanded their sport marketing efforts to broadcasting and transmission rights for global sport events.

This company, in addition to their offices in Brazil, also has expanded its reach to North America (Traffic Sports USA), Europe (Traffic Sports Europe), and across the globe (Traffic Sports International). Traffic Sports USA focuses on the logistics and production of soccer properties in North America, Central America, and South America, including the Gold Cup, CONCACAF matches, and World Cup qualifiers. In addition, one of its main goals is to actively sell and market South American and international soccer properties to the United States population.

Europe

In an effort to further the popularity of the NBA in Europe, and a desire by the NBA to expand the league into Europe in the near future, announced that in October 2006, the Los Angeles Clippers, Philadelphia 76ers, the Phoenix Suns, and the San Antonio Spurs will conduct their pre-season training campus in Europe, and will compete against top European basketball clubs in seven European cities in five countries. The event, called NBA Europe Live presented by EA Sports, is documented in the chart below:

Team	Training Site	Game Schedule
Los Angeles Clippers	Moscow, Russia	October 6 – CSKA Moscow in Moscow, Russia October 8 – Unics Kazan in Moscow, Russia
Philadelphia 76ers	Barcelona, Spain	October 5 – Winterthur FC Barcelona in Barcelona, Spain
Phoenix Suns	Treviso, Italy	October 6 – Virtus Lottomatica Roma in Rome, Italy
San Antonio Spurs	Lyon, France	October 5 – Adecco ASVEL Lyon-Villeurbanne in Lyon, France October 8 – Maccabi Elite Tel Aviv (Israel) in Paris, France

The tournament concluded with a tournament in Cologne, Germany, featuring the Philadelphia 76ers playing the Phoenix Suns, and the 2005–2006 Euroleague Basketball Champion vs. the Euroleague Basketball Champion Runner-Up on October 10. The finale featured match-ups on October 11 between the winners and the runners-up of each game.

Asia

When the New York Yankees signed Hideki Matsui to a long term contract, they were getting much more than a player. They were also opening a door to new marketing opportunities. Hideki Matsui is beloved in Japan – known as Godzilla; he was a three-time MVP in the Central League for the Yomiuri Giants. Although he has been gone from Japan for a number of years, Matsui still maintains a significant presence there. His face appears on posters and TV pushing laptop computers, beer, and other goods. His love life makes news. The Japanese fans still watch him by tuning into live TV broadcasts of Yankee night games that are shown in Japan just after breakfast.

As far as the increased marketing opportunities, look in right field during a Yankees home game. You will see the typical advertisement billboards seen in stadiums across the United States. However, there is one difference – Yankee Stadium has many advertisement signs completely in Japanese advertising a wide array of products. These signs are for their Japanese speaking fans in the stadium and for those watching in Japan. Companies including Fuji, Ricoh, Toshiba, and Sony have all had billboards in Yankee Stadium, but the most prominent is on the right field wall (as seen below) – the sponsorship by the Yomiuri Newspapers:

In turn, the Yankees are pushing their brand in Japan through licensed and branded merchandise, and by opening the 2004 MLB season in Tokyo with exhibition games vs. the Tokyo Giants and the Hanshin Tigers, and two regular season games vs. the Tampa Bay Devil Rays.

Australia

Seeking to expand the popularity of Australian Rules Football (AFL), and also trade between the United States and Australia, the Sydney Swans (the 2005 AFL grand champions) and the Kangaroos (from North Melbourne) played an exhibition match at UCLA in January 2006 as a part of Australia Week. Co-sponsored by the State of California, the Australian Government, Tourism Australia, and Qantas Airways, the purpose of Australian Week was to raise Australia's commercial and cultural profile in Southern California, while also furthering awareness and commercial return for Australian and American interests. Professional golfer Greg Norman also ran a golf day at the North Ranch Country Club in Westlake Village, California. The event, sponsored by his wine business Greg Norman Estates, was a sell out.

Emerging International and Global Sport Markets

Sport organizations are also looking at emerging international and global sport markets to expand their opportunities. Two of those emerging sport markets are Africa and the Middle East.

Africa

The sport business is rapidly growing on the continent of Africa. An example of the emergence of this market is that South Africa is going to be hosting the 2010 FIFA World Cup. This will be the first time the World Cup would be held on the continent of Africa. It is long overdue, especially with the growth of soccer on the continent. The countries of Cameroon, Nigeria, Tunisia, Senegal, Egypt, and Morocco are ranked in the top 40 of international powers in 2005. The growth is even more evident in that five African nations have qualified for the 2006 World Cup in Germany – Angola, Ghana, Ivory Coast, Togo, and Tunisia – where only Tunisia is the only country noted above in the top 40.

The NBA has also been successful finding talent in Africa. During the 2005–2006 season, there are eight players on NBA squads including Dikembe Mutombo from Congo (Houston Rockets); Michael Olowakandi from Nigeria (Minnesota Timberwolves); DeSagana Diop from Senegal (Dallas Mavericks); and Luol Deng from the Sudan (Chicago Bulls). In addition, reigning NBA MVP Steve Nash of the Phoenix Suns, while he grew up in Canada, was born in South Africa.

While there seems to be boundless opportunities, the main concern with these countries are that many still suffer from third world afflictions of developing nations. Some of the questions being asked include "What role should sport play in showcasing the problems of these nations?"; "Does the international and global sport community have a duty to foster development in these countries?"; and "Should soccer, basketball, and other sports play a role in this development?".

It seems that most of the efforts will be centered on South Africa, where many of the international and global sport opportunities seem to be based. In addition to their teams well known in international competition (cricket, rugby, and the African representative to the World Baseball Classic), they also have the infrastructure to host major global events, including the 1985 Rugby Union World Cup and the 2003 Cricket World Cup. However, probably the greatest breakthrough in sport marketing in Africa came as a result of the 1999 All-Africa Games, an Olympic-type competition hosted in Johannesburg for the 52 nations of Africa. Grinaker Sport Marketing was hired to secure sponsorship for the event, and they raised a record $10 million in sponsorships from companies including Vocacom (parent company is Vodafone of England), DHL, and Mercedes Benz. The only question is when will these sport marketing opportunities spread to all points in Africa – only time will tell.

Middle East

The Middle East sport market is rather unique in that it encompasses a cross-section of Western, Arab, and Asian culture. In addition, the range of wealth and opportunity varies greatly, from the wealthy nations of the United Arab Emirates and Bahrain, to the war-torn countries of Afghanistan and Iraq, to the sports tradition of Israel. Many correlations can be drawn between the sport marketing opportunities in the Middle East and that of Africa. Those countries with significant infrastructure, political stability, and money host the events. However, one major difference is the significant change in cultural beliefs that is taking place in the Middle East. In the past, the Arab culture was very closed minded to sport – especially the concept of team sports. However that has changed significantly with a significant growth in infrastructure over the past 10 years, as well as the desire to host or help with just about any international event.

This growth of sport is specifically being driven by the government. Their reasoning is to attract foreign business and international visitors. Some of the major events that have been hosted in the Middle East include:

- 15th Asian Games in Doha, Qatar
- FIFA World Youth Championships in the United Arab Emirates (2003); Qatar (1995); and Saudi Arabia (1989)
- Numerous events in Dubai, United Arab Emirates including:
  - The Dubai Cup (horse racing)
  - The Dubai Tennis Championships (ATP and WTA Tour stops)
  - The Dubai Desert Classic (Golf)
  - In addition, Ski Dubai opened in 2005 at the Mall of the Emirates, and Dubai Sunny Mountain Ski Dome is schedule to open in 2008.

This growth in the popularity in sport, and therefore an increase opportunity for sport marketing efforts, is not only attributable to governmental investment.

The advances in technology have served to influence the youth of these cultures, and there are many correlations that can be drawn between American youth and Arab youth. This is especially true in the way that sport figures and global brands influence the purchasing desires of Arab youth. However, as with Africa, the issue will be when will these sport marketing opportunities spread beyond the oil rich nations and political influence. Again, only time will tell.

ETHICS IN GLOBAL MARKETING: MORAL CHAMPIONS

Over the years, a number of scandals have come to light concerning production or marketing of potentially harmful products in less developed countries (LDCs). Well-known examples from the 1970s and 1980s include high-dosage contraceptives sold over the counter; baby food promoted using high-pressure sales methods; continued sales of pesticides and high-tar cigarettes after forced withdrawal from western markets; inadequate health and safety precautions during production of asbestos; and the explosion of a chemical plant due to lax safety standards. One might reasonably wonder why well-educated, professionally trained managers, who work for companies with international reputations, might take decisions that risk provoking censure by the world business community. Is it just the result of the "profit motive" run rampant? Is it merely the "ugly face of capitalism?" Or are there other reasons that might explain the apparent willingness of western managers to run the risk of jeopardizing the health and well-being of consumers in the developing world?

Marketing in LDCs is often characterized by an imbalance of power because the foreign corporation controls access to information about the product, its use, likely effects of misuse, and the availability of safer alternatives. Consumers in LDCs may be vulnerable to exploitation insofar as they lack, to a greater or lesser degree, the basic skills and knowledge that typify consumers in western markets. Also, the consumer environment in many LDCs lack agencies and organizations to monitor company action, such as the EPA, FDA, Better Business Bureaus, and Consumers Union in the US.

The term "vulnerable" is used here to describe consumers who, for various reasons, find themselves at a disadvantage relative to a global corporation in not being fully able to express, claim, or defend their rights as consumers. Since the Consumer Bill of Rights was issued in the US in the early 1960s, at least four basic rights have been identified: the right to safety; the right to be informed; the right to choose; and the right to be heard (i.e., to have one's interests fully and fairly considered in the formulation and administration of government policy).

Peter and Olson (1993) comment that even though this list appears to offer considerable protection, it assumes that consumers are willing to be

Continued

involved in purchase and consumption of a product, and that they are able to defend their rights. This assumption may not hold true in the case of the children, the elderly, or the uneducated poor because they may not have the necessary cognitive ability with which to defend their rights to information, choice, and due consideration. With regard to safety rights, the burden of responsibility would appear to fall on the sellers of goods and the local government or its agencies. Consumer vulnerability is particularly prevalent in LDCs, being associated with the poverty and illiteracy typical of lower levels of economic development. Even when willing to stand up for themselves, consumers in LDCs may not have the necessary education and confidence with which to express and claim their rights.

Use of the term "moral champion" in this article implies a high moral and ethical posture. According to Smith and Quelch (1991), ethicists identify three levels of duty to which people – and hence managers in organizations – are obligated:

1. avoid causing harm,
2. prevent harm,
3. do good.

They comment that negative duties are stronger than positive duties. This seems particularly appropriate in the context of any discussion of marketing potentially harmful products in LDCs, NEDs, and NICs. Smith and Quelch also point out that while it seems reasonable to expect businesses not to cause harm and to make efforts to prevent harm (insofar as it is within their control); there is less agreement on the need for companies to do good. McCoy's (1983) "parable of the Sadhu" illustrates the type of moral conflict that an individual can face when trying to determine what an appropriate ethical response in the face of human is suffering. While taking part in an extended hike in the mountains of Nepal, McCoy's group of companions came upon an unconscious, almost naked Sadhu, an Indian holy man. Each climber gave the Sadhu help but none made sure that he would be safe. McCoy asks himself whether someone should have stopped to help the Sadhu to safety. Would it have done any good? Was the group responsible? McCoy's ability to help the Sadhu was tempered by his own physical problems at the time, the environmental constraints (due to being halfway up a mountain), and a general lack of consensus on what to do. McCoy draws parallels between this incident and the type of ethical decisions that managers face at work.

Ciulla (1991) has drawn attention to the variability that exists in legal and ethical values, attitudes, and standards even among the developed nations of the world, leaving aside the developing world. She cites comparisons of "familial amoralism" in Italy, "national amoralism" in Japan, and "ethical imperialism" in the USA. This reminds us that there is no commonly accepted global code of ethics that applies to business (Buller *et al.*, 1991). Clearly, managers operating abroad must make some accommodation to the nature of the foreign environment in which they are operating. However, as Shue (1981, p. 600) stated, "No institution, including the corporation, has a general license to inflict harm," even in places where local laws do not specifically outlaw such behavior.

Competition is a key feature of the global market environment. Wotruba (1990) comments that "competitors' actions seem intuitively to be a possible moderator of ethical decision making since questionable behaviors may be considered more necessary under intense competition." Unfortunately, as Wotruba points out, research on this topic is lacking. In the global arena competitors bring different national ethical standards into play. Thus a manager may feel compelled to compromise ethical standards learned at home in order to "follow the crowd" and not lose ground in a foreign market.

With regard to the global company as an institution made up of peer groups, research has been conducted to assess managers' perceptions of their peers' ethical behavior. In the 1970s managers were reported to perceive their peers as being less ethical than themselves (Newstrom and Ruch, 1975; Weaver and Ferrell, 1977); in the 1980s few managers believed that their peers actually engaged in unethical behaviour (Chonko and Hunt, 1985). Zey-Ferrell *et al.* (1979) reported that marketing managers' perceptions of what their peers did had a greater influence on their behaviour than their own personal ethical beliefs. More recent research by Vitell *et al.* (1993, p. 336) reached the opposite conclusion.

The ethical climate seemed to have little effect on one's acceptance of various norms. Apparently, this is an area where individual factors dominate and whether or not one's firm espouses the importance of ethical behavior is irrelevant. On the other hand, a sense of idealism and income level were both closely linked to acceptance of all the norms tested. Since income may be a surrogate measure of success, the results may indicate that those who were more successful tended to have stronger marketing-related norms.

This last speculation does not seem to be borne out in real life if one recalls the ethical lapses of highly successful individuals like Ivan Boesky, Michael Milken, Frank Lorenzo, and most recently, Dan Rostenkowski. Moreover, contrary to Vitell *et al.*'s (1993) conclusion, Nichols and Day (1982) reported that individuals interacting in a group produce group decisions at a higher level of moral reasoning than the average of the individual members acting alone. Thus, at the present time it is difficult to determine on the evidence available whether managers in global companies are more or less likely to reach ethical decisions.

Continued

In assessing the role of the company in influencing individual beliefs and behavior, we should remember that individual ethics are also shaped by other organizations and are partly a result of the person's individual history and personality. Moreover, organizations do not reflect exactly the prevailing societal ethic. Finally, ethics are not static but change markedly over time (Buller *et al.*, 1991).

Consumer vulnerability is associated with low levels of economic development and lack of supervision of the marketplace. Consumers' emancipation is inhibited by the cumulative effects of the lack of education, lack of opportunities to acquire consumer skills through store and price comparison, lack of information about products and potential hazards, lack of availability of alternative choices, and so on. As a result many consumers in LDCs, NEDs, and NICs may be completely unprepared or insufficiently armed to evaluate marketing offers made by any company, whether global or local. A current example of vulnerability is seen among urban consumers in Russia. Although generally well educated, they have little time or energy with which to monitor the actions of companies, being daily distracted by the continuing struggle to find basic necessities.

The fact that vulnerable consumers abroad have been and continue to be victimized is explained by Shue (1981, p. 599) in these words:

[It] has a great deal to do with the discounting of the welfare of people across national boundaries, especially when the boundaries also mark cultural, ethnic, or racial differences. Harm to foreigners is simply not taken as seriously.

One may argue that discounting others' welfare results from an unequal interplay of deontological (process) and teleological (outcome) evaluations during decision making (see Hunt and Vitell, 1986 for a full discussion). However, it seems more likely that it results either from a failure to identify the existence of an ethical dilemma or choice, or from a misplaced sense of loyalty in following the lead of superiors or trying to protect company interests.

Failure to identify a moral choice may result from a low level of cognitive moral development (see Kohlberg, 1969 for details), or a lack of ethical sensitivity (Hunt and Vitell, 1993), or a lack of strength of moral character (Williams and Murphy, 1990). Candee (1975) showed that persons in moral development stages 3 and 4 were more likely to follow their superior in morally questionable action than were persons in stage 5 or 6. Ward and Wilson (1980) investigated how individual motivation (safety vs. esteem needs) interacting with the presence or absence of peer pressure affects the type of decisions taken by the individual. Esteem-motivated individuals do not submit to group pressure but display a consistent moral posture across situations. In contrast, safety-oriented individuals tend to acquiesce to group pressure and exhibit inconsistent moral action. However, when acting as individuals, both personality types make similar moral choices.

Source: Excerpts from Amine, L. S. (1996). The need for moral champions in global marketing. *European Journal of Marketing* 30(5), 81–94.

Suggested Discussion Topics

1. The author discusses the variability that exists in legal and ethical values, attitudes, and standards among the developed nations of the world. After defining the theory of marketing relativism, discuss whether this practice can be utilized when entering an international or global market. Choose any segment of the sport industry to illustrate your answer in terms of understanding and assessing cultures, business customs, and methods of negotiation.

2. How do the concepts of ethical climate, consumer vulnerability, and moral choice directly affect a sport industry's vision for entering an international or global market? Discuss the differences in the development of that vision in terms of existing markets and emerging markets. Use specific examples to elaborate your answer.

INTERNATIONAL AND GLOBAL SPORT MARKETING STRATEGIES

Throughout this chapter, the concept of international sport marketing and global sport marketing has gone hand-in-hand. However, when it comes to developing sport marketing strategies, the definitions become somewhat differentiated. International sport marketing strategy, also sometimes called multinational sport marketing strategy, focuses on cross-cultural differences and that each individual culture requires a separate sport marketing strategy adapted to the individual cultures. In contrast, global sport marketing strategy views the world as one big market, and the sport marketing strategy seeks to define and target similarities between various cultures around the world. The eventual goal is to create a diversified marketing strategy that will allow the sport organization to compete in any market in the world.

An international sport marketing strategy is a direct approach of sport marketing, where the plan is individualized for the specific sport market. The global sport marketing strategy is more of an indirect approach, where a sport marketing strategy that has worked in one country might be used and slightly modified in another because of similarities in culture and perceived product and service benefits. This ability to transfer experience from one culture to another allows sport organizations to enter new markets in a faster and more efficient manner. It also makes it easier to coordinate and control strategic operations. In addition, the economies of scale, especially in the area of advertising, are a great benefit. For example, by only having to create a few television commercials that can be used globally and targeted to similar markets, it becomes significantly less expensive as compared to developing dozens of individual television commercials for each country. By determining common themes among various country's value set, generic television commercials can be developed and only voice overlay would have to be added for the specific language of a country. As a result, a sport organization can also more easily control their global image. This is especially important in new and emerging markets, where reputational value carried a significant amount of weight because of the lack of personal experience and contact with the products and services of the sport organizations.

CONCLUSION

There are similarities and differences between sport marketing efforts in domestic sport business as compared to international sport business and global sport business. As a result of the disparity between cultures in the international and global sport marketplace, the sport marketing professional must be well versed in being able to assess these cultures. One of the common misconceptions is that as long as someone can speak the language, business can be conducted. This chapter shows that it is much deeper – including differences in verbal and non-verbal communication, history and social issues, and business customs. This requires the sport marketing professional to be able to adapt to various situations, appreciate different value and belief systems, be able to understand many different methods of doing business, and be aware of political and legal dynamics entangled throughout the international and global sport marketing processes. These situations will often be discussed through various methods of alternative dispute resolution – most often being negotiations, but also potentially including mediation and arbitration.

There are numerous opportunities in the international and global sport market. Many professional leagues and sport businesses have already taken advantage of entering foreign markets, and have also created visions of entering emerging markets such as Africa, the Middle East, and South America. All of these plans are centered on the strategic sport marketing process. Strategic sport marketing planning is utilized in matching the sport organization to a specific country or region. This is orchestrated by adapting the sport marketing mix to the specific target markets, developing a targeted sport marketing plan, and arranging for the best methods for implementing and controlling that plan. This is especially important in the areas of products and services management, channel and logistics management, integrated communications systems, and financial management.

Excerpt from "Marketing and the Globalization of Alternative Sports"

Presented by Dr. Eric C. Schwarz, Daniel Webster College and Dr. Douglas Blais, Southern New Hampshire University

---

2nd Annual Sport Marketing Association Conference in Memphis, Tennessee, in November 2004

Sport has become an international and global culture unto itself to link people around the world. As the sport marketplace becomes more technologically and industrially developed, the actions of those who operate within this marketplace become undifferentiated. Uniqueness is abandoned in favor of the rationalized world, in which the need to maximize production in the most efficient manner reigns supreme. Athletes, event managers, sponsors, and sport organizations have taken what they have learned from domestic (local, regional, and national) competition and participation, and have expanded across the world.

Internationalization and globalization efforts are only possible with the aid of the global media. Throughout the history of sports, children have evolved in their interest in sports, much of which has been controlled by media influences. In the era prior to significant media influences, children generally participated in cultural and primitive games tied to their homelands. These activities were considered tradition by the citizens of their country. As the influx of media through first print, then radio, and eventually television, there was a growth in interest in American games such as baseball and basketball, and European sports such as soccer.

As the digital technology age has evolved over the past 10–15 years, children tend to be more individualistic. As a result, another evolutionary process has taken place from traditional sports to alternative sports. This change has occurred for three reasons. First, alternative sports are more individual based than many traditional sports, so participants can take part without the restrictions placed on an activity that required teammates. Second, alternative sports are events that are relatively inexpensive to replicate, therefore affordable in various countries where the majority of the population is middle and lower class. Third, the global media is mainly responsible for bringing these alternative sporting events from all over the world into the living rooms of citizens of all social classes worldwide. By the 1990s the American-based ESPN sports network was being seen in across the globe. In fact, according to ESPN.com, through ESPN, ESPN2, ABC Sports, and ESPN International, alternative sports programming such as the X Games are broadcast to over 110 million homes, in more than 145 countries and territories worldwide.

Continued growth in the international market has resulted in positive feedback. Richard Young, Vice-President of Event Management Group stated in a

Continued

July 18, 2000 article: "The popularity of extreme sports is on the rise in Asia. We first brought the event to Asia in 1998 as a qualified for the premier sporting event of this genre, the US summer X Games. It quickly established itself as the ultimate goal for Asia's extreme athletes. Since then sponsors have been quick to see the potential of these events. Whether they are looking at an on-ground sponsorship or advertising on-air, they understand the X Games' power to capture the imagination of people of all ages."

In 2000, ESPN announced it was going to organize and televise a new global sports event. The X Games Global Challenge will take place at different locations outside of the US every other year beginning in 2002. It is the latest step in ESPN's major worldwide expansion of the X Games franchise. As a result, the X Games and many alternative sports have achieved global appeal. They, along with other alternative sports activities including the Gravity Games, the Mountain Dew Free Flow Tour, and the various events produced by Red Bull, have realized that these sports can succeed on a global level, and are becoming increasing a part of the mainstream. In addition, with snowboarding being a staple in the Winter Olympics, and BMX becoming a part of the Summer Olympics in 2008 in Beijing, China, the mainstreaming of alternative sports continues. However, in order to continue this growth and success, the key will be to continue to attract the younger demographic and market these activities constantly throughout the lifespan.

THE FUTURE OF
SPORT MARKETING

VI

15

ENTERPRISE SPORT MARKETING MANAGEMENT

CHAPTER OUTLINE

CHAPTER OBJECTIVES

The reader will be able to:

- Appreciate the difference between the art of sport marketing and the science of sport marketing.
- Understand the various aspects of the sport brand architecture: including monolithic, endorsed, and branded.

- Examine sport marketing as a part of the overall enterprise through an investigation of the concepts of enterprise sport marketing management, owning the brand experience, investment measurement, and creativity.
- Be aware of the change in the manner in which sport marketing strategies are developed as a result of the influence of enterprise sport marketing management.
- Gain an understanding of the concepts of sport consumer relationship management (SCRM) and sport consumer experience management (SCEM), and how they work collectively with sport enterprise marketing management to produce optimal sport marketing efforts by sport entities.

IS SPORT MARKETING AN ART OR A SCIENCE?

The art of marketing comes from the doing of marketing – implementing programs to attain and retain customers, and seeing what actually works. This is the territory of marketing managers, direct marketers, advertisers, and consultants. The science of marketing comes from research – about markets, customers, competitors, and how effectively various types of marketing programs work. This is the area of academicians and market researchers.

The science of marketing provides a sound foundation for good marketing practice, whereas the artistic side tends to embrace new ideas and technologies without considering the ramifications. For example, the long scientific history of the adoption and diffusion of innovations says that the Internet will take a long time to fundamentally change the way large numbers of customers buy their products and services. If more managers and investors had understood this, then many dot.coms would not have become failed.

This is also true with sport organizations. Many professional sport organizations are not willing to spend the time and resources necessary to complete proper scientific research, instead choosing to roll the dice on the potential quick fix – a new logo, a new promotion scheme, a redesign of sales options, or new innovations in technology.

But that is all starting to change. In the past, people entered the field of sport marketing because it involved not only an interest in the sport product, but also the ability to use their artistic creativity – developing copyright, designing graphics, and producing artwork. However, sport marketing has evolved into being a critical part of business, and hence more of a management science. Sport marketing professionals design campaigns based on marketing strategy, economic analysis and impact, research of societal wants and needs, ethics, and governmental regulations. While the artistic qualities are still imperative to the marketing process, scientific methodology has become the driving force behind sport marketing efforts. Scientific methodology is the process by which one gains information by a process of observation, developing a hypothesis, implementing some type of research to determine the appropriate course of action, and evaluating the results to draw conclusions, select courses of action or inaction, and modify the research and start again.

Marketers often fail in three key categories: those with (1) the inability to use their knowledge of their customers to position their brands; (2) the inability to put their brands to work beyond traditional media; and (3) the inability to build brand acceptance and understanding throughout the organization, which in turn affects how the brand is presented to the general customer. The sport brand is the business of the sport marketing professional, not just a concept or campaign that is discussed internally. It must be treated as such. However, one of the major difficulties is that sport organizations do not always understand how to position their product in relation to the sport consumer. There are some sport organizations that are not willing to spend the time, money, and other resources that explore in detail the benefits that will significantly drive sport consumers to purchase the sport product. Instead, trial and error is utilized and the hope is that the plan will eventually work. However, the evolution of sport marketing has brought about an understanding that building a relationship between the communication of benefits and sales is more cost effective and resource efficient.

SPORT BRAND ARCHITECTURE

Sport marketing professionals must work with sport entities to develop a brand structure or brand architecture that focuses on communicating the value the sport entity is creating, and the resultant benefits of the sport product as viewed by the sport consumer. This is accomplished by focusing on identifying different levels related to the brand name and/or visual associations of the brand. There are three main branding structures: monolithic, endorsed, and branded. Monolithic is when a corporation uses one name and identity worldwide (Nike). Endorsed is where the corporate name is used in association with a subsidiary or sport product brand (Starter jackets). Branded emphasizes multiple product-level brands (ESPN with brands such as ESPNU, ESPN Deportes, ESPNZone, ESPN Entertainment, ESPN Videogames, etc.). A coherent brand architecture is a key component of the firm's overall marketing strategy as it provides a structure to leverage strong brands into other markets, assimilate acquired brands, and rationalize the firm's branding strategy.

Another example is charted for Electronic Arts (EA) Sports:

Monolithic	EA Sports
Endorsed	Madden NFL by EA Sports
	NCAA Football by EA Sports
	NBA Live by EA Sports
	NASCAR Thunder by EA Sports
Branded	EA Sports (realistic sports simulations)
	EA Sports BIG (extreme sports titles)
	Pogo.com (online games site with numerous EA brand tie-ins)
	AOL games channel (operated by EA)

SPORT MARKETING AS PART OF THE ENTERPRISE

Enterprise marketing management looks to systematically link sport marketing efforts to all essential functions within an organization. This realignment seeks to put sport marketing efforts and customer service at the center of the efforts of the sport enterprise. Enterprise sport marketing allows the sport marketer to develop deeper customer understanding while delivering more personal and compelling sport marketing throughout the sport consumer life cycle. This is accomplished by improving a sport organization's ability to acquire, retain, and grow customer value, establish the corporate value proposition and brand, as well as efficiently manage the strategic planning process and marketing resources including people, time, inventory, and content.

Owning the Brand Experience

A brand is a mixture of attributes, tangible and intangible, symbolized in a trademark, which, if managed properly, creates value and influence. In traditional brand management, this involves managing the tangible and intangible aspects of the brand. For product brands the tangibles are the product itself, the packaging, the price, etc. For service brands, the tangibles have to do with the customer experience – the retail environment, interface with salespeople, overall satisfaction, etc. For product, service, and corporate brands, the intangibles are the same and refer to the emotional connections derived as a result of experience, identity, communication, and people. Intangibles are therefore managed via the manipulation of identity, communication, and people skills.

In traditional marketing management, the sport product branding process include such things as sport product extensions, merchandise, endorsements through star players and coaches, distinct trademarks and patents, advertisements, and sponsorships – to name a few. In enterprise marketing management, branding the sport event itself instead of having associated branded products has become the norm.

SPORT CONSUMER RELATIONSHIP MANAGEMENT

As the growth of Internet technologies continue, as well as the need for advanced customer services, sport marketing has entered the 21st century through the use of SCRM. SCRM is the use of various methodologies, information technologies, and Internet capabilities that help sport entities organize and manage sport consumer relationships. The goal of SCRM is to develop a system that all members of the sport marketing effort (management, sport marketers, salespeople, service providers, and consumers themselves) can utilize to access information about sport products and strive toward meeting the needs and wants of sport consumers.

The objectives of SCRM include the following:

- Helping a sport entity enable the sport marketing professional to identify and target their best customers, manage sport marketing campaigns with clear goals and objectives, and generate sales.
- Assisting the sport entity to improve telesales, consumer account management, and sales management by optimizing information shared by multiple employees, and making existing information sharing processes more efficient and effective. An example of this would be taking orders via the Internet or through mobile devices.
- Allowing the formation of individualized relationships with sport consumers. By identifying the most profitable sport consumers and providing them the highest level of service, sport entities will improve sport consumer satisfaction. The result of this will be the optimization of profits.
- Providing sport marketers with the information and processes necessary to know the sport entity's customers, understand their needs, and effectively build relationships between the sport organization, its customer base, and distribution partners.

The Nashville Predators (NHL) and the San Diego Padres (MLB) were two of the first sport organizations to extensively utilize SCRM as a cornerstone of their sport marketing effort for the future. Now, dozens of sports teams in Major League Baseball (MLB), the National Basketball Association (NBA), the National Football League (NFL), the National Hockey League (NHL), and minor league hockey and baseball teams have followed suit.

The Nashville Predators are using a customer relationship management (CRM) technology provided by AIM Technologies to collect information about the demographics and psychographics of its fans. The Predators used that information and in turn run a fan-loyalty reward card program. They use this program to market to their fans by enticing them to attend more events. This in turn increases secondary revenue from sales of merchandise and concessions. The Predators also use the information about their fans to attract advertisers and other sponsors. In addition, by tracking the number of times fans are attending, the sport marketing professionals can get a better idea of where their fans are on the "escalator," and can target market to fans based on their level by understanding which fans will more likely buy season or ticket packages in advance.

The San Diego Padres have had similar success with EDCS's Top Prospect system. Their program, called the Compadre Club, provides fans with a membership card that can be used at kiosks around the stadium, as well as when purchasing tickets, merchandise, and concessions. It has been described as a "frequent flyer program" for the baseball fan. The most the fan uses their card, the more points they get and the more benefits they receive. They also market promotions and other specials through the card. The overriding goal is to get these fans to attend at least one more game per year. To put that in perspective, if a team had 150,000 card members who attended just one more game per year at $20 per ticket, there would be additional revenue in the amount of $3 million for the organization!

New World Transactions, Technology, and Customer Relationship
Management

Ticket sales still represent a key indicator of a club's popularity despite the
fact that they represent a declining share of total revenue for many clubs in the
top European football leagues and major league sports in North America.
Sponsors and TV companies buy into teams and sports that can sell out
stadia and, while secondary event day income from merchandise and food
and beverage relies on a ticket first being sold to the fan inside the venue.
However, while the value of media rights and sponsorship packages appear to
have peaked, many teams are suffering from a decline in live audiences.

The market for ticket sales will benefit from the scheduling of two global
events in 2006, with the Torino 2006 Organizing Committee expecting 1
million spectators to be watching 63 different competitions during the
Olympic Winter Games in February and the FIFA managing the distribution
of 7 million tickets for the 64 matches of the 2006 World Cup in Germany.
Both organizations are relying on electronic ticketing systems to automate
the process of distributing massive volumes of tickets – of different types and
for multiple events – to customers who use different languages and currency.

New World Transactions

Methods of purchasing tickets have evolved from the simple cash payment
at the turnstile or box office. The first development was telephone sales,
which is still a popular method of booking a ticket having been enhanced by
Interactive Voice Response (IVR) and call centers. However, the Internet has
quickly become the most popular sales and distribution channel for many
events, with 96% of Euro 2004 tickets sold in this way. The development of
new hardware and software has enabled the introduction of seamless integration with box offices, call centers and fulfillment houses.

This technology has subsequently evolved into other forms of electronic
ticketing, such as kiosks and countertop units to allow for sales of tickets as
retail outlets. In Italy, tickets for Turin 2006 can be purchased by sports fans
from a network of 6000 banks.

More venue operators are now using the additional functionality and
reduced costs of ticketing software to enhance traditional paper-based systems, while some clubs and franchises have taken the opportunity to install
new information systems when they have either relocated, rebuilt, or refur-
bished their stadium. English Premier League club Fulham decided to install
Venue Solutions' VenueCast system at their Craven Cottage football stadium
when they returned to the venue in 2004. The club used the relocation as an
opportunity to integrate its ticketing function with its business operations
system. Matthew McGrory, head of IT at Fulham FC, says: "The applications

have enabled us to operate our business more effectively saving both time and enhancing our internal business processes."

Venue operators have been able to use e-ticketing to reduce box office operating costs and offer a better quality of service to customers. Fans can select their preferred seat, ticket type, and payment choice at a time and place that is convenient for their lifestyle. Box offices are limited by manpower and the number of customer points, such as box office windows or telephone lines, whereas ticketing systems are able to cope with peak demand and process transactions much quicker. This now means that some events can literally sell out in minutes.

Venue Solutions have further developed electronic ticketing by creating a product that integrates with venue and business management systems. Venue-Cast, which has been developed in partnership with CRM specialist Pivotal Corporation, Siemens and Sony, integrates with ticketing software supplier Synchro Systems. Dominic Berger, Managing Director of Venue Solutions, believes that ticketing data is essential to sports organizations for business planning: "Trends can be identified, ROI on marketing campaigns can be analyzed and new programs can be developed. By cross-referencing across multiple information sources, this adds value across all business departments."

Fulfillment and Access Control

Technology has revolutionized the channels via which consumers can purchase tickets as well as the ways in which transactions can be fulfilled and how sports fans enter a venue.

The traditional paper ticket is still a popular and versatile medium and has benefited from enhancements such as special inks and barcodes. This has not only improved venue safety and security by reducing opportunities for counterfeit tickets and providing more efficient access control, but has also enhanced customer service.

Some venues have introduced kiosks to supplement the box office. The kiosks are able to read credit or debit card and instantly print tickets, thereby reducing queues at box office windows. They are particularly suited for ticket collections from the box office and also generate incremental sales from walk-ups and by reducing walkaways. The NFL Atlanta Braves were one of the first organizations to introduce kiosks and can process 2000 tickets per game from the units located at their Turner Field stadium. Kiosk technology has further evolved and can now be integrated with a turnstile so that customers no longer have to queue separately to first purchase a ticket only to then queue again to access the venue.

Barcodes have also enabled print-at-home ticketing and have been applied to media such as smart cards and mobile phones. More sports fans are now

Continued

printing their own tickets and Ticketmaster reports that more than 50% of tickets for NFL Seattle Seahawks games are printed by fans using its ticketFast service.

But it is arguably the introduction of smart cards that has revolutionized ticketing more than any other medium. These cards are personalized using a barcode, magnetic stripe or chip to record data about a customer and his or her transactional history, and to allow access to a stadium or arena. Cards are now being introduced by a number of sports clubs and franchises for season tickets, membership schemes, and VIP areas.

FortressGB specializes in access control systems and has integrated smart cards with venue management systems. Clients include Liverpool and Manchester City, both of which operate FortressGB's Smart FC Scheme, plus Reading, West Ham United, and the JJB Stadium, which hosts Wigan's football and rugby league teams. As well as ticketing and access control, the FortressGB system can be used as a cashless e-purse for concessions and can be upgraded with e-commerce and CRM applications, such as secondary ticketing or the collection and redemption of loyalty points.

Philips and Sony have been championing the development of contactless smart cards that do not have to be swiped in a reader. These cards can be produced in a variety of sizes or shapes and the technology has even been integrated into watches, key fobs, and mobile phones. Roda JC, a professional football club that plays in the Dutch First Division, has been a pioneer of contactless ticketing thanks to its relationship with the Netherlands-based company Philips. The Parkstad Limburg Stadion is now a cashless environment with smart cards being used by fans as electronic cash to purchase merchandise or food and beverage from concessions.

In August 2005, Roda JC and Philips commenced a trial in which 50 season ticket holders were supplied with a Nokia mobile phone that also acts as a ticket and e-cash device. Fans are able to check their balance on the phone's screen and can top-up their account by holding the handset to credit-loading terminal. Frank Rutten, General Manager of Roda JC, is cautious but optimistic about the project: "The trial will show us how well mobile ticketing is accepted and what challenges we may face for a full-scale implementation. Of course, it is too early to draw conclusions, but initial feedback from the fans is very positive." Eventually, it will be possible to add the functionality that will enable customers to use the phone to purchase tickets and pay for credits using their mobile network phone bill. Mobile handsets could prove to be the most suitable medium for ticketing as they have the capability to integrate ticket booking, payment, fulfillment, and access control.

Customer Relationship Management

Electronic ticketing has enabled venue operators to capture more data about their customers and, through the use of customer relationship management

(CRM), has allowed them to foster more sophisticated marketing relationships with fans. This has become increasingly important as sport faces more intense competition from other leisure and entertainment brands. A number of sports organizations have used CRM systems to analyze data about each fan and then adapt their communications, products, and services to each individual's preferences.

With an effective CRM system, every transaction a customer completes is recorded wherever possible. In the case of sports venues, this may include purchases at concessions and retail outlets as well as tickets, membership schemes or other affiliated products and services. The venue can then profile customers by the recency, frequency, and value of their transaction history, and also segment the database using geodemographics metrics such as age, gender, family status, and income.

CRM facilitates the production of targeted and personalized marketing communication and the opportunity to up-sell and cross-sell. For example, an organization may target fans who have attended more than 75% of matches with a promotion for season tickets or perhaps an offer of an inclusive travel, accommodation and ticket package to occasional visitors who live more than 100 miles from the venue. By profiling the data contained within the CRM database, it is possible to implement marketing campaigns targeting the acquisition of new fans and the retention of existing customers.

Although many professional sports clubs and franchises now have access to CRM tools, there are still some doubts about whether the associated technology has generated a positive ROI. Some venues have experienced difficulties in procuring an appropriate system. The CRM market is complex with a range of options on offer, including off-the-shelf, customizable and modular systems, plus the option for systems to be developed in-house or outsourced. Managers have reported problems with implementation, which may be attributable to an over-complicated user interface or inadequate staff training.

The capture of quality of data is paramount as CRM can only be as good as the information that is recorded. Sports organizations may have to commit more time and resources to data management because so many transactions at sports venues are completed in a hurry. Dominic Berger of Venue Solutions explains the value of using CRM technology to manage customer data so that it is accurate, consistent, and complete: "Most sports and leisure venues use manual paper-based systems or disparate management systems. These processes are time consuming, open to duplication and human error and do not facilitate inter-departmental communication."

Integration

Venue operators may also not be extracting maximum value from CRM but instead treating their customer records as a homogenous database. Matthew

Continued

McGrory of Fulham FC highlights the benefits of targeted and personalized communication: "We now have information on our fans and corporate clients in a central system which enables us to more effectively communicate with our customers and increase our revenue." It is therefore essential that CRM coordinates with all customer "touch points" and not just the ticketing and box office function. This includes websites, direct and email communication, mobile phone services, food and beverage concessions, retail, media, and membership schemes.

Suppliers of CRM systems are now integrating systems with other management functions, including marketing, operations, and finance. As well as CRM functionality, VenueCast can also be linked to digital signage, CCTV, access, and temperature control as well as general management systems to improve business efficiency.

Ticketing and CRM systems will continue to be used for the sale and distribution of millions of tickets for mega events such as the Winter Olympic Games and the FIFA World Cup Finals, but have also been successfully adopted by clubs and franchises of all sizes to acquire and retain customers.

With some professional sports suffering from declining attendances as well as a stagnating market for media and sponsorship rights, it seems likely that the effective application of CRM will become increasingly important for those venues seeking to generate sustainable revenue streams.

Source: Stevens, A. (2006). Standing out for the crowd. Reprinted with Permission by *SportBusiness International*.

Suggested Discussion Topics

1. Based on your understanding of CRM and integration from this case study and the chapter, outline how would you go about designing and integrating a CRM program for a minor league baseball team in a large city where there is competition from professional sport organizations? Include in your outline a discussion of the reason you selected specific elements of the plan, the timeline for implementation, and your strategy for managing and evaluating the plan.
2. How would you integrate your CRM plan with a customer experience management plan? Discuss how the two plans can work together to maximize the experience of the sport consumer.

MORE THAN JUST RELATIONSHIPS: OFFERING SPORT CONSUMER EXPERIENCES

SCRM is often not enough to entice the sport consumer to purchase the sport product. No longer is the sport event just a game. Depending on the event or the sport, it can be viewed as either an entertainment spectacle or as an integral part of a lifestyle. Traditional sports such as baseball, basketball, and football have been looking for ways to continue to attract fans to events, but offer them a little more to enhance the value placed on the price paid for the ticket. Alternative sports such as skateboarding, snowboarding, and BMX racing have gone a different avenue. Their activities want to be more than just an activity or event; they want to be an integral part of the lifestyle and culture of the consumer.

"Traditional" Sports: More Bang for the Buck

As stated above, the sport consumer wants more, especially as related to the sport event. In general, Americans have less discretionary time. Therefore, they want to maximize their participation opportunities while minimizing the money and time necessary for participation. To address this need, sport enterprises are doing exactly that – offering event amenities to attract the sport consumer through the door.

Event amenities go beyond just the typical event promotions and giveaways – it expands the experience beyond the core sport event. At many sporting events today, there are pre-game and post-game events such as musical entertainment, live sports by radio and television broadcasters, interactive events such as climbing walls and video games, and autographic signings by former players, current players, cheerleaders, and mascots.

These mini-fan festivals are a product of the larger interactive fan festivals that have developed since the early 1990s. At this time, professional sport leagues in the United States recognized that maintaining and strengthening their fan bases would require innovative tactics that focused primarily on creating experiences and building relationships with fans rather than generating short-term revenues. As a result, leagues started a marketing trend with the development of interactive fan "festivals" which they produced at existing premier competitions such as All-Star games and championships. These interactive fan "festivals" included various forms of entertainment, food, and sport attractions that gave fans of all ages the opportunity to participate, interact and experience the sport product first-hand. The following is a list of the current interactive fan festivals in professional and amateur sport:

League	Name of Fan Fest	Year	Event?
MLB	All-Star Fan Fest	1991	All Star Game
NFL	NFL Experience	1992	Super Bowl
NBA	NBA Jam Session	1993	All-Star Weekend
NASCAR	NASCAR World	1994	Brickyard 400
NHL	NHL FANtasy	1996	All-Star Weekend
Major League Soccer	Soccer Celebration	1996	All-Star Game
National Association of Basketball Coaches	Fan Jam	1993	Men's Final Four
NCAA	Hoops City	1997	Men's and Women's Final Four

As we enter the 21st century, the advanced use of technology to market and enhance the sport event experience has arrived. An example of this would be the SkyBOX system. This system integrates emerging Wi-Fi and on-demand technologies with the Internet. *Fans* attending a sports event can tap into a wireless network from anywhere in the stadium using a handheld device that among other things, will let them: view on-demand instant replays from various cameras; access real-time analytical and graphic player, team, and game statistics; order food and merchandise; learn from *interactive* rulebooks and playbooks; play interactive games with and against other SkyBOX users; send email and graphic e-postcards; bid on in-stadium auction items; check traffic for the drive home; and make reservations at nearby restaurants.

In a competitive industry where fans have a vast number of entertainment choices, sport properties are discovering the need to create special marketing programs that reach beyond the playing field. If special efforts are made to bring the sport and its stars directly to fans, sport properties have greater opportunities to develop the relationships and positive associations required for long-term growth. This growth shows the need for sport marketing professions to move beyond sport consumer relationships (SCRM) to capture the sport consumer. They want more for their money, and are looking for multiple experiences. Embracing the concept of sport consumer experiences will allow the sport marketing professional the means to meet the needs and wants of the 21st century sport consumer.

"Alternative" Sports: Lifestyle Marketing and the Resulting Cultural Impact

Alternative sports are more than just competitions, challenges, and races – it is a lifestyle that millions of participants have embraced. Alternative sport participants do more than just participate in the sport, they live it. These sports are an extension of their lives, rather than just a way to achieve physical activity.

Especially with the youth subcultures, there are signs and styles that are easily interpretable. Subcultural style indicates to which group the individual belongs to, and distinguishes that group from the mainstream. This concept is the foundation for much of the work in sport consumer research and subcultures.

"Culture" and "lifestyle" are ways to describe the alternative sport scene. It is not only the activity or sport that an individual participates in, it is the entire culture. As an example, if you were a skateboarder, being a part of that culture means that you not only skate, but it also means you look like a skater, dress like a skater, and participate in the culture of a skater. This concept has been documented in the movie Dogtown and the Z-Boys.

Previous consumer research about sport subcultures focused on shared ethos, boundary maintenance, and hierarchical structure based on members' demonstrated commitment. Shared ethos or the shared cultural meanings of the group help to define the subculture. Shared ethos for participants of alternative sports would be individualism, rebellion, and anti-establishment. Boundary maintenance is the way members consume market goods to demonstrate acceptable behaviors to the group. Examples of market goods for alternative sports would include specific brands of skateboards, snowboards, clothing, and music.

The hierarchical structure refers to an order based on a set of criteria set by the subculture. The hierarchical structure for alternative sports would be driven by the top national stars in the various sports, the most notable being Tony Hawk. The next group in the hierarchical structure would be the local and regional stars from the sport. The final group in the structure would be the local "stars" from the skate park, snow park, or beach. These individuals are the ones who are reading the most current magazines, visiting the most "cool" websites, wearing the "in" clothing and listening to the newest bands.

Boundary maintenance and the purchase of goods are what drive the commercial aspect of alternative sports. Youth, the target segment of these companies, are becoming more sophisticated in their purchase decisions. Kids seek inherent truth in products. If brand communications lie, and the product fails to do what is said it will, the product will be rejected. The purchasing power of the youth market can be very powerful. Numerous studies show that 60% of parents state their children have some say in the purchase of food, clothes, leisure, and gifts. In addition, over 80% of teens control what they wear and what they do in their leisure time.

Understanding this unique sport market is critical to success. This has resulted in a direct relationship between culture and alternative sports. In the movie "Dogtown and the Z-Boys," a documentary that took a hard look at how surfing values, style, and culture morphed into the alternative sport of skateboarding for an outlaw gang of Southern California beach kids in the 1970s, exemplifies just how important culture and lifestyle was to alternative sports, and continues to be today. The movie portrays that it was more than just the sport, it was the art, the music, and the culture of the scene in Dogtown, a shoddy area of Santa Monica, California, that attracted people to participate in the sport and over the years create their own niche market.

Alternative sports, more importantly action sports such as skateboarding, snowboarding, and in-line skating, not only feed into the culture that performs these sports, but they are simultaneously fueled by this culture. It is a give and take relationship that is only a part of this side of the sports industry. Alternative sports is more than just the sport, it is about respecting the tradition that the sports were founded. The tradition, which is culture, style, and value based, is one that is not seen in the mainstream sports side of the industry. It is this type of lifestyle, within these types of sports that make alternative sports stand out from mainstream sports such as soccer and baseball.

Sport marketing companies across the country have gotten the message, and many companies are now specializing in marketing for alternative sports. One such company, Fuse Integrated Sports Marketing of Burlington, Vermont, is a marketing/advertising agency that connects brands with the youth market through alternative sports. Agencies like this are succeeding because of the growing impact that these types of sports are having on today's youth culture. No longer is it a myth that tattooed kids with long hair and baggy jeans are racing down a street on wooden planks attached to wheels. All you have to do is turn on the television on a Saturday afternoon to see that it is happening for real.

Kids no longer have an affinity with mainstream sports, nor do they identify with the stereotypical millionaire athletes that represent them. A 13-year-old boy does not relate to the multiple houses, yachts, and Armani suits of Shaquille O'Neal or LeBron James. However, they can relate to the skateboard ramp in the backyard, the shaggy hair, and hooded sweatshirts of skateboarder Tony Hawk. Despite the fact that Hawk and many others get paid, and get paid well, to perform these sports, they are seen as "keeping it real" and never allowing themselves to get bigger than the sports and disrespect the culture that surrounds them. This is important to a market savvy, culture conscience youth audience.

The fact is that alternative sports over the past decade have become so increasingly popular and woven into the culture of the 12–24-age demographic that participation and viewership of mainstream sports within this demographic is decreasing. In 2003, The Sporting Goods Manufacturers Association performed a survey of 25,000 American households to determine what sports are popular with today's youth. According to an analysis from this study, five of the top ten most popular sports are "X Games sports." These sports include in-line skating (1), skateboarding (2), snowboarding (4), BMX Biking (8), and wakeboarding (9). In fact, more Americans skateboarded in 2000 than played baseball. Baseball participation numbers among youths declined 13% from 2000 to 2001.

Figures released by the National Sporting Good Association (NSGA) further substantiate the premise that participation in mainstream sports among today's youth is declining, while participation in alternative sports is increasing. The NSGA figures show that from 1997 to 2002, the two sports with the most growth in participation among 7–17 year olds were snowboarding and skateboarding. Furthermore, of the seven sports that saw growth during this period, these were the only two sports that saw double-digit growth. Skateboarding grew in participation by 55.6%, while snowboarding saw an astounding 87.5% participation growth during this period.

Kids are not only choosing to participate in alternative sports over mainstream sports, but they are also choosing to watch them on television. A survey conducted by Harris Interactive in January 2000 found that ESPN's X Games is the second most appealing sporting event to watch on television for kids ages 6–17. The X Games came in just behind the Olympics, but ahead of the Super Bowl, World Series, and World Cup. On a yearly basis the X Games continue to eclipse ratings records. The eighth installment of the Summer X Games (2002) held in Philadelphia, Pennsylvania, was the most watched in history with 62.7 million viewers tuning in. This is a 37% increase from 2001. The event drew a daily audience of 676,328 households, which was an increase of 45% from the previous year.

Why do alternative sports fit in so perfectly with the youth culture and mainstream sports do not? The answer is simple: alternative sports are lifestyle driven. There is more to alternative sports than playing a game and going home after. It is more about hanging out with friends, listening to music, and wearing clothes than it is about listening to a coach and wearing a uniform. This is because the youth subculture – especially those who participate in alternative sports, prefer the individuality and freedom of the activities. In the past, kids played team sports in seasons. During the summer it was baseball season. In the fall it was soccer season. In the winter it was football season. This never gave kids a sense of individuality or identity. They were constantly switching sports according to the time of year. Alternative sports are not like this. Even if a kid cannot snowboard in the summer because of the lack of snow, he/she can still listen to music and wear clothes associated with the culture. They can have their own identity year round.

CONCLUSION: THE FUTURE OF SPORT MARKETING – IT IS ALL ABOUT YOU!

Throughout this book, you have been provided with an abundance of theoretical and practical knowledge in sport marketing. This information is compiled from some of the top educators and practitioners in the field of sport marketing. However, this information is useless if you do not know how to apply it in the real world. Hopefully, some of the examples provided in each chapter from practitioners give you a good idea of where to start. To supplement that information, we encourage you to consider the following.

Theories taught via classroom learning are integral to the philosophical and educational basis of the field of sport marketing. However, without having the opportunity to apply those theories in real-world situations, classroom knowledge is not reinforced, and results in a student's education in sport marketing not being complete. Based on discussion with professional sport organizations, non-profit sport organizations, and corporations with sport management foci, internships are considered great experiences. However, sport organizations are looking for that student who has gone a step further: one who has acquired additional practical experience through field experiences, site visitations, event assistance, and involvement with professional organization in marketing such as those offered through the Sport Marketing Association and the American Marketing Association.

Experiential learning has become an integral part of preparation in the field of sport marketing. It provides the student with the opportunity to apply theory in real-world situations, gives the student exposure to the variety of aspects within the discipline, allows the student to gain practical experience that employers' desire, provides valuable networking opportunities with professionals in the field, and increases the exposure of the students to organizations involved within the discipline of sport marketing. So how does one gain this experience while in school?

Required and Elective Coursework

Experiential learning takes various forms at an institution of higher education. As with many schools, opportunities are offered through required and elective coursework via practicum and internship.

Practicum/Apprenticeship

A practicum or apprenticeship (henceforth called a practicum) is often a "mini" internship for sophomore or junior level undergraduates. It is designed to provide structure, direction, and guidance for students who seek and accept leadership responsibility for on-campus or off-campus activities in sport management. On-campus opportunities include working with the intercollegiate athletic program, the campus intramural and recreation program, or an individualized study under the direction of a professor through sport research. Off-campus opportunities are varied, but tend to be management based under the direct guidance of a professional in the field.

Internship

An internship, which is often the capstone for many sport management programs, offers students the opportunity to gain experience in management of a sport facility, product, or service under the supervision of a professional in the field on a full-time participation basis. These opportunities, while still under the guidance of a sport management professional, tend to be more independent in nature, giving the student the opportunity to apply what they have learned in a real-world setting. These tasks often include actual sport business management and marketing tasks, as well as supervision of staff. It is the hope that when placing a student in an internship, it is with an organization that has a full-time position available in the area of the internship, and the internship is serving to "train" that individual to fill the opening.

Field Experiences

Another avenue for practical learning is through field experiences via the classroom. Field experiences yield the necessity of receiving direction, undertaking responsibility, and demonstrating competence by applying theory learned from course work. Field experiences can be offered as an extension of a class, in the form of consulting projects, site visitations, and event creation and event assistance.

Consulting Projects

There are numerous organizations that are looking for individuals to consult in various areas of sport marketing management and research. Some of the specific tasks requested by organizations involve student consultants working on a range of marketing projects including identifying target markets, conducting demographic and psychographic surveys, analyzing the appropriateness, effectiveness, reach and value of sponsorships, and aiding in the creation of a vision within marketing and sponsorship activities. While securing these consulting projects often required some searching and negotiation, they are an integral part to the learning process students in sport marketing because of the ability to apply theory in real-world situations. Mistakes that are made while carrying out a project are often correctable, and add to the reinforcement of proper application of theory.

Site Visitations

One of the easier applications of field experience is through site visitation. Whether it is an arena or stadium, a marketing firm, an event management company, or just about any sport organization, the ability to observe the organization in action reinforces the theory from the classroom. In fact, it additionally serves the purpose of giving students the opportunity to visualize themselves in a similar situation, and often gives them a better understanding of a career they may be considering. This concept of observation as a tool to reinforce theory learned in the classroom has been prevalent in the field of education, especially as related to peer coaching and teacher preparation. These site visitations also reinforce the concept that experiential learning is beneficial to students as they learn to apply classroom theory in real-world settings, as well as learn from the environment outside of the classroom.

Event Assistance

Another way to take the theory learned in the classroom and applying it to a real-world setting is through event assistance. Sports, no matter what the event, are always in need of volunteers. Volunteers are imperative to the success or failure of an event. Sport events, from the small local recreation basketball tournament, to large events such as the NBA and NHL All-Star games, need volunteers to succeed. These organizations usually will consider volunteers with varied backgrounds. However, having a volunteer with basic theoretical knowledge in sport management or marketing is more desired. While this does provide the organization with low cost or free labor, the benefits are not one-sided. The student gets an opportunity to apply their theoretical knowledge in a real-world setting, while also building a resume that is beneficial to their professional career. In addition it gives the student the opportunity to try different tasks within the field, allowing the student to discover what they like and what they do not like. While a career may sound exciting in theory, it is not until an individual experiences the career first-hand that they understand what it truly entails. This puts the student one step ahead when deciding what career path to follow. Event assistance becomes a win-win situation for all involved.

In Closing

The essential role of the curriculum in higher education is to educate students in their field of choice, and beyond, resulting in the creation of a productive member of society. This is often accomplished via the teaching of theory in the classroom. By integrating that theory with practical experiences as described in this paper allows sport management educators to further prepare students interested in the sport management field through hands-on activities, guest speakers, tours, and planning and running events.

Marc De Grandpre, Director of Field Marketing

Red Bull Northeast Business Unit Boston, Massachusetts

Owning the Brand Experience for Sponsoring and Producing Sport Events

Red Bull feels that it is an important part of our job to start at the grassroots level when we talk about events. The basic premise behind any event you will see Red Bull associated with would be to have a credible relationship within the scene. The key is to build a relationship with athletes within core scenes that we have identified as evolving extreme sports – things that really reflect the personality of our brand. We look at the athletes, try to develop relationships with them, discuss with them their sport and how it is progressing, and see how we can become a part of that sport to help them progress it further.

A perfect example that occurred recently was the Red Bull Bike Battle in Boston. It took about 2 years to develop that event concept. Two years ago, our Field Marketing Manager in Boston met up with some mountain biking athletes that went to the University of Massachusetts at Amherst. From there he developed a relationship with them, and got introduced to the right people on the scene through this relationship at UMass-Amherst. Through that, we started seeding these groups attending events that were in the back-woods and backcountry in the Northeast Business Unit in Massachusetts and Vermont. From that relationship we discussed with athletes what would take their sports to the next level.

We then developed this Urban Freeride Event concept with these mountain bikers in Boston. It took 2 years to do it, Red Bull spent a lot of money behind the development, and we at no point mass-marketed the event to the general consumer. We focused on key outlets in the market – that is mountain biking stores, mountain biking shops, and mountain biking trails. We marketed the event to these constituencies because those are the people in the scene who want to see their sport progress. But we did not put $20 million behind advertising for the event for the general consumer. We just had posters developed for the event that were posted at a few bike shops around the business unit. We wanted to make sure that the event stayed true to the scene and true to the actual sport.

If you look at the way we market our brand at these events, all the branding is functional. We do not put banners up. We do not put our logo all over the place. We make sure that wherever you find the Red Bull logo, it is either on a jump, kicker, launching pad, or start gate. We want to make sure that our logo is serving a function for that event. We also put a lot of emphasis on making sure that for TV production the branding works for the different camera angles. So when we look at events, we never do it for the mass market; we do it for the scene.

We want to make sure we have a solid relationship within a scene before developing an event concept. Whereas you look at other companies who want to reach the younger audience (12–24-year olds), they want to associate themselves with established events – that is the X Games and Gravity Games. You will see Right Guard, Target, etc. signing up and sponsoring those events, which is a great way to reach that market. However, we at Red Bull would rather start from the bottom up and build our relationship, resulting in having these events bubble up, and therefore own the event concept from start to finish. We do not want to associate ourselves with an established event, because we want to make sure that we control the content, the athletes, the media, and the TV production of the whole event, so that our brand is properly displayed throughout this event. To accomplish this, it is a three-step process: (1) identifying the right athletes and the right scenes, (2) developing those relationships, and (3) then activating those relationships to get to the major events that we sponsored around the country.

The main focus always remains the sport – either giving it a little twist or revolutionizing the scene. If you look at surfing, we have developed an Ice Break concept in the Northeast, to bring surfing to the cold waters of the Atlantic. All events are for the athletes, and they come from the athletes. We at no time try to force an event concept on athletes – we want it to come from them so that it is credible for our brand, and it reflects our brand. You will never see Red Bull sponsor football, baseball, or hockey because those are sports where it is team oriented, and we do not want to force our product on a team because we do not know if 30 athletes are going to like Red Bull. There may be one athlete on the team who likes Red Bull, but we cannot confirm that 30 athletes like Red Bull on a team. So we will not be sponsoring hockey, football, or baseball tournaments. We would like to focus on more individualistic sports, where it is one athlete we know likes the product, or multiple athletes that we know like the product, and like the fact that we are helping them to develop their sport or activity – that is BASE Jumping, Skiing, and Surfing.

So that is how Red Bull develops events. Basically we want to make sure we have the credibility within the scene before we move forward, because the worst thing we could do for our brand is to associate ourselves with a scene where we do not have credibility. If we walked into the surfing scene and we did not know any surfers, and surfers did not like Red Bull, and we tried to impose our brand on them, we would lose instant credibility within that scene. So that is the key to marketing our brand. It starts at the grassroots level, and we let the events bubble up through the scene instead of forcing events on the scene.

Note: In April 2006, Marc was hired as the General Manager of Red Bull New York of Major League Soccer (MLS).

APPENDIX:
AND NOW A FINAL
WORD ...

Nigel Jamieson, Principal Lecturer

*Centre for Recreation, Sport and Tourism at TAFE-SA North
Adelaide, South Australia, Australia*

Nigel Jamieson is currently the Principal Lecturer at the Centre for Recreation, Sport and Tourism at TAFESA North in Adelaide, South Australia and he has been a Visiting Professor at Daniel Webster College, New Hampshire, USA. He has held management positions in Rugby Union, Lacrosse, Australian Rules Football, and the YMCA in Australia and has been involved in organizing and marketing National Championships (both open and age) and a range of events and activities associated with recreation, sport, and tourism. Nigel also has been a Professional Event Organizer for a major regional center in South Australia, and has owned, operated and marketed a fitness training program, fitness organizations and served on numerous advisory boards.

He has had consultancies in recreation sport and fitness – Pheidippides Fitness (reflecting his early Bachelor of Arts in Classical Studies and History), in the Zone Sport Management (conducting sport for Primary Schools in his home state as a District Convener for the South Australian Primary School Sports Association), an event management company (Movers and Shakers which organized the SA National Aerobic Championships for 10 years), and extensive employee fitness programs, including the Adelaide Corporate Challenge which is lunchtime sport for office workers that is approaching its twentieth year of operation. In addition to this he is the President of the South Australian Chapter of the Australian Society of Sports Administrators and he has written seven books on Event Management for the Paris based Le Cordon Bleu.

You may pay lip service or false homage to the "ethical Gods," but in reality the need for ethics in sport marketing is real and powerful. In a sports world bombarded with messages, both sublime and "in your face," the need for believable, honest, and ethical marketing has never been so acute. We are an increasingly cynical and disbelieving public and rightly so with some of the less than scrupulous "operators" continuing to make outrageous claims and raising the levels of bad taste in our industry. As an industry, we also have some of the most media savvy and discerning public to market our products and services to those who can very easily see through false and dishonest marketing messages. All of these factors combine to make the need for ethics in sport marketing acute and critical in our current times.

Ethics, I believe refers to the principles and concepts of right and wrong in terms of personal and professional conduct and decisions. I have adopted my own "creed" or code of ethics and try to act in a manner that is without reproach and continue to be a "beacon" to other administrators and players that I am associated with. I believe that this is essential to my continued success in the industry over a long period of time. I also do not believe that this should be isolated only to my professional career as I continue to teach right and wrong in all aspects of my life.

I would like to suggest that everyone involved in the administration and marketing of sport should adopt a code of ethics for competition, (players, spectators, and officials) and for business practices to enable the sport, organization, or competition to be beyond reproach. Do not exhibit any bias or prejudice toward player selection and treat everyone as truly equal, officials included! Do not allow false or unethical marketing claims to emanate from your organization or sport and be true to yourself and your sport at all times.

One of the most powerful forces in sport, and indeed society as a whole, is the peer group pressure of following the "pack" and facing continual temptation to use business practices and marketing that may be less than ethical. My one piece of advice for people in the management and marketing of sport is to hold onto your good values even in the face of criticism and peer group pressure to follow the next person or organization – stand up and show your moral fiber! Act responsibly and without fear of retribution – do not blame others or shirk from your responsibilities as an administrator and "bastion" of your game – if you do not, who will? And remember in order to be considered ethical, an action must be voluntary, without fear of compromising those values you hold dear – stand up and be counted! Live your life and your sport in the most ethical manner.

Everyone is responsible for ethical behavior – it is not optional and fair play is the respect all constituents of your sport or organization must display – no one is exempt from this responsibility and make sure you impress that on your organization all the time. My strong belief is that if prospective employees do not hold ethical behavior in such high esteem as I do, then perhaps they are the wrong people to employ. I cannot instill ethical behavior in them; it must be innate and is one of the first things I look for in prospective employees. They must "walk the talk" and I value this quality highly in my current employees and I simply do not tolerate any unethical marketing practices.

What can we do as in sport to help raise ethical marketing standards?

I believe we must be united in our condemnation of the behavior that we currently see in sport marketing and general business practices that does not do our cause any good. Bring pressure to bear on those who have a role in terms of funding and "control" of the sports that have transgressed, and exercise some disdain and condemnation of those who have transgressed and do not make excuses for them. My other piece of advice is to be beyond reproach in your sport and act as a model for others in sport and society.

We are facing many challenges in sport marketing at the moment. Those challenges include restrictive privacy laws, marketing "clutter," and the get rich quick "characters" that still surface from time to time. This attracts unwanted criticisms from those who have rightly stepped up to the plate and given us a "hammering" (to borrow from the sporting vernacular). Please weather the current storm and show respect, fairness, justice, and responsibility and be caring, trustworthy, and ethical! It is the least we can do for our sport, our organization, and our employees!

Keep the faith! It will be more than worth it in the long run!

BIBLIOGRAPHY

CHAPTER 1: INTRODUCTION TO SPORT MARKETING

Branch, D. (2002). Sport marketing quarterly: A journal designed for the business of marketing sport. *Sport Marketing Quarterly* 11(2): 80–83.

Cunningham, G. B. and H. Kwon (2003). The theory of planned behaviour and intentions to attend a sport event. *Sport Management Review* 6(2): 127–145.

Desensi, J. T., D. R. Kelley, M. D. Blanton, and P. A. Beitel (1990). Sport management curricular evaluation and needs assessment: A multifaceted approach. *Journal of Sport Management* 4(1): 31–58.

Ferrell, O. C. and G. Hirt (2003). *Business: A Changing World*, 4th ed. New York: McGraw-Hill.

Horch, H.-D. and N. Schutte (2003). Competencies of sport managers in German sport clubs and sport federations. *Managing Leisure* 8(2): 70–84.

Kotlar, P. and G. Armstrong (2006). *Principles of Marketing*, 11th ed. Upper Saddle River, NJ: Prentice Hall.

Meenaghan, T. and P. O'Sullivan (1999). Playpower – sports meets marketing. *European Journal of Marketing* 33(3–4): 241–249.

Parks, J. B., J. Quarterman, and L. Thibault (2007). *Contemporary Sport Management*, 3rd ed. Champaign, IL: Human Kinetics.

Pitts, B. G. (2002). Teaching sport marketing: Notes from the trenches. *Sport Marketing Quarterly* 11(4): 255–260.

Pitts, B. G., L. W. Fielding, and L. K. Miller (1994). Industry segmentation theory and the sport industry: Developing a sport industry segment model. *Sport Marketing Quarterly* 3(1): 15–24.

Reh, J. F. (2005). Pareto's principle – the 80–20 rule. *Business Credit* 106(7): 76.

Sanders, R. (1987). The Pareto principle: Its use and abuse. *Journal of Consumer Marketing* 4(1): 47–50.

Weiss, A. (2002) *What Is Marketing?* (cited January 22, 2005). Available from http://www.marketingprofs.com/2/whatismarketing.asp.

CHAPTER 2: MANAGING THE SPORT MARKETING MIX

Burton, R. and D. Howard (1999). Professional sports leagues: Marketing mix mayhem. *Marketing Management* 8(1): 36–46.

Kotlar, P. and G. Armstrong (2006). *Principles of Marketing*, 11th ed. Upper Saddle River, NJ: Prentice Hall.

Parks, J. B., J. Quarterman, and L. Thibault (2007). *Contemporary Sport Management*, 3rd ed. Champaign, IL: Human Kinetics.

Ryan, T. J. (2005). Marketing mix. *Sporting Goods Business* 38(12): 22.

Stotlar, D. K. (2005a). Developing a marketing plan framework. In *Developing Successful Sport Marketing Plans*, edited by D. K. Stotlar. Morgantown, WV: Fitness Information Technology.

Stotlar, D. K. (2005b). Marketing mix. In *Developing Successful Sport Marketing Plans*, edited by D. K. Stotlar. Morgantown, WV: Fitness Information Technology.

Westerbeek, H. M. and D. Shilbury (1999). Increasing the focus on "place" in the marketing mix for facility dependent sport services. *Sport Management Review* 2(1): 1–23.

CHAPTER 3: SPORT MARKETING RESEARCH

Achenbaum, A. A. (2001). When good research goes bad. *Marketing Research* 13(4): 13–15.

Achenreiner, G. (2001). Marketing research in the "real" world: Are we teaching students what they need to know? *Marketing Education Review* 11(1): 15–25.

Coderre, F., N. St-Laurent, and A. Mathieu (2004). Comparison of the quality of qualitative data obtained through telephone, postal and email surveys. *International Journal of Market Research* 46(3): 347–357.

Filo, K. and D. C. Funk (2005). Congruence between attractive product features and virtual content delivery for Internet marketing communication. *Sport Marketing Quarterly* 14(2): 112–122.

Henderson, N. R. (2005). Twelve steps to better research. *Marketing Research* 17(2): 36–37.

Ilyashenko, S. M. (2004). The definition of necessary and sufficient information accumulation level to substantiate a choice of enterprise's market opportunities directions development. *Problems and Perspectives in Management* (1): 138–153.

McDaniel, C. D. and R. Gates (2005). *Marketing Research Essentials*, 5th ed. Hoboken, NJ: John Wiley and Sons.

Morgan, M. J. and J. Summers (2004). Sport consumption: Exploring the duality of constructs in experiential research. In *Sharing Best Practices in Sport Marketing: The Sport Marketing Association's Inaugural Book of Papers*, edited by B. G. Pitts. Morgantown, WV: Fitness Information Technology.

Moser, A. (2005). Take steps to avoid misused research pitfalls. *Marketing News* 39(15): 27.

Swaddling, D. C. and C. Miller (2003). Understanding tomorrow's customers. *Marketing Management* 12(5): 31–35.

Taylor, T. (1999). Audience info the key to sports marketers. *Marketing News* 33(2): 10.

Turauskas, L. and Z. Vaitkuniene (2004). Planning and conducting focus group discussions in marketing research. *Problems and Perspectives in Management* (2): 304–308.

Vriens, M. (2003). Strategic research design. *Marketing Research* 15(4): 21–25.

Wyner, G. A. (2004a). Narrowing the gap. *Marketing Research* 16(1): 6–7.

Wyner, G. A. (2004b). The right metrics. *Marketing Research* 16(2): 6–7.

Wyner, G. A. (2005). Research road maps. *Marketing Research* 17(2): 6–7.

Defining Business Objectives (2003). *Journal of Government Financial Management* 52(4): 26.

EPM Entertainment Marketing Sourcebook, 2006 ed. New York: EPM Communications, Inc.

Plunkett's Sports Industry Almanac, 2005 ed. Houston: Plunkett Research, Ltd.

Sports Marketing and the Beverage Industry by the Beverage Marketing Corporation, 2005 ed. New York: Beverage Marketing Corporation.

The 2006 Spectator Sports Industry Report. Barnes Reports. Bath, ME: C. Barnes and Company.

The 2006 Sport Business Market Research Handbook. Loganville, GA: Richard K. Miller and Associates.

The 2006 Sport Business Marketing Research Handbook. Franklin Lakes, NJ: SportBusiness Group Limited.

CHAPTER 4: SPORT MARKETING INFORMATION SYSTEMS

Ashill, N. J. and D. Jobber (1999). The impact of environmental uncertainty perceptions, decision-maker characteristics and work environment characteristics on the perceived usefulness of marketing information systems (MkIS): A conceptual framework. *Journal of Marketing Management* 15(6): 519–540.

Ashill, N. J. and D. Jobber (2001). Defining the needs of senior marketing executives: An exploratory study. *Qualitative Marketing Research: An International Journal* 4(1): 52–61.

Deveney, S. (2005). Its learning how to pan for gold in the data mine below the statistical surface. *Sporting News* 229(34): 28–29.

Evans, M. (2000). Marketing information and research. In *Oxford Textbook of Marketing*, edited by K. Blois (pp. 150–175), Oxford: Oxford University Press.

Garver, M. S. (2002). Using data mining for customer satisfaction research. *Marketing Research* 14(1): 8–12.

Hess, R. L., R. S. Rubin, and L. A. West Jr. (2004). Geographic information systems as a marketing information system technology. *Decision Support Systems* 38(2): 197–212.

Jackson, T. W. (2005). CRM: From "art to science". *Journal of Database Marketing and Customer Strategy* 13(1): 76–92.

Leonidou, L. C. and M. Theodosiou (2004). The export marketing information system: An integration of the extent knowledge. *Journal of World Business* 39(1): 12–36.

Li, E. Y., R. McLeod Jr., and J. C. Rogers (2001). Marketing information systems in Fortune 500 companies: A longitudinal analysis of 1980, 1990, and 2000. *Information and Management* 38(5): 307–322.

Lilien, G. L., A. Rangaswamy, G. H. Van Bruggen, and K. Starke (2004). DSS effectiveness in marketing resource allocation decisions: Reality vs. perception. *Information Systems Research* 15(3): 216–235.

McDaniel, C. D. and R. Gates (2005). *Marketing Research Essentials*, 5th ed. Hoboken, NJ: John Wiley and Sons.

Raab, D. M. (2004). Business intelligence systems for marketers. *DM Review* 14(8): 68–69.

Ryals, L. (2003). Creating profitable customers through the magic of data mining. *Journal of Targeting, Measurement and Analysis for Marketing* 11(4): 343–349.

Shaw, R. (2001). Marketing decision support – a new discipline for dot.coms and dinosaurs. *Journal of Targeting, Measurement and Analysis for Marketing* 10(1): 5–8.

CHAPTER 5: SPORT CONSUMER BEHAVIOR

Armstrong, K. L. (2002). Race and consumption behavior: A preliminary investigation of a black consumers' sport motivation scale. *Journal of Sport Behavior* 25(4): 309–330.

Bennett, G., M. Sagas, and W. Dees (2006). Media preferences of action sports consumers: Differences between Generation X and Y. *Sport Marketing Quarterly* 15(1): 40–49.

Brandish, C. and A. H. Lathrop (2001). Girl power: Examining the female pre-teen and teen as a distinct segment of the sport marketplace. *Sport Marketing Quarterly* 10(1): 19–24.

Debats, D. L. and B. F. Bartelds (2005). *The Structure of Human Values: A Principal Components Analysis of the Rokeach Value Survey (RVS)* (cited October 13, 2005). Available from http://dissertations.ub.rug.nl/FILES/faculties/ppsw/1996/d.l.h.m.debats/c5.pdf.

Eastman, J. K., A. D. Eastman, and K. L. Eastman (2002). Insurance sales agents and the Internet: The relationship between opinion leadership, subjective knowledge, and Internet attitudes. *Journal of Marketing Management* 18(3–4): 259–285.

Erikson, E. (1993). *Childhood and Society*. New York: W. W. Norton and Company.

Funk, D. C. and J. D. James (2004a). Exploring origins of involvement: Understanding the relationship between consumer motives and involvement with professional sport teams. *Leisure Sciences* 26(1): 35–61.

Funk, D. C. and J. D. James (2004b). The fan attitude network (FAN) model: Exploring attitude formation and change among sport consumers. *Sport Management Review* 7(1): 1–26.

Funk, D. C., L. L. Ridinger, and A. M. Moorman (2002). Understanding consumer support: Extending the sport interest inventory (SII) to examine individual differences among women's professional sport consumers. *Sport Management Review* 6(1): 1–32.

Funk, D. C., D. F. Mahony, and M. E. Havitz (2003). Sport consumer behavior: Assessment and direction. *Sport Marketing Quarterly* 12(4): 200–205.

Goldsmith, R. E. and T. S. De Witt (2003). The predictive validity of an opinion leadership scale. *Journal of Marketing Theory and Practice* 11(1): 28–35.

Gray, D. and L. Sharp, *Marketing Segmentation Strategy as Applied to Consumer Subcultures* 2000 (cited March 13, 2005). Available from http://www2.bc.edu/%7Emalec/Abstracts.

Green, B. C. (2001). Leveraging subculture and identity to promote sport events. *Sport Management Review* 4(1): 1–19.

Griffin, C. (2002). Identity check: Today's action sports consumer is the kid next door, and to understand him, just dial into youth culture. *Sporting Goods Business* 35(9): 18.

Hawkins, D. I., R. J. Best, and D. L. Mothersbaugh (2006). *Consumer Behavior: Building Marketing Strategy*, 10th ed. Columbus, OH: McGraw-Hill/Irwin.

Henry, P. C. (2005). Social class, market situation and consumers' metaphors of (dis)empowerment. *Journal of Consumer Research* 31(4): 766–778.

Herek, M. (2002). Living the lifestyle. *Sporting Goods Business* 35(9): 32–33.

James, J. D. and S. D. Ross (2004). Comparing sport consumer motivations across multiple sports. *Sport Marketing Quarterly* 13(1): 17–25.

James, J. D., R. H. Kolbe, and G. T. Trail (2002). Psychological connection to a new sport team: Building or maintaining the consumer base? *Sport Marketing Quarterly* 11(4): 215–225.

Kahle, L. R., D. Aiken, V. Dalakas, and M. Duncan (2003). Men's versus women's collegiate basketball customers: Attitudinal favorableness and the environment. *International Journal of Sports Marketing and Sponsorship* 5(2): 145–159.

Kamakura, W. A. and T. P. Novak (1992). Value-system segmentation: Exploring the meaning of LOV. *Journal of Consumer Research* 19(1): 119–132.

Kwok, S. and M. Uncles (2005). Sales promotion effectiveness: The impact of consumer differences at an ethnic-group level. *Journal of Product and Brand Management* 14(3): 170–186.

Kwon, H. H. and G. T. Trail (2001). Sport fan motivation: A comparison of American students and international students. *Sport Marketing Quarterly* 10(3): 147–155.

Kwon, H. H. and K. L. Armstrong (2002). Factors influencing impulse buying of sport team licensed merchandise. *Sport Marketing Quarterly* 11(3): 151–163.

Kwon, H. H. and K. L. Armstrong (2004). An exploration of the construct of psychological attachment to a sport team among students: A multidimensional approach. *Sport Marketing Quarterly* 13(2): 94–103.

Lam, S. S. K. and J. Schaubroeck (2000). A field experiment testing frontline opinion leaders as change agents. *Journal of Applied Psychology* 85(6): 987–995.

Lou, Y.-C. and S.-F. S. Chen (2002). Order effects on social attitude in an Eastern culture: Implications for cross-cultural consumer research. *Advances in Consumer Research* 29(1): 386.

Marsick, V. J. and K. E. Watkins (2001). Informal and incidental learning. *New Directions for Adult and Continuing Education* 89: 25–34.

Miller, T. (1998). Global segments from "strivers" to "creatives". *Marketing News* 32(5): 11–12.

Painter, G., D. Deutsch, and B. J. Overholt (1998). *Alfred Adler: As We Remember Him*, 2nd ed. Hershey, PA: North American Society of Adlerian Psychology.

Pelletier, L. G., *et al.* (1995). Toward a new measure of intrinsic motivation, extrinsic motivation, and amotivation in sports: The sport motivation scale (SMS). *Journal of Sport and Exercise Psychology* 17: 35–53.

Quick, S. (2000). Contemporary sport consumers: Some implications of linking fan typology with key spectator variables. *Sport Marketing Quarterly* 9(3): 149–156.

Russell, J. T. and W. R. Lane (2001). *Kleppner's Advertising Procedure*, 15th ed. Upper Saddle River, NJ: Pearson Education.

Schiffman, L. and L. L. Kanuk (2003). *Consumer Behavior*, 8th ed. Upper Saddle River, NJ: Prentice Hall.

Schurr, K. T., A. F. Wittig, V. E. Ruble, and A. S. Ellen (1988). Demographic and personality characteristics associated with persistent, occasional, and non-attendance of university male basketball games by college students. *Journal of Sport Behavior* 9(1): 3–17.

Steenkamp, J.-B. E. M. and H. Baumgartner (1992). The role of optimal stimulation level in exploratory consumer behavior. *Journal of Consumer Research* 19(3): 434.

Stewart, B., A. C. T. Smith, and M. Nicholson (2003). Sport consumer typologies: A critical review. *Sport Marketing Quarterly* 12(4): 206–216.

Trail, G. T. and J. D. James (2001). The motivation scale for sport consumption: Assessment of the scale's psychometric properties. *Journal of Sport Behavior* 24(1): 108–127.

Trail, G. T., J. S. Fink, and D. F. Anderson (2003a). Sport spectator consumption behavior. *Sport Marketing Quarterly* 12(1): 8–17.

Trail, G. T., M. J. Robinson, R. J. Dick, and A. J. Gillentine (2003b). Motives and points of attachment: Fans versus spectators in intercollegiate athletics. *Sport Marketing Quarterly* 12(4): 217–227.

Trail, G. T., D. F. Anderson, and J. S. Fink (2005). Consumer satisfaction and identity theory: A model of sport spectator conative loyalty. *Sport Marketing Quarterly* 14(2): 98–111.

Van Ossalaer, S. M. J., C. Janiszewski, D. G. Mick, and F. R. Kardes (2001). Two ways of learning brand association. *Journal of Consumer Research* 28(2): 202–223.

Verma, D. P. S. and S. Kapoor (2003). Dimensions of buying roles in family decision making. *IIMB Management Review* 15(4): 7–14.

Volkov, M., M. J. Morgan, and J. Summers (2005). Consumer complaint behaviour in sport consumption. In *Where Sport Marketing Theory Meets Practice: Selected Papers from the Second Annual Conference of the Sport Marketing Association*, edited by B. G. Pitts. Morgantown, WV: Fitness Information Technology.

Wilson, R. F. (2000). *The Six Simple Principles of Viral Marketing* (cited March 12, 2005). Available from http://www.wilsonweb.com/wmt5/issue70.htm.

Woodall, T. (2004). Why marketers don't market: Rethinking offensive and defensive archetypes. *Journal of Marketing Management* 20(5–6): 559–576.

Wooten, D. B. (1995). One-of-a-kind full house: Some consequences of ethnic and gender distinctiveness. *Journal of Consumer Psychology* 4(3): 205–224.

Zbar, J. D. (2002). Racing sponsors get room to stretch. *Advertising Age* 73(43): 8–9.

CHAPTER 6: SPORT PRODUCT MANAGEMENT

Barnes, R., editor (2005). Looking down the line. *Do-It-Yourself Retailing* 189(2): 28.

Bhonslay, M. (2005). Lift lines: Alpine ski and snowboard gear for 2005/06 ascends the mountain with new technology. *Sporting Goods Business* 38(1): 28–32.

Desbordes, M. (2002). Empirical analysis of the innovation phenomena in the sports equipment industry. *Technology Analysis and Strategic Management* 14(4): 481–498.

Forney, M. (2004). How Nike figured out China. *Time* 164(17): A8.

Gladden, J. M. and D. C. Funk (2002). Developing an understanding of brand associations in team sport: Empirical evidence from consumers of professional sport. *Journal of Sport Management* 16(1): 54–81.

Gladden, J. M. and M. McDonald (1999). Examining the importance of brand equity in professional sport. *Sport Marketing Quarterly* 8(1): 21–29.

Green, B. C. and T. E. Muller (2002). Positioning a youth sport camp: A brand-mapping exercise. *Sport Management Review* 5(2): 179–200.

Griffin, C. (2004). Keeping it real: Technology is bursting at the seams, but authenticity is gaining ground in marketing, as well. *Sporting Goods Business* 37(12): 30.

Holmes, S. and A. Bernstein (2004). The new Nike. *Business Week* (3900): 78–86.

Leand, J. (2004). Dog fights: A pack of small vendors are shaking up the industry in a big way. *Sporting Goods Business* 37(9): 26–27.

Lehmann, D. R. and R. S. Winer (2004). *Product Management*, 4th ed. New York: McGraw-Hill.

McGivney, A. (2003). Our bodies, our gear. *Backpacker* 31(5): 92.

Meenaghan, T. and P. O'Sullivan (1999). Playpower – sports meets marketing. *European Journal of Marketing* 33(3–4): 241–249.

Melville, G. (2005). Gym dandy. *Money* 34(2): 128–132.

Newell, K. (2003). A uniform(ed) decision: Making the right choices for team apparel. *Coach and Athletic Director* 73(3): 46–50.

Persons, D. (2001). Local inventor's brainchild on a roll. *Community College Week* 13(14): 10.

Powell, M. (2001). Technology and sporting goods. *Sporting Goods Business* 34(6): 17.

Richelieu, A. (2004). A new brand world for sports teams. In *Sharing Best Practices in Sport Marketing: The Sport Marketing Association's Inaugural Book of Papers*, edited by B. G. Pitts. Morgantown, WV: Fitness Information Technology.

Tenser, J. (2004). Endorser qualities count more than ever; the lure is strong, but athletes face resistance. *Advertising Age* 75(45): S2.

Thim, J. (2005). Performing plastics. *Chemistry and Industry* (3): 20–21.

Walzer, E. (2004). Getting personal: Product customization lets customers reveal their inner designer while vendors and retailers strengthen their on-line businesses. *Sporting Goods Business* 37(12): 50.

Walzer, E. (2005). Active fusion: The blending of sport and street style leads to subtle, sophisticated designs. *Sporting Goods Business* 38(12): 32–33.

Yiannakis, A. (1991). Training the sport marketer: A social science perspective. *Journal of Sport Behavior* 14(1): 61–68.

CHAPTER 7: SALES MANAGEMENT IN SPORT

Ashworth, A. (2005). Accelerating sales performance for Visa by closing the communications gaps. *Journal of Financial Services Marketing* 9(4): 318–328.

Baldauf, A., D. W. Cravens, and N. F. Puercy (2001). Examining business strategy, sales management, and salesperson antecedents of sales organization effectiveness. *Journal of Personal Selling and Sales Management* 21(2): 109–122.

Bundschuh, R. G. and T. M. Dezvane (2003). How to make after-sales services pay off. *McKinsey Quarterly* (4): 116–127.

Carillo, F. and P. Guliano (2001). Writer's notebook. *Public Relations Quarterly* 46(3): 48.

Clopton, S. W., J. E. Stoddard, and J. W. Clay (2001). Salesperson characteristics affecting consumer complaint responses. *Journal of Consumer Behaviour* 1: 129–139.

Dixon, A. L. and S. M. B. Schertzer (2005). Bouncing back: How salesperson optimism and self-efficacy influence attributions and behaviors following failure. *Journal of Personal Selling and Sales Management* 25(4): 361–369.

Fader, P. S., B. G. S. Hardie, and H. Chun-Yao (2004). A dynamic changepoint model for new product sales forecasting. *Marketing Science* 23(1): 50–65.

Grapentine, T. (2005). Segmenting the sales force. *Marketing Management* 14(1): 29–34.

Grewal, D., M. Levy, and G. W. Marshall (2002). Personal selling in retail settings: How does the Internet and related technologies enable and limit successful selling? Journal of Marketing Management 18(3–4): 301–316.

Howard, D. and J. Crompton (2004). Tactics used by sports organizations in the United States to increase ticket sales. *Managing Leisure* 9(2): 87–95.

James, J. D. and S. D. Ross (2004). Comparing sport consumer motivations across multiple sports. *Sport Marketing Quarterly* 13(1): 17–25.

Johansson, U. (2001). Retail buying: Process, information and IT use: A conceptual framework. *International Review of Retail, Distribution and Consumer Research* 11(4): 329–357.

Johlke, M. C. and D. F. Duhan (2001). Testing competing models of sales force communication. *Journal of Personal Selling and Sales Management* 21(4): 265–277.

Knight, C. (2004). Maximize the buying potential of current customers. *Sell!ng*: 12.

Kwok, S. and M. Uncles (2005). Sales promotion effectiveness: The impact of consumer differences at an ethnic-group level. *Journal of Product and Brand Management* 14(3): 170–186.

Lassk, F. G., G. W. Marshall, D. W. Cravens, and W. C. Moncrief (2001). Salesperson job involvement: A modern perspective and a new scale. *Journal of Personal Selling and Sales Management* 21(4): 291–302.

Locander, W. B. and D. L. Luechauer (2005). Are we there yet? *Marketing Management* 14(6): 50–52.

Luiras, T. E. and J. E. Stanley (2004). Bringing science to sales. *McKinsey Quarterly* (3): 16.

Mangan, K. S. (2003). Perfecting the sales pitch. *Chronicle of Higher Education* 49(24): A30–A31.

Marber, A., P. Wellen, and S. Posluszny (2005). The merging of marketing and sports: A case study. *Marketing Management Journal* 15(1): 162–171.

Matthews, N. (2001). Sport marketing 101. *Marketing Magazine* 106(19): 18–19.

Petersen, T. (2004). Give it your best pitch. *Public Relations Tactics* 11(10): 8.

Randall, E. J. and C. H. Randall (2001). A current review of hiring techniques for sales personnel: The first steps in the sales management process. *Journal of Marketing Theory and Practice* 9(2): 70–83.

Rigsbee, E. R. (2002). The relationship you build with your prospects and customers is more important than the close. *Cost Engineering* 44(2): 40–41.

Rouzies, D., E. Anderson, A. K. Kohli, R. E. Michaels, B. A. Weitz, and A. A. Zoltners (2005). Sales and marketing integration: A proposed framework. *Journal of Personal Selling and Sales Management* 25(2): 113–122.

Schwepker, C. and D. J. Good (2004a). Marketing control and sales force customer orientation. *Journal of Personal Selling and Sales Management* 24(3): 167–179.

Schwepker, C. and D. J. Good (2004b). Sales management practices: The impact of ethics on customer orientation, employment and performance. *Marketing Management Journal* 14(2): 134–147.

Washo, M. (2004). *Break into Sports Through Ticket Sales*. Bedford Park, IL: MMW Marketing.

CHAPTER 8: PURCHASING AND SUPPLY CHAIN MANAGEMENT IN SPORT

Anderson, J. C. and J. A. Narus (2003). Selectively pursuing more of your customer business. *MIT Sloan Management Review* 44(3): 42–49.

Barrand, D. (2005). Sports marketing: When disaster strikes. *Marketing*: 35.

Bhonslay, M. (2004). Looming ahead: With the imminent demise of apparel import quotas, much of the industry is reorienting its sourcing towards China. *Sporting Goods Business* 37(12): 8–9.

Brady, D. (2004). IMG: Show me the bottom line. *Business Week* (3891): 82.

Burke, M. (2004). X-treme economics. *Forbes* 172(15): 42.

Burton, R. (2005). Surf's up: Lessons from Down Under for sports leagues and media partners. *Mediaweek* 15(30): 17.

Carr, R. (2000). A plan to reduce supply chain time. *Sporting Goods Business* 33 (16): 7.

Cassidy, H. (2004). Tom Wilson/Craig Turnbull: Lunch pail set: Nothing but net. *Brandweek* 45(36): 42–45.

Chandra, C. and S. Kumar (2000). Supply chain management in theory and practice: A passing fad or a fundamental change? *Industrial Management and Data Systems* 100(3–4): 100–113.

Chatterjee, S. C., S. Hyvonen, and E. Anderson (1995). Concentrated vs. balanced sourcing: An examination of retailer purchasing decisions in closed markets. *Journal of Retailing* 71(1): 23–46.

Clark, K. (2005). Multiple channels, one chain: Cabela's gets serious with supply chain management. *Chain Store Age* 81(5): 37A.

Elliott, M. (2005). Bar codes are forever. *Industrial Engineer* 37(3): 28–29.

Facanha, C. and A. Horvath (2005). Environmental assessment of logistics outsourcing. *Journal of Management in Engineering* 21(1): 27–37.

Flint, D. J., R. B. Woodruff, and S. F. Gardial (2002). Exploring the phenomenon of customers' desired value change in a business-to-business context. *Journal of Marketing* 66(4): 102–117.

Greenfield, K. T. (2004). Bouncing back: A mogul hopes to revive the prospects for the megafirm of sports marketing. *Sports Illustrated* 101(14): 20.

Holmes, S. (2003). Nike. *Business Week* (3859): 98.

Janoff, B. (2004a). Dilemma of sports marketing; ATP swings deal for deuce. *Brandweek* 45(41): 12.

Janoff, B. (2004b). MLB safe at home with Ameriquest as new partner: Mortgage firm builds sports marketing with teams, All-Star Game. *Brandweek* 45(16): 8.

Janoff, B. (2004c). The world not according to Kobe. *Brandweek* 45(2): 20–23.

Kinsella, B. (2005). Delivering the goods. *Industrial Engineer* 37(3): 24–30.

Kulp, S. C., H. L. Lee, and E. Ofek (2004). Manufacturer benefits from information integration with retail customers. *Management Science* 50(4): 431–444.

Lancioni, R. A., M. F. Smith, and T. A. Oliva (2000). The role of the Internet in supply chain management. *Industrial Marketing Management* 29(1): 45–56.

Linnett, R. (2003a). Fox sports specialty: Product 'immersion'; net inks tie-ins with snapple. *Advertising Age* 74(3): 3.

Linnett, R. (2003b). Upfront: ESPN web property hawked in upfront. *Advertising Age* 74(23): 61.

Lowry, T. (2003). The NFL Machine; behind a thrilling season is a hard-nosed business run with military precision. *Business Week* (3817): 86.

Mason, D. S. (1999). What is the sports product and who buys it? The marketing of professional sports leagues. *European Journal of Marketing* 33(3–4): 402–418.

Mollenkopf, D., A. Gibson, and L. Ozanne (2000). The integration of marketing and logistics functions: An empirical examination of New Zealand firms. *Journal of Business Logistics* 21(2): 89–112.

Moore, P. (1999). Help for special Olympics. *Tech Directions* 59(1): 13.

Morgan, P. (2003). Commonwealth Games public transport wins. *Logistics and Transport Focus* 5(3): 29–35.

Palmer, I. (2004). Adidas steps up to open platform in consolidation project. *Computing Canada* 30(17): 25.

Panayides, P. M. (2002). Economic organization of intermodal transport. *Transport Reviews* 22(4): 401–414.

Schottmiler, P. (2000). Time to exchange: The new sporting goods supply chain. *Sporting Goods Business* 33(5): 14.

Siemieniuch, C. E., F. N. Waddell, and M. A. Sinclair (1999). The role of "partnership" in supply chain management for fast-moving consumer goods: A case study. *International Journal of Logistics* 2(1): 87–101.

Smith, F. O. (2005). RFID, realistically speaking. *Manufacturing Business Technology* 23(10): 2–6.

Sowinski, L. L. (2003). Skating his way to China. *World Trade* 16(11): 44–45.

Speer, J. K. (2002). Reebok International Ltd. *Bobbin* 44(4): 30–31.

Tang, N. K. H., H. Benton, D. Love, P. Albores, P. Ball, J. MacBryde, N. Boughton, and P. Drake (2004). Developing an enterprise simulator to support electronic supply-chain management for B2B electronic business. *Production Planning and Control* 15(6): 572–583.

Thomaselli, R. (2004). Will MLB sell space on player uniforms? With $500M in wings league can "never say never". *Advertising Age* 75(14): 3.

Vaidyanathan, G. (2005). A framework for evaluating third-party logistics. *Communications of the ACM* 48(1): 89–94.

van Phan, K.-Q. (2006). Strategic offshoring from a decomposed COO's perspective: A cross-regional study of four product categories. *Journal of American Academy of Business* 8(2): 59–66.

Wang, G., S. H. Huang, and J. P. Dismukes (2005). Manufacturing supply chain design and evaluation. *International Journal of Advanced Manufacturing Technology* 25(1–2): 93–100.

Yang, B. and N. D. Burns (2003). Implications of postponement for the supply chain. *International Journal of Production Research* 41(9): 2075–2090.

CHAPTER 9: COMMUNICATION MANAGEMENT IN SPORT

Alexandris, K. and C. Kouthouris (2005). Personal incentives for participation in summer children's camps: Investigating their relationships with satisfaction and loyalty. *Managing Leisure* 10(1): 39–53.

Andersson, T., A. Rustad, and H. A. Solberg (2004). Local residents' monetary evaluation of sports events. *Managing Leisure* 9(3): 145–158.

Bakamitsos, G. A. and G. J. Siomkos (2004). Context effects in marketing practice: The case of mood. *Journal of Consumer Behaviour* 3(4): 304–314.

Beaupre, A. (2003). Getting your customers to help with public relations. *Public Relations Tactics* 10(10): 9.

Boivin, C. (2005). Profiting from licensing without royalties. *Marketing Bulletin* 16: 109.

Bristow, D. and K. Schneider (2003). The sports fan motivation scale: Development and testing. *Marketing Management Journal* 13(2): 115–121.

Brown, M. T. and A. Kreutzer (2002). Reducing risk in promotion: The incorporation of risk management principles by sport marketers. *Sport Marketing Quarterly* 11(4): 252–254.

Chelladurai, P. (2006). *Human Resource Management in Sport and Recreation*, 2nd ed. Champaign, IL: Human Kinetics.

End, C. M., J. M. Kretschmar, and B. Dietz-Uhler (2004). College students' perceptions of sports fandom as a social status determinant. *International Sports Journal* 8(1): 114–123.

Eroglu, S. A., K. A. Machleit, and L. M. Davis (2001). An empirical study of online atmospherics and shopper responses. *Advances in Consumer Research* 28(1): 40.

Fink, J. S., G. T. Trail, and D. F. Anderson (2002). Environmental factors associated with spectator attendance and sport consumption behavior: Gender and team differences. *Sport Marketing Quarterly* 11(1): 8–19.

Garrison, B. (1994). *Sports Reporting*, 2nd ed. Ames, IA: Iowa State University Press.

Gaschen, D. J. (2000). Play ball. *Public Relations Tactics* 7(8): 10.

Geary, D. L. (2005). The decline of media credibility and its impact on public relations. *Public Relations Quarterly* 50(3): 8–12.

Geiger, S. and D. Turley (2005). Personal selling as a knowledge-based activity: Communities of practice in the sales force. *Irish Journal of Management* 26(1): 61–70.

Grady, J. (2005). University of Alabama case to test limits of trademark licensing in sport art cases. *Sport Marketing Quarterly* 14(4): 251–252.

Guiniven, J. (2005). Community relations – more than money. *Public Relations Tactics* 12(11): 6.

Hal Dean, D. (2002). Associating the corporation with a charitable event through sponsorship: Measuring the effects on corporate community relations. *Journal of Advertising* 31(4): 77–87.

Hardin, R. and S. Mcclung (2002). Collegiate sports information: A profile of the profession. *Public Relations Quarterly* 47(2): 35–39.

Hoffman, K. D. and L. W. Turley (2002). Atmospherics, service encounters, and consumer decision making: An integrative perspective. *Journal of Marketing Theory and Practice* 10(3): 33–47.

Hogue, J. (2000). How I spent my summer vacation: An intern's foray into sports marketing. *Public Relations Tactics* 7(9): 20.

Holt, R. (2000). The discourse ethics in sports print journalism. *Culture, Sport, Society* 3(3): 88–103.

Hopwood, M. (2005). Sports public relations: The strategic application of public relations to the business of sport. In *Where Sport Marketing Theory Meets Practice: Selected Papers from the Second Annual Conference of the Sport Marketing Association*, edited by B. G. Pitts. Morgantown, WV: Fitness Information Technology.

Hopwood, M. K. (2005). Applying the public relations function to the business of sport. *International Journal of Sports Marketing and Sponsorship* 6(3): 174–188.

Keller, K. L. (2001). Mastering the marketing communications mix: Micro and macro perspectives on integrated marketing communications. *Journal of Marketing Management* 17(7–8): 819–848.

Kurtzman, J. and J. Zauhar (2005). Sports tourism consumer motivation. *Journal of Sports Tourism* 10(1): 21–31.

Kwok, S. and M. Uncles (2005). Sales promotion effectiveness: The impact of consumer differences at an ethnic-group level. *Journal of Product and Brand Management* 14(3): 170–186.

Kwon, H. H. and K. L. Armstrong (2002). Factors influencing impulse buying of sport team licensed merchandise. *Sport Marketing Quarterly* 11(3): 151–163.

Lam, S. Y., M. Vandenbosch, J. Hulland, and M. Pearce (2001). Evaluating promotions in shopping environments: Decomposing sales response into attraction, conversion, and spending effects. *Marketing Science* 20(2): 194–215.

Lesser, J. (2001). The sports gods must be greedy. *Public Relations Tactics* 8(2): 14.

MacDonald, M. A., G. R. Milne, and J. Hong (2002). Motivational factors for evaluating sport spectator and participant markets. *Sport Marketing Quarterly* 11(2): 100–113.

Milotic, D. (2003). The impact of fragrance on consumer choice. *Journal of Consumer Behaviour* 3(2): 179–191.

Neeley, S. (2005). Influences on consumer socialisation. *Young Consumers* 6(2): 63–69.

Samsup Jo, B. (2003). The portrayal of public relations in the news media. *Mass Communication and Society* 6(4): 397–411.

Schuler, M. (2004). Management of the organizational image: A method for organizational image configuration. *Corporate Reputation Review* 7(1): 37–53.

Smith, J. M. and A. G. Ingham (2003). On the waterfront: Retrospectives on the relationship between sport and communities. *Sociology of Sport Journal* 20(3): 252–274.

Stoldt, G. C. (2006). *Sport Public Relations: Managing Organizational Communication.* Champaign, IL: Human Kinetics.

Stoldt, G. C., L. K. Miller, and P. G. Comfort (2001). Through the eyes of athletics directors: Perceptions of sports information directors, and other public relations issues. *Sport Marketing Quarterly* 10(3): 164–172.

Ward, S., K. Bridges, and B. Chitty (2005). Do incentives matter? An examination of on-line privacy concerns and willingness to provide personal and financial information. *Journal of Marketing Communications* 11(1): 21–40.

50 years of PR passion: 20 tips for success (2004). *Public Relations Tactics* 11(4): 21–29.

CHAPTER 10: SPORT ADVERTISING

Amato-McCoy, D. M. (2002). Pigskin passion! *Beverage Aisle* 11(9): 60–63.

Arens, W. F. (2005). *Contemporary Advertising*, 10th ed. New York: McGraw-Hill.

Bauer, H., N. E. Sauer, and S. Exler (2005). The loyalty of German soccer fans: Does a team's brand image matter? *International Journal of Sports Marketing and Sponsorship* 7(1): 14–22.

Bhattacharjee, S. and G. Rao (2006). Tackling ambush marketing: The need for regulation and analysing the present legislative and contractual efforts. *Sport in Society* 9(1): 128–149.

Chadwick, S. (2005). Sport marketing: A discipline for the mainstream. *International Journal of Sports Marketing and Sponsorship* 7(1): 7.

Charbonneau, J. and R. Garland (2005). Talent, looks or brains? New Zealand advertising practitioners' views on celebrity and athlete endorsers. *Marketing Bulletin* 16: 1–10.

Clancy, K. J. and L. Kelly (2001). Stemming the slide: A lesson from the Red Sox. *Brandweek* 42(14): 17.

Cohn, E. (1999). Marketwatch. *The American Prospect* 11(1): 22.

Cousens, L., K. Babiak, and T. Slack (2000). Adopting a relationship marketing paradigm: The case of the National Basketball Association. *International Journal of Sports Marketing and Sponsorship* 2(4): 331–355.

Coyle, P. (1999). NFL team scores big with DM game plan. *Direct Marketing* 62(3): 20–27.

d'Astous, A. and K. Chnaoui (2002). Consumer perception of sports apparel: The role of brand name, store name, price, and intended usage situation. *International Journal of Sports Marketing and Sponsorship* 4(2): 109–126.

Evans, D. M. and A. C. T. Smith (2004). Internet sports marketing and competitive advantage for professional sports clubs: Bridging the gap between theory and practice. *International Journal of Sports Marketing and Sponsorship* 6(2): 86–98.

Friedman, W. (2000). Brand in trouble: Hockey comeback tied to engaging its core audience. *Advertising Age* (71): 40.

Gladden, J. M. and D. C. Funk (2001). Understanding brand loyalty in professional sport: Examining the link between brand associations and brand loyalty. *International Journal of Sports Marketing and Sponsorship* 3(1): 67–94.

Grebert, C. and F. Farrelly (2005). Interview with Carl Grebert, Brand Director Nike Asia Pacific. *International Journal of Sports Marketing and Sponsorship* 7(1): 10–13.

Green, B. C. (2002). Marketing the host city: Analyzing exposure generated by a sport event. *International Journal of Sports Marketing and Sponsorship* 4(4): 335–353.

Gwinner, K. P. and J. Eaton (1999). Building brand image through event sponsorship: The role of image transfer. *Journal of Advertising* 28(4): 47–57.

Howard, D. and R. Burton (2002). Sports marketing in a recession: It's a brand new game. *International Journal of Sports Marketing and Sponsorship* 4(1): 23–40.

Hruby, P. (2001). That's entertainment. *Insight on the News* 17(17): 28.

Hyman, M. (2005). Branding the course; it doesn't come cheap, but golf tournament sponsorship earns valuable exposure. *Business Week* (3935): 96.

James, J. D. and L. L. Ridinger (2002). Female and male sport fans: A comparison of sport consumption motives. *Journal of Sport Behavior* 25(3): 260–279.

Janoff, B. (2005). ESPN brands X games goods; ING NYC Marathon sets pace. *Brandweek* 46(25): 12.

Jowdy, E. and M. McDonald (2002). Relationship marketing and interactive fan festivals: The Women's United Soccer Association's "Soccer Sensation". *International Journal of Sports Marketing and Sponsorship* 4(4): 295–311.

Lachowetz, T. and J. Gladden (2002). A framework for understanding cause-related sport marketing programs. *International Journal of Sports Marketing and Sponsorship* 4(4): 313–333.

Lefton, T. (1998). Prove it! *Brandweek* 39(27): 30.

Lorenz, T. and D. Campbell (2003). Brands treading over new ground: The demand for "sports lifestyle" products is booming. *Design Week* 18(24): 9.

Papadimitriou, D., A. Apostolopoulou, and I. Loukas (2004). The role of perceived fit in fans' evaluation of sports brand extensions. *International Journal of Sports Marketing and Sponsorship* 6(1): 31–48.

Pritchard, M. P. and C. M. Negro (2001). Sport loyalty programs and their impact of fan relationships. *International Journal of Sports Marketing and Sponsorship* 3(3): 317–338.

Richelieu, A. (2004). A new brand world for sports teams. In *Sharing Best Practices in Sport Marketing: The Sport Marketing Association's Inaugural Book of Papers*, edited by B. G. Pitts. Morgantown, WV: Fitness Information Technology.

Shannon, E. (2003). Tight skivvies: They're what everyone's wearing this season. Here's why. *Time* 161(2): A1.

Smolianov, P. and D. Shilbury (2005). Examining integrated advertising and sponsorship in corporate marketing through televised sport. *Sport Marketing Quarterly* 14(4): 239–250.

Stevens, J. A., A. H. Lathrop, and C. L. Brandish (2003). "Who is your hero?" Implications for athlete endorsement strategies. *Sport Marketing Quarterly* 12(2): 103–110.

Stone, G., M. Joseph, and M. Jones (2003). An exploratory study on the use of sports celebrities in advertising: A content analysis. *Sport Marketing Quarterly* 12(2): 94–102.

Thomaselli, R. (2004). Guarascio mixes up the NFL plays; marketing QB's mandate: "Deliver value to business partners" of football league. *Advertising Age* 75(45): S2.

Thomaselli, R. (2005). Ambushing the Super Bowl. *Advertising Age* 76(26): 3, 57.

Vakratsas, D., F. M. Feinberg, F. M. Bass, and G. Kalyanaram (2004). The shape of advertising response functions revisited: A model of dynamic probabilistic thresholds. *Marketing Science* 23(1): 109–119.

Yoon, S.-J. and Y.-G. Choi (2005). Determinant of successful sports advertisements: The effects of advertisement type, product type and sports model. *Journal of Brand Management* 12(3): 191–205.

Zid, L. A.-S. (2005). A class act. *Marketing Management* 14(1): 6.

CHAPTER 11: SPORT SPONSORSHIP

Amis, J. and T. B. Cornwell (2005). *Global Sport Sponsorship*. Oxford: Berg Publishers.

Becker, O. K. (2003). Questioning the name games: An event study analysis of stadium naming rights sponsorship announcements. *International Journal of Sports Marketing and Sponsorship* 5(3): 181–192.

Bradish, C. L., J. A. Stephens, and A. H. Lathrop (2003). National versus regional sports marketing: An interpretation of "think globally, act locally". *International Journal of Sports Marketing and Sponsorship* 5(3): 209–225.

Burton, R., P. G. Quester, and F. J. Farrelly (1998). Organizational power games. *Marketing Management* 7(1): 26–36.

Cassidy, H. (2005). So you want to be an Olympic sponsor? *Brandweek* 46(40): 24–28.

Chadwick, S. (2002). The nature of commitment in sport sponsorship relations. *International Journal of Sports Marketing and Sponsorship* 4(3): 257–274.

Chadwick, S. and D. Thwaites (2004). Advances in the management of sports sponsorship: Fact or fiction? Evidence from English professional soccer. *Journal of General Management* 30(1): 39–59.

Clark, J., T. Lachowetz, R. L. Irwin, and K. Schimmel (2003). Business-to-business relationships and sport: Using sponsorship as a critical sales event. *International Journal of Sports Marketing and Sponsorship* 5(2): 129–144.

Cornwell, T. B., G. E. Relyea, R. L. Irwin, and I. Maignan (2000). Understanding long-term effects of sports sponsorship: Role of experience, involvement, enthusiasm and clutter. *International Journal of Sports Marketing and Sponsorship* 2(2): 127–143.

Crompton, J. L. (2004). Conceptualization and alternate operationalizations of the measurement of sponsorship effectiveness in sport. *Leisure Studies* 23(3): 267–281.

Dalakas, V. and G. M. Rose (2004). The impact of fan identification on consumer response to sponsorships. In *Sharing Best Practices in Sport Marketing: The Sport Marketing Association's Inaugural Book of Papers*, edited by B. G. Pitts. Morgantown, WV: Fitness Information Technology.

De Bruin, W. (2002). Mega-bucks for sport sponsorships. *Finance Week*: 58.

Doonar, J. (2004). Sponsorship is more than just a logo. *Brand Strategy* (185): 46–49.

Fahy, J., F. Farrelly, and P. Quester (2004). Competitive advantage through sponsorship: A conceptual model and research propositions. *European Journal of Marketing* 38(8): 1013–1030.

Gladden, J. M. and R. Wolfe (2001). Sponsorship of intercollegiate athletics: The importance of image matching. *International Journal of Sports Marketing and Sponsorship* 3(1): 41–65.

Goodman, C. (2006). Brands must make most of sponsorship chances. *New Media Age* 111(7): 7.

Grohs, R., U. Wagner, and S. Wsetecka (2004). Assessing the effectiveness of sport sponsorships – an empirical examination. *Schmanlenbach Business Review* 56(2): 119–138.

Hughes, S. and M. Shank (2005). Defining scandal in sports: Media and corporate sponsor perspectives. *Sport Marketing Quarterly* 14(4): 207–216.

Irwin, R. L. and M. K. Asimakopoulos (1992). An approach to the evaluation and selection of sport sponsorship proposals. *Sport Marketing Quarterly* 1(2): 43–51.

Irwin, R. L., T. Lachowetz, T. B. Cornwell, and J. S. Clark (2003). Cause-related sport sponsorship: An assessment of spectator beliefs, attitudes, and behavioral intentions. *Sport Marketing Quarterly* 12(3): 131–139.

James, D. (2002). Athlete or competition? How to choose. *Marketing News* 36 (15): 4.

Lough, N. L. and R. L. Irwin (2001). A comparative analysis of sponsorship objectives for US women's sport and traditional sport sponsorship. *Sport Marketing Quarterly* 10(4): 202–211.

McCawley, I. (2006). FIFA vows to stop unofficial World Cup sponsorship. *Marketing Week* 29(5): 15.

McCook, K., D. Turco, and R. Riley (1997). A look at the corporate decision making process. *Cyber Journal of Sport Marketing* 1(2). Retrieved March 14, 2007, from http://www.ausport.gov.au/fulltext/1997/cjsm/v1n2/mcook.htm.

Mcgeer, B. (2003). Deciding when sponsorship can benefit a brand. *American Banker* 168(81): 8–9.

McKelvey, S. M. (2004). The growth in marketing alliances between US professional sport and legalised gambling entities: Are we putting sport consumers at risk? *Sport Management Review* 7(2): 193–210.

McKelvey, S. M. (2005). "Vice" sponsorships raise brand issues. *Brandweek* 46(7): 18.

Moler, C. (2000). Wanted: Not-for profit to take money ... marketing through sponsorship. *Parks and Recreation* 35(9): 164–166, 169–172.

Parry, T. (2005a). Crowded field. *Promo* 18(9): 25–26.

Parry, T. (2005b). What's in a name? *Promo* 18(4): 23–24.

Pritchard, B. (1998). *Sponsorship Made Simple*. Burra Creek: Sally Milner Publishing.

Pruitt, S. W., T. B. Cornwell, and J. M. Clark (2004). The NASCAR phenomenon: Auto racing sponsorships and shareholder wealth. *Journal of Advertising Research* 44(3): 281–296.

Richards, C. (1998). *Structuring Effective Sponsorships*. Sydney: LBC Information Services.

Slattery, J. and B. G. Pitts (2002). Corporate sponsorship and season ticket holder attendees: An evaluation of changes in recall over the course of one American collegiate football season. *International Journal of Sports Marketing and Sponsorship* 4(2): 151–174.

Stotlar, D. K. (2005). *Developing Successful Sport Sponsorship Plans*, 2nd ed. Morgantown, WV: Fitness information Technology.

Stuart, A. N. (2006). This is not a game. *CFO* 22(1): 54–58.

Verity, J. (2002). Maximising the marketing potential of sponsorship for global brands. *European Business Journal* 14(4): 161–173.

Willins, M. (2002). Maximize your exposure. *Aftermarket Business* 112(3): 41–43.

Sponsorship growth slows (2004). *Finance Week*: 53.

Berman, B. and J. Evans (2007). *Retail Management: A Strategic Approach*, 10th ed. Boston, MA: Pearson-Prentice Hall.

Burns, D. J. (1999). Ethics in retail buying and retail sales: Relationships between perceptions and gender of future retail personnel. *Journal of Marketing Management* 9(3): 124–136.

Cassill, N. L. (1998). Do customer returns enhance product and shopping experience satisfaction? *International Review of Retail* 8(1): 1–13.

Chiang, W. K., D. Chhajed, and J. D. Hess (2003). Direct marketing, indirect profits: A strategic analysis of dual-channel supply-chain design. *Management Science* 49(1): 1–20.

Friend, L. and S. Thompson (2003). Identity, ethnicity, and gender: Using narratives to understand their meaning in retail shopping encounters. *Consumption, Markets and Culture* 6(1): 23–41.

Grewal, D., M. Levy, A. Mehrotra, and A. Sharma (1999). Planning merchandising decisions to account for regional and product assortment differences. *Journal of Retailing* 75(3): 405–424.

Hansotia, B. J. and B. Rukstales (2002). Direct marketing for multichannel retailers: Issues, challenges and solutions. *Journal of Database Management* 9(3): 259–266.

Irwin, R. L., D. Zwick, and W. A. Sutton (1999). Assessing organizational attributes contributing to marketing excellence in American professional sport franchises. *Journal of Consumer Marketing* 16(6): 603–615.

Lam, S. L., M. Vandenbosch, J. Hulland, and M. Pearce (2001). Evaluating promotions in shopping environments: Decomposing sales response into attraction, conversion, and spending effects. *Marketing Science* 20(2): 194–215.

Merrilees, B. and M.-L. Fry (2002). Corporate branding: A framework for e-retailers. *Corporate Reputation Review* 5(2–3): 213–225.

National Sporting Goods Association (2002). NSGA's new sports equipment and footwear indices show where "best" customers live. *NSGA Retail Focus* 55(3): 19.

Neilsen, A. C. (2005). *In the News – January 2005*. (cited April 10, 2005). Available from http://www.acnielsen.ca/Insights/IntheNews/January2005.htm.

Newholm, T., P. McGoldrick, K. Keeling, L. Macaulay, and J. Doherty (2004). Multi-story trust and online retailer strategies. *International Review of Retail* 14(4): 437–456.

Reynolds, K. E. and S. E. Beatty (1999). Customer benefits and company consequences of customer–salesperson relationships in retailing. *Journal of Retailing* 75(1): 1–2.

Smolianov, P. and D. Shilbury (2005). Examining integrated advertising and sponsorship in corporate marketing through televised sport. *Sport Marketing Quarterly* 14(4): 239–250.

Sparks, M., S. Chadwick, G. Schafmeister, H. Woratschek, T. Hurley, and F. Junya (2005). Sport marketing around the world. *Sport Marketing Quarterly* 14(3): 197–199.

Steenhaut, S. and P. Van Kenhove (2005). Relationship commitment and ethical consumer behavior in a retail setting: The case of receiving too much change at the checkout. *Journal of Business Ethics* 56(4): 335–353.

Vinod, B. (2005). Retail revenue management and the new paradigm of merchandise optimisation. *Journal of Revenue and Pricing Management* 3(4): 358–368.

Young, S. (2000). Putting the pieces together at the point of sale. *Marketing Research* 12(3): 32–36.

Neilsen Business Media Retail top 100: The most successful companies continue to stress efficient operations, carefully planned store openings, and a clear point of differentiation (2002). *Sporting Goods Business* 35(6): 23.

CHAPTER 13: SPORT E-BUSINESS AND E-COMMERCE

Bart, Y., V. Shankar, F. Sultan, and G. L. Urban (2005). Are the drivers and role of online trust the same for all web sites and consumers? A large-scale exploratory empirical study. *Journal of Marketing* 69(4): 133–152.

Brandish, C. (2001). Electronic commerce. *Sport Marketing Quarterly* 10(2): 114.

Cavusgil, S. T. (2002). Extending the reach of e-business. *Marketing Management* 11(2): 24–29.

Farrelly, F., P. Quester, and S. A. Greyser (2005). Defending the co-branding benefits of sponsorship B2B partnerships: The case of ambush marketing. *Journal of Advertising Research* 45(3): 339–348.

Fay, S. (2004). Partial-repeat bidding in the name-your-own-price channel. *Marketing Science* 23(3): 407–418.

Filo, K. and D. C. Funk (2005). Congruence between attractive product features and virtual content delivery for Internet marketing communication. *Sport Marketing Quarterly* 14(2): 112–122.

Gerrard, B. (2000). Media ownership of pro sports teams: Who are the winners and losers? *International Journal of Sports Marketing and Sponsorship* 2(3): 199–218.

Hunt, E. C. and S. B. Sproat (2003). Blasting off into e-business. *Nursing* 33(12): 74–76.

Kegeng, X., T. Wilkinson, and L. E. Brouthers (2002). The dark side of international e-commerce: Logistics. *Marketing Management Journal* 12(2): 123–134.

Margolis, N. (2005). Why is B2B so far ahead of B2C in the digital marketing arena? *Precision Marketing* 17(29): 14–15.

Owens, J. D. (2006). Electronic business: A business model can make the difference. *Management Services* 50(1): 24–28.

Perrott, B. (2005). Towards a manager's model for e-business strategy decisions. *Journal of General Management* 30(4): 73–89.

Rayport, J. F. and B. J. Jaworski (2003). *Introduction to E-Commerce*, 2nd ed. New York: McGraw-Hill.

Robbins, S. (2005). In e-business, the value of every transaction increases. *Information Systems Management* 22(3): 85–86.

Rohm, A. J. and F. Sultan (2004). The evolution of e-business. *Marketing Management* 13(1): 32–37.

Sharma, A. and J. N. Sheth (2004). Web-based marketing: The coming revolution in marketing thought and strategy. *Journal of Business Research* 57(7): 696–702.

Stork, K. (2000). It pays to be different. *Purchasing* 128(3): 38.

Stotlar, D. K. (2000). Vertical integration in sport. *Journal of Sport Management* 14(1): 1–7.

Strader, T. J. and S. N. Ramaswami (2002). The value of seller trustworthiness in C2C online markets. *Communications of the ACM* 45(12): 45–49.

Tobias, H. (2002). Using e-business strategy to gain advantage. *Journal of Database Management* 9(2): 132–136.

CHAPTER 14: INTERNATIONAL AND GLOBAL MARKETING IN SPORT

Bafour, F. (2003). It's time for a new playbook. *Business Week* (3849): 56.

Bairner, A. (2003). Globalization and sport: The nation strikes back. *Phi Kappa Phi Forum* 83(4): 34–37.

Boyd, T. C. and M. D. Shank (2004). Athletes as product endorsers: The effect of gender and product relatedness. *Sport Marketing Quarterly* 13(2): 82–93.

Bradish, C. L., J. A. Stevens, and A. H. Lathrop (2003). National versus regional sports marketing: An interpretation of "think globally, act locally". *International Journal of Sports Marketing and Sponsorship* 5(3): 209–225.

Brake, M. (1985). *Comparative Youth Subcultures: The Sociology of Youth Culture and Youth Subcultures in America*. London: Routledge.

Burton, R. (2000). SMQ profile/interview. *Sport Marketing Quarterly* 9(1): 5.

Cateora, P. R. and J. L. Graham (2006). *International Marketing*, 13th ed. New York: McGraw-Hill.

Curran-Kelly, C. (2005). Stranger in a strange land: Using international student experiences to teach adaptation in global marketing. *Marketing Education Review* 15(2): 55–58.

Dyson, A. and D. Turco (1998). The state of celebrity endorsement in sport. *Cyber Journal of Sport Marketing* 2(1). Retrieved March 14, 2007, from www.ausport.gov.au/fulltext/1998/cjsm/v2n1/dyson.html

Graham, J. (2002). Where now for global sponsorship? *Sports Marketing* (78): 6.

Graves, B. (2003). In extreme sports, hardware and apparel are two sides of the same coin. *San Diego Business Journal* 36(3): 24–28.

Hewett, K. and W. O. Bearden (2001). Dependence, trust, and relational behavior on the part of foreign subsidiary marketing operations: Implications for managing global marketing operations. *Journal of Marketing* 65(4): 51–66.

Huang, X. and E. Van de Vliert (2004). A multilevel approach to investigating cross-national differences in negotiation processes. *International Negotiation* 9(3): 471–484.

Kates, S. M. (2002). The protean quality of subcultural consumption: An ethnographic account of gay consumers. *Journal of Consumer Research* 29: 383–399.

Marber, A., P. Wellen, and S. Posluszny (2005). The merging of marketing and sports: A case study. *Marketing Management Journal* 15(1): 162–171.

Mayrhofer, U. (2004). International market entry: Does the home country affect entry-mode decisions? *Journal of International Marketing* 12(4): 71–96.

McAuley, A. (2004). Seeking (marketing) virtue in globalisation. *Marketing Review* 4(3): 253–266.

Miller, T., G. Lawrence, J. McKay, and D. Rome (1999). Playing the world. *Peace Review* 11(4): 495–498.

Orejan, J. (2005). Understanding and adapting to cultural diversity in international sport marketing. In *Where Sport Marketing Theory Meets Practice: Selected Papers from the Second Annual Conference of the Sport Marketing Association*, edited by B. G. Pitts. Morgantown, WV: Fitness Information Technology.

Parry, C. and C. Jouan (2003). Mum doesn't always know best. *Marketing Week (UK)* 26(39): 32–33.

Quelch, J. A. (2002). Does globalization have staying power? *Marketing Management* 11(2): 18–23.

Rovner, M. (2000). Brands need to keep their promises if they're to win the loyalty of US kids. *Kids Marketing Report* 1(25): 18.

Schouten, J. and J. H. McAlexander (1995). Subcultures of consumption: An ethnography of the new bikers. *Journal of Consumer Research* 22(1): 43–61.

Siddall, J. (2002). A sporting chance. *Lawyer* 16(41): 31.

Styles, C. and L. Hersch. (2005). Executive insights: Relationship formation in international joint ventures. *Journal of International Marketing* 13(3): 105–134.

Thornton, S. (1995). *Cultures: Music, Media, and Subcultural Capital*. Cambridge, UK: Polity.

Till, B. D. and T. A. Shimp (1998). Endorsers in advertising: The case of negative celebrity information. *Journal of Advertising* 27(1): 67–82.

Trompenaars, F. and P. Woolliams (2004). *Marketing Across Cultures*. Hoboken, NJ: John Wiley and Sons.

Wallace, T. (2002). Reaching global extremes? Are broadcasters' claims for X games' worldwide appeal justified? *SportBusiness International* (72): 9.

Wenner, L. A. (1998). *Media Sport*. New York: Routledge.

Westerbeek, H. and A. Smith (2003). *Sport Business in the Global Marketplace*. New York: Palgrave Macmillan.

Yu, L. (2003). The global-brand advantage. *MIT Sloan Management Review* 44(3): 13.

CHAPTER 15: ENTERPRISE SPORT MARKETING MANAGEMENT

Brake, M. (1985). *Comparative Youth Cultures: The Sociology of Youth Culture and Youth Subcultures in America*. London: Routledge.

Callaghan, D. (2003). CRM game plan. *eWeek* 20(47): 31.

Cantelon, H. and S. Murray (1993). Globalization and sport, structure and agency: The need for greater clarity. *Society and Leisure* 16(2): 275–291.

Cohen, A. and R. Prazmark (1999). Future speak. *Sales and Marketing Management* 151(8): 20.

Crosby, L. A. and S. L. Johnson (2005). Managing. *Marketing Management* 14(1): 11–12.

Douglas, S. P., C. S. Craig, and E. J. Nijssen (2001). Integrating branding strategy across markets: Building international brand architecture. *Journal of International Marketing* 9(2): 97–114.

Dowling, G. R. (2004). *The Art and Science of Marketing: Marketing for Marketing Managers*. Oxford, UK: Oxford University Press.

Graves, B. (2003). In extreme sports, hardware and apparel are two sides of the same coin. *San Diego Business Journal* 36(3): 24–28.

Hayden, T. (2004). Empowering sports fans with technology. *Computer* 37(9): 106–107.

Hoover, A. and G. Bennett (2003). *From Balls to Boards: Teens Increasingly Choosing "Action" Sports* (cited October 16, 2003). Available from http://www.napa.ufl.edu/2003news/extremesports.htm.

Jones, N. (2005). Rankings demonstrate the power of event marketing. *Event*: 8–10.

Jowdy, E. and M. McDonald (2002). Relationship marketing and interactive fan festivals: The Women's United Soccer Association's "Soccer Sensation". *International Journal of Sports Marketing and Sponsorship* 4(4): 295–311.

Kates, S. M. (2002). The protean quality of subcultural consumption: An ethnographic account of gay consumers. *Journal of Consumer Research* 29(3): 383–399.

Kincaid, J. (2002). *Customer Relationship Management: Getting It Right!* Upper Saddle River, NJ: Pearson Education.

Kiska, J. (2002). Customer experience management. *CMA Management* 76(7): 28–30.

Moore, R. (2002). Games grow with their young fans. *Advertising Age* 73(43): 2–3.

Neuborne, E. (2004). Play ball. *Sales and Marketing Management* 156(1): 21.

Olins, W. (1989). *Corporate Identity*. London: Thames and Hudson.

Parr, R. (2002). The changing face of sports marketing. *Sport Marketing* (78): 16.

Parry, C. (2003). Mum doesn't always know best. *Marketing Week* 26(32): 32–33.

Peralta, S. (2001). Dogtown and Z-Boys. USA: Sony Picture Classics.

Rovner, M. (2000). Brands need to keep their promises if they're to win the loyalty of US kids. *Kids Marketing Report* 1(25): 18.

Sanchez, R. (2004). Conceptual analysis of brand architecture and relationships within product categories. *Journal of Brand Management* 11(3): 233–247.

Schmitt, B. H. (2003). Customer experience management: A revolutionary approach to connecting with your customers. Hoboken, NJ: John Wiley and Sons.

Schouten, J. W. and J. H. McAlexander (1995). Subcultures of consumption: An ethnography of the new bikers. *Journal of Consumer Research* 22(1): 43–61.

Stewart-Allen, A. L. (2000). Building a successful brand experience: Lessons of the Dome. *Marketing News* 34(16): 7.

Sutton, D., T. Klein, and S. Zyman (2003). *Enterprise Marketing Management: The New Science of Marketing*. Hoboken, NJ: John Wiley and Sons.

Thornton, S. (1995). *Club Cultures: Music, Media, and Subcultural Capital*. Cambridge, UK: Polity.

Waddell, R. (1994). Interactive sports fan festivals growing in size, popularity. *Amusement Business* 106(51): 59–60.

Waltner, C. (2000). CRM: The new game in town for professional sports. *InformationWeek* (801): 112–114.

Weinberger, J. (2004). Customers for life. *CRM Magazine* 8(7): 32–38.

GLOSSARY

Accounting Information System: See internal reports.

Adaptation: The ability to make change or modification.

Advanced Ticket Sales: Tickets that are purchased by customers before the day of the event.

Advertisements: Paid public announcements about a product or service through the print, broadcast, or electronic media that are designed to attract public attention and subsequent purchase.

Advertising: Involves paid, non-personal communications about a sport product or service through the print, broadcast, or electronic media that are designed to attract public attention and subsequent purchase.

Advertising Campaigns: A series of advertisement messages with a single mission and theme that are promoted through a variety of media options during a specified time frame.

Advertising Strategy: The formulation of an advertising message that communicates the brand's value proposition, its primary benefit, or how it can solve the consumer's problem.

Affect Referral Decision Rule: Sport consumers make a sport product choice based on previously established overall ratings of the sport product. These ratings are directly affected by brand awareness, advertisement, salesperson influence, emotions, feelings, and moods.

Affective: The attitudes, feelings, and emotions directed toward a sport activity.

Aftermarketing: A visionary sales process that encourages salespersons to communicate and service the sport ticket holders after the purchase is completed.

Aggregate Marketing Factors: The indicators of the appeal of the sport product or service in the specific segment or category.

Alternative Dispute Resolution: The collection of methods (negotiation, mediation, arbitration) utilized to hear disagreements and determine an appropriate ruling about a situation.

Ambush Marketing: It is the attempt by a third party to create a direct or indirect association of a sport event or its participants without their approval, hence denying official sponsors, suppliers, and partners parts of the commercial value derived from the "official" designation.

Amotivation: Where there is no motivational influence intrinsically or extrinsically.

Analysis of Variance: A difference analysis statistical method that assesses whether the means of more than two groups are statistically different than each other.

Analytical Skills: Proficiency in utilizing logical and critical thinking to understand the needs, wants, and desires of the sport consumer.

Anonymity: Assures the respondent that they will not be identified in conjunction with the data collected or the study.

ANOVA: Abbreviation for analysis of variance.

Antiquity: The period of history from 3000 BC until the fall of the Roman Empire around 476 (this is the period prior to the Middle Ages).

Arbitration: The process of two parties agreeing to give an independent third party the power to make a decision based on the facts of the dispute.

Arbitrator: An independent third party who oversees a hearing to determine the facts of a dispute and is authorized and given the power by all parties involved to make a decision that is final and binding.

Associative Statistics: Used to evaluate whether two specific variables within a study are related.

Athlete Endorsement: A type of athlete sponsorship where the athlete is describing their personal association with the product or service.

Athlete Sponsorship: Where a corporation seeks to become affiliated with an athlete to secure the rights to market their association and reap the benefits of that association.

Atmospherics: The design of visual communications in an environment, such as lighting, colors, music, to entice the sport consumer's perceptual and emotional responses to purchase the sport product or service.

Attitude: The state of mind or behavioral predisposition that is consistently favorable or unfavorable with respect to a product or situation.

Awareness: The measurement of the percent of the target market that knows about the organization's products and/or services, including customer recall as related to brand recognition, brand features, or brand positioning.

Backorders: An unfilled customer order in demand, immediate, or past due, against an item whose current stock level is insufficient to satisfy demand.

Bait Advertising: It states that the company shall not offer products or services for sale unless such offer constitutes a bona fide effort to sell the advertising products or services and is not a device to switch consumers to other goods or services, usually higher priced.

Balanced Scorecards: Where the companies establish their most important financial goals as well as goals throughout the company and uses supply chain metrics to identify achievements.

Balanced Sourcing: A retailer which balances its purchases between two or more suppliers.

Bandwidth: The amount of information that can be passed through a communication channel at one time.

Behavioral: The actions or reactions directly related to the internal and external stimuli sport provides.

Behavioral Incentives: Inducements that are made to consumers to entice them to purchase a product or service based on a perceptual relationship created between the consumer and the product or service.

Benefit Selling: The creation of new opportunities, conditions, or perks that will counteract the objections a potential customer may have about a product or service, and offers additional value to the consumer.

Brand: A name, term, design, symbol, or feature that identifies one sport product or service as being different from another. The mixture of attributes can be tangible or intangible, are usually symbolized in a trademark, and if managed properly, creates value and influence.

Brand Loyalty: A consumer's preference to buy a particular brand in a product category.

Branded Branding Structure: It emphasizes multiple product-level brands.

Broadcast Sponsorship: Where a corporation purchases an association with specific sport programming either via the radio or television.

Brokering Sites: A website that acts as an intermediary between one sport business wanting a product or service, and another business seeking to provide such a product.

B2B: Business-to-business.

B2C: Business-to-customer.

Business: Individuals or organizations that seek to make a profit by providing products and services that satisfy the needs, wants, and desires of the consumer.

Business-to-Business: Refers to the transactions, collaborations, and business interactions that occur between two organizations.

Business-to-Consumer: Focuses on the transactions between businesses and consumers.

Buying Process: The steps involved in making a decision to make a purchase – including identifying the need, searching for products or services that satisfied the need, evaluating options, making a decision, purchasing the product or service, and eventually reevaluating the decision to determine whether to make the same purchase again or to change.

Case Studies: These are published accounts of situations that have occurred to a business or industry, allowing the sport marketer get a first-hand view of a similar situation and see how another organization is dealt with the circumstances.

Category Attractiveness Analysis: Involves developing a general understanding of the market segment category the sport organization chooses to operate in, and whether the continued investment in that segment will yield an appropriate return.

Causal Research: The collection and analysis of information utilizing experimentation and simulations to determine the cause-and-effect relationship between the sport organization and the problem at hand; it is extremely complex because there is no certainty that the results are not being influenced by other variables.

Center of Gravity Approach: The law of the country that has the most significant relationship to a given situation has jurisdiction.

Chi-Square: An associative statistical method also known as a "goodness of fit" test; it seeks to take the obtained frequencies from the sample and compare them to the statistical hypothesis.

Classical Antiquity: The period of history that started during the 7th century BC, during the time of growth in Europe, the Middle East, and North Africa, starting with the poetry of Homer, running through the rise of Christianity, and ending at the fall of the Roman Empire.

Classical Conditioning: The process of using an existing relationship between a stimulus and response to bring about the learning of the same response to a different stimulus.

Click Streams: The tracking of the sequence of pages visited by a customer after the initial interaction.

Closed-Ended Questions: When the sport marketing researcher provides specific options of answers for the respondent.

Cluster Sampling: A probability sampling method where the population is divided into groups, any of which could be considered as a representative sample.

Cognitive: The process of acquiring knowledge about an activity.

Cognitive Abilities: The perceptual and intellectual capabilities of individuals including comprehension, judgment, learning, memory, and reasoning.

Collective Mark: A word, phrase, symbol, or design, or a combination of words, phrases, symbols, or designs, which identify and distinguish members of a cooperative, association, or group.

Commerce: An organization's ability to sell products and services using their website, including the collecting of items in a "shopping cart," and payments through secure websites.

Commitment: The process by which an individual is emotionally or intellectually bound to a course of action.

Communication Management: The planning, implementing, supervising, evaluation, and modification of the various methods of communication internal and external to a sport organization.

Communication Skills: The set of abilities that allows an individual to convey information that can be received and understood by another individual.

Community: The ability to interact with other users including email, chat rooms, and discussion boards.

Community Relations: The process of the sport organization interacting and connecting with the target population within a specific area.

Comparisons in Advertising: It states that the company shall refrain from making false, misleading, or unsubstantiated statements or claims about a competitor or his/her products or services.

Compensatory Decision Rule: How a consumer evaluates each sport product in terms of each important attribute, and then chooses the sport product or brand with the highest overall rating.

Competition Sourcing: Where suppliers study the nature of the activity, then determine the best performance for the given activity without input from customers – including elimination of an activity, modification of a product or service for greater efficiency, or outsourcing to another department, division, or company.

Competitive Set: The process of determining the direct competitors to a sport organization in the specific product or service area.

Competitor-Oriented Pricing: It is a result of researching what their competitors are charging, and react accordingly. You might decide to charge the same, to undercut, or to present your service as better in some way, so that you can charge more.

Computer-Assisted Telephone Interviews (CATI): Where survey questions pop up on a computer screen, the interviewer reads the question to the respondent, the respondent gives the answer, and the interviewer enters the answer into the computer.

Computer Networks: The system of data processing points that is interconnected to communicate data between and through the network, most often with the endpoint being a computer.

Concentrated Sport Marketing: Focusing on one specific group of sport consumers; also known as niche marketing.

Concentrated Strategy: A single-segment strategy where one market segment is served with one marketing mix, often is the strategy of choice for smaller companies with limited resources.

Confidentiality: Where the researcher knows the individual respondents, but the name of the respondent will not be divulged, or information related to the study not attached to the individual, without the expressed consent of the respondent.

Conjunctive Decision Rule: The sport consumer establishing a minimally acceptable grade for each attribute evaluated. For each sport product that falls below the established grade on any attribute, that sport product is eliminated from purchase consideration.

Connection: The ability for websites to link to other websites.

C2B: Consumer-to-business.

C2C: Consumer-to-consumer.

Consumer: An individual or organization that purchases or obtains goods and services for direct use or ownership.

Consumer-Based Integration: The involvement of the buyers and users of product and service as an integral part of the promotional process.

Consumer-to-Business: Where the consumer initiates the transaction process by soliciting organizations to compete for the individual's business.

Consumer-to-Consumer: Involves transactions between customers.

Content: The actual text, pictures, graphics, audio, and video found on a website that provides information to the user.

Context: The functionality and esthetically pleasing look of a website, including the ease of navigation, and the use of appropriate graphics, colors, and design features.

Convenience Sampling: A non-probability sampling method where the sport marketing researcher goes to a high-traffic area such as a mall or shopping center to survey potential respondents.

Conversion Rates: The measurements utilized to calculate how many viewers of a web page actually do what the organization wants.

Coordinated Integration: How all operational aspects of the organization work together to promote the products, services, and/or the organization itself.

Copyright: A type of intellectual property that provides protection by the laws of the United States (Title 17, US Code) to the authors of "original works of authorship," including literary, dramatic, musical, artistic, and certain other intellectual works.

Correlation Coefficient: See Pearson product moment correlation.

Cost-Oriented Pricing: It is a result of researching the costs, and then assesses prices, bearing in mind what percentage of profit the corporation desires.

Cost Management: The consideration of competitive manufacturing and logistics costs by optimizing the amount of stored materials, keeping capacities filled, achieving economical purchasing prices, and ensuring efficient transport and storage processes.

Creative Brief: A document designed to inspire copy writers by channeling their creative efforts toward a solution that will serve the interest of the client, and represents an informal pact between client and advertising agency that represents agreement on what an advertising campaign is intended to accomplish.

Crisis Communication: A contingency plan that is based on existing communication resources and operational capabilities, and allows sport marketing professionals to effectively respond to a crisis related to the sport organization.

Cross-Business Integration: Where the organization must coordinate with the information technologies of suppliers, sport consumers, and web-based marketplaces.

Cross-Impact Analysis: An analysis examining the relationships between outcomes.

Cross-Sectional Studies: Studies that measure factors from a sample within a population at a specific point in time.

Cross-Tabulations: An associative statistical method that involves basic tabular comparisons using raw data, frequencies, or percentages.

Culture: The principal attitudes, behaviors, values, beliefs, and customs that typify the functioning of a society.

Customary Pricing: When the sport retailer sets prices for goods and services and seeks to maintain them for an extended period.

Customer Service: The behaviors exhibited by salespersons during their interaction with customers, including the general assistance provided before and after the sale.

Customization: The ability for a website to adapt and modify itself based on the wants, needs, and desires of the user.

Database Management: The process of developing an organized collection of demographic, geographic, and other personal data (usually through a computerized program), and uses that information to maximize sales efforts.

Data Mining: The process of collecting and analyzing data from non-traditional perspectives, categorize the data, and summarize relationships.

Decline Stage: The final stage of the sport product and service life cycle; the point when a sport product or service becomes obsolete.

Delivery: The concept of producing or achieving what is desired or expected by the consumer.

Demand-Oriented Pricing: It is a result of researching what the market will bear. This means the corporation could charge more for a service which is seen as being value added or elite.

Demographics: The categories of traits that characterize a group of people. The generic categories that most sport marketing professional look at are age, gender, household size, annual income, and geographic location. In sport marketing, especially with the expansion of global influences, these concepts are expanded beyond the traditional concepts to include culture, subculture, cross-culture, and social setting.

Descriptive Research: The collection and analysis of information that describes the "who, what, when, where, and how" of a potential problem; the information is very factual and accurate, but does not take into account the cause of the situation.

Descriptive Statistics: Uses basic data reduction and summarization (mean, median, mode, frequency distribution, range, and standard deviation) to describe the respondents, the sample, and the population.

Dichotomous: A method used in closed-ended questions where the respondent is required to answer from a choice of two responses, such as yes or no or (a) or (b).

Difference Analysis: A method utilized when there are variations that exist between targeted groups – uses *t*-tests and ANOVA's for statistical measurement.

Differentiated Sport Marketing: Focuses on two or more different sport consumer groups with divergent retailing approaches for each group.

Differentiated Strategy: A selective specialization or multiple-segment strategy where different marketing mixes are offered to different segments.

Differentiation: The concept of being creating and demonstrating distinct and specialized characteristics of sport products and services as compared to those of its competitors. The concept of being distinct and specialized.

Direct Costs: These costs are defined as those which can be associated directly with the product or service.

Direct Promotional Strategy: The actual process of identifying customers, connecting with them, increasing their awareness and interest in the product or service being offered, and persuading them to make a purchase.

Direct Sport Marketing: A variety of sport retailing in which the sport consumer is first exposed to a sport product through a non-personal medium such as a catalog, television commercial or infomercial, then orders the sport product by mail, phone, fax, or Internet.

Diversification: Spreading out business activities and investments.

Domestic: Sport marketing efforts focused internally (one country).

Downward Integration: The movement of information throughout the entire organization using information technologies.

DSS: Decision support system.

E-Business: An all-encompassing term that covers the internal information technology processes of an organization including human resources, finance, inventory management, product development, and risk management.

E-Commerce: The external information technology processes of an organization including the marketing and sales functions.

E-Procurement: Where the purchasing function is often outsourced to a third party.

Ego: The balancing part of the mind between primitiveness and morality, which includes internal and external consciousness, individual character differences, and the relationship between emotions and actions.

Ekecheiria: Roughly translated means "Olympic Truce."

Elasticity of Demand: The sensitivity sport consumers have to pricing changes and the relationship to the quantity of sport product they will buy.

Endorsed Branding Structure: A corporate name used in association with a subsidiary or sport product brand.

Endorsements: The use of high profile individuals such as athletes, actors, and prominent businesspersons to use their notoriety or position to assist an organization in promoting or selling their products or services, with the result being an increase image because of the association.

Escalator Concept: Utilized to represent the movement of consumers to higher levels of involvement with a specified product.

Ethical Behavior: Attitudes focused on what is "good" or "right."

Ethical Management: It is a comprehensive program that continuously improves thinking and behavior patterns not just some high visibility issues and ethics policies.

Ethics: The philosophical study of moral values and rules.

Event Sponsorship: Creating an association between a corporation and a sport event.

Evoked Set: The sport product the sport consumer gives their greatest consideration to.

Exclusivity: The guarantee that the products or services of the sponsoring organization will be the only type in that category to have an association with the sport organization.

Experience Surveys: Refers to collecting information from those whom are considered to be experts in the field of interest as a result of being a part of direct network, through recommendations of members of the direct network, or from research conducted about the area related to the research questions or objectives.

Experimentation: The process by which an independent variable is controlled and manipulated in order to determine the change effect on a dependent variable.

Exploratory Research: The collection and analysis of information when there is little or no information about an opportunity or threat; it is the most difficult method of research because it is impossible to create a plan of action in advance, instead working with impressions and assumptions based on personal experience or expertise.

External Organizational Image: Involves the perceptions of individuals from outside an organization regarding their view of that organization.

Extrinsic Motivation: Involves rewards or incentives used by an individual to bring about desired behavior in another person.

Facility Sponsorship: Naming rights agreements for stadiums, arenas, and other sport facilities.

Factual Knowledge: Information that can be easily researched through secondary resources.

Fixed Costs: These costs are defined as those which are the same whatever the usage.

Focus Groups: An interview that involve 8–12 people at the same time in the same group, and is used to evaluate products and services, or to test new concepts.

Formal Scanning: A systematic search for information where there is a specific goal for the intelligence gathering; involves a narrow scope, but is less rigorous than a full marketing research effort.

Frequency Distribution: The number of times a value occurs during the study.

Full Market Coverage: Where an organization attempts to serve the entire market by means of either a mass market strategy or a differentiated strategy.

Functional Integration: How the design or operations of the product, service, and/or organization can be utilized to effectively promote it.

Global: A comprehensive term that refers to worldwide involvement. For this text, it will specifically refer to sport marketing efforts that involves more than 10 countries and usually a minimum of three continents.

Global Sport Marketing: Sport organizations that take the international distribution of products and services to more of a worldwide level by grouping countries into marketing units based on similar economics, political environments, legal structures, or cultural compositions, and developing sport marketing strategies and plans for each unit.

Global Sport Marketing Strategy: The strategy that views the world as one big market and seeks to define and target similarities between various cultures around the world, with the eventual goal being to create a diversified marketing strategy that will allow the sport organization to compete in any market in the world.

Goodness of Fit Test: See chi-square.

Grouping of Contacts Approach: The law of the country that is most concerned with the outcome of the case has jurisdiction.

Growth Stage: The third stage of the sport product and service life cycle; the point in the cycle when the company with the best product, price, and/or service rises to the top, and maximizes sales and profit.

Guarantees and Warranties in Advertising: It states that when the company guarantees and warranties a product it shall be explicit, with sufficient information to apprise consumers of their principal terms and limitations or, when space or time restrictions preclude such disclosures, the advertisement should clearly reveal where the full text of the guarantee or warranty can be examined before purchase.

Guerilla Marketing: The use of promotional-based marketing techniques using a low budget.

High-Analytical Decision Makers: Individuals who break down problems into smaller parts, resulting in a set of causal relationships, and then the decision variables are manipulated to address those relationships with the goal of reaching decisions that will provide optimal success for the sport organization.

Hits: The number of times an individual goes to a web page.

Horizontal Integration: The internal processes needed to bring sport products and services to market through an e-business structure.

Hyperlinks: Text or graphics placed on a web page to provide cross-referenced materials for the user.

Hypothesis Testing: The articulated expectation of the sport organization, the sport marketer, or the sport marketing researcher.

Id: The primary process of the unconscious mind that focuses on gratification (such as instant gratification and release) and primitive instinctual urges (such as sexuality and aggression).

Ideal Self: Who the consumer wants to be.

Image Integration: The relationship of the opinion of consumers and the sport product, service, and/or organization affects how it is promoted.

Impression: The receipt of third-party exposure through the media to create an association between the product or service being promoted and the reader (print or Internet), listener (radio and TV), or viewer (TV or live).

Incentives: The benefits or reduced costs that are offered to motivate a sport consumer to purchase the specified sport product or service.

Indirect Promotional Strategy: All the methods an individual or organization can create, convey, and place messages in the mind of the prospective customer.

Individualization: The customization of products and services as a function of personalized communications between the consumer and the company.

Inept Set: The sport product that the sport consumer excludes from purchase consideration.

Inert Set: The sport product that sport consumer is indifferent toward because they are perceived to have no significant advantage.

Inferential Statistics: Used to generalize the results and draw conclusions simply based on the population characteristics and the data collected.

Infomediaries: A website that publishes trade and industry standards about an industry for those who operate in that industry.

Informal Scanning: Involves a limited, unstructured effort in collecting data for a specific goal; usually involves making inquiries to individuals on an impromptu basis.

Infrequent Foreign Sport Marketing: Sport organizations that dabble in foreign markets as a result of a surplus of products or a temporary increase in demand.

Integrated Brand Promotion: The use of multiple promotional tools in a coordinated manner to build and maintain overall awareness, identify, and preference for sport products, services, and the associated brands.

Intellectual Property: A protection that is granted by law to an individual or business providing them with the exclusive rights to something they have created.

Interactivity: The ability for consumers to have additional two-way communication with companies and marketers.

Intermodal: The using of containers or sending freight via containers that are easily transferred from ship to rail car to truck as needed, without repacking.

Internal Audit: The sport marketing professional must conduct an appraisal of the internal operations and systems of the sport organization to observe and evaluate their efficiency and effectiveness in quality delivery of products and services, appropriate risk management practices, and financial control.

Internal Development: The first stage of the sport product and service life cycle; involves an idea of a new product or service or a new twist to an existing product or service.

Internal Marketing: Involves the perceptions of individuals from inside an organization and how they view that organization.

Internal Reports: The accounting information system for a sport organization, including asset and liability management, revenue and expense operations, and administration of owner's equity.

Internal Reports System: A component of the sport marketing information system that involves information that is generated by the internal operations of the sport organization.

International: Refers to those efforts that extend beyond national boundaries and involve two or more nations. For this text, it will specifically refer to sport marketing efforts that involves at least two countries to a maximum of 10, with the countries being within one or two continents.

International Sport Marketing: Sport organizations that actively engage in marketing in various markets by developing a multi-domestic sport market orientation and creating an individual sport marketing strategy and program for each country.

International Sport Marketing Strategy: The strategy that focuses on cross-cultural differences and that each individual culture requires a separate sport marketing strategy adapted to the individual cultures.

Internet: The worldwide system of publicly accessible computer networks that transmit data by a process called packet switching to standardized Internet Protocol (IP) addresses.

Internet Protocol Addresses: The unique identifiers of a computer.

Interpretive Knowledge: The meaning of facts within a society.

Interviews: Person-administered surveys where the interviewer reads the questions to respondents either in-person or by the telephone, and then records the answers.

Intrinsic Motivation: The desire to satisfy natural needs and interests, knowledge, accomplishment, and experiences.

Introduction to Market: The second stage of the sport product and service life cycle; the point at which a sport organization puts their product or service into action and starts to capture market share.

Inventory Turns: The number of times a company's inventory cycles turns over per year.

Involvement: A close connection with something.

IP: Abbreviation for Internet Protocol.

Judgment Sampling: A non-probability sampling method used when the sport marketing researcher uses either their own opinion or that of someone considered to be an expert, to determine who will be a part of the sample.

Just-in-Time Manufacturing: The concept of receiving timely and accurate supply chain information which allows the company to make or ship only as much of a product as there is a market for.

Key Performance Indicators: Those factors that influence the effectiveness of products and processes.

KISS (keep it simple, stupid) Approach: A method incorporating simple rules within the marketing strategy to allow for easy reactions to changes in the environment.

Knowledge Management: The methods utilized to create, gather, classify, modify, and apply knowledge about consumer values and beliefs to achieve goals and objectives.

Knowledge Skills: The ability to gather, organize, and share information.

KPI: Key performance indicators.

Lateral Integration: The movement of information between an organization and the consumer or business partners.

Law of the Forum: See Lex Fori Theory.

Lex Fori Theory: The law of the court in which a situation is brought to has jurisdiction.

Licensing: The creation of a strategic alliance in which the manufacturer of a sport product gives permission to a second party to manufacture that product in return for specific royalties or payments.

Life Cycle: The attitudes, values, and beliefs of individual sport consumers change as they transition through life.

Lifestyle Inventory: A system of measurement used in sport marketing research that centers on the measurement of psychographic data by taking into account the values and personality traits of people as reflected in their unique activities, interests, and opinions toward their work, leisure time, and purchases.

Local Broadcasting Contracts: Agreements that cover events of and game played by the individual sport organization; are usually for multiple years, and may include such additional broadcasts as pre-game and post-game shows.

Logistics: The coordinating of the receipt of orders from customers, develop a network of warehouses, pick carriers to get products to customers, and set up an invoicing system to receive payments.

Long-Term Value Analysis: A method for evaluating what that sport consumer is worth to the sport organization in terms of sales and profit over a period of time; usually refers to a minimum of 3 years, but can be as long as a lifetime.

Longitudinal Studies: Studies that measure factors from a sample within a population repeatedly over a period of time.

Low-Analytical Decision Makers: Individuals who look at a problem as an absolute, and seek feasible solutions to the entire problem based only on past experiences and previously solved problems.

Main Conversion: Enticing the consumer to take action such as making a purchase or contacting the organization for more information.

Marginal Cost: The total cost that is incurred based on the quantity produced.

Marginal Value: The worth to the sport organization of producing one more unit of the product in comparison to other products.

Market Potential: The process of estimating the maximum possible sales of a sport product or service so that a sport organization gains valuable knowledge about the amount of sport product or service to make available.

Market Share: The proportion of a market that you supply.

Market Specialization: Where an organization specializes in serving a particular market segment, and offers that segment an array of different products.

Market Tracking Studies: Studies that measure one or more variables over a period of time using data available from other research studies.

Marketing: The functions involved in the transfer of goods and services from the producer to the consumer. The focal point of these functions is in three specific areas known as the 3 C's of marketing analysis: the consumer, the company itself, and the competition.

Marketing Concept: A consumer-oriented philosophy that suggests that satisfaction of consumer needs provide the focus for product development and marketing strategy to enable the firm to meet its own organizational goals.

Marketing Construct: The item which is to be examined or measured.

Marketing Logistics: The management of the relationship between the marketing and logistical concepts, in order to unify their respective strategies within the context of the wider supply chain.

Marketing Relativism: This principle focuses on the realization that the sport marketing efforts are usually based on strategies, values, and beliefs formulated from experiences and knowledge.

Mass Market Strategy: Where a single undifferentiated marketing mix is offered to the entire market.

Mass Sport Marketing: When goods and services are available for sale to an extensive group of sport consumers.

Maturity: The fourth stage of the sport product and service life cycle; refers to the time at which the sport product or service has maximized profits and is seeking to maintain a stable place in the market.

Mean: The average value of a set of numbers (sum of all responses/number of respondents).

Media Relations: The activities that involve working directly with individuals responsible for the production of mass media including news, features, public service announcements, and sponsored programming.

Median: The middle value of a distribution (50th percentile).

Mediation: The process of bringing an independent person into a negotiation to hear both sides and assist the two parties to reach a mutually agreeable solution.

Mediator: The independent neutral third party brought into hear both sides of a dispute. They have no legal standing to make a decision on behalf of the facts.

Merger: The union of two or more separately owned business entities.

Metrics: The indicators that marketing professionals utilize to evaluate an organization's impact on the environment, and their level of progress and success.

Microconversions: The tracking the specific behavior a marketer would like the consumer to do to become more involved with the product or service being offered.

MIS: Marketing information system.

Mission: Developing appropriate goals and objectives to operate under based on an understanding of the philosophy of the sport organization (its values and beliefs).

Mode: The value occurring most frequently in the data.

Modified Likert Scale: A system of measurement utilized in sport marketing research in which respondents are asked to indicate their degree of agreement or disagreement on a symmetric agree–disagree scale for each of a series of statements – the most common form is the 5-point scale.

Monolithic Branding Structure: Refers to a corporation that uses one name and identity worldwide.

Motivation: Influence that initiates the drive to satisfy wants and needs.

Motive: An emotion or psychological need that acts to stimulate an action.

Multinational Sport Marketing Strategy: See International Sport Marketing Strategy.

Multiple Category: A method used in closed-ended questions where there are more than two response options.

Mystery Shopping: See secret shopping.

National Broadcasting Contracts: Agreements with a series of local radio or television networks to broadcast the games of leagues; usually multiple year deals, and broadcasting dollars are split evenly across all teams within a league.

Negotiations: The process utilized by two parties to resolve disputes or to complete transactions.

New Economy: The use of information, communication, and digital technologies for manufacturing, selling, and distributing products and services.

Niche: A special area of demand for a product or service.

No Direct Foreign Sport Marketing: Sport organizations that are not involved in marketing efforts outside their own country.

Non-compensatory Decision Rule: The positive evaluation of an attribute of a sport product does not counteract a negative evaluation of another attribute belonging to the same product.

Non-probability Sampling: A sampling category when there is no way to guarantee the representation in the sample.

Official Sponsor: Refers to the sport organization's public acknowledgment of the association between the sponsor and the organization.

Offshoring: The transference of manufacturing, customer service centers, and other labor-intensive work to other nations.

Online Communication: The ongoing dialog between users and the website including customer service requests, email notifications of specials and opportunities, and instant messaging.

Online Offering: The products, services, or information to be placed on the Internet and World Wide Web.

Open-Ended Questions: When the sport marketing researcher provides no answer options.

Operant Conditioning: Sometimes also called instrumental conditioning, this is where no automatic stimulus–response relationship is involved, so the sport consumer must first be induced to engage in the desired behavior and then this behavior must be reinforced.

Operational Definition: How a construct will be measured; usually is in a question format that will be used in a specific measuring tool.

Opinion Leadership: The process by which the sport marketer, or the opinion leader, informally influences the consumption actions or attitudes of sport consumers.

Order-to-Payment Cycle: The focal point of the internal records system; includes all of the activities associated with the completion of a business transaction.

Organizational Image: The combination of how the internal organization believes others view the organization, and the beliefs and perceptions the external organization actually has of the organization.

Organizational Skills: Expertise in planning and managing the sport product and service information in an efficient and effective manner.

Overheads: These are costs that a business incurs so that production is continued. Overheads can be cut if limits to production are made, or if production is halted completely, although some overheads are incurred whether there is production or not.

Packet Switching: The method of moving data through computer networks in the most efficient and effective manner possible by splitting the data up into smaller units, each labeled with the destination address, sent individually, and reassembled at the destination.

Panels: A group of individuals who have agreed to being involved with market research studies at periodic intervals to measure changes over time with a consistent sample.

Pareto Principle (80/20 Rule): A rule that assumes that 20% of customers generate 80% of sales or that 80% of merchandise comes from 20% of the vendors.

Participant Consumer Behavior: Actions performed when searching for, participating in, or evaluating the sport activities the consumer believes will satisfy their needs.

Participants: Individuals who take part in an activity.

Partnership Sourcing: The commitment between customers and suppliers to create a long-term relationship based on understood and agreeable objectives that work toward maximizing capability and competitiveness.

Patent: A type of intellectual property that grants property rights to an inventor for their invention. The term of a new patent is 20 years from the date on which the application for the patent was filed in the United States or, in special cases, from the date an earlier related application was filed, subject to the payment of maintenance fees.

Pearson Product Moment Correlation: An associative statistical method also known as the correlation coefficient; creates a linear association between two variables.

Perceived Self: How the sport consumer believes they are viewed by others.

Perceptions: Involves gaining an understanding of the individual values, attitudes, needs, and expectations of the sport consumer by scanning, gathering, assessing, and interpreting those insights.

Personal Contact: One-on-one communication between a representative of the sport organization and the sport consumer that should result in achieving promotional objectives ranging from providing information about products and services, to generating sales.

Personality: The unique and personal psychological characteristics of an individual which reflects how they respond to their social environment.

Phonorecords: A technology that allows musical works to be played, recorded, and stored in a digital format for use on computers or other devices.

Place: The method of distributing the product to consumers.

Plan: The strategy for managing all the resources that goes toward meeting customer demand for your product or service.

Pluralistic Research: When both qualitative and quantitative data are used concurrently.

Point-of-Purchase Displays: Special exhibits involving a product or service at the point of sale, such as cardboard cut-outs, end caps, kiosks, and signage.

Point-of-Sale Systems: A sales information computer system for internal reports that provides sport marketing professionals with more comprehensive information at their fingertips by providing instant access to information about their prospects and customers.

POP: Point of purchase.

Population: Refers to the entire group that is defined as being under study as per the research questions.

POS: Point of sale.

Positioning: The process of influencing the perceptions of potential and current customers about the image of the company and its products and services. This is accomplished by applying the 4 P's of marketing with the goal of strategically placing the product or service firmly in the mind of the consumer.

Predictive Statistics: Used in prediction and forecasting of the future by evaluating previously collected data.

Price: The value a consumer equates to a good or service or the amount of money or goods asked for in exchange for something else.

Price-Based Incentives: The benefits derived from lowering the retail price of a product or service.

Price Claims in Advertising: It states that the company shall avoid price claims which are false or misleading, or saving claims which do not offer provable savings.

Price–Quality Matrix: The relationship between price and quality in positioning the sport product as compared to others.

Primary Data: Information collected by the sport marketer specifically for the research project; normally collected via personal contact, either by mail, telephone, email, or face-to-face.

Primary Intelligence: Information collected by the sport organization through direct contact with customers, the distribution network, competitive analysis, and the internal sport organization itself.

Probability Sampling: A sampling category utilizing random selection from the known population.

Processing Power: The amount of information that can be handled by a website at any given time.

Product: Tangible (goods) or intangible (services) merchandise.

Product Specialization: Where an organization specializes in a particular product or service, and tailors the product or service to different market segments.

Production: The schedule of activities necessary for making, testing, packaging, and preparation for delivery.

Projective Techniques: Used to allow respondents to verbalize their true opinions or beliefs about products and services.

Promotional Integration: The actual creation and delivery of the promotional message that involves defining how the message is to reach the consumer, ensuring that the promotional message will be received and understood, and that the promotional message will lead to the purchase of a product or service.

Promotions: An element of the sport marketing mix that involves communicating information about the sport product or service to consumers.

Prospecting: The process of identifying potential customers to purchase products and services.

Public Relations: The collection of activities, communications, and media coverages that convey what the sport organization is and what they have to offer, all in the effort to enhance their image and prestige.

Publicity: The use of unpaid, non-personal promotion of a sport product or service through a third party that publishes print media or presents information through radio, television, or the Internet.

Publicity Campaign: The use of communications, activities, and media coverages to convey specific information to a targeted market over a specific period of time.

Puffery: Refers to exaggerated, subjective claims that cannot be proven true or false.

Qualitative Research: Involves collecting, analyzing, and interpreting data by observing what people do, or how they answer open-ended questions utilizing a small number of respondents that represent a segment of the population, and focusing on the qualities of a sport product or service by articulating the values and beliefs they perceive the specific brand to have.

Quantitative Research: Involves collecting, analyzing, and interpreting data collected from a larger sample via a structured questionnaire or survey, with the data being analyzed in statistical terms, and the results produced in a numeric form.

Questionnaire: A form containing a set of questions used to gather information for a survey.

Quota: A number or percentage that constitutes an upper limit (such as maximum inventory available), or in most cases for sales, a targeted minimum.

Quota Sampling: A non-probability sampling method that seeks to balance the proportion of selected respondent characteristics by setting quotas on how many individuals from a specific group can respond.

Radio Frequency Identification Tag: A digital technology that can tell what the product is, where it has been, when it expires, whatever information someone wishes to program by global positioning satellites.

Range: The distance between the lowest value and the highest value in a distribution.

Reference Group Self: How the sport consumer interacts with their reference group.

Referral Sampling: A non-probability sampling method where the respondents to a survey are also asked to identify other individuals who would likely qualify to take the survey.

Referrals: Recommendations made by one individual to another about a specific product, service, or organization.

Regression: A predictive statistical method used to measure a dependent variable and its relationship to one (bivariate) or more (multiple) independent variables.

Regular Foreign Sport Marketing: Sport organizations that have a permanent presence outside national borders, but their primary market (50% or above) is domestic.

Relationship Management Integration: How the aspects of a series of promotional strategies work cooperatively to effectively and efficiently promote the sport product, service, or organization.

Reliability: The ability to show that the results of the experiment are trustworthy, and if the same experiment were run again, the results would be either similar or comparable.

Renvoi: Where a court utilizes its own laws, and has the option of adopting the center of gravity laws from another country.

Research Method: A plan for a study that steers the collection and analysis of information gathered.

Resource System: The process of selecting and utilizing resources to provide the benefits valued by the consumer.

Return on Equity: The amount of profit earned on an organization's common stock over a given period, which tells investors how effective their money is being utilized by the organization.

Return on Investment: The amount of profit earned based on the quantity of resources used to produce the profit.

Returns: The network for receiving defective and excess products back from customers and supporting customers who have problems with delivered products.

Revenue Models: The methods of securing earnings for the sport organization.

RFID: Radio frequency identification tag.

RFM: Recency, frequency, monetary.

RFM Analysis: A method for evaluating the most profitable customers for the sport organization based on: (1) if the customer has purchased recently; (2) how often the customer has made a purchase; and (3) how much the customer spends with the sport organization.

ROE: See return on equity.

ROI: See return on investment.

Royalties: A share of income, in accordance with the terms of a license agreement, paid by a licensor for the right to make, use, or sell a product or service.

Sales Force: The individuals responsible for selling sport products and services.

Sales Incentives: The offering of a premium to attract first time or bulk buyers of products and/or services, but more often are used to reward those repeat customers.

Sales Management: The process of directing and controlling the sales force, and achieving the desired level of exchanges between the sport organization and sport consumers.

Sales Pitch: A communication process where the salesperson outlines and explains the benefits of a product or service to a potential customer in order to stimulate interest and motivate them to make a purchase.

Sales Process: The steps that focus on taking the sport products and services available for sale, and developing the best methods for luring the sport consumer to make a purchase.

Sales Promotion: A unique promotional method that is utilized to generate immediate interest in a product or service.

Sample: The most basic element of sport marketing research, as it is the factor taken from a small group that is representative of the characteristics of an entire population.

Sample Frame: A master list of the entire population.

Sample Frame Error: The degree to which the sample frame does not encompass the entire population.

Saturation: The fifth stage of the sport product and service life cycle; the stage when gaining market share begins to slow.

Scale: A standard of measure developed by the sport marketing researcher.

Scaled-Response Questions: When the sport marketing researcher develops a scale and the answers from the respondent are based on both their perception and the scale defined.

Scanning: The collection of intelligence acquired through informal observations and conversations.

Scientific Methodology: The process by which one gains information by a process of observation, developing a hypothesis, implementing some type of research to determine the appropriate course of action, and evaluating the results to draw conclusions, select courses of action or inaction, and modify the research and start again.

Screening: The process by which a research can conduct a preliminary appraisal of the potential respondent to determine their suitability for the study.

Season Ticket Equivalencies: The combination of season tickets sold and partial season ticket packages.

Secondary Data: Information that has been collected by another source or for another purpose prior to the current research project, and is being evaluated for use to solve the problem at hand.

Secondary Data Analysis: Involves using existing data that has been collected by another source or for another purpose prior to the current research project.

Secondary Intelligence: Information collected by the sport organization from previous published sources such as books, trade journals, newspapers, and reliable sources on the Internet.

Secret Shopping: A tool utilized in market research to investigate products and services of competitors by sending individuals to act as buyers.

Segment Factors: The underlying opportunities and threats that affect the segment or category.

Segmentation: The concept of dividing a large, diverse group with multiple attributes into smaller groups with distinctive characteristics.

Self-administered Survey: A survey where an individual respondent completes the form on their own.

Self-concept: A concept that includes a consumer's ideal self, perceived self, and reference group self.

Semi-focused Scanning: When there is no specific intelligence being sought or goal to attain, but a general inquiry is conducted to discover any piece of intelligence that may become evident.

Sense and Respond Approach: A method utilized to quickly respond to changes in the market as a result of strategic thinking need to be intuitive, reactionary, and simple.

Service Mark: A word, phrase, symbol, or design, or a combination of words, phrases, symbols, or designs that identifies and distinguishes the source of a service rather than a product. Similar to a trademark.

Servicing: A process that involves a salesperson providing work or a duty to a customer in response to a need or demand, and then creating a relationship that helps a customer make an initial or repeat purchase.

Shopping Intercept: A survey method utilized when a researcher stops shoppers at malls, supermarkets, outlets, and other retail establishments to get individual opinions.

Simple Random Sampling: A probability sampling method where a chance method is used to guarantee each member of the population has an equal chance to be selected into the sample.

Single Sourcing: The retailer who concentrates most of its stock purchases in one wholesale supplier.

Skip Interval: A number representing how many names would be skipped when selecting the sample – is calculated by taking the entire population list, and dividing it by the desired sample size.

Socialization: The process by which individuals acquire attitudes, values, and actions which are appropriate to members of a particular culture.

Sourcing: Choosing suppliers that will deliver the goods and services you need to create your product.

Spam: An unsolicited email.

Spectators: Individuals who observe a performance, such as a sporting event.

Sponsee: The term that refers to the sport brand that desires to enter into an agreement with a corporate sponsor.

Sponsor: A term that refers to the corporation that desires to enter into an agreement with a sport organization.

Sponsorship: The relationship between a corporation and a sport organization as a tool to develop brand image and customer loyalty as a result of the association.

Sport: Activities, experiences, or business enterprises that center on athletics, health and wellness, recreation, and leisure time opportunities. It is an all-inclusive term covering all aspects that go beyond the playing field, including all the various operations that make the games happen.

Sport Advertising: One of the primary elements of the promotional mix that involves the process of attracting public attention to a sport product or sport business through paid announcements in the print, broadcast, or electronic media.

Sport Business Ethics: The values and principles within a commercial setting that applies to those individuals engaged in commerce.

Sport Consumer Relations: The use of various methodologies, information technologies, and Internet capabilities that help entities organize and manage the interaction between the sport consumer and the sport organization.

Sport Consumer Relationship Management (SCRM): The use of various methodologies, information technologies, and Internet capabilities that help sport entities organize and manage sport consumer relationships. The goal of SCRM is to develop a system that all members of the sport marketing effort can utilize to access information about sport products and strive toward meeting the needs and wants of sport consumers.

Sport Governing Bodies: Sport organizations that are responsible for developing the rule structure for the specific activity as well as organize competitions at levels from local youth to international.

Sport Journalism: Encompasses all types of reportage and media coverage of current events in the world of sport.

Sport Management: The collection of skills related to the planning, organizing, directing, controlling, budgeting, leading, and evaluating of an organization or department whose primary product or service is related to sport and its related functions.

Sport Market Opportunity Analysis Framework: A methodology utilized by marketers to identify and evaluate the attractiveness of an opportunity in the marketplace.

Sport Marketing Decision Support System: A component of the sport marketing information system that encompasses the primary and secondary data previously collected by the sport organization, the tools and techniques utilized to interpret that data, and the process by which that information is used in the decision making process.

Sport Marketing Information System: A structure that consists of all aspects of the sport organization (people, equipment, goals and objectives, policies and procedures, etc.) being responsible for gathering, organizing, analyzing, evaluating, and distributing marketing information across the sport organization for the purpose of efficient and effective decision making.

Sport Marketing Intelligence System: A component of the sport marketing information system that involves the procedures and sources that the organization utilized to obtain everyday information about developments regarding external opportunities and threats.

Sport Marketing Planning Process: This process involves the development of the sport organization's products and services marketing strategies, including the tactics and programs to be implemented during the lifespan of the plan.

Sport Marketing Research: The collection and analysis of information about sport consumers, market niches, and the effectiveness of sport marketing initiatives.

Sport Organization Resource Planning: Assimilating all functions of an organization through information technology methods to become more efficient and effective in planning, manufacturing, marketing, and selling sport products and services.

Sport Product: A bundle of attributes which are bought or sold.

Sport Product and Service Life Cycle: The defined stages that a sport product goes through during its lifespan. The six stages are initial development, introduction to the market, growth, maturity, saturation, and decline.

Sport Product and Service Management: Focuses on the approach taken by sport marketers and organizations to define and market their products and services.

Sport Promotional Mix: Advertising, sponsorship, public relations, licensing, personal contact, incentives, and atmospherics.

Sport Promotional Strategy: The process of building brand loyalty and product credibility, developing image, and positioning the brand.

Sport Retail Management: The process of directing and controlling the business activities related to the sale of the sport product to consumers for their personal consumption.

Sports: Refers to individual, dual, and team sports activities such as soccer, baseball, golf, and tennis.

Sports Information: The gathering of results and other pertinent sporting information on individuals, teams, departments, and leagues.

Sport Service: The process of providing quality, value, and satisfaction to the sport consumer.

Sport Sponsorship: Acquiring the rights to be affiliated with a sport product or event in order to obtain benefits from that association.

Standard Deviation: Measures the spread of values throughout the data – for a normal curve, which is used most often, the midpoint is the mean and the standard deviation is measured from that point.

Standard Error: An inferential statistical method used to measure the variability in the sample distribution – calculated by taking the standard deviation from the mean and dividing by the total number of respondents (SD/N).

Stakeholder: Those with a vested interest in the outcomes of a sport marketing effort.

Stakeholder-Based Integration: How the ownership and employees of the organization have a vested interest in the efficient promotion of the product, service, and/or organization.

Stratified Sampling: A probability sampling method where there is a large divergence in the population that would cause a skewed distribution.

Substantiation in Advertising: It states that the company's claims shall be substantiated by evidence in possession of the advertiser and advertising agency, prior to making such claims.

Superego: The morality of an individual, which in turn formulates the ethical framework of individual values, beliefs, and codes of conduct.

Supply Chain Management: The process of coordinating the movement of sport products, sport services, and other pertinent information from raw materials to manufacturer to wholesaler to retailer and eventually to sport consumer.

Supply Chain Metrics: A set of measurements that helps the company to understand how well it is operating over a given period of time.

Support Media: The use of non-traditional media efforts to connect with members of the target audience who have not been reached through traditional media (print, radio, television).

Survey: A form used to collect information from respondents about their attitude, values, opinions, and beliefs via telephone, mail, face-to-face, and online.

SWOT: Acronym meaning strengths, weaknesses, opportunities, and threats.

Systematic Sampling: A probability sampling method that starts with a list of the entire population, each is given a number, a skip interval is calculated, and names from the list would be entered into the sample based on the skip interval.

Targeting: Finding the best way to get a product's image into the minds of consumers, and hence entice the consumer to purchase the product.

Taste and Decency in Advertising: It states that the company shall be free of statements, illustrations, or implications which are offensive to good taste or public decency.

Team Sponsorship: An agreement between a corporate partner and a team; usually more appropriate for local or regional companies that have smaller marketing budget but have a desire to become the official sponsor of a team.

Technology Integration: The modification of the traditional processes of order handling, purchasing, and customer services with the specific needs of the consumers and the unique abilities of the organization in mind.

Telemarketing: Marketing goods and services by telephone.

Test Marketing: The process of determining the sales potential of a new product or service, or the acceptance of a product previously entered into the marketplace.

Testimonials: The words and experiences of past users of the products or services being promoted.

Testimonials in Advertising: It states that advertising containing testimonials shall be limited to those of competent witnesses who are reflecting a real and honest opinion or experience.

Third-Party Logistics: Services added onto regular transportation activities, including freight forwarding, which is the handling of freight from one form of transport to another.

Time Management Skills: The ability to control time.

Trademark: A word, phrase, symbol, or design, or a combination of words, phrases, symbols, or designs, that identifies and distinguishes the source of the goods of one party from those of others.

Transactional Data: Information collected from the exchange process between a buyer and a seller.

Trend–Impact Analysis: A forecasting method that allows sport marketing researchers and the organization to track trends.

Truth in Advertising: It states that the company shall tell the truth, and shall reveal significant facts, the omission of which would mislead the public.

***t*-test:** A difference analysis statistical method that assesses whether the means of the two groups are statistically different than each other.

Unfocused Scanning: Exposure to information the sport marketing professional deems to be useful based on what they have read, heard, or seen.

Uniform Resource Locators: More commonly known as main web addresses, are the actual location of an Internet item.

Upselling: The movement of customers from less profitable products or services in a specific category to either a more profitable one in the same category, or into another, more profitable category.

URL: Abbreviation for uniform resource locators.

User Interface: The ability to create a digital representation of the theme of the store, the ease in which the consumer can navigate around the website, and provide a pleasurable experience for the consumer.

Validity: The ability to show the accuracy of the methodology, and that the results are logical, reasonable, and sound.

Value: What the consumer is willing to pay for a product; or an amount of goods, services, or money that is a fair price or return for something of an equivalent amount.

Value Chain: The activities adding value directly to the consumer while adding indirect value through the support of other organizational operations.

Value Propositions: How an organization will differentiate itself to consumers in terms of the value to be offered.

Variable Costs: These costs are defined as those which vary according to usage.

Variable Pricing: When a sport retailer changes their prices as a result of changes in costs or demand.

Vertical Integration: The speed in which information is delivered through internal and external information technology processes.

Viral Marketing: Seeks to pass marketing messages about the sport marketer to as many people as possible, creating the potential for exponential growth in the influence the sport marketer has, as well as exposure of the sport product.

Word-of-Mouth: Spoken communication that does not come from the primary party.

World Wide Web: The collection of interconnected documents that are connected by uniform resource locators (URL's) and hyperlinks.

WWW: Abbreviation for World Wide Web.

INDEX